ANIA HERITAGE

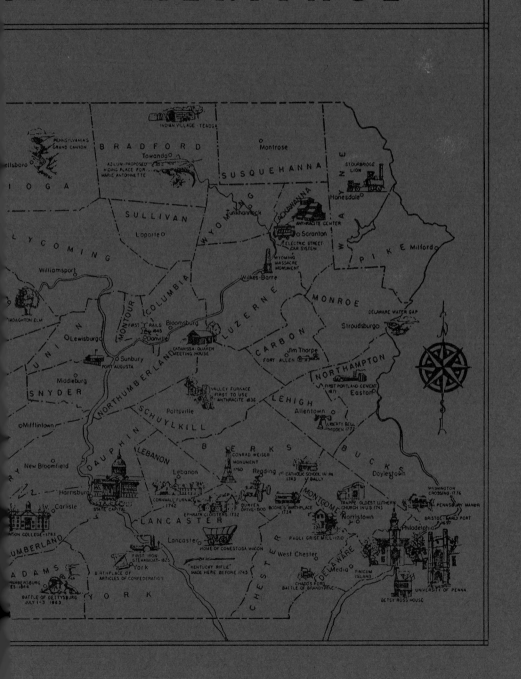

OUR PENNSYLVANIA

HERITAGE

OUR

PENNSYLVANIA

HERITAGE

Thirteenth Edition

by

WILLIAM A. CORNELL
Pennsylvania Student,
Teacher and Writer

with activities by

MILLARD ALTLAND
Former Teacher
West York Area Schools

PENNS VALLEY PUBLISHERS
Lansdale, Pennsylvania

Copyright 2003 by Penns Valley Publishers
International Standard Book Number 0-931992-44-3

All Rights Reserved

Printed in the United States of America

Contents

	Page
Preface	7

chapter I
Pennsylvania Today 11

chapter II
Earning a Living in Pennsylvania 33

chapter III
Indians of Pennsylvania 59

chapter IV
The Early Years 81

chapter V
Colonial Life 107

chapter VI
Conflict on the Frontiers 133

chapter VII
The New Nation Is Born 153

chapter VIII
Keystone of the Nation 179

chapter IX
Saving the Union 215

chapter X
The Age of Big Business 231

chapter XI
Entering the 20th Century 255

chapter XII
The Later Decades *275*

chapter XIII
Living in Our Local Communities *317*

chapter XIV
The Citizen and the Voter *331*

chapter XV
Local Government in Pennsylvania *345*

chapter XVI
Government of the Commonwealth *359*

appendix
List of Executives of Pennsylvania *385*

index *387*

Preface

"All world history is simply local history 'writ' big," a teacher said. All history happened some place which was local. Our federal system of government makes it important for citizens of all ages to study and understand how their state fits into the development of the national history and government of the United States. The everyday life of the citizens of Pennsylvania is influenced most by local and state events, laws, and history.

In 1943 The General Assembly of Pennsylvania mandated by law that the history and government of the Commonwealth be taught to all students in the secondary schools of the State. This law affects both public and non-public schools. No law should be necessary for educated persons to know that children and adults alike learn best that which affects them most. The study of the materials in this book can be meaningful and exciting to those who are taught to understand their surroundings.

Most Pennsylvanians want to be proud of their state. To be truly proud one must appreciate and understand the subject of his affection. The authors are pleased that favorable comments have been received from students, parents, and persons not related to schools at all.

This edition has been re-written to be used in schools at any grade level or for the general reader. It can be read from cover to cover or read by chapters in any order. For those who wish it might be used as a reference book.

The author has used the most up to date materials from the latest available census and the latest constitutional changes of the State. When used in conjunction with older editions of this book, teachers can teach students how to determine and use updated facts and material.

The first chapter on the geography of the State provides a setting for the history that follows. The second chapter indicates that geography is vastly changed by man's activities. This is borne out by studying the Indians of chapter three.

The facts of history and government are brought up to date in this edition so that the student can relate to history and developments of his own lifetime. New reading materials are listed.

Teachers and students are encouraged to supplement the materials of this book by the many fine local and county histories. Where such histories are not up to date students should be encouraged to help write their own materials. Learning to write history is one of the finest ways of understanding it.

Teachers should get the annual Book and Publication List from the Pennsylvania Historical and Museum Commission. Free historic leaflets are available from the Commission also. Every classroom should have a Pennsylvania Manual, published annually, which can usually be obtained free from your legislator. The Pennsylvania Abstract, published by the Pennsylvania State Data Center at Penn State Harrisburg, is helpful for facts on population figures and industry to keep all facts up to date. Teachers should consider joining the Pennsylvania Historical Association to get its publications.

The authors wish to thank those who encouraged the writing of this new edition and also those who gave permission to use pictures, charts, and graphs.

Particular thanks go to Laura Cornell for her aid.

William A. Cornell

Signers of the Declaration of Independence.

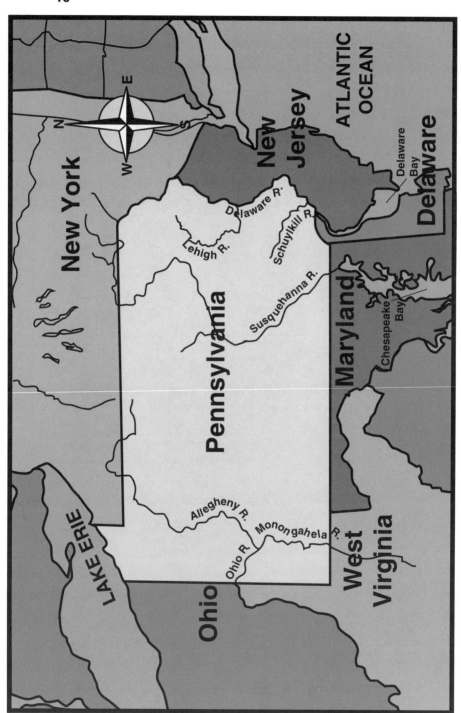

View of Pennsylvania with surrounding states and waterways.

chapter 1

Pennsylvania Today

Pennsylvania is a popular place. Over 12 million people live there. Pennsylvania was 300 years old on March 14, 1981 which makes it ninety-five years older than the United States. Millions of people from all over the world visit the Commonwealth each year. Long known as the "Keystone State," Pennsylvania remains so because of its central location, history, diverse and distinctive culture, scenic beauty, agriculture, business, and industry.

In the first chapter we shall look at Pennsylvania as it is today. What is the geography of Pennsylvania? What produces the wealth of the State? What types of people are there in Pennsylvania? Where do they live?

LOCATION OF PENNSYLVANIA

Where is Pennsylvania located? How do you describe its location?

It is in North America 40 degrees north of the equator. That is almost half way to the North Pole. It is in the northeastern part of the United States.

The United States is about 2,600 miles wide. Pennsylvania is about 300 miles wide. Pennsylvania is about 150 miles from north to south. The area of Pennsylvania is 45,333 square miles. There are 32 states larger than Pennsylvania. Texas is five times as large. There are 17 states smaller. Pennsylvania is five times as large as Vermont.

To understand better its location, let us learn the boundaries of Pennsylvania. The entire eastern boundary is the Delaware River. Notice that the river flows from the north in New York State. New

York is east of the river as far south as the town of Port Jervis.

Most Pennsylvanians do not realize that New York City is farther south than the northern half of Pennsylvania.

From Port Jervis south along the Delaware River, Pennsylvania is bordered by New Jersey. Notice on the maps in this chapter that the river is not straight and neither is the border.

About 25 miles south of Philadelphia there is another state line. Notice that it is semicircular. The border is called the New Castle Arc. It separates Pennsylvania and Delaware. The history of this border is discussed later.

The border between Maryland and Pennsylvania is 39°43' north latitude. This border is better known as the Mason-Dixon Line. It was named for the men who originally surveyed the line. All states south of Pennsylvania are in "Dixie."

The Mason-Dixon Line was extended to 80°31'36" west longitude to form the West Virginia boundary. Notice on the map that West Virginia forms the western boundary of Pennsylvania as far north as the Ohio River north of Pittsburgh. This same border extended to the lake forms the Ohio-Pennsylvania boundary.

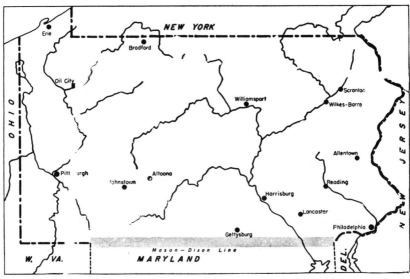

After looking at the map, it's easy to see why Pennsylvania is regarded as the Keystone State. It is bounded by New York, New Jersey, Delaware, Ohio, West Virginia, and Maryland. The Mason-Dixon Line, the official boundary between the Commonwealth and Maryland, has now become the dividing line between North and South.

Lake Erie borders the State for 50 miles along the northwestern part of the State. Thirty miles out into the lake is part of Pennsylvania. At that point, Pennsylvania borders the Canadian province of Ontario. Few Pennsylvanians realize that their State borders on a foreign country.

The 42nd parallel forms the remaining boundary of Pennsylvania and New York from near Lake Erie to the Delaware River.

GEOGRAPHY

The shape of the State is almost rectangular. Drawing a map is thus made very easy. Notice that it is twice as far from New Jersey to Ohio as from Maryland to the New York state border.

ELEVATION MAP

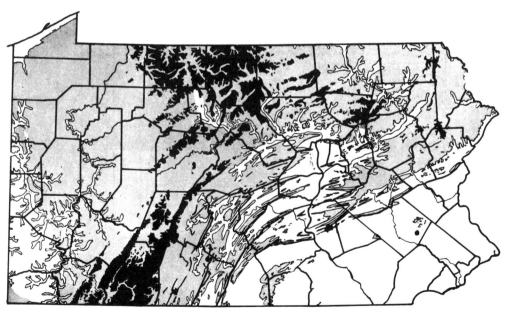

Black - 2,000 to 3,213 feet above sea level.
Grey - 1,000 - 2,000 feet above sea level.
White - Sea level to 1,000 feet above sea level.

Source: **Pennsylvania State Planning Board, Topographic and Geologic Survey,** *Elevations in Pennsylvania*

The Mountains of Pennsylvania

The surface of Pennsylvania is quite varied. Near Philadelphia and Erie the surface would be described as a plain. Most of the rest of the State is mountainous. At Philadelphia the surface is only 26 feet above sea level. The land rises slowly across the Piedmont plain to Harrisburg. Harrisburg is 317 feet above sea level.

North and west of Harrisburg are the mountains which form part of the Appalachian Mountain region. This chain extends from central New York State to Alabama. All of Pennsylvania, except that part southeast of Harrisburg, and the plain along Lake Erie, is part of the Appalachian Mountain region.

Pennsylvanians should know the names of the important ridges of mountains in their State. The mountains play a big part in the history and development of the State. Note how the ridges generally curve in an arc from the northeast to the southwest.

The first mountain of any size, found in traveling west from Philadelphia, is the South Mountain. It extends into Pennsylvania from Maryland between Gettysburg and Chambersburg. Its ridges reach up to 2,000 feet, but it dips to the plain before it extends to Harrisburg. Most travelers go north of the mountain.

The next mountain cannot be missed. It is the Blue Mountain which extends from Maryland southwest of Chambersburg to the New Jersey border south of Stroudsburg. This mountain reaches a height of 2,240 feet and formed a wall for the early settlers to climb.

In northeast Pennsylvania there is a short range of mountains called the Poconos. These mountains extend up to 2,000 feet but the ridges are not long.

Another mountain with a ridge extending up from Maryland is the 2,200 foot Tuscarora that parallels the Blue Mountain.

The 2,300 foot Jack's Mountain extends from the Maryland border to near Bloomsburg. From Maryland north and east to Lock Haven is the Allegheny Mountain, the highest of the mountain chains, rising up to 2,979 feet near Bedford.

West of the Allegheny Mountains is the Allegheny Plateau. It is not a level region, however, as there are more ridges. To the west is Negro Mountain which rises to 3,213 feet at the highest point in the

S. W. Kuhnert

Cultivated valleys lie between the long mountain ridges. The Susquehanna River cuts through both.

state at Mount Davis, south of Somerset. Farther west is the 3,000 foot Laurel Ridge and the 2,300 foot Chestnut Ridge.

The ridges fall away to the west. Somerset has an elevation of 2,100 feet, Johnstown 1,214, Pittsburgh 749 and Erie 655. The mountains in the northern counties rise at places to 2,300 feet, but there are no long ridges.

These mountains of Pennsylvania seem high to those who live on the plains of Illinois. Compared to the mountains of North Carolina that rise to 6,600 feet, or to the 14,000 foot peaks of the Rockies, Pennsylvania mountains are small. We shall see that the mountains of the State are very important.

Climate, Rain and Growing Season

The climate of Pennsylvania is the humid continental type. There is plenty of rain and the summers are hot and winters cold. Most of the wind currents come from the west. The mountains cause a difference of climate in various parts of the State. Northern Pennsylvania is generally cooler than southern.

In areas where the elevation rises over 1,000 feet, the summers are cooler and winters colder. Northern Pennsylvania averages 22-26 degree temperatures in winter and 66-70 in summers. There are usually about 40 inches of rain and 54 inches of snow each year. Snow lies on the fields about three quarters of the winter days.

The higher mountain areas of the State receive up to 50 inches of rain and up to 88 inches of snow. The greatest snowfall is in the Somerset area. The growing season ranges from 130 days in the Poconos to 165 in the upper Susquehanna Valley.

The most moderate temperature is that southeast of Harrisburg. There is plenty of rainfall, 38-46 inches, and about 30 inches of snow fall each year. Here the growing season is the longest with 170-200 days.

Western Pennsylvania has the most changeable weather. It has the most frequent rains and snow storms. Rainfall is about 40-44 inches and snow 50. The temperature varies from 0 to 100 degrees with the year's average about 52.5.

Weather along Lake Erie is the most unusual in the State. Although it is the most northern part of the State, summers are long. The lake's water keeps the weather moderate along the shores. Large areas of water warm slowly and keep adjacent land cool longer in the spring. In fall the water cools slowly and holds back winter weather. This gives Erie County 175 growing days. Only the area around Philadelphia has more.

This would indicate that Pennsylvania has about five distinct climate regions: the northern counties, the mountains, the western section, Erie County, and the southeastern region. In all cases the climate is pleasant and agreeable.

Pennsylvania's rainfall is very important. Generally there is enough for agriculture and for human use. Sometimes, however, floods occur and wash away the valuable topsoil that grows our food. Pennsylvania's average rainfall of 42 inches would fill a flat swimming pool the size of our State with three and one-half feet of water. That much water weighs 138,000,000,000 tons. Where does all this water go?

PENNSYLVANIA TODAY

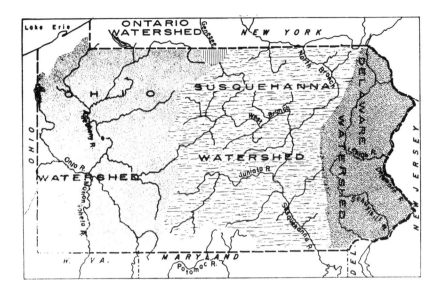

The cross-hatched areas show the watersheds drained by the principal streams of Pennsylvania. The Susquehanna drains nearly half the State. The Ohio has the second largest river basin, followed by the Delaware, which borders the State for two-thirds its course.

Rivers and Lakes

Pennsylvania is drained by three major river systems: the Delaware, the Susquehanna, and the Ohio. The Susquehanna drains central and northern Pennsylvania. It drains 46.4 per cent of the State's surface. The Ohio River and its branches in Western Pennsylvania drain 35.4 per cent of the State. The Delaware River system in the east drains 14.3 per cent of the State's surface. In south central Pennsylvania the Potomac drains 3.5 per cent. Lake Erie drains 1.1 per cent, and 0.2 per cent flows north into the Genesee River and later Lake Ontario.

At this time we should learn as many of the various major rivers that flow into the three drainage systems as we can. The Schuylkill and Lehigh flow into the Delaware. Both branches of the Susquehanna should be traced. Into the Susquehanna flow the Juniata, Lackawanna and numerous creeks of local importance. Into the Ohio flow the Allegheny, Monongahela and Beaver Rivers. Into these rivers flow others of importance. Locate the Kiskiminetas, Youghiogheny, Conemaugh and Clarion.

There are more than 1,000 square miles of lakes and rivers in Pennsylvania. If Lake Erie's 735 square miles are discounted there are 367 square miles of inland waters. Conneaut Lake in Crawford County is the largest natural lake with 928 acres. Harvey's Lake in Luzerne County is second with 659 acres. Some artificial lakes created by dams are bigger than natural ones. Pymatuning, 16,400 acres; Kinzua, 12,000 acres; Raystown, 8,300 acres; and Wallenpaupeck, 5,600 acres, provide water reserves, flood control, recreation and in some cases electric power. Practically all the lakes of the State are located in northern Pennsylvania. Ancient glaciers gouged out the lakes and swamps and rounded many of our hills.

Soils and Forests

Pennsylvania's soil varies as much as the surface elevation. In the southeast is a fertile reddish sand and clay loam. Westward to the mountains it becomes a very fertile brown silt loam. In the mountains is a brown gravelly and stone loam that is not too good for farming. Western Pennsylvania has a yellowish silt which is somewhat sandy from sandstone. In the Erie region the soil is greyish to brown silt loam of good quality.

A large area of the state, where the mountains provide poor soil, has been turned back to forest in many places. It will surprise some that Pennsylvania still has 58 per cent of its area covered with forests (26,291 of the 45,333 square miles are forests). Cameron County has 93 per cent of its area in forest. Forest County is 90 per cent forest. Over 80 per cent of Clinton, Elk, McKean, Pike, Potter and Sullivan Counties is forest land.

The forests of Pennsylvania are black cherry, pine, hemlock, maple, beech, and birch in the higher areas. In the more fertile areas are found mixed hardwoods such as oak, hickory and walnut.

Of the forest land, 10 per cent is owned by the State and 2 per cent by the National government. The 468,991 acres Allegheny National Forest is in Warren and McKean counties. Many acres are owned by coal companies, forest industries and private hunting clubs. Many farmers keep part of their land in woodland.

Preque Isle State Park protects the harbor of Erie and attracts almost 4,000,000 visitors for swimming, picnics, fishing, boating, and hiking. It is the most popular park of the State.

Nine-tenths of Pennsylvania is either farmland or forest. This means that if only one-tenth of the people are farmers, then nine-tenths of the people live in one-tenth of the area. A visitor traveling through central Pennsylvania north and south, or across northern Pennsylvania, would think Pennsylvania to be a state of forest and poor farmland.

WHERE DO PENNSYLVANIANS LIVE?

Pennsylvania has only 1 percent of the United States land area but 4.4 percent of the nation's population. In 2000 there were 12,281,054 people in Pennsylvania. Only the states of California, New York, Texas, Illinois and Florida had more people. There are 274 people per square mile in Pennsylvania. Alaska has only 1.3 persons in each square mile. New Jersey has 1134.5 people per square mile.

OUR PENNSYLVANIA HERITAGE

The 274 people per square mile in Pennsylvania are not evenly distributed. Over 95 percent, over 11 million people, live in 15 metropolitan (metro) areas. The remaining area which covers 34 counties has less than five percent of the population.

Populations of cities, boroughs, and townships are counted within State recognized municipal boundaries, so that on the list on the next page one will note that nationally recognized metropolitan area populations are higher. The metropolitan area combines the municipal area with that of closely related municipalities. The twenty largest municipalities are included in the ten largest metro areas. Upper Darby Township is the fifth largest municipality, but it is part of the Philadelphia metro area. The five smallest metro districts include simply the municipality and the host county. Philadelphia remains the largest municipality and metro district. The metro district includes almost five million people in five Pennsylvania counties, not including parts of New Jersey, Delaware and Maryland.

The metro area of Pittsburgh is the State's second largest with over two million people in five counties.

STANDARD METROPOLITAN STATISTICAL AREAS IN PENNSYLVANIA
2000

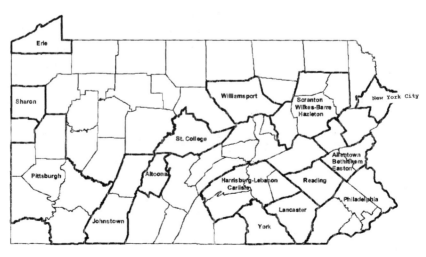

PENNSYLVANIA TODAY

The population areas shift as practically every city lost population in the 1980s and the 1990s. New metro areas were recognized around the industrial cities of Beaver, Sharon and Williamsport and the educational center at State College. The metro centers of Scranton and Wilkes-Barre were combined. It is now the fifth largest metro. The Allentown-Bethlehem-Easton (A-B-E) metro is now the third largest population. York, Lancaster and Harrisburg metros are the fastest growing.

Municipality	Population Name	Metro Area
1,517,550	Philadelphia	3,849,647
334,563	Pittsburgh	2,358,695
106,632	Allentown	637,958
103,717	Erie	280,843
81,821	Upper Darby Twp.	(Phila. Metro)
81,207	Reading	373,638
76,415	Scranton	624,776
59,850	Lower Merion Twp.	(Phila. Metro)
58,434	Bensalem Twp.	(Phila. Metro)
56,348	Lancaster	470,658
56,105	Abington Twp.	(Phila. Metro)
55,521	Bristol Twp.	(Phila. Metro)
52,129	Millcreek Twp.	(Erie Metro)
49,523	Altoona	129,598
48,950	Harrisburg	629,401
48,498	Haverford Twp.	(Phila. Metro)
46,809	Penn Hills Twp.	(Pitts. Metro)
44,424	Lower Paxton Twp.	(H-L-C Metro)
43,123	Wilkes-Barre	(S-WB-H Metro)
40,862	York	381,751
38,420	State College	135,758
30,706	Williamsport	120,044
23,908	Johnstown	232,621
16,328	Sharon (Mercer Co.)	120,293
5,028	Beaver (County)	181,412

Erie continues to be the state's third largest city, but as a metro district it is ninth in population. It is exceeded by the York metro, even though York ranks twentieth as a municipality.

Even though you do not live within a metropolitan area you probably feel the effect of at least one. You may watch its television stations, use its airport, read its daily newspaper or shop in its stores.

On the map of metropolitan areas, check the one which includes or aids your community. Some students may find that their communities are really a part of the metropolitan areas outside of Pennsylvania, such as New York City. Pike County of the Pocono region had a 257 percent growth between 1980 and 2000 and became part of the New York City metro area.

About 70 percent of the people of Pennsylvania live in dense urban areas. About eight of every eleven people live in municipalities with over 2500 people. The whole of Philadelphia County is the City of Philadelphia. Allegheny County, with the City of Pittsburgh, includes 127 other municipalities with 82 boroughs, 42 townships, and three other cities. Almost five percent of the population of Allegheny County is still rural.

Almost four million people live in rural municipalities that have less than 2500 population each. Over 300,000 people moved from urban to rural places in the decades since 1970. Forest, Fulton, Juniata, Pike, Sullivan, Susquehanna and Wyoming Counties are totally rural.

Pennsylvanians, like other Americans, move often for economic and social reasons. After 1980, 35 counties lost population while 32 had growth. Philadelphia lost over 102,000 population, while the adjacent counties of Bucks gained about 62,000, Chester, 60,000, and Montgomery 35,000.

The cities of Johnstown, Wilkes-Barre and Pittsburgh lost 15, 9.3 and 9.5 percents of their populations in the 1990s. Also, in the 1990s, Limerick Township in Montgomery County experienced a 102 percent growth. Meanwhile, Penn Hills Township in Allegheny County lost nine percent of its population. Overall, the State population grew only 3.4 percent.

PEOPLE OF PENNSYLVANIA

There are different ways of classifying the people of Pennsylvania. The United States census of 2000 changed racial classifications by adding "Two or More Races" and "Hispanic". Also changed was the use of the word "Asian" instead of "Oriental" and the interchangeable use of the words "Afro-American" and "black". Adding the classification "Hispanic" caused the reported numbers for "Afro-Americans" and "whites" to change significantly.

Between 1990 and 2000, the population of the United States increased by 13.4% while the population of Pennsylvania grew by only 3.4%. The number of "white" persons decreased by 65,998 during the ten years between 1990 and 2000. The number of Afro-Americans in Pennsylvania fell by 36,790 during this ten year period. Now appearing as a separate classification, Hispanics totaled 394,088 or 3.2% of the total population. The number of Asians grew from 1.2% in 1990 to 2.0%. The new classification of persons of two or more races now makes up 1.2% of Pennsylvania's population. With 18,343, Pennsylvania's population of Native Americans equals only one-tenth of one percent of Pennsylvania's population.

Philadelphia has the most diverse population in Pennsylvania and the largest numbers of minority groups. Philadelphia is 45% White, 43% Afro-American, 7.5% Hispanic, 4.5% Two or More Races and 4% Asian. Philadelphia has the largest Native American population of any city or county with 4,073. This amounts to less than one-tenth of a percent of Philadelphia's total population. By comparison, Cameron County's population is 99% white with all other races combined equalling less than 1%.

Bucks County has the largest percentage of Asians with 6%. Centre and Montgomery counties are only 4% Asian and only seven Asians live in Cameron County.

The greatest percentage of Hispanics are in Lehigh County with 10%; Dauphin County has 8.4%; Philadelphia has 7.5% and Monroe County has 7.4%.

Pennsylvania's population has continued to become more diverse with each ten-year census. In 1910, non-whites or minorities made up only 2.5% of Pennsylvania's total population. Today, Pennsylvania's non-white population amounts to 14.9%.

who also were born in this nation. However, 337,111 persons living in Pennsylvania in 1980 were born in another nation. Most of these people are now American citizens. However, of the foreign-born, the greatest number, 67,289 are Italian; 38,071, German; 26,599, Russian; 21,214 Polish; 18,214, English; 13,626 Canadians and 12,960, West Indians.

Although the majority of Pennsylvanians are still descendants of German, Irish and British parentage, each decade sees more Italians and Poles taking active roles in the State.

Between 1970 and 1980 an average of about 10,000 immigrants per year moved into Pennsylvania. The new immigrant groups include groups were Koreans, Hindus, Vietnamese, Cambodians, and Cubans.

TRANSPORTATION

Water Routes

A far-flung transportation system ties all the cities and towns of Pennsylvania together and connects them with the rest of the world.

The earliest type of transportation was by water. Philadelphia, on the Delaware River, remains the second greatest ocean port along the Atlantic Coast. Three-fourths of its trade is carried over water with other American cities and one-fourth of its ocean trade is with foreign nations. Petroleum products from Norway, Venezuela and Saudi Arabia are the greatest value of imports. The greatest value of exports are machinery, transportation equipment, grain and chemicals. The countries of Australia, Netherlands and Belgium are Pennsylvania's best customers. Over 100 nations trade through Philadelphia.

The Delaware River channel, as far north as the location of the new steel plant in Bucks County, is deep enough for some ocean vessels.

Pittsburgh is another great shipping port. The Ohio River and its tributaries, the Monongahela and Allegheny, have navigation dams and locks that allow river vessels pushing barges to navigate up river as far as West Virginia and north to above Kittanning.

The Monongahela River is the busiest river in the United States and carries more tonnage than the Panama Canal. Millions of tons

Philadelphia Electric Company

Philadelphia's greatest import product is petroleum. Crude oil is refined into numerous usable products in one of the world's greatest refinery centers.

of coal and coke are shipped down the Monongahela to the hungry mills of the Pittsburgh district. The finished steel products are shipped sometimes as far as New Orleans.

The Allegheny is used to ship sand and gravel dredged from its river bottom. Some of the coal from along the Allegheny River is shipped by barge.

Erie is the third great port of the State. It has a natural harbor from which the State exports electric powered locomotives, coal, and wood. Erie thrives as the State's only St. Lawrence Seaway port.

Railroad Network

Railroads bind Pennsylvania with gleaming bands of steel. All but one of the counties are served by one or more rail lines. The greatest and largest of the railroad systems are Norfolk Southern and CSX. Its main line runs from Philadelphia to Pittsburgh and then on to Chicago. Branches of the system reach practically all important Pennsylvania cities and connect them with New York, Washington, St. Louis and Chicago.

26 OUR PENNSYLVANIA HERITAGE

One of the chief expenses of State government is providing highways. Millions of dollars are spent for one interchange. Taxpayers demand good roads and pay for them with gasoline taxes.

There are about 4,000 miles of railroad trackage in the State. Other large lines are the Chessie System, Pittsburgh and Lake Erie, Norfolk Southern, and Bessemer and Lake Erie.

Amtrak passenger trains connect Philadelphia and Pittsburgh with nationwide trains. The state subsidizes a train a day between the cities as well. Erie in on another nationwide line of Amtrak.

Highways and Vehicles

Pennsylvania's modern highway system has become the greatest in the world. There are over 81,664 miles of roads in the State, a distance that would reach four times around the world. The famous Pennsylvania Turnpike is a toll road that connects Philadelphia, Pittsburgh and Scranton.

Federal interstate freeways east-west and north-south were begun in 1959. Pennsylvania travelers are now able to drive throughout the State on the new freeways. The new Keystone Shortway, I-80; Erie-Pittsburgh Expressway, I-79; the Erie Thruway, I-90; the Susquehanna Expressway, I-83; and I-81, I-95, I-76 and 1-78 are a few of the major arteries.

Pennsylvania needs many highways to serve the 7.3 million licensed drivers with their 8.6 million private, commercial, public and government motor vehicles. There are 235 bus lines with the Greyhound and the Trailways companies running the length of the State. There are about 3,000 truck lines in Pennsylvania with Roadway and Yellow being large nationwide ones. Subsidized mass transit bus, trolley and in some cases subways service 15 large cities of the state.

Airlines and Airports

Major airlines serve all the large cities of the State. Over 74 air transport companies do business in Pennsylvania. Philadelphia and Pittsburgh have international airports that handle the greatest number of people and amount of mail and air freight in the state. Over three million people use each airport each year.

The USAir, formerly Allegheny Airlines, with its headquarters in Pittsburgh, provides jet service to and from Allentown, Erie, Harrisburg, Philadelphia, Pittsburgh, and Scranton-Wilkes-Barre. All these cities are connected directly to New York, Chicago, and other major cities. Philadelphia and Pittsburgh are served by other national and international airlines such as American, Continental, Delta, Northwest, TWA, and United as well as British, Canadian, Italian, German, Mexican and other nations' airlines. USAir Express airline connects 15 smaller Pennsylvania cities with larger ones.

There are over 759 civil airports in the State. Many Pennsylvanians have their own private planes. Bucks and Montgomery County each have over 50 airports. Heliports now number over 200.

ENJOYING PENNSYLVANIA

Pennsylvania is viewed by visitors as a State of natural beauty, interesting cities, historical sites, and fine recreational facilities. Millions of visitors from other states and around the world come to view and enjoy the attractions. Pennsylvania is the third most popular tourist state in America. Millions of Pennsylvanians visit the attractions of the State also.

The great metropolitan attractions of the cities of Philadelphia and Pittsburgh are the State's most magnetic areas. Their historic sites, museums, parks, zoos, sporting events, theatres, universities, and cultural attractions draw millions of visitors. The greatest recorded number of visitors use the more than 100 State-owned and operated parks that are found throughout the state. The most popular are the recreation parks of Presque Isle, Pymatuning, Moraine, Codorus, Ohiopyle, Promised Land, and Point which attract over a million persons each in a year. The aim of the state is to have such a park within 25 miles of any citizen of the state. Picnicking, swimming, boating, hiking, camping and fishing are the main recreational uses of the parks.

The state's 53 historic sites attract over a million visitors with Washington Crossing, the State Museum, Railroad Museum, Brandywine Battlefield, Old Economy, Bushy Run Battlefield, Ephrata Cloister, Somerset Museum, and Drake's Well as the most popular. The state distributes maps for visitors to locate parks and historic sites.

The National Park Service administers eleven historic sites in the state that attract about 10 million visitors a year. The most popular are Valley Forge Park, Delaware Water Gap Recreation Area, Independence National Park, Gettysburg Military Park, Eisenhower's Home, and Hopewell Village. The AlleghenyPortage Railroad Site, Fort Necessity, and the Johnstown Flood Memorial are also drawing cards.

Practically every county maintains its own parks, museums, historical sites, recreational areas and attractions. Some communities provide parks, museums, art galleries, and theatres. As more and more people have more leisure they will have time, and should have the interest, to visit such sites for understanding, appreciation, and pride in the state.

REVIEW QUESTIONS

1. The latitude of State College is 41 degrees north and its longitude is 78 degrees west. What does this tell us about its location in Pennsylvania?
2. Why do many people spend their summer vacations in the mountains.?
3. Explain all the natural and artificial boundaries of Pennsylvania.
4. Name the geographic regions of Pennsylvania beginning with the Coastal Plain and ending with another plain. Name one industry important to each region.
5. Is the growing season longer in the interior of Pennsylvania or near the coast? Why?
6. List Pennsylvania's three drainage systems with their major rivers and tributaries.
7. In what regions of the state do most of the people live?
8. What services does a metropolitan area provide for its region?
9. Identify the four major units of transportation in Pennsylvania.

Do You Know the Meaning? Write a sentence containing the following words or phrases and explain their relation to Pennsylvania. Example: Anthracite - Pennsylvania has the only anthracite coal mines in America.

1. natural harbor
2. sea level
3. artificial lake
4. Presque Isle
5. foreign-born
6. metropolitan
7. Oriental
8. nationality
9. Allegheny Forest
10. Black
11. Nigeria
12. USAir
13. Conrail
14. Interstate 80
15. Pocono

Maps to Help Us Learn

1. On a map of Pennsylvania locate the following places:

Bucks County	Altoona	Bensalem Township
Harrisburg	Chester	Penn Hills
Pittsburgh	Lancaster	Philadelphia
Erie	York	Valley Forge
Scranton	Johnstown	Lower Merion
Reading	Wilkes-Barre	Williamsport
Allentown	State College	Gettysburg

2. Study the rivers on a Pennsylvania map. Where do the following rivers end: Delaware, Lehigh, Susquehanna, Allegheny, Monongahela, Ohio, Genesee?

3. Obtain a map of Pennsylvania from your local service station, then with the help of pictures found on the map, plan a trip through Pennsylvania.

What Do You Think? Use the knowledge gained thus far to discuss the following statements.

1. Pennsylvania is a wonderful place in which to live.
2. At one time Pennsylvania ranked second in population in the United States. Why does it rank lower now?
3. Our transportation system is a number of years behind most of our neighboring states.
4. Pennsylvania can rightly be termed the "melting pot" of the United States.
5. Study the geography of a region thoroughly before attempting to study its history.

ACTIVITIES

(Individual, committee or class projects and class reports)

1. You are making an automobile trip across Pennsylvania from east to west. Starting with Philadelphia, describe the most important features of the country that you observe. Take any route you wish. Several are suggested in this chapter.

2. Have students or committees compile notebooks on current affairs in Pennsylvania, reporting weekly or monthly. An example

would be the work of the General Assembly.

3. Construct a relief map of Pennsylvania from clay, plaster of Paris, or flour, salt and water. Show the geographical regions and the drainage systems.

4. On a map of Pennsylvania show where people of European ancestry live, making these locations with appropriate picture symbols.

5. Arrange your bulletin board in keeping with Pennsylvania today. Display postcards, pamphlets, maps, pictures, newspaper clippings which the students have been able to collect.

6. Pennsylvania is blessed with stone. Collect as many different kinds as you can find near your home.

7. Organize a weekend camping trip. Report to your class on the Pennsylvania mountains, rivers, flowers, birds, animals, and other features you noted on your trip.

8. Follow your local radio or TV weather report and keep a chart on changes and differences in temperature in your area.

9. Make your own crossword puzzle. You decide your limitations on words used. Here is an activity that can be continued a week, month, or entire school year, depending entirely on you. Always go down or to the right with a word: Any two or more open blocks connected must spell out a word.

READING MATERIALS

Allan, Keith B., *Pennsylvania, A Geographic Survey*, Shippensburg State College, Shippensburg, Pennsylvania, 1963.

Beers, Paul B., *Profiles from the Susquehanna Valley*: Past and Present Vignettes of Its People, Times and Towns, Harrisburg, Stackpole Books, 1973.

Bodnar, John, ed., *The Ethnic Experience in Pennsylvania,* Lewisburg, Bucknell University Press, 1973.

Common Trees of Pennsylvania, Department of Forest and Waters.

Cuff, David J. etal, Atlas of Pennsylvania, Philadelphia, Temple University, Press, 1989.

Department of Education, *American Diversity*, Harrisburg, Pa., 1973.

Fairharn, (3. Don, *Philadelphia, Fabulous City of ''Firsts, "* Wyncote, Pennsylvania, Kirsh Publishing Company, 1976.

Guide to the Historical Markers of Pennsylvania, Pennsylvania Historical and Museum Commission, 19S2.

Mining and Preparation of Anthracite, Hudson Coal Company, Scranton, Pa.

Murphy, R.E., and Murphy, M.F., Pennsylvania Landscapes, A Geography of the Commonwealth, Penns Valley Publishers, 1974.

Nutting, Wallace, *Pennsylvania Beautiful*, (Eastern). New York, Bonanza Books, 1974.

Pierce, Neal, R., *The Magistrates of America; People, Politics and Power in the Ten Great States*, Norton, N.Y., 1972.
Pennsylvania Teaching Guide to Natural Resources Conservation, Department of Public Instruction Commonwealth of Pennsylvania, Harrisburg, Pa., 1962.
Ruppert, Elfriede E. *A Historical and Folklore Tour of the Pennsylvania Grand Canyon*, Dorrance, Philadelphia, 1964.
Story of Champion Coal, Pennsylvania Coal Company, Koppers Building, Pittsburgh, Pa.
Shires, H. B., and March, R. N., *Adventures in Pennsylvania*, Penns Valley Publishers, 1961.
Stevens, S. K., *Pennsylvania, Titan of Industry*, Lewis Historical Publishing Co., 1948.
Pennsylvania Abstract, Pennsylvania State Data Center, Penn State Harrisburg, 1992.
Pennsylvania Manual, The Commonwealth of Pennsylvania, (odd numbered years).
Pennsylvania Forest Facts, The Pennsylvania Forest Industries Committee, Harrisburg, Pa., 1961.
Pennsylvania Today, Department of Public Instruction, Commonwealth of Pennsylvania, 1962.
Voight, William Jr., *The Susquehanna Compact Guardian of the River's Future*, N. J. Rutgers University Press, 1972.

chapter II

Earning a Living in Pennsylvania

OUR ECONOMIC SYSTEMS

"What does your father do?" is a question young people often are asked. Pennsylvanians are "doing" people. In some countries people may be proud not to work, but Americans are proud of their work. Pennsylvanians are proud to be doing a job to earn a living for themselves and their families.

In our study of Pennsylvania history we will learn that at one time most Pennsylvanians were farmers. At that time most families raised their own food, made their own clothing, and built their own homes. Transportation for most people was limited and usually they went no farther than the nearest town. Communication was limited and most families knew only nearby neighbors and usually lost contact with those who moved away. Little real money was seen or exchanged as the farmers traded their surplus crops for goods.

Over 65 per cent of Pennsylvania families today own their own homes. Almost 60% of Pennsylvania's families own television sets. Over 40% of the families have air conditioning. See if you can find comparable figures for Russia, China, England, Sweden, or any country in the world.

Our economic system has grown and changed considerably since colonial times. It is a "free enterprise system" in the sense that privately-owned capital and profit-motivated enterprise are the dominant forces. Under this system each person is encouraged to work, accumulate capital, and assume responsibility for the production of goods and services with minimal governmental ownership, operation and regulation. Capitalism, as this system is widely known, often is contrasted with socialism, communism, and other arrangements where the degree of governmental ownership, operation and control is greater.

Legally and organizationally, privately-owned enterprises take several forms, including proprietorships, partnerships, corporations, and cooperatives. Such enterprises vary widely in size but increasingly huge corporations, many of which are organized on an international scale, dominate the economic scene. Added to these privately-owned enterprises is a considerable number which are owned and operated by our national, state, and local governments. Within Pennsylvania, for example, the Federal Government owns and operates the postal service, and a mint for the manufacture of coins; the State owns and operates a liquor monopoly and several colleges; and local governments own and operate numerous utilities which provide such services as water, sewers, electricity, and mass transit.

While American businesses operate with less governmental involvement in economic affairs than in many other countries, they are not free to do as they please. Competition and public opinion are formidable controls. The prospect of losing money or going into bankruptcy also serves as a constraint. Added to these are governmental controls of many types. Besides, privately owned enterprises are dependent upon governments for innumerable public services and even subsidies. Indeed, private businesses and government are today so intertwined that instead of being a "free enterprise system" ours can more appropriately be described as a "mixed economy." Even so, it rests upon a long history and tradition of capitalistic assumptions, and private pursuit of profit remains the primary driving force.

RAW MATERIALS OF PENNSYLVANIA

Pennsylvania was blessed by having 4% of the minerals of the United States. Pennsylvania ranks in the top 10 states in mineral production. A great number of the industries of the State are related to mineral production. The minerals which bring the greatest wealth to the State are coal, stone, natural gas and oil, sand and gravel, clays and zinc. These minerals help make Pennsylvania a wealthy State by creating opportunities for employment and producing products for sale throughout the world.

Value of Mineral Production in Pennsylvania, 2000

Mineral	Dollar Value
Bituminous Coal	1,604,870,000
Anthracite Coal	159,605,000
Natural Gas	753,401,000
Stone	522,000,000
Cement	514,800,000
Sand and Gravel	120,000,000
Lime	95,900,000
Oil	43,200,000
Clay	1,760,000
Peat	185,000
Total Value	3,815,422,000

Source: Pennsylvania Department of Energy and U.S. Geological Survey

Coal Fields

Most students know that Pennsylvania is famous for its coal production. Hard coal, anthracite, is found in 10 eastern counties. The most coal is mined in Schuylkill, Luzerne, Northumberland, Carbon, Columbia, and Dauphin Counties. Soft, bituminous, coal is mined in over 30 central and western counties of which the leading producers are Washington, Greene, Cambria, Clearfield, Allegheny, Indiana, and Westmoreland Counties. As noted in the chart, more soft coal than hard is mined and thus produces more money value. Production of cheaper coal in western states has hurt Pennsylvania production.

Although coal is used less than in previous years, it is still the State's major mineral and became more important with the growing oil problems. Most of the coal is used to help produce electric power or in the production of steel. Many of the mines are owned by electric, steel and railroad companies. Several electric plants are built at coal mines. Several of the largest electric plants are in Indiana County to take advantage of the huge coal reserves there.

Stone

Stone is found in all counties but the most valuable is the limestone of Northampton, Lehigh, Butler, Adams and Berks Counties. Limestone is used to produce cement and lime. Limestone is processed also in Armstrong, Lebanon, and Chester Counties for use in blast furnaces in the making of steel. Centre and York Counties are large lime producers also. Some limestone is cut in several of the southeastern counties for use in buildings. Beautiful limestone homes are found in that area.

Slate is quarried in Lehigh and Northumberland Counties for use on roofs, floors and chalkboards. Montgomery, Delaware, and Chester Counties have valuable deposits of granite and other harder stones as well as limestone.

Crushed stone from over 50 counties is used for road building.

Natural Gas and Oil

Natural gas and oil usually occur in the same areas. They are found in more than 20 counties of northern and western Pennsylvania from Tioga to Greene Counties.

The gas is piped to homes and industry to provide clean, convenient heat. Pennsylvania produced over 207 million dollars annually. The increased use of gas for winter heat has led to the setting up of a unique plan. Texas gas is piped into exhausted gas wells in western Pennsylvania during summer months and the gas is distributed in winter for use. By drilling as much as a mile into the earth new gas pools were recently discovered in what were previously considered exhausted fields.

Oil is found in 23 counties today with over 25,000 wells producing oil worth over 99 million dollars in annually. Warren, McKean, and Venango counties are the greatest producers of oil. Higher prices brought about increased production. Elk, Forest, Washington, Butler, and Allegheny Counties each produce over 60,000 barrels annually. The amount of oil used in Pennsylvania exceeds the amount produced, but the specially refined Pennsylvania oils are in demand in many parts of the world.

EARNING A LIVING IN PENNSYLVANIA

Sand and Gravel

Sand and gravel are found in about half the counties of the State. In northern counties both products are found together in hills left by ancient glaciers. Constant dredging is done in the Allegheny, Monongahela and Delaware Rivers for the sand and gravel that has drifted into the streams. Ships are sent out from Erie to dredge the Lake Erie bottom also. In Huntingdon County one can see whole mountainsides of sand. Sand and gravel are used in the making of concrete products.

Special sand, used for the making of glass, is made by grinding up rock found in Huntingdon, Mifflin, Bedford, Beaver, Fayette, Mercer, and Venango Counties.

Clay

Over 25 counties produce some kind of clay products from one type of clay or another. Berks, York, Adams, Clearfield, and Jefferson Counties have a silica clay for tile and brick. The clay of Blair and Huntingdon Counties is a rare type used for ganister fire

Stone for road building, steel making, fertilizers, and buildings is second only to coal in mineral value. Pictured is blue stone quarrying in Bradford County.

brick in blast furnaces. In southwestern Pennsylvania, some clays are dug for making pottery and china. Over 28 counties produce clay for building brick. Are there many brick houses in your community? If so, a brick clay is probably found nearby.

Zinc and Other Minerals

Zinc deposits are found in Lehigh and Carbon Counties. There is more zinc processed in Pennsylvania than in any other state. Much of this mineral is imported for processing.

Peat moss is produced in parts of Lackawanna, Luzerne, Monroe, and Erie counties. It is used for agricultural and horticultural purposes. Other minerals are found in Pennsylvania including cobalt, copper, gem stones, gold, graphite, iron, mica, and silver. Cobalt formerly was thrown away, but is now used for medical purposes.

CAPITAL IN PENNSYLVANIA

Capital is needed to produce wealth. Capital is defined as money available to promote the production of goods and services. Pennsylvania has built up a reserve of capital (money) that can be used to promote industries. These industries will produce things for sale to gain money to pay wages, salaries and profits. The sale of the products must also produce enough money to pay for machinery and needed buildings.

If a person has enough capital (money) he may use his own. If he needs more than he has, he may borrow the money from a bank. He repays the money over a period of time. The bank charges interest for the use of its money. In this way the bank makes a profit.

Sometimes a person needing money for his industry may ask a friend to join him in a partnership. If more money is needed, others may be asked to put their money into the company. If a person wishes to sell part of his company, he may give a certificate of stock. To help companies get money, stock certificates are sold in stock exchanges as well as by the owners. Stock exchanges are found in

Philadelphia and Pittsburgh. Stocks also are sold in smaller cities through stock brokers.

Persons, banks, and stockholders decide where to invest their money. If a company improves its sales and profits, its stock sells for higher prices. No stock is guaranteed to pay profits, but persons who are willing to invest their money aid industries. Lending institutions and stockmarkets are strictly regulated by Federal and State governments.

JOB OPPORTUNITIES IN PENNSYLVANIA

As you progress in your education you must begin to think about the work you will do after graduation. Many years ago most Pennsylvanians were farmers. In later years there was more development of various businesses and industries. Some people believe that Pennsylvania is a coal mining state. Others believe that manufacturing is the major industry. Others believe that office jobs are the best chance of employment in Pennsylvania.

The facts are that one must study the development of various industries constantly to understand job opportunities in the State. Job opportunities change and you must be alert to those changes in order to select a career.

The chart below shows the percentage of persons employed in various industries. Railroad employees, farmers, and other self-employed persons were not included in this survey.

Percentage of Employment by Occupation in Pennsylvania

Occupation	%	Occupation	%
Service Industries	26.6	Finance, Insurance and Real Estate	5.9
Wholesale and Retail Trade	22.6		
		Construction	5.1
Manufacturing	20.7	Transportation, Communication and Public Utilities	4.8
Government Administration	13.1	Mining	0.4

Source: PA Dept. of Commerce

Employment in Service Industries

Service industries employ more people, over 1,200,000, than any type of industry in Pennsylvania.

The health service industry is made up of hospitals, offices, and clinics of medical doctors, dentists, and other health practitioner, nursing and personal care facilities, home health care services and medical and dental laboratories. The health service industry employs over 230,000 people.

A doctor used to practice his profession from a room in his home, but today he may be the president of a health care corporation. A doctor may have five different offices with professional and supporting employees to help treat patients.

Nursing and personal care facilities employ over 73,000 people. Medical doctors employ over 52,000 people and hospitals over 30,000 persons.

Corporations may own four or five hospitals with professional administrators, accountants, and all types of staff. Corporations that own a medical college, a hospital, research laboratories, a nursing home, a financial corporation and a nursing school also employ many staff members. An example is the Geisinger Medical Center of Danville which is probably the largest employer of Montour County.

Harrisburg Hospital Photo

Harrisburg Hospital, pictured above, is part of the growing health care industry that often is the largest private employer in a community.

Business services are the second highest employer of service people. Almost 200,000 people work in advertising, credit reporting and collection, mailing, reproduction and stenographic services; services to buildings, equipment rental and leasing, computer and data processing services, and personal supply services. About 2,000 new computer and word processing jobs are added in the state yearly.

Educational services, not counting public schools or universities which are government agencies, hire over 111,000 people who work in kindergartens, elementary and secondary schools, colleges and universities, libraries, and vocational schools. The University of Pittsburgh and Temple University may be the biggest employers in their cities. There are over 75,000 persons employed in Pennsylvania's non-public colleges and universities.

Engineering and management services, including public relations, employ over 101,000 people.

Social services, including individual and family services, job training, child day care, and residential care, employ over 94,000 people. More and more of such services are being performed by agencies outside the family. More and more such facilities are owned by corporations.

Hotels and lodging places employ almost 52,000 people throughout the State from central cities to the most remote places. Individuals, the Hershey Entertainment and Resort Company, and nationwide and foreign organizations operate hotels/motels within the state.

services, which include laundry, cleaning and garment services, photographic studios, beauty shops, barber shops, shoe repair, and funeral services and crematories, employ over 51,000 people.

Over 45,000 people work in membership organizations. The Harrisburg telephone book lists over 250 associations that range from the AAA to church groups to labor unions to the YWCA. Each group promotes programs, membership, and favorable legislation. Labor organizations employ more than 10,000 people. Over 5,000 employees work for business and professional organizations such as chambers of commerce and medical societies.

Amusement and recreational services employ almost 40,000 people in orchestras, bowling centers, dance studios, and commercial sports. The professional athletic clubs like the Philadelphia Phillies and Pittsburgh Steelers, as well as the Williamsport baseball or Johnstown hockey teams, employ a total of 3,000 people. Amusement parks employ several thousand more people.

Producing motion pictures, then distributing, projecting and renting them through videotape stores employ an additional 10,000 people.

Lawyers and/or their law firms employ almost 40,000 people to help provide legal services to Pennsylvanians. This service has changed from the lawyer who had an office in his home and typed his own letters to groups of lawyers whose partnerships may be a professional corporation with over 100 lawyers, additional paralegals, legal secretaries, and others.

Automobile repair services employ over 38,000 people. Two large nation-wide transmission repair shop companies are headquartered in Philadelphia.

Almost 2,500 people who work in museums and zoos provide for our interests. The Carnegie in Pittsburgh and the Museum of Art in Philadelphia are well known, but smaller museums employ people too. Zoos need veterinarians, managers and attendants.

The number of people employed in the service industries increased by over 43% in the years between 1979 and 1989 while over 53% of the jobs in mining were eliminated.

Wholesale and Retail Trade

Over a million workers in Pennsylvania are employed in the wholesale and retail industries, the second largest employer of people in Pennsylvania. Wholesale dealers sell finished products to retailers who sell them to individuals.

The wholesale distribution of food requires over 100,000 people, and retail food stores another 160,000 people. Eating and drinking establishments need 264,000 people to serve food. The 15,000 eating establishments employ more people than any other Pennsylvania business. Twice as many people are employed in distributing food than growing it, and four times as many are required to serve it in restaurants.

Wholesale companies sell such things as automobiles, television sets, and household appliances to retailers. The wholesale distribution of machinery is the largest employer of durable, lasting goods with almost 38,000 persons. There are 25,000 persons in wholesale and 201,000 in retail and fixing automobiles in Pennsylvania. The automobile plays an important part in the Pennsylvania economy.

Wholesale warehouses are found in all metropolitan areas. One of the nation's largest hardware store wholesalers is in Butler County. From Cumberland County, Rite-Aid, one of the nation's largest drug store chains, distributes its wares, and the Book-of-the-Month Club distributes its books to America.

Often the large retail department stores of Philadelphia and Pittsburgh have retail stores in smaller cities and municipalities. The Blair Company of Warren is one of the nation's largest mail order houses and is the county's largest employer.

Retail stores selling clothing employ over 50,000 people, furniture 35,000, and building materials over 32,000. Apparel stores vary from the owner-operated type to the outlets of Luzerne County. Building material stores vary from the smallest to warehouse-sized retail stores.

The number of wholesale and retail jobs increased 17% in the years 1979-1989.

Harold Corsini, Photographic Library

Night and day the steel furnaces of Pennsylvania are turning out products for the use of the world's population. Pittsburgh, pictured above, has become the steel capital.

Manufacturing Industries

The number of jobs in manufacturing industries in the United States decreased in the 1980s, but in Pennsylvania such jobs decreased by 24%. Pennsylvania still ranks third in the number of employees in such industries, with only California and New York having more.

There are over a million workers in over 16,000 factories. The following chart indicates the types of manufacturing industries, the number of plants, and the number of employees:

Manufacturing Industries of Pennsylvania, 1989

Industry	**Number of Plants**	**Number of Employees**
Metal	2480	175,000
Paper and Printing	2820	124,000
Textile	1780	110,000
Machinery	2650	109,000
Food Products	1130	91,000
Electrical Products	830	90,000
Chemicals	580	59,000
Transportation Equipment	320	58,000
Lumber and Furniture	1400	54,000
Leather, Rubber and Plastic	760	51,000
Stone, Clay and Glass	880	48,000
Instruments	470	39,000
Petroleum and Coal Products	170	10,000
Miscellaneous	360	22,000

Source, Dept. of Commerce

Metal Products

Pennsylvania continues to rank first in producing primary metals and has the headquarters of ALCOA (aluminum), USX (formerly United States Steel), and ARMCO Steel. These companies have plants throughout the state and across the nation. There are numerous other smaller metal companies throughout the state. In the early 1980s, Pennsylvania steel companies laid off almost half their employees and closed obsolete and surplus plants because of decreased demand and foreign imports. There has been some turn around and in the year 1988-1989 there were almost 2,400 new jobs created. There are over 500 metal making plants employing over 82,000 people making steel, aluminum, copper, zinc and brass.

The larger part of the metal industry is fabricating metal into usable products. Pennsylvania has about 2,000 such plants employing about 100,000 persons. There are such plants throughout the state manufacturing everything from nuts and bolts and brass door knobs to aluminum cable, prefabricated buildings and metal doors, automobiles frames, and huge forged parts for electric generators. There are rails made for railroads and pipes for transporting oil, gas or water. The largest number of jobs are in Philadelphia, Allegheny, Montgomery, Lancaster, and York counties.

Paper and Printing Industries

Pennsylvania's paper plants use pulp from local forests to produce paper and paper board in 25 mills employing over 8,500 persons. The largest paper plants are in Erie, York, Blair, and Elk counties.

Another 30,000 people are employed to convert the paper and paperboard into products that range from stationery products and sanitary paper products to corrugated paper boxes. Scott Paper is one of the largest such employers.

More than 83,000 people are employed in more than 2,400 plants to produce printed and/or published materials. The greatest number of people, 31,000 in about 1,900 shops, do commercial printing for others.

The 328 newspaper plants publish about 100 daily and over 300 weekly newspapers and employ over 28,000 people. As might be expected, the largest cities employ the greatest number for printers to produce the metropolitan newspapers that are read in their areas.

Philadelphia employs about 20 percent of Pennsylvania's printers to produce two daily papers, 36 weeklies, and 249 periodicals. America's most popular magazine, TV GUIDE, is published in Delaware County, along with 50 other magazines. There are over 660 periodicals published in Pennsylvania. There are 75 book publishers employing over 2,000 persons, while 38 plants employee 4,000 persons to print books.

Textile Related Industries

Pennsylvania ranks second to New York in producing textile products. There are almost 1,800 plants employing over 110,000 people producing fabrics, clothing, woven and tufted carpets, and rugs. The Philadelphia College of Textiles is devoted to the industry.

Clothing is produced in over half of the counties. The largest clothing factories are found in Berks, Philadelphia, Lehigh, Lackawanna, Luzerne, and Northampton counties. A men's clothing factory in Lehigh County manufactures suits sold under more than a hundred labels. Vanity Fair manufactures women's clothing and also attracts outlet shoppers from several states. Many small communities have sewing factories that employ mostly women to make various articles of clothing.

The largest floor covering plants are those of Masland in Carlisle and Magee in Bloomsburg. Their products are used in automobiles as well as homes and offices.

There are several textile companies in Southeastern Pennsylvania that manufacture American flags.

Industrial Machinery and Equipment

Factories that manufacture machines to perform duties for people are important. There are over 2,500 plants that employ over 100,000 people to manufacture engines and turbines. Machinery for farm and garden, construction, metal working, refrigeration, computers and industry are also produced.

Allegheny, York, Montgomery, and Lehigh counties produce machinery of greatest dollar value. York Corporation's refrigeration machines, Grove's mobile cranes, and Ford's New Holland farm machinery plants are some of the nation's largest of their types.

The Unisys Corporation of Montgomery County manufactured the first successful computer and its many plants and offices employ many Pennsylvanians. Zurn Industries manufactures machinery for improving environmental quality.

EARNING A LIVING IN PENNSYLVANIA

Food Products

There are many more persons who prepare food products than grow them. There are over 1,100 food product plants employing over 91,000 people. Pennsylvania is America's fourth largest producer of food products. Practically every county has some type of food plant, but Philadelphia, Dauphin, Allegheny, Berks, York, Lancaster, and Montgomery counties have the largest employment of such food workers.

Philadelphia is known for its bakery products, its ice creams; and its candies. Hershey and Heinz are some of the nation's largest food companies. Hanover Foods processes most of its food in York County, but grows some of its crops as far away as Central America. Fruit is canned in Adams County, vegetables in Northumberland, and meat is processed throughout the State.

Food products include Alpo pet foods made by Allentown Products.

Electrical and Electronic Products

There are over 90,000 people working in over 850 plants in the expanding electrical and electronic business. Everything from electric light bulbs to electric motors and generators are manufactured. Westinghouse, with its headquarters in Pittsburgh, has plants throughout the State, as does General Electric.

Telephone, radio and television parts and sets are manufactured by ITT, General Electric and others. Caloric manufactures electrical home appliances in Berks County. Montgomery, Berks, Lehigh and Allegheny Counties manufacture the largest amounts of electrical equipment.

Manufacturing electronic components worth over a billion dollars employs over 37,000 workers. TYCO (AMP) of Dauphin County has numerous plants in several counties and nations.

Chemical and Allied Products

The number of chemical and allied product plants has increased in Pennsylvania. The center of this activity is in Allegheny, Montgomery, Chester, and Philadelphia Counties.

Two thirds of the value of manufacturing is for pharmaceutical products, medicines and needed drugs. Some of these plants are those of E.R. Squibb and Sons, Eli Lilly, and Smithkline Beckman of Southeastern Pennsylvania. Allegheny County is the headquarters of Bayer USA and the Calgon Corporation. Pennsylvania employs about 10 percent of all such workers in America.

A related industry is that of Dentsply International in York which manufactures artificial teeth.

There are over 50 paint producing plants and 37 fertilizer plants. Soaps, cleaners, glues, inks, and explosives are other types of the 150 chemical plants in the state.

Transportation Equipment

Transportation equipment is made in over 320 plants which employ over 58,000 people. The types of equipment included are motor vehicles, aircraft, ships and boats, railroad, motorcycles and bicycles, and guided missiles and space vehicles.

The motor vehicle made in Pennsylvania that are most noticeable are the small mail delivery trucks made by Grumman LLV in Lycoming County for the U.S. Postal Service. The headquarters and a factory of Mack Trucks is located in Lehigh County. Truck trailers are made in Berks and Lawrence counties and travel trailers in Lancaster County. Of the more than 80 factories that make motor vehicles parts, the largest is the General Motors' Fisher Body works in Allegheny County. The only American owned motorcycle assembly plant is Harley-Davidson in York County.

Boeing helicopters are manufactured in Delaware County in a former locomotive factory. There are almost 40 aircraft related manufacturing plants in Pennsylvania. Over 8,000 people are employed in manufacturing parts for guided missiles and space vehicles in the plant of General Electric in Valley Forge.

Ship building along the Delaware River has fallen to foreign competition. There is still some ship repairing in Delaware County and at the Philadelphia Navy Yard. Pleasure boats are made in Lancaster County.

Diesel-electric locomotives are manufactured at General Electric's plant in Erie County, and railroad cars are manufactured in Mercer and Cambria counties.

Lumber and Furniture

The forests of Pennsylvania provide the raw materials for over 1,400 lumber and furniture factories that employ about 45,000 people.

Logging and sawmills employ over 8,000 people. There is an international market for Pennsylvania's walnut, oak and cherry woods. There is a State lumber museum in Potter County.

Wood millwork employs another 12,000 and even more people are employed to make wooden containers, plywood and mobile homes. Several companies produce kitchen cabinets, wooden roof trusses, doors, and even modular homes.

There are more than 70 home furniture factories, with the Pennsylvania House of Union County being the largest. Ethan Allen and Armstrong World Industries also make furniture.

Leather, Rubber and Plastic

Pennsylvania's State tree, the hemlock, has always been an important source of tannin for finishing leather. A large factory in Tioga County and 15 others tan and finish leather. 50 Shoe factories, with intern, now employ 7,000 of 10,000 leather workers. The shoe factory is in Hanover of York County. A related industry is the luggage plant in Lawrence County.

Rubber and plastic plants employ about 42,000 workers. Rubber manufacturing has changed in Pennsylvania from automobile tires to industrial related products. Westmoreland, Erie, Allegheny, and Lackawanna Counties have rubber plants. Bicycle tires are made in Cumberland County.

Plastic products of all sorts are made in large numbers in Montgomery, Erie, Bucks, Chester, and Lancaster Counties. Rohm and Haas is a major producer. The Polymer Corporation of Reading has factories in seven countries. There are increases in the number of employees needed to produce plastic products.

Stone, Clay and Glass

About 50,000 people are employed in the stone, clay and glass products industries.

Pennsylvania's sand heated by its natural gas has long provided a glass industry that today employs 20,000 persons making flat glass, glassware, and pressed and blown glass. Pittsburgh Plate Glass Company (PPG) has factories in Allegheny Crawford and Cumberland counties, and Lenox Crystal is in Westmoreland County. Others make glass containers in Clarion, Jefferson and Fayette Counties.

Sand is dredged from the bottom of Lake Erie and a similar operation takes place in the Allegheny River.

Pennsylvania's clay has always provided jobs for persons making pottery tableware. The largest number of jobs are in York, Lawrence and Jefferson counties. The clay of Clearfield County is manufactured into ceramic refractory products.

The stone product that produces the most jobs is crushed stone used for building roads and buildings. Some building stone is also produced.

Cement is a major industry in Lehigh, Northampton, and Lawrence Counties. Northampton County is the home of Pennsylvania's slate industry. Lime is produced for agricultural and industrial uses in many counties.

Instruments and Related Products

In 470 plants about 39,000 people produce search and navigation equipment, measuring and controlling devices, medical instruments, photography equipment and watches and clocks.

The Tele-Dynamics plant in Montgomery County produces search and navigation equipment. Robertshaw of Westmoreland County produces heat measuring devices that are found on most stoves. Fischer and Porter of Bucks County makes process control instruments. American Sterilizer of Erie manufactures medical instruments.

Petroleum and Coal Products

Changing crude oil into usable products employs over 10,000 Pennsylvanians. The largest refineries located along the Delaware River, using imported oil, are operated by Atlantic, BP, Chevron, formerly Gulf, and Sun. The Sun Company (Sunoco) of Delaware

County is one of America's largest companies. It refines, distributes and often retails gasoline and other products. Pennsylvania oil is refined by Kendall and Quaker State in McKean County and Pennzoil in Venango County. Refineries in Allegheny, Beaver and Warren counties use other oils.

Asphalt products are produced in connection with road paving and roofing companies throughout the State.

Other Manufacturing

Over 22,000 people are employed manufacturing other types of products.

Manufacturing signs and advertising displays employs 2500 people, while making fine and costume jewelry about 1000 people.

Northampton County produces pencils, pens, office and art supplies for home, schools and industry. Bedford County has a plant that makes toys, baby carriages and playground equipment. Brooms and brushes are made in Berks County. Musical carillons are made in Bucks County.

Government Administration

Pennsylvania's 2500 local governments employ from one person to the 33,000 in Philadelphia. The State government employs over 85,000 persons under the Governor's direction. Over 30,000 work for the Department of Public Welfare and 12,600 for the Department of Transportation. The General Assembly and the State judicial system employ additional people. Public school districts employ over 120,000 and the 14 public universities have 2500 professional employees. Thousands more are hired as support personnel.

In Dauphin County 15,000 people work for the state. In Centre County, the state-related Penn State is the largest employer. In some counties, the public schools are the largest employers.

The federal government employs people in each community to deliver the mail and to operate the post offices. The federal buildings in larger cities have court rooms and offices for social security employees, agricultural agents, internal revenue agents and military recruiters.

The federal government employs thousands of employees to maintain military installations within the State from the Philadelphia Navy Yard, New Cumberland Army Depot, the Mechanicsburg Defense Depot, Letterkenny and Tobyhanna Depots, the Willow Grove Naval Air Station and the Pittsburgh Air Force Unit.

Finance, Insurance and Real Estate

The number of jobs in finance, insurance and real estate increase yearly. Banks and related financial institutions such as savings and loan units employ over 100,000 people. With the advent of state-wide banking, PNC Financial and AllFirst, both multi-state banks, have become the state's largest financial institutions.

There are still over 300 banking institutions, 130 private financial companies, 1400 credit unions and 200 savings and loan companies.

The largest insurance employer is the Pennsylvania Blue Shield, which also administers much of the federal government's Medicare program in Pennsylvania. The various regional Blue Cross programs are large employers as well. Several large insurance companies have their headquarters in Philadelphia and throughout the State. There are 1200 insurance agencies employing over 11,000 people in Pennsylvania.

The exchange of real estate requires the employment of over 35,000 people.

Construction

Construction of buildings, roads and bridges employs over 260,000 Pennsylvanians. The number of employees has grown over 32 percent in the past 10 years. Pennsylvania has exceeded the average growth of the nation in this important business for several years.

The construction of buildings employs over 210,000 people, including those who remodel homes, build homes, and those who build tall office buildings, factories, and warehouses.

Other than the builders, there is a need for about 140,000 special trade contractors to install plumbing, heating and air conditioning; to paint, hang wallpaper and decorate; and to do electrical work.

EARNING A LIVING IN PENNSYLVANIA

Over 20,000 masons are needed to lay brick and stone, 10,000 roofers and 9,000 carpenters.

Building highways and local streets for the state and local governments employs over 7,000 people, not counting those employed by the government.

Transportation, Communication and Public Utilities

Transportation, including trucking, warehousing, passenger transit on land and by air employs over 157,000 people.

One half of the transportation jobs are in the more than 2,000 trucking companies. Their terminals have replaced railroad yards in size and activity. Roadway and Yellow double trailer rigs represent two of the larger companies.

Most Pennsylvanians travel by personal automobile, but public transportation by local and long distant buses, railroad trains, and airlines employ over 40,000 people. About the same number of people, 16,000 are needed to provide school bus transportation as it does to provide airline transportation.

Greyhound and Trailways buses provide state-wide-bus service, while government owned Amtrak trains provide some passenger service.

US Airways of Pittsburgh employs the most persons and provides the most service in the State.

Norfolk Southern and CSX serve most of the State and 49 other railroads haul freight and employ over 30,000 people.

Communication

Providing telephone, radio and television service employs over 50,000 people with the telephone industry providing over three-fourths of the jobs.

The Verizon headquarters are in Philadelphia. However there are still 49 other phone companies from the large Sprint to the Denver and Ephrata Company.

Practically every community has a radio station. Large cities may have over 20. Television stations are found in all metropolitan areas. Broadcasting employs over 10,000 people. Cable companies pro-

54 OUR PENNSYLVANIA HERITAGE

vide more stations for viewers and employ over 5,000 people.

Public Utilities

Providing electric, gas, water and sanitation services employs 55,000 people, with over half in electric service.

Electric companies generate electricity in coal-steam plants at mine heads in Indiana County, by water power by the Safe Harbor Company on the Susquehanna, or by nuclear power by PP&L, GPU, Duquesne and PECO. Additional employees are needed to have the power transmitted to homes, offices and industry.

Natural gas, found in Western Pennsylvania, is widely used there for heat. Gas is manufactured by the Philadelphia Gas Works. Additional gas is piped in from other states. Over 8,000 persons are employed to complete these tasks.

Over 2,000 people, not including those of community owned systems, are employed by private water companies, and sewage and solid waste' disposal by companies require another 5,000 employees.

Pennsylvania State Department of Commerce

Corn is Pennsylvania's largest crop. Rich Lancaster County soil produces more corn than any other county, but the crop is grown in practically all counties.

Mining, Oil, and Gas Extraction

Mining, which once employed over 100,000 persons, now employs less than 20,000 in coal mining. Less than one person in 200 works in mining, oil and gas extraction in Pennsylvania.

The Consolidated Coal Company of Pittsburgh and the Rochester and Pittsburgh Coal Company of Indiana County are two of the 500 bituminous coal companies. The once thriving anthracite coal business now employs about 1250 people in 50 companies.

There are five small iron mining companies and one zinc mining company. Akzo of Lackawanna County mines, manufactures and sells salt.

There are over 370 small oil and natural gas companies extracting those products. Companies that service the wells employ 2500 people.

Agriculture

Employment in agriculture is not listed separately since most of the 53,000 farms in Pennsylvania are run by individual families. The crops produced by such farmers provide many more jobs as the crops become food products, are manufactured into other products, and are distributed through wholesale and retail outlets. Farms also provide jobs indirectly from the products they use.

Employment in the Future

Possibilities for employment in Pennsylvania are numerous. The types of jobs change with the needs of the people and the creative minds of people who dream up new industries.

The computer was developed in Pennsylvania. Pennsylvania's hospitals attract patients from all over the world. Entertainers from Pennsylvania on television and in sports create new jobs.

One reality of employment is that more and more jobs require more and more education. There are few jobs that require less than a high school education. Community college, college and university educations are often needed for the better jobs. The better jobs are for those who are best educated.

REVIEW QUESTIONS

1. What is the meaning of economics?
2. What is meant by the term "free enterprise"?
3. What functions do banks serve in our State?
4. Name four of the major minerals in Pennsylvania and tell how they are used.
5. Name as many uses of limestone as you can.
6. What is the meaning of the word "labor" to the people of Pennsylvania?
7. Identify some businesses conducted by the government.
8. Which industry hires the greatest number of workers in Pennsylvania?
9. The textile industry in Pennsylvania is centered in what area of the State?
10. Name some of the major producers of transportation equipment in Pennsylvania and list their products.
11. Where is the center of the lumber industry in Pennsylvania?
12. Why has the opportunity for jobs in the farming industry decreased?
13. In what areas of employment have we had the greatest growth of job opportunities?

Do you know the meaning of or can you identify?
Write a sentence containing the following words or phrases:

1. capital
2. profit
3. communism
4. socialism
5. capitalism
6. mixed economy
7. corporation
8. bituminous
9. anthracite
10. natural gas
11. stockholder
12. manufacture
13. service
14. electronics
15. plastic
16. public utilities
17. automation
18. Pittsburgh Pirates
19. Hershey Bears
20. Philadelphia Eagles

EARNING A LIVING IN PENNSYLVANIA

Maps to Help Us Learn

1. On a Pennsylvania outline map shade all the cities that have steel factories.
2. On an outline map of Pennsylvania indicate and identify all the areas of the major mineral deposits in Pennsylvania.
3. On an outline map of Pennsylvania indicate the forest areas of Pennsylvania.
4. On an outline map of Pennsylvania locate all radio and television stations of Pennsylvania.

What Do You Think?

1. A person earns his living by doing something that another person is willing to pay him to do.
2. Pennsylvania has the minerals, money and men to be wealthy.
3. One must work harder physically today than ever before.
4. The United States has the highest standard of living in the world.
5. Private enterprise needs less (or more) government regulation.
6. Trucks are taking the place of the railroads in the transportation of more and more items of our economy.
7. There is a definite future today in the chemical industry.
8. Pennsylvania produces some of the finest oil in the world.
9. Television will become an important part of our future educational system.
10. Grapes could grow just as well in Adams County as apples could in Erie County.
11. Job opportunities have increased continually in real estate.
12. The greatest and the best opportunities exist today for those young people who are best educated.
13. The local country store will eventually replace the department store.

ACTIVITIES

1. Draw a circle graph showing the percentages of employment by occupations in Pennsylvania in 1981.

2. Through research, trace the major railroad, truck, bus, and the airplane routes in Pennsylvania. What areas are lacking in transportation facilities? Why?

3. Make a list of the famous entertainers who were born in Pennsylvania.

4. Draw a cartoon illustrating the work that your father does.

5. Dramatize the effect of television on the future of education in Pennsylvania.

6. Do a research project about the largest manufacturing companies that are located in Pennsylvania or have branches in Pennsylvania. Another person could take one company and study it in detail.

7. Write a composition entitled "Why I am proud of Pennsylvania."

READING MATERIALS

Annual Report, Pennsylvania Department of Agriculture, Harrisburg, PA

Billinger, Robert D., *Pennsylvania's Coal Industry*, Pennsylvania Historical Association, Gettysburg, Pa., 1954.

Bining, Arthur C., *Pennsylvania Iron and Steel Industry,.* Pennsylvania Historical Association, Gettysburg, Pa., 1954.

Fey, Arthur W., *Buried Black Treasure; The Story of Pennsylvania Anthracite*, Bethlehem, Pa., 19S4.

Fuller, Theodore E. and Smith, Stephen M., *Road to Renaissance V*, Bell of Pennsylvania, et al, Harrisburg, PA, 1990.

Jaworlk, W. G., "Petroleum in Pennsylvania - Today and Tomorrow" *Pennsylvania Business Survey*, August, 1959.

Pellow, Randall, *Pennsylvania Geography*, Penns Valley Publishers, Lansdale, PA, 1992

Pennsylvania Abstract, (Published biennially), Penn State Harrisburg, Middletown, PA

Pennsylvania Chamber of Business and Industry, *The 1989 Pennsylvania Business Guide*, Harrisburg, PA, 1989.

Report on Forest and Waters, Land and People, 1954-1958, Department of Forest and Waters, Harrisburg, Pa., 1959.

Roscoe, Edwin Scott, *The Textile Industry in Pennsylvania*, Pennsylvania State University Park, Pa., 1958.

Young, Joseph S., *The Lehigh Story (Cement) 1897-1955*, Allentown, Pa., 1955.

chapter III

Indians of Pennsylvania

Indians were the first people to live in Pennsylvania. It is thought that the Indians had been living in Pennsylvania for more than five thousand years before the white man came from Europe.

Indians have the physical characteristics of the people of Asia except that their skin is redder than other Orientals. Their thick, black hair and high cheekbones are characteristics of the people of Asia. They walk erect and their faces are beardless like the face of Asiatics.

Most historians agree that Indians migrated to North America from Asia. Perhaps the two continents were at one time joined at what is now the Bering Strait. They may have passed over this strip of land as long ago as fifteen thousand years before some of them found their way to Pennsylvania.

The Allegewi

The earliest known Indians to live in Pennsylvania were the Allegewi. From them we get the name Allegheny. They are believed to have been the builders of the great mounds found along the Ohio River and its tributaries. By the time the whites arrived, they had disappeared. Their burial mounds have been found in Erie, Crawford, Westmoreland, Fayette and Allegheny Counties. It is thought that the Cherokee Indians of the South were their descendants.

The Allegewi left no writings. They had no written language. They probably lived like the later Indians, but their clothing and weapons were not quite so well developed.

THE INDIAN TRIBES

The Algonquins

The Europeans found two major groups of Indian nations in Pennsylvania — the Algonquin and the Iroquois. Each of these groups spoke a basically different language. The Algonquin group at one time consisted of 40 tribes. When they moved into Pennsylvania from the west some stayed behind. Other tribes of the Algonquin moved south. The leading representatives of the Algonquin nations in Pennsylvania were the Lenni Lenape. The name is said to have meant the Original People. The Europeans found these Indians in the Delaware River Valley and called them Delaware Indians.

The Delaware Indians in the river valley were divided into three large clans. The Munsees, or Wolf Clan, lived north of the Lehigh River. They were generally more warlike than the other clans and often acted independently of them. The Unami or Turtle Clan, whose chief was regarded as the King of all the Delawares, lived between the Schuylkill and Lehigh Rivers. Their special importance to the Delaware nation is revealed by their totem symbol, the turtle or tortoise. In the Delaware religion the tortoise was the symbol of

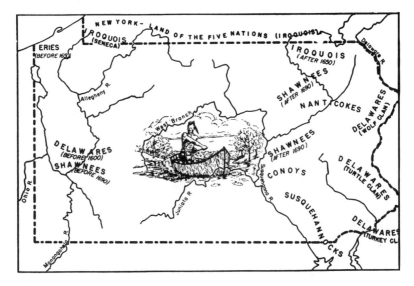

This map shows where the different tribes lived and hunted in the wilderness that was Pennsylvania before the arrival of the white settlers changed their lives.

University of Pittsburgh Press

Bark wigwams were used for homes by the Algonquin tribes of Pennsylvania. The woman to the left is stretching a deerskin before curing it by smoke. The man is trying to start a fire. The woman to the right is trying to make a mat from fibers or rushes.

life, of the earth, and of the origin of things. The Unalachtigo or Turkey Clan lived south of the Unami around Delaware Bay and are sometimes identified with the Nanticokes.

The fact that the colonies to the south were started by Englishmen long before William Penn established Pennsylvania forced other Algonquin tribes to invade our state. In addition to the Nanticokes, the Shawnees wandered north of Pennsylvania. The Shawnees were one of the most restless of American tribes, seldom stopping for long in any one place. They entered Pennsylvania from the southwest and reached the Susquehanna country by 1690. The Conoys migrated into the same general area a little later.

The Iroquois

In northern Pennsylvania and New York State lived the Iroquois Indians. Indian lore tells of the Iroquois and Delaware coming east together, but that they became enemies. There were many clans of the Iroquois and they often fought with one another. According to Indian legend a wise Indian by the name of Deganawidah finally succeeded in getting the Iroquois tribes to work together as a confederation. He preached to them about justice between men and nations, healthy minds and bodies, and the power of authority through laws and customs. He had little success until helped by the great Indian orator, Hiawatha, who was later made famous by the poem written by Longfellow. Some years before the first white settlers came to Pennsylvania, the Iroquois created the Confederacy of Five Nations with the Cayuga, Mohawk, Oneida, Onondaga and Seneca Tribes. Later, about the year 1713, the Tuscaroras joined the Confederacy which was then known as the Six Nations.

Because of the Confederacy the Iroquois were able to live in peace with themselves, but they did have wars with other tribes that refused to join with them. The Erie Indians, who lived in northwestern Pennsylvania and spoke an Iroquoian language, were almost entirely destroyed by the Iroquois Confederacy. The spark was ignited when an Erie Indian killed a Seneca. In return the Senecas killed several Eries. The Eries captured the Onondaga chief Annanraes. He was given to the mother of one of the dead Eries. The mother refused him and asked that he be tortured. Finally he was burned at the stake.

University of Pittsburgh Press

Iroquois long houses were the most advanced homes to the Indians in eastern United States. The one at the left shows the method of construction. Note the coverings over the smoke holes in the completed house. Women in the foreground are grinding corn, making pottery, roasting corn, and the one to the right is storing the dried corn.

The Five Nations in 1654 attacked the Eries' fortified village called Rique at the present site of Erie city. The Iroquois and Eries both suffered great losses, but in the end the Eries were defeated. Those who were not killed either fled west or joined the Iroquois. This defeat of the Eries left western Pennsylvania practically deserted of Indians. For some time the land was simply a hunting ground for the Iroquois.

Another once powerful tribe who spoke an Iroquoian language, the Susquehannock Indians, met a similar fate after resisting the Confederacy for many years. In the 1670s their forts and villages along the lower Susquehanna River were destroyed. They retired to the Conestoga Valley which is now Lancaster County. There they lived peacefully until settlers became embittered with all Indians in 1763. At that time many Conestogas, as they were called, were massacred.

INDIAN WAY OF LIFE

With the tribes mentioned, one might think there were many Indians in Pennsylvania. Most historians agree there were not over 20,000 at any one time. If the Indians had been evenly distributed, there would have been only one for each 2 1/4 square miles. Today there are about 600 people for every 2 1/4 square miles. Early traders had to search out the Indians to make their trades.

When the white man arrived, they found the Indians of the Delaware Valley living peacefully. The Unami chief of the Delawares was respected as the leader. They were living in clans in villages along the river bank. Their civilization would be described as that of the later stone age; that is, their tools and weapons were still made of stone. They had no guns, used no wheels, and had neither alphabet nor writing.

The most advanced tools of the Indian were hatchets of stone and knives of flint. His weapons were spears and arrows tipped with flint stone. The stone was tied to wooden shafts with rawhide. Bows were made of wood strung with rawhide to shoot the arrows. These weapons were crude and not effective at any great distance.

Home and Villages

By the time of the white man's arrival, most Indian tribes had given up their earlier nomadic wanderings and settled down to village life. An Indian village generally contained from 10 to 50 families. A white visitor counted 18 hunters, 13 squaws, and "numerous" children in the camp he visited.

Most villages were located near a stream where the soil was fertile. The stream also provided fish and if large enough could be used for canoe travel. In the evening the game from the woods would come to the stream for water where it could be killed more easily.

The Delaware and other Algonquin tribes built individual houses for each family. They were not the teepees usually pictured in movies. The Indians of the east needed all the skins they had for making clothing. The Delaware home was made by bending over saplings or young trees. These were bent and tied together at the top to make it rounded. The saplings were then interwoven with split poles crosswise. These were covered with bark or brush.

Iroquois Indians lived in what are known as long houses. A whole clan might live in one house. These houses were 50 to 100 feet long and 6 to 8 feet wide. Logs were placed upright in the ground 4 to 6 feet high and smaller logs were placed across the top to give it a rounded effect. All logs were lashed together with rawhide and then covered with bark.

The inside of the long house was dingy and dark for there were no windows. The door was an opening which was covered in the winter with a bear skin. Holes were left in the roof so that fires could be built in the aisle down the center. Smoke would find its way out the top in time. On each side of the aisle down the center, compartments were made by hanging deer hides every 6 or 8 feet. Each family had a separate compartment. Beds were simply bear skins, deer hides or even soft boughs.

Around each permanent village a palisade was built. A palisade was a fence of upright logs lashed together with grapevines or tree branches. The palisade would keep the panthers and other dangerous animals outside. It served as a fort against attacking enemies. The farm land of the Indians was outside the palisade.

The Work of the Men

It was the job of the men to protect the village and to kill the animals that would serve for food and provide skins for clothing. At a very young age all boys were taught to hunt and to defend themselves. Boys were taught to wrestle, use a knife, and to use bow and arrows properly.

Indian battles usually involved a small number of braves. Often a fight would involve less than 30 men. The men learned to move through the woods as silently as possible. They crept up on their foes and endeavored to surprise them.

Indians killed foes in warfare only when they thought it absolutely necessary. If possible they took their enemies as prisoners. The prisoners were given to widowed women or to young women without husbands.

Animals were killed only when necessary as Indians did not kill for sport. Food was usually scarce and practically the whole animal was eaten. Hunting was quite a skill. The bows and arrows were clumsy by our standards. Remember that the arrows were made by attaching a sharpened piece of flint stone on a shaft that was hand made. Making a balanced point was almost impossible. The hard flint stone did not chip easily. To hit anything the hunter had to be very close to it.

The white-tailed deer was the most common Indian prize. The deer provided plenty of meat and the hides were fine for clothing. Antlers and bones were used for tools. The intestines were used for binding and for glue. To kill deer, the Indians set traps, or the men would steal up and pounce upon them. The latter method is called stalking. It required great skill.

The forests covered practically the whole area of what is now Pennsylvania. In them the Indians could find elk and black bear in addition to the deer. Hunters had to be on guard against the bobcats and panthers that lurked ready to pounce upon them.

Smaller animals frequently served as food. The raccoon, opossum, fox, squirrel, ground hog, and even rabbits, chipmunks, mice and shrews were often eaten. Along streams beavers and muskrats lived in great numbers. These animals were often clubbed to death by the Indians. To get beavers they used special methods. A hole would be broken in the beaver dam. When the beaver came to repair it, he was killed.

Birds were often killed by the use of blow guns. The larger ones were shot by arrow. Wild turkey, ruffed grouse, partridge, goose and dove were found throughout the state. Turkey calls were used by the Indians to lure the birds into a trap or to get them close enough to shoot with arrows.

Some writers have claimed that buffalo and moose were found in Pennsylvania, but investigation has revealed that moose probably never lived in the State. The remains of only one buffalo have ever been found, uncovered in what is now Somerset County.

The Indians were fishermen also. In the streams and rivers there could be found trout, perch, pike, catfish, sturgeon and bass. Turtles and eels also served as food for the Indians.

Europeans found that the Indians also maintained gardens. The men cleared the space for the garden, but the women were the gardeners. To clear a patch of land, an Indian would remove a band of bark from around the tree. This would kill the tree and allow the sun to shine on the crops. Sometimes the deadened trees were burned, but often they were simply left standing.

The Work of the Women

Women were very important and respected in the Indian civilization. When a man married, he moved in with his wife's family. The oldest woman was the umpire of all family problems. The family would include the grandparents, uncles, aunts, parents and children.

Women were the housekeepers. They skinned the animals and cooked or preserved the meat. Meat was preserved by smoking or drying. Women also tended crops and made the clothing.

Most of the clothing was made from deer skins. The skins were buried until the hair rotted off, then tanned into the well known buckskin. The women made the men shirt-like garments that reached to the knee. Leggings were made of the same material to protect the wearer from bushes. Women wore dresses of the same material, long loose-fitting garments that reached below the knees. Both men and women wore moccasins made of buckskin. Such foot coverings allowed them to move quickly and quietly through the woods.

Unlike the people of today, one set of clothing was plenty for an Indian. In summer the men wore only loin cloths. Adults and children went without foot covering in the summer. Children dressed as the parents did.

Gardening was done in a primitive manner. The ground was not plowed as it is today, but with the use of a sharp stick the soil was crudely prepared for sowing. The Indians did not plant corn in rows but in "hills" or mounds of soil drawn up around the kernels. When possible, fish was used as fertilizer. When the corn plants appeared, pumpkins, squash and beans were planted to vine among the stalks. Tomatoes also were planted.

Practically every Indian garden in the State had some tobacco plants. Tobacco was smoked in clay pipes at all important occasions. Indians had the mistaken idea that tobacco smoke was good for their health.

Women in the summers would spend time in the woods hunting for wild fruits, berries and nuts. Huckleberries, strawberries, raspberries, elderberries, grapes, choke cherries, sunflower seeds and persimmons were gathered to be eaten immediately or dried. Acorns, chestnuts, hickory nuts and walnuts also were eaten for food.

Food for the Indians

When the corn of the fields ripened, it was guarded closely for it would have to last for the winter. It was dried and placed in pits where it would be safe from animals. The dried corn would often be soaked in lye water, then made into hominy. Lye water was obtained by running water through the ashes of burnt wood. Hominy was easier to eat than the dried corn. The lye water would eat off the hard part of the kernel.

A white man described eating with the Indians as follows: "At this time, hominy, plentifully mixed with bear oils and maple sugar, or dried venison, bear oils and sugar, is what they offer to everyone who comes in any time of the day; and so they go on until their sugar, bear oil and venison is all gone, and they have to eat hominy by itself. Yet they invite everyone that comes in to eat while they have anything to give....

"When the warriors left town to hunt, all we had to live on was corn pounded into coarse meal or small hominy—this they boiled in water, which appeared as well-thickened soup without salt or anything else. At length we were brought to very short allowance. The warriors did not return as soon as expected. We were in a starving condition. The children were crying bitterly because of pinching hunger."

"Soon the warriors returned. About the same time the green corn became of use. The green corn and venison brought by the Indians allowed for good living."

When game became too scarce or the crops poor, the village was moved. This was not a complicated process. There was no furniture. All the valuables could be carried quite easily. Crop rotation was unknown to the Indians. They had no domestic animals except the dog. Walking was their only overland method of transportation. So when they moved it was not for any great distance.

How the Indians Shared

Life in the Indian village was usually peaceful and happy. Indians liked to sing, dance, play games and eat. Children were taught early to care for themselves. There was no formal schooling. There was no reading or writing to learn. Boys learned the problems of life from the men. Girls learned from the women.

Indians owned practically nothing. There was no money. Food belonged to all. The only possessions of an individual would be his clothing, weapons and a few bead ornaments. The Indian was taught to believe that the land belonged to all of them.

There was great cooperation among the Indians. They hunted together and shared their catch. The women helped one another in planting, weeding and harvesting the corn crops. When there was food, no one went hungry. If a strange Indian happened into the village he was given the best. When a white man living with the Indians gave one of the best pieces of meat to a stranger, the Indians praised him. They further asked, "Did you give him sugar and bear oil too?" When they found he had not they scolded, "Do you not know that when a stranger is in camp, we ought to give him the best we have?"

The Indians used wampum for gift-exchange and ceremonial purposes. Wampum was a belt of colored beads. The beads were made from sea shells that were cut up and pierced. They were then strung into belts three fingers, or seven beads, wide. They were worn by men or women as belts, tablets, bands for womens' hair, bracelets, necklaces or links to hand in their ears.

Sometimes the wampum was used to picture a deed, treaty or tradition. A treaty might show a white man and a red man holding hands to indicate friendship and agreement. A message of friendship was at times sent by messenger.

Indian Government and Worship

Indian government was simple and democratic. Each village or clan elected one of its members as chief. He was usually a good warrior or hunter. He had no great power and could be voted out as well as in to the position. He led his people in hunting and in war.

Government extended beyond the village to the tribe also. The chief from each village was a member of the tribal council. In the case of the Delawares the chiefs of the Munsee, Unami, and Unalachtigo made up the ruling council. The chief of the Unami was usually the head chief. This chief had to get the agreement of the others before he could make any important decisions.

There were no judges or written laws among the Indians. They established the simple right and wrong for law. Stealing was wrong. Lying was wrong. If a man stole from you, you were to get his property. A murderer was to be murdered by the victim's family. In case of large disputes, the council of chiefs settled the problem.

Pennsylvania Indians worshipped nature. They thought of the sun, moon, thunder and lightning as gods. But the gods of all gods was the Great Spirit. Most Indians were extremely devout and had a keen sense of religious values. Hunting and fishing success depended upon the wishes of the Great Spirit. Celebrations to the gods were held in springtime and at harvest time. Corn roasts were often part of a religious ceremony.

Religion was handed down from father and mother to children

by song, story and legend. When Europeans brought the Christian religion it was accepted by many Indians. They accepted the Christian God as the Great Spirit, but they saw no need for the Bible. "Indians have no need for such a book to let them know the will of their maker," they said. "Indians find it engraved in their hearts. "

THE INDIANS AND THE EUROPEANS

When the Indians first came into contact with the Europeans, they were friendly. Indian relations with the Swedes and the Dutch were generally peaceful. Susquehannocks met the English on the Chesapeake Bay and were friendly with them. Before the English arrived in Pennsylvania, the French had tried to gain control of the Iroquois. The English befriended the Iroquois in order to decrease the power of the French.

The Great Treaty

In 1682 the English found the Delawares living peacefully in the Delaware Valley. At this time the great chief of the Delawares was Tamenend or Tammany. His home was in the village of Shackamaxon in what is now northern Philadelphia.

An old tradition claims that William Penn and Tammany signed a Great Treaty in 1683. At this meeting Penn is believed to have said, "We meet in the broad pathway of good faith and good will; no advantage shall be taken of either side, but all shall be openness and love. We are the same as if one man's body was divided into two parts; we are one flesh and one blood."

The Indian chief replied, "We will live in love with William Penn and his children as long as the creeks and rivers run, and while the sun, moon, and stars endure. "

Both sides held to this treaty which gave the land near the Schuylkill and Delaware Rivers to the whites. For 70 years the peace thus established between the two people was carefully maintained. Both signers were long dead when the treaty was first broken.

INDIANS OF PENNSYLVANIA

Pennsylvania Academy of Fine Art

William Penn believed the Indians and white men could live in peace. Benjamin West, a Quaker from Swarthmore who became court painter to King George III, painted this scene showing Penn's meeting with the Delaware chiefs under a great elm at Philadelphia.

It was the white people who were to break the treaty. White men began to take advantage of the simple wants of the Indians. The Indians traded furs, food, and large pieces of land for a few beads, trinkets, or pieces of colored cloth. Other treaties were made later, but they too were eventually broken. More and more Europeans arrived in the new country, and the demand for Indian lands became greater and greater.

Purchasing the Land

Pennsylvania purchased nearly all the land of the state from the Indians at one time or another. In all there were thirty-three treaties and purchases. The early purchases were personal affairs between William Penn and the various chiefs who lived on the land. Much of the land of Bucks, Philadelphia and Chester (including present Delaware) Counties was purchased from the Delawares in 1683. The dealings were fair and not disputed. Penn received land "to run two days journey with a horse up into the country as said river doth go." In return the Indians were to receive, "so much wampum, so many guns, shoes, stockings, looking glasses, blankets and other goods as said William Penn shall please to give." Since both men were honorable there was no argument.

The next land purchases in 1684 gave Penn the land between Reading and Allentown in southern Berks and Lehigh counties and northern sections of Montgomery and Bucks. But Penn's health failed in 1712 and his wife assumed control of Pennsylvania affairs in England before Penn's death in 1718. In 1718, the Penn family purchased the land between "the Delaware and Susquehanna rivers from Duck Creek to the Lehigh Hills." This would include most of the area of York and Lancaster counties of today.

Following a small purchase in 1732, the Penns in 1736 bought what is now Franklin, Adams, Cumberland and parts of Dauphin, Lebanon and Berks counties. The goods given in return were thought to be fair exchange. Most of the Delawares moved to the west though a few stayed behind to live alongside the white settlers.

The Walking Purchase

But the purchase of 1737 was the turning point of all Indian relations in Pennsylvania. By then William Penn's sons were in charge of the colony. The young men said they possessed a treaty signed in 1688 by the old Delaware chiefs. By this treaty the Penns were to receive lands north of central Bucks County as far as a man could walk in a day and a half. The Indians denied that any such treaty existed. Finally the walk was agreed upon and Penn's sons hired three men who were known to be very strong and swift to make the walk. A path was cut ahead of them. The Indians, of course, expected a leisurely, friendly walk, but the three white men ran so fast the Indians did not try to keep up. One of the whites died of exhaustion along the way and the others finished by "walking" over sixty miles from Wrightstown, Bucks County to Lehighton, Carbon County. Then instead of drawing the northern line of the new boundary directly east to the Delaware River, as the Indians had understood the agreement, the Penns insisted that the upper boundary be drawn northeastward, at a right angle to the direction of the "walk."

The Indians thus lost practically all of the land that included their villages along the Delaware River. The Munsee Clan of the Delawares and the Shawnees were enraged and the Indians then refused to leave their lands. In 1742 the Penns called in the Iroquois chiefs and asked for their help. Gifts were given to the Iroquois and the Iroquois then informed the Delawares they would have to move westward. Hereafter, the Delawares were told, the Iroquois would do all the dealing with the white men. The Delawares were insulted when the Iroquois said, "We conquered you, we made you women, and you can no more sell land than women."

The Retreat of the Red Man

By the purchase of 1749, the Penns bought what was to become the southern part of the great anthracite coal region, including parts of Schuylkill, Carbon, Dauphin, Northumberland, Columbia and Luzerne Counties. This purchase, and all those thereafter, was made from the Iroquois. In 1754 south-central Pennsylvania, from Centre County south to the border and all lands west to the Allegheny mountains, was added.

At a treaty at Fort Stanwix in New York in 1768 the Iroquois sold the huge area that included all northeast and southwest Pennsylvania. By another treaty at Fort Stanwix in 1784 the remainder of the State, except the Erie triangle, was purchased. When Pennsylvania bought the Erie triangle from the federal government in 1792, the Iroquois were paid for their claims also.

After the Walking Purchase of 1737 the Delaware and Shawnee Indians were bitter toward the English. Some settlers always moved beyond the purchase lines, and these squatters, as they were called, would get into fights with the Indians. During the French and Indian and the Revolutionary Wars, the Delawares and Shawnees avenged these long-standing injuries by attacking frontier settlements.

In return some frontiersmen like Sam Brady became very bitter against the Indians. Brady's father and brother had been killed by Indians near Muncy, and in return Sam Brady became a famous Indian killer. Western Pennsylvania and eastern Ohio legends tell of the hundreds of Indians that Brady was supposed to have killed.

Tales of his daring are retold in each generation and towns, townships and streets have been named for him.

When the French came into western Pennsylvania they talked the embittered Indians into fighting the English colonists. The British enlisted the Iroquois to fight first the French and later the rebellious American colonists. The Indians became confused. "If the French own west of the Ohio, and the English own east, where do the Indians live?" they asked.

As the settlers moved into the interior of the State, the Indians were forced to move more and more to the west. By 1763 the Indians were west of the mountains and set up villages with names familiar to us today: Conewango, Punxsutawney, Kittanning, Kiskiminetas, Conemaugh and Shenango.

The Iroquois continued to rule over all Indians in this part of the country. In 1747 they sent down chiefs from New York to rule over western Pennsylvania Indians. One such ruler was Tanacharison, known to the whites as Half-King. He was a friend of George Washington as we shall find in a later chapter.

Each advance of the settlers sent the Indians farther west. The noisy and expanding invasion of the white men made it more and more difficult to hunt game in Indian fashion. Indians came to rely on guns and gun powder from the white men.

What the Indians Did for the White Men

Indians guided the settlers into the new lands and pointed out the springs of water, salt deposits, and paths through the wilderness. Each time they helped the settlers, they had less for themselves.

The white man's diseases reduced the Indian population even more. More Indians died from the common cold, influenza, and tuberculosis than in battle. These diseases had not been known before the coming of the white man.

By 1763 there were only about 5,000 Indians left in Pennsylvania and by 1776 there were but 1,000. At that time there were probably more than 300,000 white settlers in Pennsylvania. The Delaware and Shawnee Indians were forced to move into Ohio. Today their descendants live in Oklahoma. The Iroquois moved into western New York and those who fought for the British moved into Canada

INDIANS OF PENNSYLVANIA

after the Revolutionary War.

One group of Seneca Indians, under the leadership of their chief, decided to stay in Pennsylvania. This famous and beloved chief was called Cornplanter. The legislature of Pennsylvania awarded him 1,500 acres of land on the upper Allegheny River in 1789, and here he lived until his death in 1836 when he was believed to have been over 100 years old. He asked that the Quakers send his people teachers so his people could be "taught by the same principles by which your fathers were guided." Seventeen descendants still lived on the reservation in Warren County in 1950, but they and some 600 New York State Senecas were forced to move again by 1965 to make way for the Kinzua flood control dam on the Allegheny River.

When the Indians were gone, much remained to remind Pennsylvania of them. Numerous towns, counties, townships and rivers have Indian names. Erie, Juniata, Lackawanna, Lehigh, Lycoming, Tioga and Wyoming are all counties whose names come from the Indians. Allegheny, Susquehanna, Conemaugh, Conestoga,

Pennsylvania Historical and Museum Commission

Chief Cornplants was the last of the fighting Iroquois chiefs to have lived in Pennsylvania. The few remaining Indians of Pennsylvania lived in Warren County on the Cornplanter Reservation until about 1965.

Kiskiminetas and Conewango are but a few of the streams named by the Indians. Aliquippa, Punxsutawney, Nanticoke, Kittanning, Pocono and Pymatuning are interesting Indian place names.

Indians taught the settlers to grow maise and we now call the grain corn. In the first chapter we learned that corn is Pennsylvania's major crop today. Potatoes, beans, squash, pumpkins, tomatoes and tobacco were introduced to the white men by the Indians. Frontiersmen often followed the Indian method of clearing land and tilling soil.

Indian trails were used by the settlers and just about every major highway in the State today follows an earlier Indian trail. Nemacolin's path became Braddock's Road, later National Road, and today U.S. Route 40. The Lincoln Highway, Route 30, follows another path. The William Penn Highway, Route 22, is another example. In many places railroads have followed the trails that the Indians had carefully marked out.

No native American Indian reservations exist in Pennsylvania today. Children of Seneca Indians are pictured in the doorway of their 1950 home of the Cornplanter Settlement in Warren County before the Indians were moved to new homes in New York state. The 14,700 Native Americans in Pennsylvania in 1990 lived as Americans.

INDIANS OF PENNSYLVANIA

REVIEW QUESTIONS

1. By what route did the Indians first reach the Americas?
2. Explain how the members of the tribe worked for the common welfare?
3. How did the different Indian tribes of Pennsylvania feel about each other before Penn came? After the death of Penn?
4. Describe the homes of the Algonquin and Iroquois.
5. What do we have today that reminds us of Indian civilization?
6. Why did relations between the Indians and whites deteriorate to the point of armed conflict?
7. What was the basis of Indian religion? Why?
8. At most, how many Indians lived in Pennsylvania at one time? In 1776? Today?
9. Were the Indian trails of any use to the early settlers? to us today?
10. Compare William Penn's policy of land acquisition to that of his sons.

Do you know the meaning? Write a sentence containing the following words or phrases and explain them.

1. Allegewi
2. Lenni Lenape
3. Seneca
4. late stone age
5. palisade
6. to stalk
7. buckskin
8. venison
9. wampum
10. Great Spirit
11. Cornplanter
12. Tammany
13. Sam Brady
14. tribal council
15. confederacy

Maps to Help Us Learn

1. Find the name and location of each of the tribes of Indians in Pennsylvania at the time of Penn's arrival. Place them on a map of Pennsylvania at their proper location.

2. Draw your own map of Pennsylvania, then locate the following:

Conestoga River Walking Purchase of 1737
Schuylkill River Punxsutawney
Pymatuning Cornplanter Reservation
Shackamaxon Pocono Mountains

What Do You Think? Use the knowledge gained thus far to discuss answers to the following statements.

1. I would have liked being a mother rather than a father in an Indian family.
2. The American Indians are strikingly similar in many ways to the people of Asia.
3. Because the Iroquois were stronger and fiercer than other Indian tribes, they became the conquerors of most Pennsylvania Indian tribes.
4. The Indian loved his way of life and the white man is entirely responsible for disturbing it.
5. When the Indian was treated with fairness and respect, he returned the same to the white man.

ACTIVITIES
(Individual, committee or class projects and class reports)

1. Imagine you are an Indian living in eastern Pennsylvania about 1686. Write your impression of the white man.
2. Imagine you are an Indian and tell whether you would prefer to live as Indians live now or as they lived before the white man came.
3. Indian place names are probably common in your locality as they are throughout the State. Make a collection of such names, giving, their English meaning if you can.
4. Arrange for a talk and exhibit by a collector of Indian relics in your community.
5. Make a survey of the racial and national origins of your class. Keep the report for use in later chapters also.
6. Arrange a visit to the local historical society or museum to view the exhibit on Indian life. If the class cannot go as a group,

arrange to go alone.

7. Draw a picture of the great Indian orator Hiawatha.

8. Arrange for separate committees to list what they think are the contributions of the Indians to your local community. Compare the reports.

9. Do some research on physical characteristics of Pennsylvania Indians. Then in a class period or at an evening party hold a contest to see who is best at recreating an Indian in soap, clay or wood.

READING MATERIALS

Baity, E.C., *Americans Before Columbus*, Viking Press, 1951.
Bleeker, Sonia, *Indians at the Longhouse*, Morrow, 1950.
Buck, S.J., and E.H., *Planting of Civilization in Western Pennsylvania*, University of Pittsburgh Press, 1939.
Carr, Kurt and Adovasio, James, *Ice Age People of Pennsylvania,* Pennsylvania Historical and Museum Commission, Harrisburg, 2002.
Donehoo, George Patterson, *Indian Villages and Place Names in Pennsylvania*, Baltimore Gateway Press, 1977, Reprint.
Downes, R.C., *Council Fires on the Upper Ohio*, University of Pittsburgh Press, 1940.
Embree, E.R., *Indians of the Americas*, Houghton-Mifflin, 1939.
Grumet, Robert S, *The Lenapes*, Chelsea House Publisher, Philadelphia, 1989.
Huntingdon, E., *The Red Man's Continent*, Yale University Press, 1921.
National Geographic Society, *The World of the American Indian*, Washington, D.C., 1993
Seneca Indians, The Conservation Society of York County, Inc., York, Pa., 1944.
Sipe, Chester Hale, *The Indian Chiefs of Pennsylvania*, New York, Arno Press, 1971.
Thompson, Ray, *The Walking Purchase Hoax of 1737*, Fort Washington Bicentennial Press, 1973.
Wallower, Lucille, *Indians of Pennsylvania*, Penns Valley Publishers, 1976.
Wallace, A.F.C., *King of the Delawares: Teddyuscung*, 1700 63, University of Pennsylvania Press, 1949.
Wallace, P.A.W., *Indian Paths of Pennsylvania*, Pennsylvania Historical and Museum Commission, 1952.
Indians in Pennsylvania, Pennsylvania Historical and Museum Commission, 1961.
Weslager, Clinton Alfred, *The Delaware Indians*, New Brunswick, New Jersey, Rutgers University Press, 1972.
Wittholf, John, *Indian Prehistory of Pennsylvania*, Pennsylvania Historical Society, 1965.

The oldest street in United States is Elfreth's Alley in Philadelphia. The street and its homes are today as they were at the time of William Penn.

chapter IV

The Early Years

Pennsylvania was not really the name of any place until the time William Penn set up his colony. What we know as Pennsylvania was found first by explorers sent out from Holland. Nearly 70 years passed after the first European set eyes on Pennsylvania before William Penn came to Pennsylvania.

THE DUTCH AND THE SWEDES

Jamestown, Virginia, was founded in 1607 as the first permanent English settlement in North America. Two years later the government of Holland sent over explorers to North America. Henry Hudson, an English explorer, was hired to sail for them.

Dutch Explorers

In his ship, the Half Moon, Hudson found what is now known as Delaware Bay. He explored the bay far enough north to see that it was formed by a river. It was named the South River since what is now the Hudson River in New York was already named the North River.

In 1616, the Dutch explorer, Cornelis Hendricksen, sailed up the Delaware beyond the mouth of the Schuylkill River. He named it Schuylkill, which means hidden river, because he had first sailed by without seeing it.

Soon afterward the Dutch West India Company was formed and sent over explorers and settlers who set up trading posts. The first of these was along the Delaware Bay in what is now New Jersey and Delaware. The first Dutch attempt to settle in present-day

Pennsylvania occurred when the Dutch established Fort Beversrede in 1647 at the mouth of the Schuylkill in what is now Philadelphia. However, this was abandoned when Swedish traders to the south took away the trade.

The Dutch in general were not interested in settlements but only in trading with the Indians. With the coming of the Swedes, however, the real settlement of Pennsylvania began.

Swedish Settlers

Sweden was a rich and powerful nation in the early part of the seventeenth century and her king, Gustavus Adolphus, was one of

the great military leaders of the world. Sweden's boundaries had been extended into Russia and Germany. When Dutchmen offered to help the Swedes set up a colony in the New World, the king was delighted.

The necessary arrangements were made for a Swedish trading company to be set up in 1626, but Sweden became involved in another war, King Gustavus Adolpus was killed in battle and plans were postponed. Finally in 1637 Queen Christina chartered a new company and another Dutchman, Peter Minuit, was hired to head the expedition.

Two Swedish men-of-war, the Kalmar Nyckel (Key of Calmar) and the Fogel Grip (Bird Griffin) set sail in December of 1637 with the aid of experienced Dutch seamen. Minuit knew the land of the Delaware Bay well for he had been a Dutch agent there before. Minuit was known for his shrewd bargaining and it was he who purchased Manhattan Island for $24 from the Indians. His ships arrived in Delaware Bay in March of 1638.

For some cloth, beads and trinkets, Minuit purchased the land along the west side of the Delaware River from the Indians. It was to include the land from the present site of Wilmington, Delaware, to the Schuylkill and west to "where the sun sets. " The settlement at what later became Wilmington was called Fort Christina in honor of the queen.

Minuit set about making the settlement secure. The Dutch in New Amsterdam made a protest against the settlement, but to no avail. Crops of corn and tobacco were planted. Trade was set up with the Indians to obtain furs which were in great demand in Sweden.

By fall the tiny settlement was established. Minuit took the two ships by way of the West Indies to return to Sweden, but the ship he was sailing, the Fogel Grip, never reached Sweden. The Kalmar Nyckel mastered the voyage and gave Sweden its first New World profits in the form of tobacco and furs.

The settlers were strengthened by the return of the Kalmar Nyckel in 1640. More farmers, tools, domestic animals and supplies arrived, and the severe hardships suffered by the colony for three years were overcome. The second expedition also brought a new governor, Peter Hollender, and the Reverend Roerus Torkillus, the first Lutheran minister in America.

New Sweden's Golden Age

In 1643 a new governor arrived by the name of Johan Printz, who became the outstanding leader in the history of New Sweden. As a colonel in the armies of Gustavus Adolphus he had learned to be a forceful leader. It was his opinion that the capital should be moved to Tinicum Island, about 20 miles south of Philadelphia, and this became the first permanent white settlement in Pennsylvania.

The new capital was named Fort New Gothenburg in honor of the port of departure in Sweden. The fort and its inner buildings were made from large hemlock trees found growing nearby. Four small copper cannons were placed ready for use against invaders. Printz erected a log fort, a governor's mansion called Printzhof, a church, and a storehouse.

The Swedes never succeeded in building up an extensive Indian trade but spent most of their energy in farming. From the Indians

American Swedish History Museum

Ceiling mural in the American Swedish Historical Museum by Christian von Schneidau. "See how good friends these are who have brought us such gifts. We shall be as one body and one heart," said Chief Hackaman, of the Delaware Indians, in a speech to the Swedes.

THE EARLY YEARS

they learned to plant corn, pumpkins and beans, and also how to stalk game. The Swedes introduced the growing of flax to America. Finland was at that time part of Sweden, and many of the settlers were Finns. Printz later said of Pennsylvania, "It was a remarkably beautiful country with all the glories that a person could wish on earth. It was adorned by all kinds of fruit trees. The soil was suitable for planting and sowing."

A crop failure in 1652 led Printz to sail for Sweden the next year to win better support for the little colony. In 1654 the biggest of the expeditions arrived. There were about 100 Swedes living in the colony in 1653, and the new expedition brought 350 immigrants. The number of Swedes continued to increase even after Sweden lost control of the colony.

With the new group came a new governor, Johan Classon Risingh. He had not yet arrived at Tinicum Island before he made the mistake that was to cost him and his country their colony. As his ship proceeded up the bay, he captured the small Dutch Fort Casimir, across the river from Tinicum. The 350 Swedes captured the 22 Dutch soldiers in charge. Until this time the Dutch and Swedes had lived in peace, the Dutch on the east side of the Delaware and the Swedes on the west.

The Dutch Again

Meanwhile in Europe, Sweden lost most of its great military power. Holland at the same time had risen to be a great power. The Dutch resented the Swedes in the Delaware Valley from the first. Risingh's capture of the Dutch fort now provoked them into action.

Peter Stuyvesant, the one-legged governor of New Netherlands, gathered an army at New Amsterdam (New York). With 300 soldiers in seven ships, he proceeded to the Delaware Valley and recaptured the fallen Dutch Fort Casimir. The Swedes at Tinicum Island say they had no chance of winning, and on September 16, 1655, Governor Risingh surrendered all New Sweden to the Dutch.

The terms of the surrender gave the Swedes the right to return to their homeland if they chose or to stay if they wished. The Dutch promised to allow them to keep all the property they owned.

Although the Reformed Church was the official church of Holland, the Swedes were permitted to keep their Lutheran Church. All but 37 of the Swedes decided to stay.

Sweden's rule lasted only 17 years, 1638-1655. The Swedes are to be remembered as the first real settlers of Pennsylvania. They were the first to build homes and churches, and establish civil government. They imported the first livestock, cultivated the first farms and set up the first civil court system. The Swedes liked living in the area so well that they continued to come, even under Dutch rule. They remained the largest nationality in Pennsylvania until the coming of the English with William Penn. Their introduction of log cabins for homes established the famous log cabin tradition of America.

The Dutch and English, meanwhile, had become rivals throughout the world. In both the East and West Indies the Dutch and English competed for power. In North America the Dutch took the Hudson and Delaware Valleys in violation of the English claim. From the time of John Cabot, the English claimed all of North America. Now the Dutch began to tamper with English trade. The Dutch separated New England from Virginia.

Dutchmen never moved into Pennsylvania in large numbers. Perhaps there never were more than 100 Dutch settlers in Pennsylvania. Their colony in Pennsylvania was governed by the Dutch West India Company. A deputy was named by the governor in New Amsterdam to govern over the Delaware Valley. The sole desire of the Dutch seemed to be to conduct trade with the Indians, but this trade did not flourish as expected. Actually the Swedes were the only ones making any progress under the Dutch rule.

The English Take Control

In 1644 the King of England, Charles II, gave all the land between Connecticut and Maryland to his brother, James, Duke of York. When England got involved in a far-flung war with Holland, an army was sent to take the Dutch colony in America.

At New Amsterdam, Peter Stuyvesant surrendered without a shot when the large British army appeared. The British commander, Colonel Nicolls, changed the name of the community to New York and dispatched another group under Sir Robert Carr to capture the Delaware Valley forts. The Dutch at Fort Casimir resisted and had to be attacked. The deputy governor, D'Hinojossa, and the people had to give up their moveable property for resisting the capture. The British commander, Carr, then changed the name of the community to New Castle.

The bay and the river were now officially called Delaware. In 1610 an expedition from Jamestown, Virginia, had visited the region and so named it. The Dutch had called it the South Bay and River. The name Delaware originated from the governor of Virginia at this time, Sir Thomas West, Baron de la Warr.

The Dutch in 1673 recaptured the region in another war but gave it up in the peace treaty of the following year. English laws were set up in the Delaware Valley. Courts were set up at New Castle, Hoornkill (Lewes, Delaware) and Upland (now Chester). The Upland court served the area of Pennsylvania. Some Englishmen moved into the Upland area, but the number was less than 100 in 1681. The Swedes were the largest nationality group in the area. Some Dutch, Finns, German, French, and Scotch were also present.

PEACEFUL WILLIAM PENN AND THE ENGLISH SETTLEMENT

We have used the term Pennsylvania to denote the area of the present State, but the area was in reality part of New York until 1681. It was only with William Penn that the real Pennsylvania began.

William Penn was born in London, October 14, 1644, the son of a distinguished admiral in the British navy, Sir William Penn, who was a favorite of the King and his brother, James. The admiral had been made a knight for his services and awarded a seat in the House of Lords. Sir William owned a great deal of land in both England and Ireland. The great land owners were the richest men of the country. Sir William lent money to King Charles II to carry on wars.

Pennsylvania Department of Commerce

William Penn's portrait, showing him clad in armor, was painted when he was twenty-two years old before he became a Quaker.

Penn the Quaker

Young William was sent to the famous Oxford University. He attended some meetings of Quakers near the university and came under their influence. When school officials discovered this, young William was dismissed from the university. There was only one official Church of England, headed by the King. The King's officials distrusted all who, like the Quakers, did not conform to the rules of the official church.

William's father sent him off to France hoping he would change his religious convictions, but William was to remain faithful to Quaker belief. When he was 23 years of age he officially joined the Society of Friends, the official name for the Quaker church, and became a preacher for the Quakers. He suffered arrest and imprisonment many times in England. He wrote a great deal about the religious and political questions of his day. He was a fine speaker, and had a manner that won him numerous friends.

When William joined the Quakers, his father disinherited him. However, William's charm and manners were such that he was even able to win the friendship of the King. In spite of his nonconformist ideas he was able to get the King to grant him favors. Many Quakers were released from prison after William Penn used his influence at court.

Before the elder Penn died in 1670, he relented in his will and at his death, William inherited the great lands and fortune of his father. Part of the legacy was a claim against the King for money loaned for Dutch wars. When a Quaker group moved to New Jersey in 1674, Penn contributed money to the venture and helped write its constitution.

The Founding of Pennsylvania

Penn thought it would be better if the Quakers had a colony completely their own. In 1680 he petitioned the King to give him a grant in the New World in return for canceling his claim against the King. After a year's delay, the King granted the request.

On March 14, 1681, Charles II signed the charter granting Penn the land from the Delaware River westward for five degrees longitude. It was to be "bounded on the north by the beginning of the three and fortieth degree of northern latitude, and on the south by a circle drawn at twelve miles distant from New Castle, northward and westward, and then by a straight line westward to the limits above mentioned."

The King had kept the power of taxation and the right to veto laws. The Bishop of London had insisted that the worship of the Church of England should be permitted. Otherwise, Penn was to be the "true and absolute proprietary of the country aforesaid. " The King's authority was to be recognized each year by a token payment of two beaver skins. He also was to get one-fifth of all the gold and silver found in the colony.

The charter names the colony "Pennsilvania." Penn himself was going to call the land New Wales or Sylvania, but the King insisted otherwise. Penn said it was against the Quaker religion for a man to name a place for himself, but the King insisted the colony was being named for Admiral Penn. Sylvania means a place abounding in forests and trees; thus, Pennsylvania means Penn's forest land. At that time the colony was nearly all forest land so it was well named.

Penn was then the largest landholder in the British Empire, owning over 45,000 square miles of land in the New World, in addition to his holdings in Ireland. He feared that his colony might be cut off from the ocean, so he petitioned the Duke of York to give up his claims to what is now Delaware. This was done in August, 1682. For some years the territory was called the "Lower Counties," but in 1703 the counties were set apart as a separate colony. However, the Penn family owned the land and named the same person governor over both colonies until the Revolution. In 1750 the "Lower Counties" took on the name Delaware.

Establishing a Government

William Penn did not waste time setting up his government. In April, 1681, he named his cousin, Captain William Markham, as deputy governor. In June Markham arrived in Upland, where he set up a council of nine men, seven Englishmen and two Swedes, to conduct the business of the colony.

That winter Penn sent over four surveyors to select the site for a new capital. The men, under the leadership of Thomas Holme, located the city where Philadelphia now stands. Penn had his own ideas on the layout of the city, using what is called the checkerboard plan. Penn selected the name for the capital to be Philadelphia, meaning "brotherly love." Upland he renamed Chester.

Over a year passed from the time the charter was signed until Penn came to see his Pennsylvania. While still in England, he drew up the First Frame of Government and advertised his land to attract settlers. Finally in September of 1682 he set sail on the Welcome with 100 other passengers bound for Pennsylvania. One third of the passengers died of smallpox on the six-weeks' voyage. Penn arrived at Chester October 19, 1682, and a few days later went on to inspect the progress in the building of Philadelphia. Penn quick-

THE EARLY YEARS

Atwater Kent Museum

A model of the Welcome, *the ship that brought William Penn to his new province in 1682. Ships like this brought Pennsylvania's first settlers.*

ly turned to thought of government and called for all land owners to appear at Chester for a general assembly. He then divided the colony into three counties. The first three counties of Pennsylvania were Bucks, Chester and Philadelphia. The lower three were New Castle, Kent and Sussex. It should be noted that the Legislature of Pennsylvania ever since has been called the General Assembly. The county system, too, has been maintained ever since.

The Great Law

The Assembly decided to unite the Lower Counties with Pennsylvania for the present, to make aliens citizens, and enacted the so-called Great Law. The aliens were the Swedes, Dutch, and Finns who lived in the colony when the Quakers arrived.

York Film Library

Quaker meeting houses were not fancy. The one pictured here was built in the eighteenth century in York County. Quaker dominated Pennsylvania government until the time of the French and Indian War.

The Great Law was the basis of government. Enacted on December 7, 1682, it remained the basic government for the next 94 years and established religious freedom. All religions were allowed but only Christians could hold office. Working on Sunday was forbidden. Provision was made to care for the poor and the orphans. Prisons were to be workhouses, whereas in England they were simply lockups. In England there were over 200 crimes punishable by death. Only murder and treason were punishable by death in Pennsylvania.

The court system provided the basis for the courts of Pennsylvania today. Such terms as common pleas and quarter sessions courts were used from the beginning of the colony. The Supreme Court was first called the Provincial Court.

Most of the ideas for the government were Penn's and many of them were based on Quaker ideals. The laws reflected the Quaker spirit to regulate morals and at the same time protect individual rights.

Penn did everything possible to maintain friendship with his neighbors. He went to visit the Lord Baltimore in Maryland and while there tried to get the boundary of the two colonies defined. He went over into New Jersey and New York to indicate his friendship toward those colonies also, but his most noted gesture of friendship was that toward the Indians.

From the beginning Penn was a friend of the Indians. In the chapter concerning the Indians we read of his sentiments. Penn and the Delaware Chief Tammany agreed to permanent peace. During the lives of these men there was no trouble between the two races, and peace with the Indians was to last for almost 80 years.

Selling the Land

Penn then began the task of selling his land. He was a good businessman and expected to get a nice income from land sales. He advertised the land as fertile and beautiful and told of the democratic nature of its government. Sales were not hard to make. For 100 English pounds one could purchase 5,000 acres which would be about four cents an acre. An annual quitrent of twenty cents per 100 acres was supposed to be paid but rarely was. Quitrent was rent paid in money instead of services as in the feudal system still in effect in many parts of Europe.

Penn tried to sell off large portions of land to companies. One such group was the Free Society of Traders, a Welsh colonization company that bought 20,000 acres. The group was composed mostly of Welsh Quakers who settled on the west side of the Schuylkill River north of Philadelphia. This land included what is today over 11 townships in Delaware, Chester and Montgomery counties. At first the Welsh settlers were self-governing, but later they became part of the regular township and county governments.

Another such organization was the Frankfurt Land Company of Germany. The advance agent for this company was Francis Daniel Pastorious who directed the settlement of Germantown, now a part of Philadelphia. The Germantown settlers received from Penn a grant of 28,000 acres. Their tract of Germantown, which contained 6,000 acres of this grant, soon became a center of German life in America.

The area around Philadelphia grew fast. Within a year 3,000 new inhabitants moved into Pennsylvania. Counties were divided into townships for political purposes. Penn continued to appoint the most important officers, but the government was the most democratic in America.

From its beginning Pennsylvania was a colony of varied nationalities and religious beliefs. The major part of the people who came were of three nationality groups: English, German and Scotch-Irish. The fact that each of these groups settled in distinct areas of the colony tended to point out its special religious beliefs, customs, traditions, and ways of living and working together.

The English Settlers

The largest group to enter Pennsylvania were the English. Most of them came directly from England, but a large number came from the West Indies and from other colonies. The majority of the early English settlers were Quakers who wanted to escape religious persecution in England. Most other Englishmen who came to the colony did so because they hoped for better opportunities in the new country. The majority of the Quakers came to Philadelphia between 1682 and 1684 on the 50 immigrant ships. These men were not penniless and were able to establish a prosperous community in a short

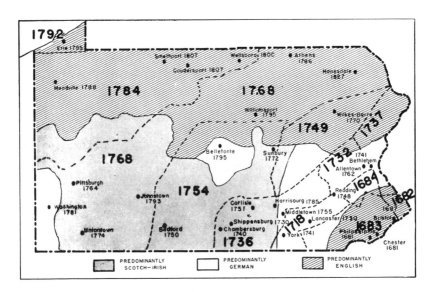

Great blocks of land were purchased from the Indians during the Colonial days. The early settlements were principally of English, German, and Scotch-Irish extraction. This map shows their movement and the development of this land.

time.

The Quaker religion allowed them to live peacefully with the Indians, and their humility caused them to treat the Indians as equals. The Indians learned that Quakers were honest and did not believe in war. Quakers believed that each person had right and wrong revealed to him personally thus making it impossible for anyone to use religion to gain power and position. Quakers held the major offices of the colony for 80 years.

The other Englishmen who came settled in all parts of the colony, but the majority of them settled in the original counties of Philadelphia, Bucks and Chester. Many of these Englishmen belonged to the Episcopal, Methodist and Baptist Churches. After the frontier was pushed westward, some Englishmen from Connecticut moved into the colony. By the time of the Revolutionary War, 5,000 settlers had moved into the upper Susquehanna Valley.

Pennsylvania Department of Transportation

The Amish and other plain sects still use only horse and wagon for transportation and send their children to one room schools for a minimum of formal education. They dress as they did in the eighteenth century.

Englishmen from Maryland moved into York County, and from Virginia, English settlers moved into what was to become Fayette, Greene, Washington and Allegheny Counties. From the English we have received numerous political, social and economic institutions, handed down to become accepted as part of our life today.

GERMAN AND SCOTCH-IRISH

The Germans were the second largest group in number to come to Penn's colony. German culture and ideals have greatly influenced the development of the State. Most early Germans came to gain greater religious and political freedom. Later, many German immigrants came to improve their economic positions.

The Dutch in New York disliked the Germans there and forced them to move out of the Hudson Valley. They crossed overland to the Susquehanna and floated down to settle in what was to become Lancaster County. The Germans found the limestone soil like that of their homeland and wrote their friends and relatives to come over. Between 1727 and 1776 more than 68,000 Germans entered Pennsylvania through Philadelphia.

The Sectarians

The early Germans came prepared to buy their own land. They came in groups and stayed in those groups. Usually they brought their own pastors with them. Many early groups belonged to sects that had broken away from the Roman Catholic, Lutheran or German Reformed Churches to form their own congregations. They had been driven from their homelands and were happy to be allowed to live where they could worship as they pleased. The Mennonites and Amish are the best-known of the sects. Most of these sects trace their origins back to the Anabaptists of Switzerland, who taught that Christians should follow the simple, peaceful ways of the early church of the first apostles. One of these groups, the Amish, still wear much the same style clothes, work their farms in the same manner, and conduct themselves the same as when they first came to Pennsylvania. The Mennonites and Amish are concentrated mainly in the rural sections of eastern Pennsylvania.

THE EARLY YEARS

Pennsylvania Department of Commerce

Among the religious sects of early Pennsylvania were the German Seventh-Day Baptists who built the community pictured at Ephrata, in Lancaster County. The Cloister buildings are now owned by the state.

The Moravians came in the 1740s to set up settlements in Bethlehem and Nazareth in Northampton County and Lititz in Lancaster County. They were great missionaries and converted many Indians to Christianity. Moravians introduced their fine music to the colony and set up some of the first schools.

Other sects like the German Baptist Brethren and the Schwenkfelders also moved into communities of their own to live and worship as they chose. A group under the leadership of Conrad Beissel set up the famous Ephrata Cloister where German Seventh-Day Baptists shared all things equally and established one of the most interesting communities of early America.

Lutherans and Reformed

Most Germans, especially those who came in such great numbers after 1750, belonged to the established state churches of their German homeland. Most of them were Lutherans and German Reformed, but some were from Catholic areas. Since most of the Germans had lost heavily in wars and political wrangles in the homeland, they were content to follow Quaker leadership in the colony. Many of the sects agreed with the Quakers in opposing all war. Most of the Germans were farmers, but quite a few were skilled workmen who had made excellent wagons, boats and rifles. The German farms outproduced the others in the colonies.

Scotch-Irish Presbyterians

The third largest nationality group to settle in Penn's colony were the Scotch-Irish. They were so called because they were Scotchmen who had migrated to Ireland. There they found that their Presbyterian beliefs caused friction with both the Irish Catholics and the English Church. The largest group of them moved to Pennsylvania. The Scotch-Irish came about the same time as the Germans but moved farther to the west. They were more individualistic than other groups and pushed on beyond the last settlements. In their hurry to move westward, they often moved beyond the boundaries of land legally purchased from the Indians, and thus were first to feel the wrath of the frontier Indians. They also resented Quaker friendship for the Indians, and were at last successful in putting an end to Quaker control of the government.

Other Settlers

Jews, who were forbidden settlements in other colonies, came to Pennsylvania, settling mostly in Philadelphia and Lebanon Counties. Schaefferstown in Lebanon County was thought to have been settled by Jewish tradesmen from Portugal. French Protestants also came in small numbers, as did a few later Dutch and Swedes. Welsh settlers were quickly absorbed with the English.

TRIALS OF THE HOLY EXPERIMENT

The Second Frame of Government

The General Assembly met in March, 1683, to review the needs of government and establish new laws. They first set up the Second Frame of Government by which to operate. The Council, whose members assisted the Governor, was to have three members from each county and the Assembly was to have six members from each county. The vote of the Deputy Governor was reduced from three to one. Council members were elected for three years. Assembly members for one year. The Deputy Governor was appointed at the pleasure of the Governor, William Penn himself.

New laws were drawn that are important to us today. The ancient law of primogeniture, whereby the oldest son inherited all the land of his father, was abolished. Import and export custom duties were set. All children were to be taught to read and write, and everyone was to be taught a useful trade. Provisions were also made to provide "cartways" and ferries.

Penn liked to call his colony the "Holy Experiment." He believed he was laying the foundation for a free colony for all mankind, realizing that governments in themselves are only as good as the people. In the preface to the First Frame of Government he had written, "Governments, like clocks, go from the motion men give them, and as Governments are made and mov'd by men, so by them are they ruin'd too; wherefore Governments rather depend upon men than men upon governments. Let men be good and the Government can't be bad."

Thinking that his government was in good hands, Penn returned to England to defend his interests. The Stuart Kings, Charles II and James II, had been friendly to Penn, but in 1688, James II had been driven from his throne and new rulers were brought in from Holland. The new rulers, William and Mary, were suspicious of anyone friendly toward the former rulers. This was especially true when France declared war on England to get James's throne back for him.

A Royal Colony

Using the excuse that Penn was not conducting the government properly, the new British rulers took away all Penn's governmental power. From 1692 until 1694 Pennsylvania was thus a royal colony, under the direct control of the British Crown. It was governed through the Governor of New York, Benjamin Fletcher. Fletcher was a friend of Penn and did nothing to take away his rights. As

Deputy Governor of Pennsylvania, he named William Markham who knew the job and Penn's wishes.

Governor Fletcher visited Pennsylvania to raise money to fight the French and Indians. He tried to force the Council and Assembly to provide the money, and it was only after much argument that the Quakers voted money for a war. In the end, they voted the money to the Governor who used it for the war.

The bickering between the Assembly and the Governor was reported to London. The Assembly refused to pass a militia bill and balked against the power of Governor Fletcher. In London it was decided the best thing to do would be to send Penn back to take over the government. On August 20, 1694, his governmental powers were returned. Penn promised to return to the colony as soon as possible and to get the Assembly to reconsider the defense needs of the colony.

Penn found himself unable to return to the colony immediately, so Markham was put in charge. He asked the Assembly to provide money for defense. They refused to do so unless the Assembly was given more power. Markham agreed to the changes which were to be reviewed by Penn and the Assembly then gave the money for defense purposes.

The changes that the Assembly gained in 1696 were called Markham's Frame. The Assembly was given the right to draw up its own legislation for the first time. Previously, only the Council could begin legislation. The Governor agreed to perform no public act without the consent of the Assembly. This was another step in the development of more democratic government in Pennsylvania.

In December, 1699, Penn returned to Pennsylvania for his second visit, and brought with him his second wife, Hannah Callowhill Penn. It seemed that Penn had come to stay. Crowds greeted him with great feeling of welcome and admiration. He had his country home completed and ready for him.

Penn's country estate, Pennsbury Manor, was probably one of the most beautiful homes in America at that time. The manor included 8,000 acres along the Delaware in Bucks County. There Penn entertained like an English nobleman. Indians and colonial leaders loved his generosity.

Pennsylvania Department of Commerce

Pennsbury Manor on the banks of the Delaware River in Bucks County was built for William Penn to live in when he arrived for his second visit in 1699-1702. It is open to the public today.

Charter of Privileges

Penn decided he would try to settle the problems of government and called a special meeting of the Assembly. After much debate a Charter of Privileges was adopted October 28, 1701. It was the most democratic government of its day. The Assembly was given all the law-making power. There was to be only one house in the Legislature. The Governor was forbidden to interfere in the work of the Assembly, but he did retain the power of veto on all laws.

The three Lower Counties were given the right to withdraw from Pennsylvania if they chose before 1704, and in 1703 they did so.

An important part of the Charter of Privileges was the renewed pledge of freedom of religion. It was the first article of the Charter and stated that the article could never be amended. Any other part of the Charter could be amended by a vote of six-sevenths of the Assembly and the consent of the governor.

Many years later the Charter of Privileges was so valued by the people of Pennsylvania that they wished to honor its fiftieth birthday in 1751 with a celebration. A special bell was cast in London and sent to Pennsylvania the following year. On the bell was inscribed, "Proclaim liberty throughout all the land unto all the inhabitants thereof." This bell which was made to celebrate Pennsylvania's liberties under William Penn later would gain even greater fame as the Liberty Bell.

Penn's Death

William Penn was recalled to London to protect his rights in 1702. While he was there his money seemed to disappear. His colony and his estates in Ireland also lost money. Too late it was discovered that he had a dishonest manager. Penn was thrown into prison for his debts for nine months in 1708. He was freed when his friends raised 7,600 pounds ($38,000) to pay his debts. He was unable to raise the money to repay his friends before he died July 30, 1718.

With the death of Penn, his wife took over as manager of the affairs. Although Penn's sons had the titles, she controlled the colony's affairs until 1727 when she died. In that time she paid off his debts, appointed governors and answered all important questions. The children of Hannah Penn acted as proprietors and governors. John Penn was Governor 1727-46. Richard and Thomas were joint owners until the death of Richard in 1771. Richard's son John was owner until the time of the Revolution. At that time, all the Penn family's rights were ended by a payment to John. Details of the settlement will be found in the chapter concerning the Revolution.

Political Troubles

From the time William Penn left Pennsylvania, political problems constantly troubled the province. The various members of the Assembly split over their political beliefs, in much the same way that political parties developed in England at the same time. Like the Tories in England who favored the king, the Proprietary Party in Pennsylvania backed the policies of the Penn family. This group was made up of the more educated and wealthy Quakers of the Philadelphia area. It was led by James Logan.

A second party, similar to the Whigs of England, was the Popular Party. Just as the Whigs wished to give more power to the people of

England, so the Popular Party wished to control the powers of the proprietor. This group was led by the Welsh Quaker, David Lloyd. Most of its adherents lived in the country districts.

This political difference between the city and country people was to continue in various guises even beyond the Revolution. The people in the interior were not satisfied until the capital was moved from Philadelphia, and they were given better representation in the government.

After the death of William Penn, relations with the Indians grew steadily worse. During his life, Penn treated the Indians equally. The Quaker Assembly also was generous to the Indians and constantly gave gifts to the Indians. Other settlers did not look upon the Indians in the same manner. Those who wanted the Indians' lands simply moved in on them. The Assembly warned that such moves were unlawful, but it did not have the power to force out the illegal settlers. More and more, the Indians complained that the settlers were taking their lands.

The long peace with the Indians was soon to be broken. Perhaps the trouble was inevitable. The number of white men was growing. New settlers moved into the western wilderness. If the Indians did not like the new civilization, they would have to move, but it was only natural that they would do so grudgingly.

REVIEW QUESTIONS

1. What contributions did the Swedes make to Pennsylvania?
2. The Dutch West India Company was founded partly to aid in settling the New World. How well did it succeed?
3. The English claim to the lands around the Delaware was based upon whose explorations?
4. What part of the land claimed by England was settled by Penn and his Quaker friends?
5. Describe William Penn's relationship with his father. How did his father enter into the naming of Pennsylvania?
6. In what ways did Penn show his friendship to the Indians and the other colonies?
7. How did Penn attempt to attract settlers to Pennsylvania?
8. How did the Holy Experiment help create what some people

might call a melting pot of peoples?

9. Why were the Quakers able to control the government for as long as eighty years?

10. What motive brought the different national groups to Pennsylvania? Why were there so many different German groups?

Do you Know the Meaning? Write a sentence containing the following words or phrases.

1. Society of Friends
2. Lower Counties
3. freeholder
4. brotherly love
5. Peter Minuit
6. Tinicum
7. Great Law
8. "inner light"
9. quitrent
10. nonconformist
11. proprietor
12. "Holy Experiment"
13. Scotch-Irish
14. Charter of Privileges
15. Pennsbury
16. Liberty Bell

Maps to Help Us Learn

1. Draw your own outline map of the eastern part of the United States. Now locate the boundaries of Penn's grant as defined in his charter.

2. On an outline map of Pennsylvania dot the original entrance of each nationality on Pennsylvania soil. Then by arrows and crayon show the progress and the areas populated by each.

3. On an outline map of the eastern coast of the United States show the Swedish, Dutch and English claims. Now look at the map and explain why the English were anxious to conquer the Dutch.

What do you think? Use the knowledge gained thus far to give your opinion of the following statements.

1. Trading posts were usually the beginning of permanent settlements.

2. Pennsylvania could rightly be called the melting pot of the United States.

3. It seems possible that many of Penn's ideas in his Holy Experiment could be applied just as well today.

4. Pennsylvania has always been a refuge for oppressed people.

OUR PENNSYLVANIA HERITAGE

5. The early settlers in Pennsylvania made permanent impressions that still affect the lives of people living in the same region today.

ACTIVITIES
(Individual, committee or class projects and class reports)

1. To understand better the constitutional development of Pennsylvania, organize committees to study each of the following and report to class:

The Great Law	Markham's Frame
First Frame of Government and Second Frame of Government	Charter of Privileges

2. Draw sketches of Dutch, Swedish and English colonial houses.

3. Bring to class postcards and pictures illustrating the costumes worn by the Plain Sects, the early Quakers, and other distinctive groups of settlers.

4. Describe, as though you were an eyewitness, the taking of New Netherlands by the English in 1664.

5. Make a chart with the different nationalities of Pennsylvania placed at the top. Now in parallel columns place the contributions of each to our society today.

6. Are there any religious sects living near you that are distinctive? If so, describe anything about them that makes them distinctive.

7. Draw a poster that might have been used by Penn to attract settlers to his colony.

8. Make a drawing or model of the Welcome.

9. Try to make a cartoon showing the political differences between the Quakers in Pennsylvania and other groups.

10. Make a bar graph to show the population of different nationalities in 1776 as compared to the same groups today. An almanac will help.

READING MATERIALS

Altland, Millard, *The Pennsylvania Citizen*, Penns Valley Publishers, 1964.

Amish, The, Historic Pennsylvania Leaflet, Pennsylvania Historical and Museum Commission, 1952.

Applegarth, Albert Clayton, *Quakers in Pennsylvania*, New York, Johnson Reprint Corporation, 1973.
Beatty, Edward Corbynobert, *William Penn as Social Philosopher*, New York, Octagon, 1972 (Reprint).
Bowden, James, *The History of the Society of Friends in America*, New York, Amo Press, 1972, Reprint.
Brand, Miller, *Local Lives*, New York, C.N. Potter, 1975. (Poems about the Pennsylvania Dutch.)
Comfort, W.W., *The Quakers*, Pennsylvania Historical Association, 1948.
Endy, Melvin B. Jr., *William Penn and Early Quakerism*, Princeton, Princeton University Press, 1973.
Fantel, Hans, *William Penn, Apostle of Dissent*, New York, William Morrow, 1974.
Frost, Jerry William, *The Quaker Family in Colonial America; a Portrait of the Society of Friends*, New York, St. Martin's Press, 1973.
Gilbert, R., *Picture of the Pennsylvania Germans*, Pennsylvania Historical Association, 1947.
Governor Printz Park (pamphlet), Pennsylvania Historical and Museum Commission, 1948.
Holm, Thomas C., *Description of the Province of New Sweden*, New York, Kraus Reprint Co., 1975.
Klees, Frederick, *The Pennsylvania Dutch*, Macmillan, 1950.
Klett, G.S., *The Scotch-Irish in Pennsylvania*, Pennsylvania Historical Association, 1948.
Myers, A.C., *Narratives of Early West New Jersey, Pennsylvania and Delaware*, Barnes and Noble, 1952.
Nash, Gary B., *Quakers and Politics*; Pennsylvania 1681-1726, Princeton University Press, 1968.
Parsons, William T., *The Pennsylvania Dutch, A Persistent Minority*, Boston, Twayne, 1976.
Pennsbury Manor, Pennsylvania Historical and Museum Commission, Leaflet.
Remember William Penn, Pennsylvania Historical and Museum Commission, 1945.
Richards, H.M., Muhlenberg, *The Pennsylvania German in the Revolutionary War, 1775-1783*, Baltimore, Genealogical Publishing Co., 1978 Reprint of 1908 ed.
Tributes to William Penn, Pennsylvania Historical and Museum Commission, 1946.
Wallower, L., Wholey, E., *They Came to Pennsylvania*, Penns Valley Publishers, 1976.
Ward, Christopher, *The Dutch and Swedes on the Delaware, 1609-1664*, University of Pennsylvania Press, 1930.
Zielinski, Joseph M., *The Amish: A Pioneer Heritage*, Des Moines, Iowa, Wallace-Homestead, 1975.

chapter V

Colonial Life

The colonial period in Pennsylvania lasted for almost 100 years, from the time Pennsylvania was established as a province to the time when it joined the other colonies to revolt from Great Britain's control. In the period from 1681 until 1776 we should not forget that the King of Great Britain was the ruler of the colony. In that period the Penn family had charge of both the colonial government and the land sales. During this period the eastern part of the colony was to change from a great forest area to a fine farm land.

Different living conditions were found throughout the colony. On the end of the frontier the settlers fought the elements, animals and savage Indians. In eastern areas, farmers were busy turning the forest into productive farms. Philadelphia life was as fine as any city life anywhere in the world at that time.

PENETRATING THE FRONTIER

The Blue Mountains formed a barrier to settlers for 50 years after the formation of the colony. It was not until about 1720 that the first settlers ventured into the Cumberland Valley west of the Susquehanna. Thirty years later a settlement was made as far west as the present town of Bedford. Actually, the first settlers west of Laurel Ridge came north from Virginia.

The Hunters

Settling the area beyond the original counties followed pretty

Traders following the old Indian paths carried trade goods to the Indians as a step in the settlement of the land beyond the frontiers. Note the various types of packs and try to decide what would be in the packs.

much the same pattern. The first men who ventured into the forests were the hunters. With their pack horses they would follow the original Indian trails. Slowly they widened the trails, mapped the regions, the streams, valleys, Indian villages and trading posts. From the Indians they learned where to find salt, fish and food. They found clay for brick and pottery, and learned where the best soil was to be found.

In Europe hunting was generally unlawful. Only a rich land owner could hunt for game. Few common people had ever tasted the meat of deer, bear or even rabbit. In Pennsylvania there seemed no end to the number of deer, bear and rabbits that one could kill easily. In Europe it was often unlawful to own a gun, but every person who lived on the Pennsylvania frontier could own and use a gun. The hunter soon learned to dress and hunt as the Indians did. He wore a hunting outfit of doeskin, moccasins and coonskin cap, and carried a rifle, a powderhorn, a leather bullet bag and a tomahawk. For food he carried a small bag of cornmeal which could be mixed with water and baked into a hard cake on a rock beside a fire.

COLONIAL LIFE 109

The woodsman tracked the woods alert for every type of animal. He learned the properties of the plants and herbs and the habits of birds and animals. He was geographer, botanist, astronomer, geologist, and knew how to cook, butcher and doctor. All this knowledge he used to wrest a living from the wilderness. He learned to hunt deer on quiet sides of the hill in stormy weather. He turned his ears for every snapping twig, scuffle of leaves and every call or cry of bird or animal.

He knew the trading posts and traded his pelts for guns, gunpowder or food. Some hunters were to become traders, some farmers, some went farther west and others returned east to settle down.

There was lots of land. When a hunter wanted to settle down, he would simply pick out a good piece of land and do so. Many times he did not bother to record his claim. He killed the trees and planted a crop of corn. If the legal owner appeared, the hunter often accepted a small amount for his improvements and moved on.

The most famous of such men was Daniel Boone. Born in Berks

Pennsylvania Department of Commerce

Daniel Boone was born in a log cabin in Berks County where his family built this fine Boone homestead. They later moved south and west.

County, Pennsylvania, he and his family moved farther west into the wilderness. He became a famous hunter in the woods of Pennsylvania, Virginia, Kentucky, and finally Missouri. Such men as he were the vanguard of the farmers to follow.

The Traders

The actual settlers were preceded by another group, the traders. There were two types of traders: those who visited the Indian villages, and those who lived in frontier communities and furnished supplies to the men who went out to the Indian settlements. Some traders who had supply depots on the frontier were agents of Quaker merchants in Philadelphia. Shippen, Lawrence and Lev's post was to become Shippensburg. Frank and Simon set up a post at Lancaster. The men who carried on from there would take the goods on credit and trade it to the Indians.

These traders who went out among the Indians were brave, adventurous and hard. All too often they were also cruel, mercenary, and without principle. Some did not hesitate to defraud the Indians. However, the Indians tried to seek out those they knew were honest. Following the Shamokin Path, Frankstown Road, and later the Raystown Path, the traders sold the Indians guns, ammunition, shirts, hats, shoes, blankets, hatchets, knives, scissors, needles, pots and kettles, combs, mirrors, ribbons, beads, pipes and tobacco, dolls and toys for the children. The sale of rum was unlawful but it sold well.

Most traders built cabins in or near the Indian villages to serve as temporary homes, trading posts, storehouses, blacksmith shops, and meeting places. As a rule the traders went back east in the winter. The most noted of the traders were George Croghan, John Fraser, and James Lawrey. The Indians trusted them and at one time or another saved the life of each. Croghan had great influence over the Indians and helped in settling Indian wars.

In exchange for goods, the traders received from the Indians products of their hunting. The Indians offered the traders deerskins, beaver, fox and raccoon furs.

THE FRONTIER FARM

Following the traders came the frontier farmers who most often were Scotch-Irishman. They moved west as the other settlers moved into the neighborhood. When they could see the smoke of a neighbor's fire or hear a neighbor's dog, it was time to move again. Living in a crude log hut, the early frontier farmers might raise only one crop before moving.

Permanent farmers moved in and prepared to stay. The men of the family would go west to find a likely place for a farm. The smarter ones would choose the place with the largest trees as they knew it took good soil to grow big trees. In order for crops to be raised on the land, the trees had to be killed. Sometimes, the Europeans cut down the trees, but most of the farmers learned from the Indians that it was easier to kill a tree by cutting a ring around the bark. After trees were dead and dry, the women and children could burn them down.

The Frontier Cabin

The first home of the farmer was generally a lean-to or shed to protect him from the weather. After a crop of corn was planted, the men returned east to work until fall. They would return to reap their crops and build more permanent log cabins. On their second trip to the east they would sell their eastern homes to new settlers, and then entire families moved to the new homes.

The first houses of the frontier were built of logs. Usually they were less than 20 by 30 feet. They did not pretend to be anything but honest cabins which were made with the crude materials at hand. Between the logs were stuffed plain rails and chips of moss or straw mixed with mud. The roof was made of split logs about five inches wide. The first chimneys were often built of logs covered with mud. When more time was at hand to dig out rocks, a new chimney was built. Usually there was only one window, covered with greased paper to allow the light to come through. For a door, logs were split into rough boards. The doors were often what are known as Dutch doors. These doors were of two sections, upper and lower. In the summer and during the day, the top section could be kept open and the bottom closed.

Inside the cabin the light was dim. Smoke from the fireplace usually filled the room. Dried meat, fruit, corn and herbs dangled from the roof. The area around the cabin was kept clear of trees and bushes to protect the family from surprise Indian attacks.

Friends settled near one another. Relatives went out in groups and community life slowly developed. As settlers multiplied, they fixed up their log cabins by putting clapboard over the logs, or in some cases a whole new house was built. Floors of sawed boards replaced the dirt floors and stone chimneys replaced the wooden ones. Oak shingles were nailed on the roof and windows of glass replaced the oiled paper. When the cabin was replaced by a new house, the second house was often of stone or brick. An example of this type was the home of Daniel Boone's family. When he was born his family lived in a log cabin but when the family moved from Pennsylvania 16 years later, their house was an ample structure of stone. The house is still standing in good repair in Berks County.

Utensils and Clothing

The first utensils in the home were made of wood: spoons, forks, dippers, buckets, and shovels. Iron utensils and tools came slowly as iron had to be imported from England. Gradually, iron was made more and more in Pennsylvania and was sought after by every farmer. It was used for making rifles, kettles, griddles, spoons, skillets, waffle irons, hooks for the fireplace and andirons to hold the logs in the fireplaces. Some of the early settlers brought their kettles with them from Europe, but others had to buy them at high prices.

Early settlers dressed according to their resources. The wealthy people of Philadelphia could import their clothing from England while the frontier men and women often wore clothing made from deerskin. Frontier families, of course, made their own cloth. Since there were not enough sheep to supply everyone with wool, the wool was often woven in with linen. Linen was made from flax grown on the farms. The wool and linen together was called linsey-woolsey. Since dyes were impossible to buy on the frontier, forest dyes were used. From walnut hulls a rusty black color could be made, and the bark of the white walnut would give a yellow color. If some money was available, indigo could be bought in

COLONIAL LIFE

Bethlehem Historical Museum
Spinning wheels that once belonged to early Moravians are exhibited by a girl in Moravian dress.

Philadelphia to make the color blue. Good clothing was scarce on the frontier. The history of one frontier church records that 19 men wore the same blue coat with brass buttons during their wedding ceremonies. Clothing in general was plain and simple. Salt, gunpowder, nails and bullets were needed more than fancy clothing.

Frontier Farming and Crops

Farming was crude at first. The early farmer might own only an ax, hoe and sickle. The early plows were made of wood. Horses were scarce and men, women and children were sometimes hitched to the plow. Oxen were introduced by those who could afford them. Seeds were planted by hand and covered by dragging a small log over the field. Weeds were pulled by hand or cut with a hoe. Grain was threshed from the straw by a flail, consisting of a long leather thong. The grain was then beaten from the plant on the floor of a barn or on hard ground. The grain was then gathered and thrown into the air. The chaff blew away and the grain was caught in a sheet. If one man could thresh more than four bushels of wheat in one day, he was doing very well.

Corn was grown everywhere. It served as food for humans, horses, cows, pigs and sheep. Ground into meal, it was then boiled as mush or made into johnny cakes or pone. Dried corn could be made into hominy as the Indians had done. Corn cobs could be burned as fuel or made into toys for children or pipes for the men. Husks were used for stuffing cushions or dried for bedding. Flax and hemp were important crops and flax grew easily, producing linseed oil for many uses. The fibers of the plant were made into linen or combined with wool for linsey-woolsey. Hemp was raised for making rope and sacks.

Winters seemed very long in the early settlements. Men and boys were kept busy cutting logs for fuel or for splitting into boards and fence rails. Tools were made or repaired in the cold months and new plows, flails and sickles were made ready for the next growing season. If possible, a piece of iron was purchased and the spare time could be spent in making nails. Extra nails could be sold to new settlers who passed through. Grinding corn, tanning leather and mak-

University of Pittsburgh Press

Wooden farming implements were used in Pennsylvania in many cases until the time of the Civil War. Wood was always available and iron was expensive and hard to get.

ing candles were a few of the jobs that could be done while the weather was bad outside. The light was poor in the cabins as about the only light was a piece of cane or reed soaked in grease. The next step was a candle made from tallow of animals. The earliest form of lamp was the Betty lamp. It was a small bowl filled with tallow, grease or oil and a piece of rag or homemade wick hung over the edge to be lighted. The light was dull, smoky and ill-smelling.

At first the only means of making fire was by striking flint and steel together. If the fire in the fireplace was allowed to go out, a child was sent to the nearest neighbor to bring home a live coal on a shovel or on a broad strip of green bark. If there was no neighbor the long job of starting a fire by flint was begun. The family probably kept the flint-steel and some tinder in a small tin box called a tinder box. The tinder was usually a bit of dry linen rag. The striking of a light from such equipment took much skill and often a great amount of time. Sending someone to bring home some fire was much easier.

THE RURAL COMMUNITY

As an area became more settled, life improved. Roads cut through the forests brought more settlers and soon towns sprang up. Stores appeared in the towns with many new products for sale.

Farmers grew more than was needed and traded off the surplus in the stores for goods they could not grow or make. Better tools, clothing and furniture were purchased with surplus corn, wheat, or flax seed.

Colonial Prosperity

The farmers who settled in Philadelphia, Bucks and Chester Counties prospered from the first. They were close enough to sell their fresh vegetables in Philadelphia and other towns. These farmers did not live in log cabins very long but soon built large permanent homes of brick from nearby clay. Sometimes abundant limestone was used to build fine homes. Carpenter tools were imported, and houses were built that still today are copied by people wanting fine homes.

Life in southeastern Pennsylvania was pleasant from the beginning. There was no near starvation as there had been in Virginia and Massachusetts. Pennsylvania Indians originally were friendly and helpful and the population grew rapidly. The rich soil of the region produced such a great surplus of wheat that Pennsylvania soon became the breadbasket of America. The wheat was exported from Philadelphia to other colonies, England and the West Indies. Sometimes it was made into flour, biscuits or bread for shipment. It did not matter that the bread or biscuits became hard because they did not spoil easily and could be kept for months before use.

The Mills

In the country the chief center of activity beyond the home was the neighborhood mill. Located along a stream where water was dammed to turn large wheels, the mills did numerous jobs. Many think of the mills only as places where grain was ground between the mill stones to make flour, but mills also did much more. Corn was ground into meal, rags were ground to make into paper, soft stones were ground for plaster. The big wheels were used to break flax and full (compact) leather. Rifles were bored, iron slit, and sickles, scythes and knives sharpened.

The Conestoga Wagon

If the farmers grew surplus crops, wagons were needed to carry crops to town. A wagon large enough to make the trip profitable was needed, and thus was developed the great covered wagon, known as the Conestoga wagon. When it was first built is unknown, but in 1750 the Pennsylvania Gazette of Philadelphia wrote of the Conestoga Wagon Inn. These noted wagons were first built in the Conestoga Valley of Lancaster County by the Germans. They were huge carriers for their day, being 16 feet long and 4 feet high and deep. Wheels were 3 to 4 feet high with iron tires 4 inches wide. These high wagons were covered with homespun or canvas stretched over a series of wooden hoops and carried up to 6 tons. To pull them a special breed of powerful horses was developed, also

COLONIAL LIFE

Pennsylvania Department of Commerce

Conestoga wagons and their six-horse bell teams carried the farm produce of Lancaster County to Philadelphia's port. In return loads came the imported materials that helped lighten the work of the inland farmers.

called Conestogas. With their wide wheels, the wagons were able to roll on the dirt roads before them. Flour and iron ore were the most common products carried. On the return trip from Philadelphia, the wagoners brought the new tools, clothing, furniture and imported products that were wanted so much in the interior. The unknown Germans who developed the great wagons made a great contribution to American history. The boat-shaped bodies were to carry men and materials the whole way to the Pacific Ocean in later years.

The Pennsylvania Rifle

Another development of the Lancaster County Germans was the Pennsylvania long rifle. Martin Meylin of the Pequea Valley gets credit for the development of this famed rifle, but it was developed from a rifle used by the Germans in Europe. Englishmen were using smooth bore muskets. A rifle causes the shot to turn or twist as it goes out the barrel. This increased the range and accuracy. The typical Pennsylvania rifle was up to 5 feet long and shot a .45 caliber ball. A man or beast could be killed from 300 yards. This was far superior to the type of musket used by the British army even at the time of the War in 1812. Pennsylvania Germans were making the rifles in the early 1700s. Lancaster was the first riflemaking center, but soon they were made in all German counties. Albright, Boyer, Roesser, Butler, Dechard, Lemon, Lefevre, Dreppard and Pannabecker were manufacturers of rifles before the American Revolution. William Henry was a famed gunsmith who produced fine rifles and pistols in Nazareth. His company continued in business through the Civil War.

These rifles were attractive as well as useful with stocks of beautifully grained maple. Often they were ornamented with etched brass or even silver and gold. The barrels were forged from iron bars in charcoal fires and the rifling was done on a primitive hand-powered machine. Daniel Boone and others carried this rifle to Kentucky where it was copied and became known as the Kentucky rifle. Pennsylvania rifles were used to subdue the Indians, to defeat the English twice, and helped to establish a continental nation. They were replaced by the percussion rifles before the Civil War but are still favorite collectors' items.

University of Pittsburgh Press

From the founding of Pennsylvania until the coming of the automobile, the blacksmith was a very important person in every community. Name the jobs that he did for the settlers.

Beginning of the Iron Industry

Iron was badly needed as we have already seen. Tools, cooking utensils, guns, wagon parts and horseshoes were but a few of the things that had to be made from iron. At first all iron was imported from England or other colonies at great cost. Soon iron ore was found and small forges were set up to smelt the iron and make it into many products. Ore was plentiful, and limestone was everywhere. Heat for melting the products was created from the hardwood trees found nearby. Streams provided water power and ran the bellows for small blast furnaces. In some cases plantations were set up to mine the ore, quarry the limestone, cut the trees, prepare the charcoal, make the iron and fashion it into numerous products. The most noted of these plantations was the Cornwall Furnace in what is now Lebanon County.

The first iron furnace was set up by Thomas Rutter in 1716 along the Manatawney Creek in Berks County. Others soon followed such as the Coventry Furnace in Chester County, Colebrook Furnace in Berks County, and Durham Furnace in Bucks County. Small furnaces appeared in every river valley. These furnaces were of stone, usually built against a hillside so that the ore and limestone could be poured in the top from wagons. The charcoal fire was built in the bottom, and when the limestone and iron ore melted it was drawn off the bottom into forms called pigs. This pig iron was then made into iron products by being reheated at a forge. By 1750 Pennsylvania was the leading producer of iron in the colonies, and this leadership has continued to the present day.

COLONIAL PHILADELPHIA

While the inland country was developing, Philadelphia was growing rapidly. It soon surpassed Williamsburg (Virginia), Baltimore, Boston and New York to become the largest city in America. Only London surpassed it in the British empire. From its 4,000 inhabitants in 1700 it grew to more than 50,000 by the end of the Revolutionary War.

Philadelphia was much more attractive than most European cities or those in the other colonies. William Penn had planned it to be so. The streets, wide for their day, ran at right angles so that all blocks were square. Parks were designed so their natural beauty would remain. Philadelphia was to be a model for all the planned inland cities of the colonial era. The products of the farms and workshops of the interior, of the iron plantations and of the frontier fur trade were channeled to the city so that Philadelphia soon became a great trading center.

Expansion of Trade

Most of the merchants of the city were Quakers. Many of them equipped and sent out the frontier traders and received furs and hides in return. These were shipped to Europe where there was a ready market for such goods. Soon it was found there was much more money in the exchange of Pennsylvania farm products. Wheat, beef, pork and flax were bought up and exported to other colonies and to Europe. Lumber was shipped in large amounts. Someone discovered that wood ashes could be turned into potash which could be exported to Europe for use as fertilizer, for bleaching and for use in dyeing cloth.

The merchants had to be careful in their trading. There was very little actual money. Banks did not exist and all credit was a personal affair. The Quakers, because of their religious reputation for honesty, were deemed trustworthy. Most of the trade was carried on by barter, one person trading what he had for what another owned. Real money, hard money in forms of coins, was scarce. Actually most of the gold and silver money came from Spain which had a surplus from its colonies. The Spanish pieces of eight often were cut into halves, quarters, and bits. Two bits made a quarter, hence our slang expression of today. The lack of real money led to the use of paper money. This Pennsylvania currency was based upon the value of property owned. There was soon so much money in Philadelphia that it was invested in small industry to put the money to "work" for the owner.

The wealth of the city of Philadelphia, soon known all over the civilized world, provided money for the development of science, art and education far beyond that in other colonies. Pennsylvania became a magnet for those seeking their fortunes in many fields. Men came from other colonies and from Europe to visit the city or to settle permanently.

Benjamin Franklin

Perhaps the best known example of such a person was Benjamin Franklin, who was born in Boston in 1706. He was the fifteenth child in the family of a poor candlemaker. As soon as he was old enough to work, his father apprenticed him to his brother in a print shop but before the apprenticeship expired, Ben ran off to Philadelphia at the age of 17.

He arrived with what would be a few pennies of today's money. Going to work in a print shop, he owned it by the time he was 23. His newspaper, the Pennsylvania Gazette, became the most widely read paper in America. He published Poor Richard's Almanac which he filled with the wise sayings of the day. Many, such as "A penny saved is a penny earned," are still quoted today. Elected to the

Harvard University

Forty-two-year-old Benjamin Franklin was already a successful Philadelphia printer and a leading public figure when this portrait was painted in 1748.

Assembly he became one of its most influential members. He was sent to London and Paris where he became world famous as America's "wise man." In Philadelphia he helped start the first public library, the first hospital, first fire department and the first American college not connected with a church. In 1742 he developed an iron stove that became widely used as the first major advance in home heating in centuries. He invented the lightning rod, after discovering that lightning was a form of electricity. Bifocal glasses were another of his inventions. After the beginning of the Revolutionary War he contributed greatly to the success of the founding of the new nation.

THE ATHENS OF AMERICA

Philadelphia's wealth that attracted men of genius from many countries and colonies made the city and the surrounding area the cultural center of early America. It soon became known as "The Athens of America" because the genius of the colonies was concentrated here, just as that of ancient Greece was gathered at Athens.

Men of Science

Pennsylvania was the scientific center of America. David Rittenhouse was a mechanical and mathematical wizard who mapped movements of the planets with instruments he developed himself. He measured the movement of the planet Venus in 1769 and the comet of 1770. John Bartram at his botanical gardens along the Schuylkill developed the study of botany to such an extent that the King of England awarded him a job studying plants in Florida. His studies in plants, fossils and other objects of interest made his home the meeting place for people of science who visited Philadelphia. An inventor of the mariner's quadrant, Thomas Godfrey, was also a resident of colonial Philadelphia. His invention of 1730 was to make the navigation of the seas much safer.

Philadelphia also became the medical center of the New World. Penn had brought two doctors with him on the Welcome in 1682. All doctors were educated in Europe until 1765, when Dr. William

Morgan set up the first courses in medicine at the College of Philadelphia. William Shippen, Jr., and Dr. Benjamin Rush helped in the development of the medical school and were the leading physicians of America. Dr. Morgan was to become the Physician-in-Chief for the entire American Army in 1775-1777.

The Fine Arts

Art was slow to develop in Pennsylvania as it was elsewhere in the New World. Art cannot exist until there is wealth to support it and Philadelphia, because of its wealth, became the first artistic center in the colonies.

The first painter of note was Benjamin West, a Quaker born in Swarthmore. Educated at the College of Philadelphia, he painted portraits of noted people in Philadelphia. He went abroad to study further in Italy, and returned by way of London where he exhibited his paintings in the famous Spring Garden. His works were so well received that he was asked to become the painter for the King. He remained to paint what some people consider the greatest historical paintings of the eighteenth century. His famous Penn's Treaty With the Indians and the Death of Wolfe have been admired by millions. Americans who wanted to become painters went to London to study under the famed Benjamin West. These artists will be considered in a later chapter.

The art of music developed slowly. Francis Hopkinson was Philadelphia's chief promoter of musical life. He was a church organist, psalmodist and harpsichordist. "My Days Have Been So Wondrous Free" was composed in 1759 and is still sung on concert stages today. It was the outstanding song of the colonial period. Hopkinson also was known as a witty poet and essayist. Most of the finer music of the colonial era was developed inland by the Germans. At Ephrata, in Lancaster County, the members of the religious Seventh-Day Baptists composed over 1,000 hymns. Under the leadership of Conrad Beissel, the community became known for its unique music and produced a printed hymnal of their works in 1747. The Moravians of Bethlehem developed church music also. Unlike other religious groups they used entire brass bands in their church services. They developed outstanding music that made Bethlehem the music center for religious music. Today the Bach Choir of Bethlehem attracts thousands to its great music festival each year.

The Written Word

Philadelphia led the colonies in the production of drama and literature, and the first theatre opened in Philadelphia in 1766. The initial theatre, the 'Southwark," in 1767 produced the first American play, The Prince of Parthia by Thomas Godfrey, Jr. Books were published in Philadelphia and Germantown throughout most of the colonial period, but few won such worldwide fame as Benjamin Franklin's Autobiography of his years 1706-1759. Newspapers were the most common reading matter. The first newspaper was Andrew Bradford's American Weekly Mercury which began publication in 1719. The second was Samuel Keimer's Pennsylvania Gazette which began in 1728, but was sold in 1729 to Benjamin Franklin.

No power machinery helped the colonial printers as much as did Benjamin Franklin.

Building

In architecture Philadelphia was the leader of America. The Georgian style, as it was called after the Georges who reigned in England in this period, has maintained popularity until today. In 1724 the Carpenters' Company began as an organization of master carpenters of Philadelphia and their famous Carpenters' Hall is a fine example of colonial architecture. A more noted and excellent example of Georgian Architecture is the famed Pennsylvania State House or, as it is better known, Independence Hall. Built in 1732-1741, it became a model for public buildings throughout America.

The major lines of these buildings were simple, but their beauty stemmed from the carpentry work. The doorways, cornices, mantlepieces, stairways and wainscoating are copied and admired to this day. Some of the most outstanding homes of the time were Pennsbury Manor, James Logan's Stenton, the Chew House and Mount Pleasant. The home of Robert Morris was to become the residence of two Presidents who were to live in Philadelphia.

The Schools

Education was a factor of Pennsylvania life from the beginning of the colony. Penn required that the first government erect public schools so children might learn to read and write by the time they were 12 years of age. The first school was set up in Philadelphia by Enoch Flower in 1683, but the government stopped its support of education in 1689. For a time education was left largely in the hands of the parents, and it was not until 1834 that free public schools would be introduced. The Quakers and other religious groups set up their own schools. One of these is the William Penn Charter School which still provides educational opportunities in Philadelphia. Moravians set up schools for both boys and girls at Lititz and for boys at Nazareth Hall in early times. Presbyterian schools were taught by their ministers. Lutherans and German Reformed groups set up church schools also. The greatest exponents of free public education were the Connecticut settlers in northern Pennsylvania. They had such schools in Connecticut before they moved to Pennsylvania.

OUR PENNSYLVANIA HERITAGE

Pennsylvania Department of Commerce

The beautiful Philadelphia home "Mount Pleasant" built for the wealthy colonial sea captain John Macpherson is now a museum open to the public.

CONTRASTS OF COLONIAL LIVING

Bucks County Historical Tourist Commission

At the same time in Bucks County, less than 50 miles away, a colonial farmer lived in this log home.

Early Pennsylvania schools were generally conducted by church groups. The only reading book was usually the Bible.

Higher education was one of Benjamin Franklin's chief concerns. He published a pamphlet in 1743 entitled *Proposals Relating to the Education of Youth in Pennsylvania*, which urged the founding of an academy. The resulting "Academy and Charitable School" purchased a building, and in 1751 the school opened to develop into the College of Philadelphia, later the University of Pennsylvania.

COLONIAL TRAVEL AND TRANSPORT

Philadelphia became a shipbuilding center almost from its founding. William West's yards in 1683 were turning out fine ships used in the ocean trade. The nearby forests of fine hardwoods provided the lumber for building strong fast ships to carry Pennsylvania's exports to Europe and to the West Indies.

River Transportation

The first method of transportation was by way of the rivers in canoes fashioned like those of the Indians. When the farmers and iron makers of the Delaware and Schuylkill Valleys wanted to send their wares to market, they needed larger boats. Above Philadelphia there are falls on the Delaware, so a flat-bottomed boat had to be developed. A sharp-nosed, flat-bottomed boat was developed by the Moravians of the Bethlehem district in the early 1700s. By 1737 the Durham iron furnace owners had a fleet of the boats, called Durham Boats, carrying iron products to Philadelphia. These boats were up to 60 feet in length and 8 feet wide. Their best quality was the fact they needed only 2 feet of water to carry 15 tons of cargo.

The First Roads

Roads had been slow to develop since it took such great effort to cut the trees and keep down bushes. Stumps had to be cleared, rocks moved and mud and ruts were a constant problem. As early as 1677, before the arrival of Penn, a road was started from New York to Upland (Chester). A road was cut from Philadelphia to Morrisville in 1686, to Chester in 1706, to Easton in 1722, to Lancaster in 1733, to Harrisburg in 1736, and one was begun from Harrisburg to the Potomac River through the Cumberland Valley in 1735. These early roads were constructed to connect streams and settlements. An act of 1700 set up a plan for King's highways with a width of 50 feet. Overseers, like township road supervisors of today, were placed in each area to keep the roads in good repair. These roads were all dirt. There were few bridges in Pennsylvania. All but the smallest streams and rivers had to be forded or crossed at ferries.

Before 1750 there were few travelers who were willing to pay someone to haul them. If anyone wanted to go anywhere he walked or used his own means of transportation. The first stage line was opened between New York and Philadelphia in 1756. These early stagecoaches were simply covered buckboards with no windows, springs or cushions. The closed stagecoach was a thing of the future. These early stagecoaches went about 40 miles a day in the

COLONIAL LIFE 129

summer and only 25 in winter. The trip to New York from Philadelphia could be made in two days in good weather.

NEW COUNTIES ARE ESTABLISHED

As settlers moved to the unsettled parts of the colony they soon established towns and townships. However, all legal business had to be done in the courthouses of the three counties, which meant a trip to the Delaware River. Western settlers complained. As their numbers grew, their complaints against Quaker control of the government increased, but at last they were able to establish their own governments. The first additional county was set up in 1729, when Lancaster County was carved from Chester County. The county seat took on the same name in 1730 and grew quickly to become the largest inland city in the colonies. Now it would be possible for the farmers of that county to take care of all their legal business without going all the way to Chester. The county was given representation in the Assembly.

Not until twenty years later, 1749, was an additional county added. When the people west of the Susquehanna River convinced the colonial government that they needed a separate government, York County was formed with the county seat at the town of York. The community had been in existence since 1741. The Cumberland Valley became a settled region and was set up in 1750 to include all lands north and west of York as Cumberland County. Carlisle was designated as the county seat, and here all business was carried on for the huge area to the west until Bedford County was founded in 1771. Westerners had to travel over Laurel Ridge to the courthouse at Bedford until Westmoreland County was organized in 1773 with Hannastown as its county seat.

Settlers in the northern and western sections of Bucks and Philadelphia Counties asked for their own counties, and in 1752 two additional counties were added. The upper western portion of Philadelphia County became Berks County with its seat at Reading. The lands to the north of Bucks County were designated as Northampton County with its courthouse at Easton.

In 1772 the areas that remained in the colony at that time were designated as Northumberland County with headquarters at Sunbury. The huge county of that time has been reduced in size to become one of the smaller counties, but its county seat is still in Sunbury.

REVIEW QUESTIONS

1. Describe the steps by which the white man penetrated and took over the lands of the Indians.
2. Describe the home of the frontier farmer.
3. Compare the dress of the wealthy easterner and the frontiersman.
4. Why was the neighborhood mill so important in colonial times?
5. Why did the iron industry develop so rapidly in Pennsylvania?
6. Why were many Philadelphia Quakers so important to the frontier trader?
7. What is meant by the statement, "Pennsylvania became a magnet for those seeking their fortune in many fields."
8. Benjamin Franklin was a versatile man. Explain.
9. Explain the meaning of the term "Athens of America."
10. Give the reasons why areas west of Chester County, such as Lancaster and York, requested their own county governments.
11. Mention four kinds of work which the colonists did by hand but which we now do by machine.

Do You Know the Meaning? Write a sentence containing the following words or phrases.

1. Conestoga
2. hominy
3. trading post
4. lean-to
5. quadrant
6. doeskin
7. Scotch-Irish
8. sickle
9. almanac
10. tinder box
11. forge
12. linsey-woolsey
13. lightning rod
14. Durham Boat
15. ferry

COLONIAL LIFE

Maps to Help Us Learn

1. Study your maps of Pennsylvania. Notice the rivers, harbors, mountains and plains. Answer the following questions.
    a. Why was Pennsylvania at one time 99 percent forest land?
    b. Why did Philadelphia grow so large?
    c. Which routes did the settlers take when they went over the Blue Mountains?
    d. Why was life in southeastern Pennsylvania more pleasant than in southwestern Pennsylvania?
    e. What trail would you follow to cross Pennsylvania east to west in a Conestoga Wagon?
2. On an outline map of Pennsylvania show the original counties and then each new county added until 1776.

What Do You Think? Use the knowledge gained thus far to comment on the following statements.

1. The frontier farmer was practically self-sufficient.
2. Indirectly the wealth of Philadelphia could be traced to the prosperous farmer.
3. I would think life on a farm today would be dull compared to life on a frontier farm.
4. Was the most noteworthy contribution of the Pennsylvania German to Pennsylvania the long rifle or the Conestoga wagon?
5. Around Philadelphia log cabins of the farmers gave way to large permanent homes of brick or stone.

ACTIVITIES
(Individual, committee or class projects and class reports)

1. A rifle-conscious member of the class may be able to show on the blackboard or demonstrate the difference between a musket and a rifle.
2. Visit a local farm. Examine the modern barn and equipment. Then ask the farmer to compare it with older methods of farming. If grandfather is there, he can tell you of old-fashioned farming methods almost like those used by the frontier farmer.

3. Arrange for students of German, French, English, and Irish extraction to tell how and when their ancestors came to Pennsylvania, where they lived and their contributions to Pennsylvania.

4. Have a panel discussion on the following: "The Colonies had more pressing problems than we have today."

5. Report to the class on the life of important men of this chapter, such as Daniel Boone, Benjamin Franklin, John Bartram, Benjamin West, George Croghan, David Rittenhouse or Benjamin Rush.

6. If there are any old mills in your locality, visit one of them and try to get its history from the beginning until today.

7. Make a drawing or model of a Conestoga Wagon or of a Durham Boat.

8. Write a short play. Base it on Philadelphia in the eighteenth century. Show how it became the scientific and cultural center, and how great men were drawn there as if by a magnet.

9. Imagine you are the son of a frontier farmer and have just reached the spot along a creek where your log cabin will be built. Tell us what might happen in the next few months.

READING MATERIALS

Beyer, George R., *Pennsylvania's Roads, Before the Automobile*, Historic Pennsylvania Leaflet No. 33, Harrisburg, Pennsylvania Historical and Museum Commission, 1972.

Bining, Arthur Cecil, *Pennsylvania Iron Manufacture in the Eighteenth Century*, 2ed., Harrisburg, Pennsylvania Historical and Museum Commission, 1973.

Block, Symour S., *Benjamin Franklin: His Wit, Wisdom and Women*, New York, Hastings House, 1975.

"Charcoal Burning Industry," *Magazine*, Pennsylvania Department of Forests and Waters, January, 1952.

Cornwall Furnace, Pennsylvania Historical and Museum Commission, 1946.

The Conestoga Wagon, Historic Pennsylvania Leaflet, No. 5, Pennsylvania Historic and Museum Commission, 1951.

"Early Grist Mills," *Bulletin*, Pennsylvania Department of Internal Affairs, May, 1947.

Eaton, J., *That Lively Man, Ben Franklin*, Morrow, 1948.

Franklin, Benjamin, *Benjamin Franklin, A Biography in His Own Words*, ed., by Thomas Fleming, New York, Harper and Row, 1972.

Lichten, Frances, *Folk Art of Rural Pennsylvania*, Scribner, 1946.

Long, Amos, *The Pennsylvania German Family Farm*, Pennsylvania German Society Publications, Vol. 6, Breinigsville: The Society, 1972.

Pennsylvania's State House and Capitols, Historic Pennsylvania Leaflet, Historical and Museum Commission, 1953.

The Pennsylvania Rifle, Historic Pennsylvania Leaflet, No. 4, Pennsylvania Historical and Museum Commission, 1953.

chapter VI

Conflict on the Frontiers

Quakers, because of their religion, opposed war, so from 1682 until 1754 there was no war in the colony. England had been involved in three wars with the French during the period: King William's War 1689-1697, Queen Anne's War 1702-1710, and King George's War 1743-1748. None of these wars directly affected the colony. There were no militia in the colony. The Quaker government believed they were unnecessary.

THE FRENCH IN WESTERN PENNSYLVANIA

On the western side of the province's mountains the French of Canada became interested in the Ohio River Valley. Virginia at the same time was interested in settling the region and laid claim to it. In 1750 as the Virginians were becoming entangled with the French, Pennsylvania considered the area west of the Laurel Ridge as part of the Indian domain.

Frenchmen Explore the Ohio

The French had been settled in Canada since 1608 with settlements north of the Great Lakes and the St. Lawrence River. At the same time they had established trading posts along the Mississippi river from New Orleans northward. In 1739 they decided to unite their holdings. They sent an army from New Orleans north along the Mississippi. A second one was sent down the Mississippi from Mackinac Island. A third force was sent from Montreal to Lake Erie, the Allegheny River, the Ohio and the Mississippi to join the others at Fort Assumption (Memphis, Tennessee). By this latter expedition the French asserted their claim to the Allegheny and Ohio Valleys.

Their army of 422 men came into Pennsylvania by way of Lake Erie up the Chautauqua Creek to Lake Chautauqua, over land to the Conewango Creek and down the creek to the Allegheny River. With the army was an 18-year-old French soldier, Sieur Chaussegros de Lery, who mapped the route for the French. This was the first known real map of western Pennsylvania. It was the first map to show the curves of the various rivers and to indicate where Indian villages were located. The French would use the map soon again.

Virginia's Claim

At the same time in Virginia men were becoming interested in the lands of the Ohio Valley. Virginia claimed southwestern Pennsylvania since their original charter had allowed them all lands "up into the Land, throughout Sea to Sea, West and Northwest." A group of wealthy Virginians headed by Thomas Lee and Lawrence and Augustine Washington, brothers of George, wanted the land. They petitioned the governor of Virginia for all the land south of the Kiskiminetas and Ohio Rivers.

Colonial America's great Indian agent and interpreter, Conrad Weiser, lived in this handsome stone house in Berks County.

The request was forwarded to London where the group was granted 500,000 acres in 1749. If the group could get 100 families to move into the land within seven years and build a fort along the Ohio, the land was theirs. The land seekers called themselves the Ohio Company. The next year they hired Christopher Gist to go into the area, map it, and find the best areas for settlement. He talked to the Indians of the region, got their permission to build. trading posts, and then built his own cabin in what is now Fayette County.

Pennsylvania was warned by the Indians and the traders of the French and Virginia moves. Two famous Pennsylvania scouts, George Croghan and Conrad Weiser, were sent out into the west to convince the Indians that their best friends were still the Pennsylvanians. Lewis Evans was sent out at the same time to map the region for Pennsylvania. He published his map of the entire middle colonies and the Ohio country in 1755, the first accurate map of its kind. He found that the Indians were friendlier to the Pennsylvania traders than to either the French or the Virginians.

Celoron's Expedition

In 1749 the French decided to send a second expedition under Celoron de Blainville to assert their ownership of the Ohio Valley. He took with him 20 Frenchmen, 180 Canadians, 30 Iroquois, and 25 Abnaki Indians. This group tried to get the Delaware and Shawnee Indians of the region to trade with the French. They buried lead plates at the mouth of each stream flowing into the Allegheny and Ohio Rivers. The plates claimed the land for the French king. A copy of the French coat of arms was affixed to trees along the route. English traders who were in the region were warned to get out of French territory. Indians were called before the French commander and informed they would be expected to trade only with French traders thereafter. The Indian chiefs told the French they preferred the English traders. Celoron continued his expedition to the Mississippi Valley, but sent word that stronger means would be needed to convince the Indians.

In the period 1750-1752 six Pennsylvania traders were captured by the French. Two escaped to tell the story to eastern authorities, and three were taken to France before they were released. These cases called the attention of English and colonial leaders to the serious French problem.

Virginia continued to press its claim. In 1752 a road was cut from Wills Creek (Cumberland, Maryland) to the Youghiogheny. The route was pointed out by a Delaware Indian named Namacolin whose name was given to the road. It would be used by Washington and Braddock, and later became the National Road. The Indians in 1752 gave the Virginians permission to erect a fort on the south bank of the Ohio.

The French Fortify the Allegheny

That same year a new governor arrived in Canada, with orders to "arrest the progress of the English along the Belle Rivere." (The French name of "Beautiful River" applied to both the Allegheny and the Ohio). Marquis DuQuesne de Menneville took his post in Quebec and ordered an expedition sent into the Allegheny Valley to erect forts to maintain the French claims. In April 1752 a force of 250 men started out under the command of Chevalier Pierre Paul Marin. They discovered the fine harbor of Erie and built a fort on the peninsula which they named Presque Isle (meaning "almost an island"). They went overland where they built a second fort on the headwaters of French Creek at LeBoeuf. This is now the site of the community of Waterford in Erie County.

At the mouth of French Creek was an Indian village of the Delawares called Custaloga. A Pennsylvania trader by the name of John Fraser had conducted a post there for some time but fled before the French who moved in to build Fort Machault at the junction of French Creek and the Allegheny River. Today this is the site of the city of Franklin, Venango County.

George Washington Warns the French

In England, the political leaders knew stronger measures must be used. All colonial governors were directed, in October 1753, to demand that the French withdraw from English territory. If the requests failed, the colonial governors were to "repel Force with Force." Governor Robert Dinwiddie of Virginia was the first to act. He selected young George Washington to deliver a letter to the

Pennsylvania Historical and Museum Commission

George Washington kept a complete diary of his travels. Shown is a map he made of his trip from Wills Creek, Cumberland, MD, to the French Fort Machault. (Franklin, PA)

French along the upper Allegheny. George's brothers were not interested in having the French invade the lands of the Ohio Company. George had acted as a surveyor of their lands and at the age of 21 was already a major in the Virginia militia.

At Wills Creek (Cumberland, Maryland), he engaged Christopher Gist to be his guide. A French interpreter was a member of the party also. Near the forks of the Ohio they found John Fraser where he had set up his trading post after being driven from Custaloga. About November 23, 1753, Washington passed the forks of the Ohio and wrote in his journal that this location seemed "extremely well situated for a Fort." Twenty-five days after leaving the Virginia capital at Williamsburg, Washington arrived at the Indian village of Logstown, near the present town of Ambridge. There Half-King, an Iroquois chief, and three other Indians agreed to lead the party to the French. By following the Venango Trail, the party reached Fort Machault six days later. The Frenchmen directed the party to the commander at Fort LeBoeuf

On December 11, 1753, Washington delivered Dinwiddie's letter to Legardeur de St. Pierre, the French commander. The Frenchman declared that he would not withdraw. Further, the French were determined to take possession of the entire Ohio Valley. St. Pierre wrote a letter to the Virginia governor in which he said that Dinwiddie's letter would be sent to DuQuesne, but the forts would be held until he was ordered to do otherwise. Washington took note of the forest, the number of men and their equipment, and especially of the large number of canoes ready for the soldiers to use in making their invasion.

Washington and Gist decided to hurry back to Virginia. They took a short cut to Fraser's post, and along the way Washington twice came close to losing his life. In the forest he was narrowly missed by a bullet shot by an angry Indian. Then, as he and Gist tried to cross the icy Allegheny on a crude raft, it overturned. Fortunately, they swam to an island where they stayed until the river froze over that night. This crossing has been marked by a memorial bridge at the spot in Pittsburgh.

THE FRENCH AND INDIAN WAR

Washington gave the French reply to Governor Dinwiddie. The journal kept by Washington was published throughout the colonies and in England. Colonists were aroused. Washington was promoted to the rank of colonel and in the spring of 1754 was sent to help build a fort at the forks of the Ohio. Fort Prince George, named in honor of the future George III, was never finished. Before Washington and his men arrived, the French appeared with 500 soldiers. The 41 men building the fort were forced to surrender, but were permitted to return to Virginia. The French built a fort on the same site which they named Fort Duquesne.

A French party of 32 men was found in a ravine of Fayette County by Washington's group. Ten Frenchmen were killed, including their leader, Coulon de Jumonville, 21 were made prisoners and one escaped. This encounter was the beginning of a war which was to spread all over the world between Great Britain and France. "A shot fired in the woods of North America drenched all Europe in blood," wrote the English author Carlyle.

CONFLICT ON THE FRONTIERS

Pennsylvania Department of Commerce

Fort Necessary has been reconstructed as above. It was originally built under the direction of George Washington in 1754. French forces captured it July 4 of that year.

Washington and his men retired to the nearby "Great Meadows" where he had his men erect a stockade called Fort Necessity. The escaped Frenchman aroused his countrymen at Fort Duquesne. Jumonville's brother swore revenge and led 1,000 men to surround the 140 Virginians at Fort Necessity. On July 4, 1754, Washington agreed to withdraw back to Virginia and the French were then in control of western Pennsylvania.

Braddock's Tragic March

In England the British army leaders decided that a regular army was needed to defeat the French. General Edward Braddock was sent to America with 1,000 Irish troops. The colonies were asked to provide many of the supplies needed to send an army on an expedition into the forest. Benjamin Franklin convinced the Assembly to send numerous Conestoga wagons loaded with supplies to Fort Cumberland at Wills Creek. James Burd of Pennsylvania supervised the building of a new road from Shippensburg to Raystown (Bedford) and west to Redstone (Brownsville) over which to send supplies to Braddock.

With 2,000 troops, half of which were colonials, Braddock set out along the Nemacolin path from Fort Cumberland. His large artillery and wagons demanded the road be widened into what was then called Braddock's Road. The British troops in their scarlet uniforms marched proudly through the thick forest over the newly cut road. The Indians, mostly Shawnees in the pay of the French, kept the army under watch. On July 9, 1755, at the site of the present town of Braddock, the French and Indians struck. Two hundred French and 500 Indians hid behind trees and picked their targets among the 2,000 men in the open field. Washington, who was Braddock's aide-de-camp, advised the men to take cover in the woods. Braddock refused because the European armies at that time were trained to fight their battles in open fields.

Finally Braddock saw that the situation was hopeless and ordered a retreat. In the retreat Braddock was shot. About a third of the British army was killed and another third was wounded. Sixty-three of the 86 gaily-dressed officers, bright targets for the tree-hidden Indians, were killed. The French ordered the Indians to attack the retreating English, but instead they rushed in to gather the plunder from the fallen. In the retreat Braddock died and was buried in the roadway so that his grave would be concealed from the Indians. Colonel Thomas Dunbar, who was next in command, took the army to Philadelphia to await orders from England. The whole west was left at the mercy of the French and Indians.

Now was the chance for the Indians who had been cheated out of their lands. Many of the western Delawares joined with the French. Indian bands roamed the forests as far east as the Blue Mountains. Homes were burned, settlers killed or taken prisoner, and property looted. Frontier farmers rushed back across the mountains to the more settled regions. The French tried to control the Indians, but they had no way of doing so.

Quakers Lose Control of the Assembly

The Scotch-Irish and Germans in the western regions called upon the Assembly for protection. The Quakers always had been able to deal with the Indians peacefully and refused to set up an army. In the past they had been willing to send money and supplies as "a gift to the Queen" or "to aid the frontier and for other purposes." Now an army seemed to be the only answer to the problem.

Governor Robert Hunter Morris, however, was not a Quaker but a member of the Church of England. Without the consent of the Assembly, he placed a bounty on all Indian scalps, men, women, or children, and declared war on the Delaware and Shawnee tribes. Rather than refuse to support the war, and since they did not want to give up the principles of their religion, the Quakers began to resign from the Assembly. By 1756 the Quakers had turned the control of the Assembly over to others.

A militia was quickly formed. Local communities set up companies of rangers. Benjamin Franklin was again one of the prime movers and participated in the planning and erection of over 200 forts from Easton to the Maryland border along the Blue Mountains. Some forts were really just log houses, but others were good-sized stockades, manned with from 30 to 70 men. In case of an impending Indian attack, the settlers would rush to the fort. Slowly the attacks within the circle of forts ceased.

Counter-attack

With the ring of forts completed, the time had come for counter-attack. Kittanning, along the Allegheny River, was the base of many of the Indian attacks. Colonel John Armstrong of Carlisle was selected to lead an attack on the town. Beginning at Fort Shirley, in the Juniata Valley, 300 Pennsylvania militiamen followed the Kittanning trail to the Delaware town. On September 8, 1756, the Indians were surprised by the attackers, the town was burned, large quantities of French ammunition and supplies destroyed and cornfields wrecked. Eleven English prisoners were released, and the danger of attack was greatly reduced.

The Quakers, believing the Indians could be persuaded to stop their attacks, sent word to the Indian chiefs through trader George Croghan and Moravian missionary Christian Frederick Post. These men went out among the Indian villages of western Pennsylvania and convinced the chiefs that they should attend a conference at Easton in 1757. In 1758 the Treaty of Easton was signed. This treaty altered the terms of a purchase made by the Penns in 1754, and it returned a large tract west of the Alleghenies to the Indians.

The Forbes Expedition

General John Forbes, who had been busy fighting the French in Canada, was sent to take over command of the troops of Great Britain in the region of Pennsylvania, Maryland and Virginia. A new prime minister had taken over in Great Britain. He was William Pitt, who wanted to defeat the French as quickly as possible. Forbes was ordered to attack Fort Duquesne. More troops were sent from England to Philadelphia. In 1758 over 1,500 red-coats arrived in Pennsylvania. Forbes planned his campaign carefully, deciding to cross the mountains through Pennsylvania. James Burd was ordered to cut a road directly toward the fort. Proceeding slowly from Carlisle, forts were built along the way: Fort Loudon, Fort Littleton and Fort Bedford. Part of the army advanced over Laurel Ridge and built Fort Ligonier.

Forbes led an army of 6,000 troops, including 2,500 Pennsylvanians led by Colonel Armstrong and 1,500 Virginians led by Colonel Washington. When Forbes became quite ill, the army was headed by Colonel Henry Bouquet, a Swiss-born officer of the British army. The French at Duquesne thought perhaps they could defeat this army as they had Braddock's. When an advance detachment of British troops led by Major James Grant attacked Fort Duquesne prematurely, one-third of Grant's 750 troops were killed or taken prisoner. Grant was one of the prisoners. The French then sent out 600 troops to attack the British at Ligonier. Neither side won the battle that followed, but the French retired to their fort.

A captured prisoner told General Forbes that the French at Duquesne were in poor shape to defend the fort. He reported that the number of troops had been reduced and there were few supplies. Forbes ordered an attack. The French saw there was no chance of success, burned their fort, and retreated first to Machault and finally into Canada. On November 25, 1758, the British marched to the burning Fort Duquesne. Forbes ordered a new fort erected. He wrote of his success to Prime Minister Pitt, dating the letter at "Pittsborough," and he named the new outpost Fort Pitt.

The remaining French forts were abandoned and burned by the French as they retreated into Canada before being finally defeated. The British moved troops into the area and rebuilt the forts.

CONFLICT ON THE FRONTIERS 143

Machault was renamed Venango, but LeBoeuf and Presque Isle retained their French names.

Pontiac's Conspiracy

With the French gone, the Indians asked the British to withdraw but they refused. The Indians asked for more gifts, guns and food, but the English tried to cut expenses. The forts were strengthened. Fort Pitt was build to cover eight acres. One complete wall was built of brick and a moat dug from the Allegheny River to surround the fort with water. Facilities were set up for 1,000 men.

Meanwhile an Ottawa Indian, Chief Pontiac, secretly set out to organize a league of all the Indian tribes to drive the English out of the lands west of the mountains. Aided by Chief Guyasuta in southwestern Pennsylvania and Chief Custaloga in the northwestern part of the colony, attacks were made on all forts.

On June 16, 1763, Fort Venango fell; two days later LeBoeuf was taken; and two days later Presque Isle surrendered to the rampaging Indians. The Delawares, Mingos, and Shawnees, as well as many Senecas, were in the attacking forces. Fort Ligioner was attacked June 21, but held out. The next day Fort Pitt was unsuccessfully attacked. Settlers again found it was unsafe beyond the line of Blue Mountain forts. The Indians roamed as far east as the Susquehanna in their burning and plundering. Carlisle and Shippensburg were filled with thousands of refugees.

Battle of Bushy Run

Colonel Henry Bouquet was ordered to the aid of the surrounded Fort Pitt. General Forbes had died shortly after his return from the Duquesne campaign. Assembling wagons, supplies and men at Carlisle, Bouquet got under way with 500 men in July, 1763. Following Forbes Road, the army marched to Fort Ligonier. Bouquet decided that he would leave the wagons there and pushed on with packhorses and troops. The Indians were determined that he would not reach Fort Pitt.

On August 5, 1763, at Bushy Run, near the present city of Jeannette, Westmoreland County, the Indians attacked. The British troops were caught in the open, and it looked like certain defeat, but Bouquet's men lasted the day by hiding behind the bags of flour their horses were carrying. In the flour bag fort, Bouquet spend the night planning his next day's battle. Part of his men pretended retreat, and others hid themselves in the woods and attacked the advancing Indians. It was a great victory for the British. The Indians fled in disorder. The rest of the journey to Fort Pitt was uneventful. The defeat of the Indians at Bushy Run is the most important Indian battle in Pennsylvania history. Had Bouquet failed, possession of the whole Ohio River valley would have been delayed indefinitely. The State of Pennsylvania has made the battlefield a State Park.

Revenge of the Backwoodsmen

Indian attacks on frontier settlements slowed down for some time. However, the attacks soon became more frequent. Frontiersmen began to look upon all Indians with suspicion. The feeling grew among the Scotch-Irish that the only good Indian was a dead one. A mob of men from Paxton, near present Harriburg and Donegal in Lancaster County, attacked the 20 harmless, peaceful Conestoga Indians living under the white man's protection in Lancaster County. Swooping down upon them, the 57 "Paxton Boys" killed every Indian man, women and child. The action was viewed by the colonial government as a great crime. Warrants were issued for the arrest of the men, but no one would make the arrests.

Christianized Indians living near the Moravians were suspected of being in league with their Delaware relatives to the west. The frontiersmen set out to attack them also. A thunderstorm delayed the attackers long enough to have the Indians sent to Philadelphia for protection. To the Scotch-Irish, it looked as if the government was more interested in protecting the 140 Indians than they were the frontiersmen.

The Scotch-Irish decided they would go to Philadelphia and kill the Indians. At the same time they would take the government out of the hands of those who would do nothing to protect the frontier. About 600 backwoodsmen set out for Philadelphia in January, 1764. The city dwellers called upon the British troops for protection, and a volunteer army was set up to man the defenses. All ferry boats were drawn to the east shore of the Schuylkill. The invaders crossed up the river and were going to enter the city by way of Germantown when the versatile Benjamin Franklin was sent to meet them. He convinced them that armed might would get them nowhere. They agreed to send a petition to the government and return home.

Grievances of the frontiersmen were spelled out in the petition. They expressed their dissatisfaction with the protecting of the Moravian Indians. They asked that all Indians be removed from the colony in time of war. They demanded that the newer counties be given equal representation in the Assembly. The three original counties of Bucks, Philadelphia and Chester had 26 members and the five others had only 10 members. More people lived in five counties than in the other three. Such representation was unfair. The men returned home with no action on their demands.

Colonel Bouquet Marches to the West

British army leaders were determined to put an end to the Indian menace. It was decided to send a large army into the Indian country west of Fort Pitt to punish the Indians. Colonel Bouquet was again called upon to do the job. In the fall of 1764 Bouquet set out with 1,500 men from Fort Pitt to attack the Indians. He marched into the middle of the Indian country in what is now the State of Ohio. The army put fear into the heart of the Seneca Indians who sent their chiefs to sue for peace. The Shawnee, Delaware and Seneca chiefs promised to surrender and to turn over all white prisoners held by their tribes. Over 200 white men, women and children were brought back by Bouquet in his triumphal return to Fort Pitt. All the Indians, including Pontiac, soon made peace with the British.

Bouquet's fine work and that done by his men was appreciated by the Pennsylvanians. The Pennsylvania Assembly passed a resolution of thanks to Colonel Bouquet "for services rendered during our late war with the French and the barbarous Indians, in the remarkable victory over the savage Enemy, united to oppose you near Bushy Run, August, 1763; as also in your late march to the country of the savage nations,...striking terror through the numerous Indian Tribes around you, laying a Foundation for a lasting as well as honorable Peace and rescuing from savage captivity upwards of 200 of our Christian Brethren, Prisoners among them...The grateful Tribute of Thanks from all good men,"

The defeat of the Indians left the frontier clear for settlement and trade. Settlers began to flock across the mountains. Traders could not wait to resume the rich Indian trade. Boatmakers were sent from Philadelphia to Pittsburgh so that river trade could be started.

ESTABLISHING PENNSYLVANIA'S SOUTHERN AND NORTHERN BOUNDARIES

Serious questions as to the boundaries of Pennsylvania had been advanced since the time of William Penn. Now would be a worthwhile time to study the solving of those problems. The only boundary not disputed was the eastern one which is the Delaware River. The boundary separating Pennsylvania from the State of Delaware had been defined in Penn's charter as a circle drawn twelve miles distant from New Castle, Delaware. This line had not been defined for many years because Lord Baltimore claimed that land as part of Maryland. A question arose also as to how such a line could be drawn. Finally in 1732 David Rittenhouse, the famous Philadelphia astronomer, supervised the laying out of the line.

Cresap's War and the Mason-Dixon Line

Penn's Charter had further stated that westward from the New Castle arc the boundary would be drawn. This was disputed for many years by the various Lords Baltimore. In 1735 a Maryland settler named Thomas Cresap was appointed as the Baltimore land agent in territory claimed by Pennsylvania. Cresap led a group to expel Pennsylvania settlers in the region that is now southern York County. One Pennsylvanian was killed and others were jailed in Maryland. The area in dispute was part of Lancaster County at the time, and the Lancaster sheriff took 20 men to Cresap's home, arrested him, and burned his home. He was taken to Philadelphia and charged with murder. The dispute was taken before the King and both sides were cautioned to use no violence. In 1745 a bound-

CONFLICT ON THE FRONTIERS 147

ary dispute near Hanover resulted in another death.

The boundary was finally settled when in 1763 the two colonies agreed to extend the line from the New Castle arc westward. Two surveyors, Charles Mason and Jeremiah Dixon, were sent from England to do the job. By 1767 they had completed the boundary as far as present day Greene County. The Mason and Dixon Line was approved by the King and has become the traditional boundary between the North and the South of the United States.

Virginia Claims Southwestern Pennsylvania

Actually the Mason and Dixon Line did not complete the boundary of southern Pennsylvania, for Maryland only extends 230 miles toward the west. As seen earlier in this chapter, Virginia claimed the land west and north of there to the Kiskiminetas and Ohio Rivers. Before the French and Indian War there was not much dispute about the area. But after the capture of Fort Duquesne, both Virginia and Pennsylvania claimed the territory. In 1773 Pennsylvania set up the county of Westmoreland to include all land west of the Laurel Ridge. In January of 1774 a group of Virginians acting on orders of their governor, Lord Dunmore, said Fort Pitt and the area west of Laurel Ridge were part of Augusta County, Virginia. Pennsylvania established a courthouse and jail at the village of Hannastown, and the prothonotary, Arthur St. Clair, went to the Virginia seat of government at Fort Pitt and arrested the Virginia leader, Dr. John Connelly. Connelly was released, but returned with a group of 200 Virginians to arrest the Pennsylvania judges. The confusion continued until after the Revolutionary War when it was mutually agreed to extend the Mason and Dixon Line the five degrees called for in Penn's Charter. From that point the line was extended north to Lake Erie for the western boundary. The many Virginia settlers who lived in southwestern Pennsylvania were given the right to maintain their land titles.

Connecticut's Claim and the Pennamite War

The case of the northern boundary was one of the most vexing. Connecticut, which does not touch Pennsylvania, claimed the

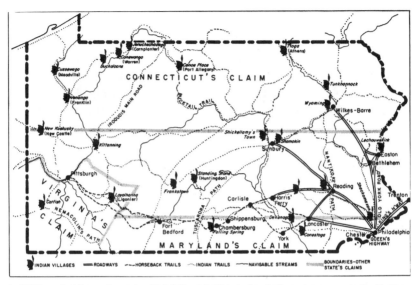

In 1775 most of the main roads which followed either Indian trails or rivers were in the Eastern part of the State. Note those parts of the State which were claimed by Maryland, Virginia, and Connecticut.

northern third of the State. Its charter of 1662 had given that colony north and south boundaries extending to the Pacific ocean, except for land already "occupied by another Christian prince." That exempted New York. But Pennsylvania was not established at that time, and so Connecticut, because of its earlier grant, claimed northern Pennsylvania. In 1753 the Susquehanna Company was set up in Connecticut, and in 1762 they set out to settle the Susquehanna Valley. They found the Indians unfriendly but in 1769 returned with a larger force to set up Forty Fort and Fort Durkee. In the meantime, settlers from Pennsylvania had moved in. Pennsylvania had purchased the land from the Iroquois in 1768, but the Connecticut Yankees outnumbered the Pennsylvanians for many years. In 1774 there were 2,000 Connecticut settlers, in 1783, 5,000. The Susquehanna Company set up townships and settlers were sold farmland. The Pennsylvanians tried to drive them out, but were unsuccessful. These feuds were called the Yankee-Pennamite Wars and lasted from 1769-1771 and again from 1775 until the beginning of the Revolutionary War.

In 1782 a group of Federal commissioners met at Trenton, New

Jersey, to render the verdict that Pennsylvania's northern boundary should be the 42nd parallel. But the numerous New Englanders who settled there left deep impressions on the upper Susquehanna River area. The influence of their architecture and their educational ideas may still be observed in that area today.

The Erie Triangle

With the boundaries thus established, Pennsylvania was left with only four miles of lake front and no harbor on Lake Erie. In 1781 New York had given up all claims to land west of the western tip of Lake Ontario. The man who surveyed the boundary for the Federal government was General William Irvine of Pennsylvania. He saw the value of the triangle of land and the longer shore line thus left available to Pennsylvania, especially the harbor of Presque Isle. Through his efforts as a Pennsylvania congressman, the triangle became part of Pennsylvania in 1788. In 1789 the boundary of western New York was surveyed and Pennsylvania paid the Federal government $151,640.25 for the 202,187 acres. The price of 75 cents per acre was paid in March of 1792.

REVIEW QUESTIONS

1. Both England and France attempted to secure control of the Ohio Valley. Explain how one finally won control of the valley.
2. The French and the English each had some advantages over the other in the wars in North America. Name some of these.
3. For what reasons did England suffer defeats early in North America and what changed the final outcome?
4. Why was Virginia interested in the Ohio Valley? Who warned the Pennsylvanians of the French and Virginian moves?
5. Could the defeat of Braddock have been prevented? How?
6. The Quakers resigned from the Assembly to such an extent that by 1756 they lost control. Why?
7. Why was the Forbes Road built? What do we call the road today?
8. Why was the defeat of the Indians at Bushy Run the most important Indian battle in Pennsylvania history?
9. The Scotch-Irish were angry. Explain what happened until

they decided to go home peacefully.

10. The location of the boundaries of Pennsylvania was a continual headache to the authorities. Why did Pennsylvania seem to win most of the arguments?

Do You Know the Meaning of/or Can You Identify? Write a sentence containing the following words or phrases.

1. ambush	9. Governor Dinwiddie
2. bounty	10. John Armstrong
3. frontier	11. Christian Frederick Post
4. Duquesne	12. Henry Bouquet
5. Pontiac	13. General Braddock
6. Fort Necessity	14. Yankee-Pennamite War
7. Christopher Gist	15. William Pitt
8. Conrad Weiser	

Maps to Help Us Learn

1. Make an outline map of your county and surrounding counties. Then by research locate all the frontier forts in the area.

2. Show in color the North American colonies of France and England before war began between the two nations in 1754. Indicate also the disputed territory that was claimed by both nations. Then show England's gain after the peace treaty.

3. Using an outline map of North America, trace the French and English routes into Western Pennsylvania and the location of the important battles.

4. Suppose Pennsylvania had lost all her boundary disputes. With that in mind, on a map of Pennsylvania draw the smaller Pennsylvania with a red pencil. What state would you probably be living in today.

What Do You Think? Use the knowledge gained thus far to comment on the following statements.

1. Regardless of the outcome of the French and Indian War our lives would not have been affected.

2. The English would have been better off to follow the Indian policy of the Pennsylvania Quakers.

CONFLICT ON THE FRONTIERS 151

3. With the French troops leaving Pennsylvania, the Indians were right in asking the British to withdraw.

4. The Scotch-Irish saying, "The only good Indian, is a dead Indian," was justified during this period.

5. The information Washington was able to get of the Ohio country was more important than the letter to the French commander.

ACTIVITIES
(Individual, committee or class project and class reports)

1. Remember the letter George Washington had to deliver to the French along the upper Allegheny. What do you suppose he and Gist thought about in planning the trip and as they started north? Do you suppose they thought they were in danger? Write a short paper on "The Journey of Washington."

2. As a class project, appoint committees to make scaled miniatures of a Pennsylvania frontier fort.

3. Have a committee report on boundary disputes. If the class asks for it, be able to justify each boundary with the proper explanation.

4. Visit your local historical association and report on your county's activities during the French and Indian War.

5. Consider the phases of the French and Indian War that might cause friction between Colonists and England. Then show how the outcome of the War helped lay the foundation for the American Revolution.

6. Write a paper justifying Pontiac's conspiracy.

7. Hold a panel discussion on the question, "Were the English or French more entitled to the Ohio Valley?" You may include the Mississippi Valley to broaden the discussion.

8. Imagine that you are an Indian in Illinois in the 18th century. Tell a white captive whether you like the French or the English better and why.

9. General Braddock and Washington are arguing about the advisability of seeking cover when fighting the red men. Dramatize.

OUR PENNSYLVANIA HERITAGE

READING MATERIALS

Adams, Paul K., *"Colonel Henry Bouquet's Ohio Expedition in 1764,"* Pennsylvania History SO: 139-147, April 1973.

Bailey, Kenneth P., *Christopher Grist, Colonial Frontiersman, Explorer, and Indian Agent*, Hamden, Conn., Shoe String Press, 1976.

Bailey, K., *The Indian Wars of Pennsylvania, Including Supplement*, New York, Arno Press, 1971 (Reprint).

Buck, S. J. and E. H., *Planting of Civilization in Western Pennsylvania*, University of Pittsburgh Press, 1939.

Downes, R. C., *Council Fires on the Upper Ohio*, University of Pittsburgh Press, 194~.

Henry Bouquet, Historical Pennsylvania Leaflet, No. IS.

Kent D., *Washington's Journal*, Pennsylvania Historical and Museum Commission, Historic Pennsylvania Reprint.

Nixon, L. L., *Jarnes Burd, Frontier Defender, 1726-1793*, University of Pennsylvania Press, 1941.

Peckham, H. H., *Pontiac and the Indian Uprising*, Princeton University Press, 1947.

Sipe, Chester Hale, *The Indian Chiefs of Pennsylvania*, New York, Arno Press, 1971 (Reprint).

Stevens, S. K., *The Pennsylvania Colony*, New York, Growell-Collier Press, 1970.

Stevens, S. K., and Kent, D. H., *Wilderness Chronicles of Northwestern Pennsylvania*, Pennsylvania Historical and Museum Commission, 1941.

Swetnam, George, *Pittsylvania Country*, Duell, Sloan, and Pearce, 1951.

Thompson, Ray, *The Walking Purchase Hoax of 1737*, Fort Washington, Bicentennial Press, 1973.

Wallace, Paul A. W., *Conrad Weiser, 1696-1760, Friend of Colonist and Mohawk*, New York, Russell, 1971 (Reprint).

Wright, J. E. and Corbett, D. S., *Pioneer Life in Western Pennsylvania*, University of Pittsburgh Press, 1940.

Russ, William A., Jr., *How Pennsylvania Acquired its Present Boundaries*, University Park, Pa. Historical Association, 1966.

Weslager, Clinton Alfred, *The Delaware Indians*, New Brunswick, New Jersey, Rutgers University Press, 1972.

chapter VII

The New Nation is Born

All wars are terrible and expensive. The French and Indian War caused Great Britain to go into the greatest debt in its history. Pontiac's War of 1763 and 1764 caused a still greater drain on the treasury. To keep from becoming involved in further Indian Wars, it was decided that the Indians and colonists should be kept separated. To pay for past wars and maintain an army in America meant that new taxes had to be found. Both of the measures were opposed and resented by the colonists.

PENNSYLVANIA DISAGREES WITH THE BRITISH

By 1754, as the French and Indian War was about to get under way, the Iroquois had lost all the land in the State west of Sunbury. During the war that followed, Pennsylvania decided to give up its claim to lands west of the Alleghenies. At the Easton Conference of 1758, Pennsylvania agreed to forbid settlers from living in the Indian territory, but as soon as the French were driven from the area, settlers flocked in.

In October, 1761, Colonel Bouquet forbade all settlers to stay west of the line decided on. The British government in London decided that the land of the Indians and the whites should be separated by the Appalachian Mountains. Any settlers already there were "forthwith to remove themselves." Frontiersmen were furious. British troops were dispatched to burn the cabins of all violators of the Proclamation Line. These frontiersmen felt that the troops were more interested in helping the Indians than the colonists.

153

Taxes Hurt Business

While the frontiersmen were upset about the Proclamation Line, colonists in the east were troubled by the new British taxes. As early as 1650 the British Navigation Acts had regulated colonial trade, but in most cases they were not enforced. In April of 1764, the first specific tax on the colonies was passed by the British Parliament. This so-called "Sugar Act" taxed sugar, molasses, coffee, indigo, wines and non-British textiles. Certain goods shipped through England were to be double-taxed. Taxes were placed on iron, hides, potash, and pearl ash. There had always been import taxes, but few importers had paid them. Tax collectors' salaries sometimes exceeded the amount of taxes collected.

Under such a system new taxes would have meant nothing. However, the new British financial leader, George Grenville, hoped to make sure that his taxes were collected. At Halifax, Nova Scotia, he set up a court to hear all cases involving ocean commerce in the New World. This meant that if a Chester importer was suspected of smuggling he would have to go to Nova Scotia for trial. Under the new setup the accused person had to prove that he was innocent. This was just opposite to the English-American tradition that a person is innocent until he is proved guilty. To further assure collection, tax collectors were sent to America. Formerly they lived in England and hired agents to be collectors in America. Merchants in Philadelphia soon discovered their prices rising sharply as a result of these measures.

Paper Money Forbidden

Another law was passed to forbid the issuing of paper money in the colonies. Pennsylvania had been issuing paper money since 1723. Over 950,000 pounds ($4,750,000) had been printed. In 1764 all this paper money had to be withdrawn. This brought business to a standstill. The lack of paper money forced many merchants to accept other goods for the products they sold. This was called the barter system. Farmers who formerly sold their surplus for export found that increased prices brought them less for their crops. Thus taxes raised prices, the new customs collectors made trade expensive and the abolishing of paper money left the colony with practically no money.

In 1765 the British Army commander got permission from Parliament to force all colonies to provide British troops with barracks and supplies. The troops that 10 years before were welcomed as protectors from the French and Indians, were now a heavy burden. Colonists were to provide "fire, candles, vinegar, salt, bedding, cooking utensils and liquor. " This was the first time that colonists had to tax themselves to aid the British government.

Leaders Fight the Stamp Act

In March of 1765 the notorious Stamp Act was passed to help pay for the troops stationed in America. This tax, plus the others already noted, raised almost one-third of the estimated 300,000 pounds needed each year. The Stamp Act taxed newspapers, almanacs, pamphlets, legal documents, ship's papers, licenses and playing cards. All collections were to be used for colonial defense. American colonists were to be the collectors but opposition developed immediately. The leaders in the community were hit by this tax: lawyers, printers and land speculators. Businessmen were already enraged. The idea of a direct tax, one which was to be paid in addition to the price, was unpopular. Many people in Philadelphia thought that Britain was trying to punish the colonies.

A Congress was called in New York to oppose the taxes. John Dickinson represented Pennsylvania. He was called upon to write the Declaration of Rights and Grievances agreed upon by the members from all the colonies. Dickinson claimed that Americans had all the rights of British subjects, and that since the colonists were not represented in Parliament such taxation was a violation of these rights. The Declaration called for the repeal of the Stamp Act and other taxes of 1764. Copies were sent to the King, the House of Lords and the House of Commons.

To fight the taxes, most Philadelphia businessmen agreed not to purchase any European goods until the taxes were repealed or modified. On November 1, 1765, when the Stamp Act was to go into effect, all business came to a standstill. British trade fell off. Benjamin Franklin, who was in London, argued before Parliament for the repeal of the acts. He pointed out that Pennsylvania had spent 500,000 pounds on the wars and was hard pressed for money. William Pitt praised the colonies for their action. Finally, the Stamp Act was repealed in March, 1766.

Other Taxes Spread a Spirit of Revolt

Pitt soon became prime minister again and his party decided to set up new taxes. These Townshend Acts proved unpopular too. John Dickinson wrote essays against the new external taxes. His "Letters From a Farmer in Pennsylvania to the Inhabitants of the British Colonies," were printed in the Pennsylvania Chronicle. In this series Dickinson denied that Parliament had any right to tax America to raise revenue. Reprints of the "Letters" were read widely in Jamaica and England. By February, 1769, the Philadelphia merchants banned all British goods until the Townshend Acts were repealed. Philadelphia imports were cut in half in a year.

Another prime minister came into power. In 1770 Lord North had all the Townshend Acts repealed except for one on tea. American tea traders were inflamed when it was discovered that British merchants were going to undersell the Americans by shipping cheap tea. This led Boston merchants to strong resistance, and the famous Boston Tea Party resulted on December 16, 1773. In Philadelphia angry citizens caused the merchants to refuse to accept the tea. When a tea ship arrived on Christmas Day, 1773, the captain of the ship was persuaded not to land his ship. The British government took the act at Boston as an act against the British Crown. To punish the city, the port of Boston was closed.

The people of Massachusetts then appealed for aid from the other colonies. Paul Revere arrived in Philadelphia to plead for help. The Pennsylvania Assembly on May 21, 1774, called for a meeting of all the colonies. The others agreed to meet in Philadelphia. Pennsylvanians were further angered when the news reached them that the Quebec Act of May 20, 1774, had given all land west of the Alleghenies south to the Ohio to the Canadian province of Quebec. Another act of June 2 required that British troops be quartered in private homes when other quarters were not provided.

PENNSYLVANIA BECOMES A BATTLEFIELD

Continental Congress Meets in Philadelphia

On September 5, 1774, all the colonies, except Georgia, sent delegates to meet in Philadelphia. Since the Pennsylvania Assembly was in session, the group met in Carpenters' Hall near the State House. John Dickinson, Joseph Galloway and James Wilson were the leading Pennsylvania deligates. Charles Thomson was secretary for the group that took on the name Continental Congress. Galloway wanted to compromise with the British. Wilson declared that Parliament had no power over the colonies. John Dickinson was again elected to write up the views of the deligates. He wrote the "Address to the Inhabitants of Quebec," the "Address to the Armies," the "Address to the United Colonies" and a "Declaration of Rights and Grievances." The last was sent to the King asking his aid in relieving the colonies from the acts of Parliament.

Before adjourning, the Congress formed Continental Associations to try to stop the importing of all British goods. Each colony

Independence Hall in Philadelphia looked like this when the colonies declared their independence in 1776. Farmers still used the two-wheel cart and gentlemen rode on horseback.

was advised to set up a militia. If Great Britain did not repeal the repressive measures, Congress agreed to meet in Philadelphia May 10, 1775. Benjamin Franklin had returned to Philadelphia and became a leader in setting up the Pennsylvania Associators, an armed militia. Citizens in the interior reformed their old Ranger groups which they used to fight the French and the Indians. When the British and the Massachusetts Minute Men became involved in battles at Lexington and Concord April 19, 1775, the Pennsylvania militia was ready to go to their aid.

In May the Second Continental Congress met as scheduled. All the colonial armies were united under the command of George Washington of Virginia. The war that started as a battle for American rights within the British Empire soon became a battle for independence. As early as January of 1776, Thomas Paine, a brilliant writer recently arrived in Philadelphia from England, called for independence. His pamphlet, "Common Sense," was widely read and helped to prepare the way for open revolt against England.

Congress Adopts a Declaration of Independence

In June of that year the Continental Congress set up a committee to draw up plans for independence. Thomas Jefferson of Virginia headed a committee to draw up the document. He wrote the Declaration with some help from Benjamin Franklin. On July 4, 1776, the Declaration of Independence was adopted in the Pennsylvania capitol, now know as Independence Hall. The bell in the tower rang out the news, and the Pennsylvania bell was thereafter called the Liberty Bell for all America to revere. The inscription on the bell, "Proclaim Liberty throughout the land unto all the inhabitants thereof" took on new meaning.

When the Declaration of Independence was adopted, colonies were advised to set up new state governments. Pennsylvania had already known that the break with England was coming. They had been operating under various extralegal organizations for some time. Included were Committees of Correspondence, the Committee of Safety, headed by Benjamin Franklin, and various provincial conventions. Franklin headed a committee that approved the Declaration of Independence for Pennsylvania. Charles Thomson,

THE NEW NATION IS BORN

The Liberty Bell in Independence Hall, Philadelphia, was made in 1752. It was always rung on important occasions. On July 8, 1776, it summoned all Philadelphians to hear the Declaration of Independence read. The bell cracked on July 8, 1835.

Other towns besides Philadelphia had their own Liberty Bells. This is Easton's that rang out independence on July 8, 1776, and is still in use today in the court house.

as Secretary of the Continental Congress, was the first person to sign the document after John Hancock, the president. Thomson was called the "Life of the Cause of Liberty," and kept the records of the entire two Congresses. Other Pennsylvanians who signed the document were Benjamin Franklin, Robert Morris, John Morton, George Clymer, James Smith, Benjamin Rush, James Wilson, George Ross and George Taylor. John Dickinson, however, did not approve the action and withdrew from the government for some time.

The War Moves Into Pennsylvania

Pennsylvania had been in the Revolution since the beginning of April of 1775, but there was no fighting in the State until 1777. Most of the fighting had taken place in Massachusetts, New York and New Jersey. In December of 1776 the British army forced Washington and the Americans to retreat across New Jersey and the Delaware River to Pennsylvania. Congress fled to Baltimore but the British stayed in New Jersey.

Pennsylvania Academy of Fine Arts
General George Washington posed for this portrait by the famous Philadelphia artist, Charles Willson Peale, during the hard days of the Revolution.

THE NEW NATION IS BORN

Fighting for the British at various times were 30,000 German troops. These were men hired by the British from the rulers of the various German states. Since over half of them were from the state of Hesse-Cassel, they were all called Hessians. About 1,400 of these Hessians were encamped at Trenton, New Jersey, along the Delaware River, Christmas night in 1776. Washington and part of his army made their famous crossing of the Delaware from Pennsylvania and attacked the Hessians who were celebrating the holiday. Over 1,000 Germans were captured. In January, Washington defeated the British army at Princeton, New Jersey, and captured more Hessian prisoners. Some of the prisoners were sent to take Carlisle Barracks where they built buildings that are still in use today. Other Germans were turned over to Pennsylvania farmers, iron foundrymen and millers who put them to work. Other Hessians deserted the British army to move to Pennsylvania. At the end of the war many of these men settled permanently in Pennsylvania.

In August, 1777, a British army from New York sailed up the Chesapeake Bay and landed at Elk Ferry, Maryland. Led by General William Howe, the troops started for Philadelphia. General Washington decided to stop them at Chadd's Ford along the Brandywine Creek. When they met September 11, 1777, the Americans were forced to retreat. The British troops led by Lord Cornwallis and German General von Kynphausen had outflanked the rebels to kill 1,000 Americans while the British lost less than 600.

Ten days later the British routed an American army of Pennsylvania at Paoli west of Philadelphia. By then the Continental Congress had fled again. This time they went first to Lancaster and later to York. Government records were moved to Easton, and the Liberty Bell was hauled to Allentown. Horses and cattle were driven from the city to keep them from the British. York was to remain the capital of the United States until June 28, 1778. While at York the Congress adopted the Articles of Confederation and signed a treaty with France.

The British troops moved into Philadelphia on September 26, 1777. The fort which had guarded the Delaware River to the south was captured. Ships of the British navy could then sail into Philadelphia harbor. Washington's troops attacked from the north-

Pennsylvania Historical and Museum Commission

The Battle of Germantown raged furiously for several hours in and around the houses of the residents. In this model can you make out which side is attacking the fine old mansion?

west and met the British in the Battle of Germantown on the night of October 3, 1777. The next morning, in the confusion of fog, the Americans at times found themselves shooting one another. Retreat was the only answer and Philadelphia was to remain in British hands for the winter.

Troops Spend a Dismal Winter at Valley Forge

Washington was forced to find a winter camp. The British settled in the city where they were welcomed by those who were against the war. Gay parties and celebrations were held. Plenty of food was brought in by nearby farmers who wanted the British gold. Washington in the meantime moved up the Schuylkill Valley to Valley Forge. There he decided, December 11, to stay for the winter. His 11,000 men were ill-fed and ragged. A camp was laid out by the French General Duportail. From the trees that were everywhere, log huts were built. Nine hundred huts and a few earthen fortifications were put up. Over 3,000 troops died of exposure and illness that winter. Washington wrote at that time, "Naked and starving as they are, we cannot enough admire the incomparable patience and fidelity of the soldiery."

The French officially joined the Americans in the war May 6,

THE NEW NATION IS BORN 163

Pennsylvania Historical and Museum Commission

At Valley Forge in the winter of 1777-1778 Washington's troops hastily built huts such as the one above. Many men froze to death or died from exposure during the hard winter.

1778, and new money, men and supplies reached Washington's troops. Foreign officers arrived in the camp during the winter to teach the Americans better military organization and discipline. A German officer from the state of Prussia, Baron von Steuben, introduced regular formation and exact discipline. The British in Philadelphia feared the reports of a French fleet approaching, so they left the city. Washington's new army marched out of Valley Forge to pursue the redcoats. Catching them at Monmouth, New Jersey, they forced the British to flee to New York. It was now possible for the Congress to return to their capital in Philadelphia.

Indians Raid the Frontier

New dangers appeared for the State from another direction. The Iroquois Indians had been friendly to the British throughout the colonial period. When the Revolutionary War broke out, the Iroquois remained loyal to the British. Indian agents and other men that remained loyal to England led the Indians on raids against the frontier settlements of the upper Susquehanna Valley. In June, 1778, Indians attacked homes near what is now Williamport. All settlers who had not fled were killed. Men, women and children of the area fled by foot, horseback and raft to the downstream settlements. This was called the Great Runaway.

Most of the able-bodied men of the area had gone off to aid Washington. News that the Indians and Loyalists were going to attack again spread to the settlements near Wilkes-Barre. All the old men and boys of the area were gathered under the leadership of Colonel Zebulon Butler. With 300 men, July 3, 1778, the settlers met 1,100 Indians and Tories led by Colonel John "Indian" Butler. The Americans were crushed, and all the men captured by the Indians were killed. The Indians roamed throughout the Wyoming Valley burning all homes and killing every man, women or child found. Some settlers were burned at the stake. Women and children who escaped to settlements farther south gasped out the story of the Wyoming Massacre.

Congress was shocked at the reports. Members of the English Parliament spoke out against using savages against fellow Christians. Washington chose one of his most trusted generals to punish the Indians for their deeds. General John Sullivan gathered an army of 2,000 men at Easton. In June of 1779 they set out for the Indian country. At Tioga (Athens) they burned the Indian town of Chemung. A force of 2,000 New Yorkers joined the army under General Clinton. Near what is now Elmira, New York, the Indians under Colonel John Butler and the Mohawk Chief Joseph Brant attacked. The Indians were routed. Every Indian town east of the Genesee River was laid to waste. Forty villages, thousands of bushels of grain, and all crops were burned or wrecked. Sullivan wrote, "I am well persuaded that...there is not a single town left in the country of the Five Nations."

In southwestern Pennsylvania Fort Pitt was the headquarters for the defense. During the early part of the war the Indians were kept friendly with gifts. By 1778 the Shawnees and the Wyandots had been convinced that the British would win and went over to their side. The Delawares remained friendly until 1781. However, small raids on the frontier and the Wyoming Massacre gave Colonel Daniel Brodhead at Fort Pitt reason for alarm. Led by Scout Sam Brady, whose father and brother had been killed during the Great Runaway, Brodhead's men cleared the upper Allegheny of the Senecas. His troops burned the Indian villages, ruined their crops

THE NEW NATION IS BORN

and took over $30,000 worth of British supplies found in the towns. This quieted the western frontier until 1781. In that year the Delawares turned against the Americans. Brodhead then took his Pennsylvania troops to attack the Delawares in the Ohio country.

The Indians were constantly being stirred up by the English at Fort Detroit and by frontiersmen, who stayed loyal to the British. Men such as Alexander McKee, Simon Girty and Dr. John Connelly used the Indians to fight their enemies among the Pennsylvania frontiersmen. After the end of the fighting at Yorktown in the east, Chief Guyasuta and Connelly gathered a force of Senecas and Canadians to attack Hannastown. Connelly was still angry about the time he had been jailed there by Pennsylvanians. The Pennsylvania county seat for Westmoreland County was warned, and the settlers ran to the fort. Their log homes and barns were plundered and burned and the area ravaged. The damage was so great that the town was never rebuilt, and the county seat was moved to Greensburg.

Even the end of the war did not end the frontier attacks. The British kept control of the forts at Detroit and Niagara. The soldiers there kept the Indians supplied with guns and ammunition. In the spring of 1783, several frontiersmen were killed or captured. The next year the Iroquois were forced to agree to sell their claims to the remainder of Pennsylvania. All were forced to move out except Chief Cornplanter and his clan who were given a small reservation.

Pennsylvania's Participation in the War

At last the war came to a close in 1783. Some Pennsylvanians, as in other colonies, actively opposed the war because they did not believe the colonists had a right to break away from the authority of the British Crown. Many of these Tories or Loyalists lost their homes and property and left with the British. Ova 1,400 Pennsylvanians joined the British army. Many more did not aid the British, but they refused to join the fight for independence. These were the Quakers and other religious sects which believed that war was contrary to the Christian religion.

However, the big majority of Pennsylvanians supported the war. Thousands of Associators, great numbers of Ranger Companies, and thirteen regiments of the Pennsylvania Line were engaged in action from the siege of Boston in 1775 to Yorktown and the final Indian wars on the frontiers. Perhaps the greatest Pennsylvania general was "Mad Anthony" Wayne. He had led troops in Canada, at Ticonderoga, Brandywine and with Washington until the end of the war. Other Pennsylvanians served as generals including John Armstrong, Philip Benner, Ephraim Blane, John Cadwalader, Thomas Mifflin, Edward Hand, William Irvine, Peter Muhlenberg and Arthur St. Clair.

John Barry had set up the Pennsylvania Navy and headed the unit when it became part of the U.S. Navy. With his crew on the Lexington he is credited with capturing the first British man-ofwar taken by the Americans. Twice his crew captured two British ships single-handedly. After the war he was named head of the entire U.S. Navy.

Molly Pitcher is remembered as a symbol of the numerous women who aided the revolutionary cause. Molly, whose real name was Mary Ludwig Hays, followed her husband from Carlisle to the Battle of Monmouth. When he was killed, she took up his post on the front line.

Leadership Behind the Lines

Behind the lines Pennsylvanians were leaders in the functions that are necessary for the winning of wars. Robert Morris of Philadelphia had the very necessary job of raising the money for the war. Soldiers had to be paid, supplies bought and diplomats sent abroad. Morris lent all his own money and raised a great deal from his friends. He was named superintendent of finance for the government. Paper money was issued but it was almost worthless at times. Morris advised the government to set up a bank. By getting the wealthy men of Philadelphia to place their money in the bank, a more satisfactory money system was established. Haym Salomon, also of Philadelphia, helped to get Holland to give a large loan to the new nation. Benjamin Franklin helped to get the French treaty and loans. He also helped complete the Paris Treaty of 1783.

Many of the soldiers during the war had no uniforms and wore their regular clothing. Many others wore uniforms made by the tex-

THE NEW NATION IS BORN

tile mill of Samuel Wetherill of Philadelphia. This Quaker saw to it that many men had clothing to wear at Valley Forge even when he was not paid. Sarah Bache, daughter of Benjamin Franklin, organized 2,000 women in Philadelphia in 1781 to sew clothing for the soldiers. Betsy Ross, according to legend, made the first official flag of the United States at her home in Philadelphia. It had 13 stars and 13 stripes and was adopted by Congress, June 14, 1777.

At the beginning of the Revolution there were no arsenals. Rifles were made in the Lancaster area, and cannons were soon made in Philadelphia and at various iron furnaces. Carlisle was chosen as the first army arsenal. The army post established there has been continued until the present. Pennsylvania rifles distributed from the post made American soldiers better equipped than the musket-carrying British. Conestoga wagons were invaluable in transporting supplies to the American army.

Many of the German sects that would not enter the fighting served the cause by caring for the wounded. In 1777 the large hall

Pennsylvania Department of Commerce

The home of Betsy Ross in Philadelphia flies a flag similar to the one she made for the 13 independent states.

of the Moravians at Bethlehem and Lititz were opened as hospitals. The Ephrata community also took in numerous wounded.

A NEW GOVERNMENT IS ESTABLISHED

When the Declaration of Independence went into effect, the old Pennsylvania Assembly was dissolved. The Committee of Safety, headed by Benjamin Franklin, took over the government of the State. It levied taxes to help conduct the war. A committee was set up to draw up a State Constitution to replace the one used under the Penns. By September, 1776, the group completed their job and proclaimed it to be in effect. This was an extremely democratic document. All power was taken from any one person and divided among a large number.

Pennsylvania Adopts a New Frame of Government

Instead of a governor, an Executive Council of 12 members was set up. One member was elected in each county and one in the city of Philadelphia. The Council chose one of its members as President. This President of Pennsylvania was simply chairman of the meetings but had no more power than the other 11 members. Laws were passed by the People's Assembly. Initially each county and the city of Philadelphia had equal representation in the Assembly. Later representation was determined by taxable population. A unique feature of this new government was the Council of Censors which was set up instead of a Supreme Court. This council, with two members from each county, was to meet every seven years to review the laws and the Constitution. It had the right to amend the Constitution on a two-thirds vote of its members. Judicial authority was placed in the hands of an appointed judiciary.

Any free man who was 21 years of age, paid taxes, and lived in the State for one year was eligible to vote by secret ballot. This Plan or Frame of Government for the Commonwealth or State of Pennsylvania followed closely Penn's Charter of Privileges. The people were given the power to "alter, reform, or abolish their gov-

THE NEW NATION IS BORN

ernment in such manner as they may think proper. " The rights found in Penn's document were continued. Trial by jury, freedom of speech, press, and assembly, right to bail, and habeas corpus were guaranteed. Jewish residents were allowed to hold office for the first time as the religious requirement for holding office was changed to a belief in one God.

Thomas Wharton of Philadelphia was elected as the first President of Pennsylvania and served until 1778 when he died. He was succeeded by George Bryan, Joseph Reed, William Moore, John Dickinson, Benjamin Franklin, and George Mifflin. Joseph Reed was one of the outstanding men of the period. He had been an aide to Washington during the early part of the war, a Congressman, and a signer of the Articles of Confederation. He opposed slavery and the proprietary system of government. Under his leadership the Divesting Act and gradual abolition of slavery law were enacted.

The Penns Are Divested of Their Lands

The Divesting Act of November 27, 1779, required that all land owned by the Penn family in Pennsylvania should be turned over to the new State government. All quitrents were abolished and all money owed to the Penns was made payable to the State. Heirs of William Penn were paid for their claims. The act stated "the freemen of the Commonwealth, being desirous to manifest not only a regard for their own safety and happiness, but their liberality also, and the remembrance of the enterprising spirit which distinguished the founder of Pennsylvania," hinted that the new Government appreciated the work of the great founder of the State. After the end of the war Penn heirs were to receive 130,000 pounds sterling (about $650,000). Actually it was not necessary for anything to be paid for the Penn family had not supported the Revolution. Many other loyalists had had all their property taken without a penny being returned. But the State felt obligated to the Penns, so the money was paid.

Slavery Is Abolished

Slaves had been brought to Pennsylvania almost since the beginning of the colony. Most people opposed the use of black slaves, and on February 29, 1780, former President George Bryan introduced a bill to abolish slavery gradually. Passed by vote of 34-21, it provided for all children born of slave mothers to be free when born. Those children already slaves were to be set free when they reached the age of 28. All slaves were to be registered by November 1, 1780, or be set free. Pennsylvania was the first state to pass any sort of abolition law. This did not completely outlaw slavery, but the number of slaves in the State became smaller each year.

Political Leadership Becomes Divided

During the Revolution and afterward, the political leaders were of two groups. The Constitutionalists developed and supported the Constitution of 1776. Led by Bryan and Reed, they were radical, vigorous and always patriotic. They took a lot of power for themselves. As revolutionists they were opposed by more conservative men like Robert Morris, James Wilson, and John Dickinson. They were firm supporters of the war and kept control of the state government until the end of the fighting. At that time, the Anti-Constitutionalists were elected to leadership with John Dickinson as President. These men thought that the government should have more power. They advocated a whole new constitution. Dickinson and his Anti-Constitutionalists also believed that the Articles of Confederation were too weak to govern the new nation. They advocated a new constitution for the United States. When a call was made for a new Federal constitution in 1787, the conservatives were in power in the state. Although Benjamin Franklin was President of Pennsylvania at that time, most of the delegates to the convention were believers in stronger government. When the delegates from 12 states met in Philadelphia in May, 1787, Pennsylvania was represented by Benjamin Franklin, James Wilson, Robert Morris, Gouverneur Morris, George Clymer, Thomas Mifflin, Thomas Fitzsimons and Jared Ingersoll.

THE NEW NATION IS BORN

Pennsylvanians Help Frame a New National Constitution

James Wilson, a Scotch immigrant with a university education, was Pennsylvania's leading delegate. He was on the committee with Madison to frame the constitution. A strong national government with the support of the people was his ideal. His ideas are found throughout the document. Gouverneur Morris did outstanding work in the actual writing of the constitution. His sentences and phrasing are so clear that few questions of meaning have ever arisen.

When the new Federal Constitution was finished, all states were asked to ratify it. The old Constitutional Party of Pennsylvania refused to support the new document. They claimed that it gave too much power to the national government. They soon took on the name of Anti-Federalists. Wilson and those for the new Constitution were called Federalists. When it came time to vote for a constitutional ratifying convention, the Anti-Federalists stayed away. There were not enough members present, therefore, to make the vote legal. Officers were sent out to find two AntiFederalists

United States Department of State

George Washington presided at the Constitutional Convention at Philadelphia's Independence Hall when the present United States Constitution was adopted 1787.

and dragged them to the State House. In this manner, the quorum was gathered and the Assembly voted for a convention.

Most of the delegates from eastern Pennsylvania were for the new Constitution. Those from the west were against it. James Wilson and Thomas McKean of Philadelphia were leaders for the acceptance. William Findley of Westmoreland County and John Smilie of Fayette County led the opposition. There were 46 Federalists at the convention and 23 Anti-Federalists. When the vote was held, the acceptance was 46-23. Since it took weeks to come to a vote, Delaware became the first state to ratify. Pennsylvania ratified the Constitution on December 12, 1787, to gain the second star on the national flag.

The new Federal Constitution went into effect in 1789 with George Washington as the first President of the United States. The national capital was moved to New York City for one year, then returned to Philadelphia. The Pennsylvania State House, now called Independence Hall, was the United States capitol building until 1800. Congress met in one wing and the Supreme Court in the other. Frederick A.C. Muhlenberg of Pennsylvania was elected as the first Speaker of the House of Representatives. James Wilson was appointed by Washington to become one of the original members of the United States Supreme Court. When the first United States mint was set up in Philadelphia in 1792, David Rittenhouse was named as the first director of the Federal Coin Manufacturing Plant. Presidents Washington and John Adams lived in the home of Robert Morris while the capital was in Philadelphia. In 1800 the capital was moved to Washington, D.C., along the Potomac River.

The State Sets Up a Stronger Government

Men who had opposed the 1776 State Constitution demanded that it be replaced too. Since the Constitution had been drawn up in the midst of the Revolution, some thought if hastily drawn and too democratic. The idea of 12 men trying to be the executive was considered confusing. The Council of Censors was accused of being "capable of only making trouble." The one house Legislature gave signs of being too quickly responsive to public clamor. A second house was thought necessary to provide a check on the measures of the first. Most constitutions are changed to take power from the government, but in this case the proponents of change wanted to provide the government with more power.

The Pennsylvania Assembly was dominated by Federalists in 1789 when a vote was taken as to whether a constitutional convention should be held. Therefore, a vote to hold the convention November 4, 1789, in Philadelphia passed without any problem. Thomas Mifflin, as President of Pennsylvania, acted as president on the convention. James Wilson was the great guiding hand. The State Constitution then was modeled on the recent new Federal Constitution. The chief executive was to be a Governor elected for three years. He was limited to three terms in each 12 years. The Council of Censors was eliminated. A Supreme Court was set up with judges to be appointed by the Governor for a term of good behavior. The one house Legislature was changed to include both a House of Representatives and a Senate. Senators were to be elected for four years, House members for one year.

Anti-Federalists knew that they could not keep the Constitution from being adopted. Findley and Smilie, aided by Albert Gallatin

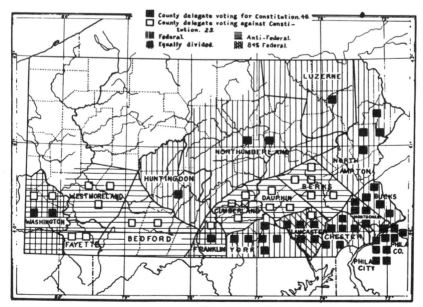

Pennsylvania Historical and Museum Commission

Most populared districts favored the Federal Constitution of 1787. Berks, Dauphin, Cumberland, Bedford, Westmoreland and Fayette Counties opposed ratification.

of Fayette County, were the leaders of the Anti-Federalists who tried to keep the new Constitution as liberal as possible. On September 2, 1790, the new Constitution was proclaimed to be in effect. Thomas Mifflin, the last President of Pennsylvania, was elected as the first Governor of the State and served three terms.

In the period 1775-1790 Pennsylvania changed from a colony of Great Britain and became a State in the United States. From the proprietary government of the Penn family, the State took on a democratic form of self-government. Many Pennsylvanians were killed, homes ruined, and bitterness raised between Revolutionists, Loyalists and non-combatants. After the war serious-minded men saw reason to strengthen the governments on both state and national levels. These constitutions, drawn up with the leadership of Pennsylvanians, are still the basis of our government today. In the war and in the making of successful peace efforts, Pennsylvanians always played an important part.

REVIEW QUESTIONS

1. Regarding the American colonies, what were the two major goals of Great Britain following the French and Indian War?

2. List at least four measures enacted by the British government between 1764 and 1774 that set the colonies on the road to revolution.

3. When and where was the First Continental Congress held? What was its purpose?

4. What were the attitudes of the different groups of Pennsylvania toward Independence at the beginning of the War?

5. State how Washington was aided by men such as Robert Morris, Lafayette and Baron von Steuben.

6. Why is Valley Forge endeared to the hearts of the American people today?

7. Enumerate the many contributions of Pennsylvania to the Revolution against England.

8. Explain the difference between the Pennsylvania constitutions of 1776 and 1790.

9. Briefly describe the contributions made by Pennsylvania in the formation of the Federal Constitution and the establishment of the government it created.

THE NEW NATION IS BORN

Do You Know the Meaning of or Can You Identify the Following Words and Phrases? Write sentences to prove it.

1. embargo
2. direct tax
3. "Common Sense"
4. Cornplanter
5. Divesting Act
6. revolution
7. amend
8. Federalists
9. loyalists
10. Carpenters' Hall
11. John Dickinson
12. Rangers
13. John Barry
14. Hessians
15. Wyoming Massacre
16. Associators
17. Samuel Wetherill
18. commonwealth
19. James Wilson
20. William Findley

Maps to Help Us Learn

1. On an outline map of Pennsylvania indicate American victories with blue stars, defeats with red ones. If you like, also trace the two armies across Pennsylvania.

2. Get a service station map of Pennsylvania. Then find all objects of interest pertaining to the Revolutionary period. Make a pictorial map of your own for the benefit of the class.

What Do You Think? Use the knowledge gained thus far to comment on the following statements.

1. The Quakers would have made better neighbors of the Indians west of the Alleghenies than of the Scotch-Irish.
2. The colonists should have been happy to pay the soldiers who so recently had helped defend them.
3. The Committee of Safety which took over the State government was not a legal government.
4. The heirs of William Penn should not have received one penny for their confiscated property.
5. The Federalists received more support in western than in eastern Pennsylvania.
6. The Federalists had no right to force the Anti-Federalists to attend the Assembly to create a quorum.

ACTIVITIES
(Individual, committee or class projects and class reports)

1. Get a copy of the Declaration of Independence. Then count the abuses charged against George III. How many?

2. Look in your school encyclopedia for a description of the Liberty Bell and its history. Make a report to be given in class.

3. Prepare a chronological table of important Revolutionary events in Pennsylvania thus:
Date   Event   Names of Leaders   Effect on Colonies

4. Give a conversation between a "Tory" boy and the son of a "Patriot" during the British occupation of Philadelphia.

5. Imagine that you are thirteen years old during the winter of 1777-1778, and that you live near Valley Forge. Write a short paper on what your actions might be during this time.

6. Dramatize the parting of Washington and Lafayette at the close of the War.

7. Make a chart on the causes of the Revolution. Divide it into remote and immediate causes.

8. Make a cartoon suggested by the effect of the Declaration of Independence on the Scotch-Irish of Pennsylvania.

9. Write a "Who Am I" of eight clues of a Pennsylvania leader. Then see if the class can guess who you are.

10. If your county was formed before the Declaration of Independence was signed, give a report on the role your county played in the Revolution.

READING MATERIALS

Anthony Wayne: Man of Action, Historic Pennsylvania Leaflet, No. 2, Pennsylvania Historical and Museum Commission, 1953.

Balderston, Marion, *Lord Howe Clears the Delaware*, Pennsylvania Magazine 106:326-345, July 1972.

Baldwin, Leland, *Whiskey Rebels*, University of Pittsburgh Press, 1939.

Brenneman, Gloria E., The Conway Cabal: Myth or Reality, Pennsylvania History 50: 169-177, April 1973.

Brunhouse, R. L., *The Counter Revolution in Pennsylvania, 1776-1790*, Pennsylvania Historical and Museum Commission, 1942.

Buck, S. J., and E. H., *Planting of Civilization in Western Pennsylvania*, University of Pittsburgh Press, 1939.

Busch, Noel Fairchild, *Winter Quarters: George Washington and the Continental Army at Valley Forge*, New York, Liveright, 1974.

Carousso, Dorothee Hughes, *How to Search for Your Revolutionary Patriot in Pennsylvania*, Philadelphia, Genealogical Society of Pennsylvania, 197S.

Coleman, John M., *Thomas McKean, Forgotten Leader of the Revolution*, Rockaway, New Jersey, American Faculty Press, 1975.

Egle, William Henry, *Pennsylvania Women in the American Revolution*, Cottonport, La., Polyanthos, 1972 (Reprint).

Gough, Robert, *Notes on the Pennsylvania Revolutionaries of 1776*, Pennsylvania Magazine 96:89-103, January, 1972.

Mayer, Jane, *Betsy Ross and the Flag*, Random House, 1952.

Neuenschwander, John A., *The Middle Colonies and the Coming of the American Revolution*, Port Washington, N.Y., Kennikat Press, 1973.

Pennsylvania and The Bill of Rights, Pennsylvania Historical Association, 1990.

Pennsyvlania and The Federal Constitution, Pennsylvania Historical Association, 1987.

Peterson, C.E., "Carpenters' Shrine," *American Heritage*, Fall, 1951.

Selsam, J.P., *The Pennsylvania Constitution of 1776; a Study in Revolution Democracy*, University of Pennsylvania Press, 1936.

Stevens, S.K., *"William Penn and the Declaration of Independence,"* American Heritage, Fall, 1951.

Thayer, Theodore, *Pennsylvania Politics and the Growth of Democracy*, 1770-1776, Pennsylvania Historical and Museum Commission, 1953.

Thompson, Ray, *Benedict Arnold in Philadelphia*, Fort Washington, Bicentennial Press, 1974.

Thompson, Ray, *Betsy Ross, Last of Philadelphia's Free Ouakers*, Fort Washington, Bicentennial Press, 1972.

Thompson, Ray, *Washington at Whitemarsh: Prelude to Valley Forge*, 2nd ed., rev. and enl., Fort Washington, Bicentennial Press, 1974.

Tinkcom, H. M., *The Republicans and Federalists in Pennsylvania, 1790 1801*, Pennsylvania Historical and Museum Commission, 1950.

New settlers often found rivers the best way to travel. Pictured are immigrants floating down the Susquehanna.

chapter VIII

Keystone of the Nation

The majority of the people in Pennsylvania were farmers until after the time of the Civil War. With the close of the Revolutionary War period, Pennsylvania rapidly developed into a greater farming area than ever before. But expansion called for better transportation and communication. Mineral resources began to be developed, and these resources helped to make Pennsylvania the industrial center of the new nation. Villages developed into towns and towns into cities. As cities grew, people demanded a more direct voice in government, and on this demand the Democratic Party controlled the State for half a century. By 1860, Pennsylvania's political and economic power was a decisive factor in the growth of the young nation.

POPULATION SPREADS WESTWARD

In the 10-year period 1790 to 1800 the population of Pennsylvania jumped from 434,000 to 602,000 people. Although many new settlers came from Europe during the period, most of the increase came from large families. Farm families not uncommonly had 10 to 14 children. When the children of these large families married and had large families of their own, population increased rapidly.

More Counties Are Set Up

The southeastern and southwestern parts of the State benefited most from the rapid increase of population. This in turn caused new counties to be created. From Westmoreland County, Washington

180 OUR PENNSYLVANIA HERITAGE

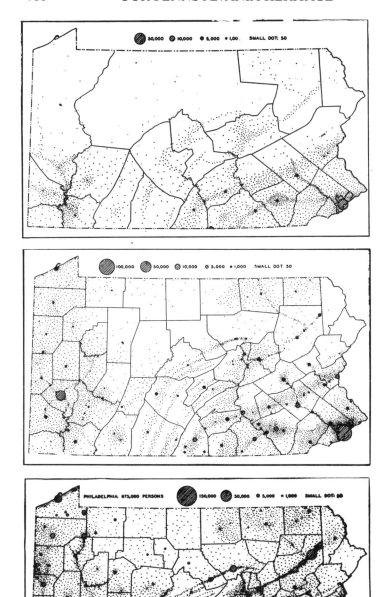

Population grew in numbers and density as shown for 1800, 1840, and 1880.

County was cut in 1781 and Fayette in 1783. Franklin County was cut from Cumberland in 1784. In the same year Montgomery County was formed from Philadelphia. In 1785 Dauphin County was created, in 1786 Luzerne, in 1787 Huntingdon, in 1788 Allegheny, and in 1789 Delaware and Mifflin Counties were set up. In 1790 there were 21 counties in the State, and for the first time the whole State was divided into counties.

The population west of the Alleghenies grew from 75,000 in 1790 to 139,000 ten years later. Most of these settlers were in Washington, Fayette and Westmoreland Counties. However, in 1795, Somerset was cut from Bedford and Lycoming from Northumberland. The next year Greene was carved from Washington County. Wayne County was formed from Northampton in 1798. Ten new counties were set up in 1800: Adams, Armstrong, Butler, Beaver, Centre, Crawford, Erie, Mercer, Venango and Warren. This brought the total of 34 counties in the State at the beginning of the new century.

The Indian Threat Ends

Although the Indians had agreed to give up all claims to Pennsylvania, fear of the redmen slowed settlement of northwest Pennsylvania. An Indian war broke out in 1790 along the western border of Pennsylvania. That year General Josiah Harmer led Pennsylvania troops into the Miami River area in Ohio and was defeated by the Indians. The next year General Arthur St. Clair of Ligonier was sent by President Washington to settle the Indians. He led his 2,100 men into a trap and the Indian menace grew worse.

Finally General Anthony Wayne was sent to Pittsburgh where he drew up an army in 1792. After drilling his men at Legionville, near Beaver, he set out for Ohio. At Fallen Timbers, in northwestern Ohio, Wayne defeated the Indian forces. By the Treaty of Greenville, 1795, the Indian boundary was set well west of Pennsylvania. No further Indian trouble would threaten Pennsylvania thereafter.

Soldiers and Speculators Open Up Northwest Lands

In order to pay Pennsylvania soldiers for their services in the

Revolutionary War, and to hurry the settlement of unused land, it was offered to veterans. In 1783 veterans were allowed to take up land west of the Allegheny River north of Butler. Soldiers who had back pay owed to them by the State were given certificates for a certain amount of land. Many veterans were content to sell their certificates to land speculators for cash. The speculators then bought up the choice land to sell later for a profit.

Beginning in 1785 the state gave away land to all veterans. A private could acquire 200 acres, a major-general could have 2,000 acres. This donation land disposed of 600,000 acres of state property. Though many soldiers sold their land rather than move to it, many also established homesteads on the donation lands. Even today some farmers in Butler, Crawford, Lawrence and Mercer Counties can proudly say that they are living on farms given to their ancestors for service in the Revolutionary War.

Land in north central Pennsylvania was sold for as little as seven cents an acre. Much of this land, however, was returned to the State. Men like Robert Morris formed land companies to buy up great blocks of land in northcentral and northwestern Pennsylvania. At one time the Dutch bankers who owned the Holland Land Company owned over 1,500,000 acres of Pennsylvania property. Profits were small. Taxes soon caused the companies to sell all their holdings, often at a loss. Robert Morris lost his fortune in the land business. The Holland Land Company finally sold out.

Northcentral Pennsylvania, with its mountains, poor soil and short growing season is not heavily populated to this day. In northwestern Pennsylvania, however, the town of Erie was important from the first. It was laid out in 1795, and had 81 people by 1800, 394 by 1810 and 635 by 1820. In 1808 there was an academy and a newspaper in operation there. Meadville was established by settlers who came west from Sunbury. In 1810 it had 426 people, and by 1820, 649, with a Presbyterian Church organized in 1799, a newspaper in 1805 and Allegheny College in 1815. The county seats of Butler, Mercer and Kittanning were founded in 1803, Clearfield in 1804, Indiana in 1805 and Smethport in 1807.

Philadelphia Loses Government Centers

In the east, the cities continued to grow and prosper. Philadelphia was the largest city in the United States in 1790 with 28,522 people. Its medical, literary and scientific leadership of the nation continued far into the nineteenth century. But in 1793 along with the summer came a terrible epidemic of yellow fever that hit the city with such effect that 5,000 people died. Many thousands left the city, for at that time no one knew the cause or cure of the disease. In 1799 the State Legislature moved the capital of the Commonwealth to Lancaster. The inland population wanted a more centrally located seat of government. Many rural people distrusted the idea of a big city capital. By 1810 the State capital was moved farther west to Harrisburg. There it has remained ever since.

Because of a political compromise the capital of the United States was moved from Philadelphia to Washington in 1800. Independence Hall was sold to the City of Philadelphia and the political leadership of the nation moved from the city. This loss hit the city hard.

However, Philadelphia was to remain the cultural "Athens of America" for many years. In 1805 the Academy of the Fine Arts was founded by Charles Willson Peale. He had been operating America's first museum since 1785. Later he rented part of Independence Hall to display his collections. Charles Peale and his son Rembrandt helped to make Philadelphia the art capital of America. The father painted portraits of Washington, Hancock, Franklin and Jefferson. Washington's portrait by Rembrandt Peale hangs in the United States Senate. Thomas Sully, who moved to Philadelphia from England in 1808, was noted for his famous portraits of Queen Victoria, Thomas Jefferson and many other prominent people. John James Audubon, who lived for several years on a beautiful estate near Norristown, began his study of American wildlife in this area. Today his pictures of American birds are regarded throughout the world as unsurpassed masterpieces.

Philadelphia also long remained the medical center of the nation. In 1821 the first college of pharmacy in America was set up there, and in 1849 the world's first women's medical college was founded. Philadelphia led the nation in scientific progress. By 1801 there was a public water system for the city. Steam pumped the water to buildings through hollow log pipes. By 1836 the streets of the city were lit with gas lights, and by 1858 horse drawn street railway cars were in operation.

Western Pennsylvania Rebels Against Whiskey Tax

All progress in the State was not smooth and peaceful. The settlers west of the Allegheny mountains found shipping crops eastward extremely difficult. To raise their standards of living they had to sell their surplus grain to buy the things that they wanted. To ship grain over the mountains profitably was practically impossible. Finally, some one discovered that the solution was to turn the grain into whiskey. Whiskey in barrels could be hauled over the mountains on the backs of animals and sold for high prices in the east. Many farmers in the Pittsburgh area grew prosperous from this trade.

The new Federal government was looking about for new sources of revenue and among the new taxes suggested was a tax on liquor. Congress put a tax of four cents per gallon on distilled liquor in

Western Pennsylvania stubbornly resisted collectors of the new Federal government's tax on whiskey — until Washington led an army to put down the revolt.

1791. This tax was to be collected at the place of manufacture. The Scotch-Irish of the Pittsburgh region thought the tax unfair and considered it a punishment on the region that had become the major distilling area for the whole country. In Congress the members from the area, Congressmen Smilie, Findley and Gallatin, opposed the measure. When it was passed, they advocated that all residents oppose the tax in every legal way possible. Delegates met and drew up resolutions against the tax, just as merchants had done in the east to oppose British taxes earlier. Inspectors and tax collectors were almost impossible to find for the area. Popular General John Neville was finally persuaded to take the job as collector. A mob appeared before his house and demanded that he resign his commission. The leader of the mob, a Revolutionary War major, James MacFarlane, was shot and the mob burned Neville's house and barn.

Tax collectors were hunted down and tarred and feathered. Farmers refused to pay their taxes. Congressman Gallatin returned home and called for peaceful opposition. But Western Pennsylvania militia members decided to take matters into their own hands. David-Bradford of Washington County was elected to lead the opposition. The Federal mails were intercepted and letters with names of the rebels were burned. Alexander Hamilton, Secretary of the Treasury, called upon the President to enforce the collections. Washington asked the states of Pennsylvania, New Jersey, Maryland and Virginia to send troops to put down the so-called Whiskey Rebellion. The President went with the 12,500 troops as far west as Bedford. When the distillers heard of the army approaching, the leaders fled. The other men quickly agreed to pay their taxes.

Some of the leaders were rounded up and taken to Philadelphia for trial. Bradford had escaped down the Ohio River. Those arrested were found guilty, but pardoned. The new Federal Government thus gave warning that it would enforce the laws. Meanwhile, farmers found that it would be easier to sell their grain to a central distiller and let that person pay all the tax. This marked the beginning of large distilleries. Perhaps of more importance, the farmers of the region were determined to elect a westerner as President. In 1800 they helped to elect Jefferson as the third President of the

United States, and he rewarded the area. The tax on liquor was then lifted.

Eastern Farmers Rebel Against House Tax

Under the administration of the second President, John Adams, a tax was placed on houses throughout the country. This time it was the Germans of Northampton and Bucks Counties who objected. John Fries, who had been a militia man sent to quiet the whiskey rebels, led opponents of the new tax. Tax collectors agreed to tax houses according to the number of windows. This was a common thing in European nations at that time. Fries and his lieutenants told the farmers not to allow the collectors on their properties. When collectors appeared, some women threw scalding hot water on them, and for that reason the rebellion is often called the "Hot Water Rebellion. " Those who refused to pay their taxes were thrown into jail. Fries and a mob forced the United States marshal to release his prisoners. Armed troops were sent to the area and Fries was caught. He was tried of treason, but his lawyer, Alexander James Dallas, got the charge reduced to rioting. Fries was pardoned by Adams, but the Federalists again were charged with oppressing the poor.

DEMOCRATS CONTROL STATE POLITICS

Pennsylvania political activity in this period was dominated by the Anti-Federalists, who eventually changed their label to Democrats. The first Governor, Thomas Mifflin, was elected three times as a member of this party. In his last election, 1796, he won by a 30-1 margin over the Federalist candidate. The following Governors: Thomas McKean, 1799-1808; Simon Snyder, 1808-1817; and William Findlay, 1817-1820, were also Democrats.

When the Democrats gained control of the national government in 1800 with Thomas Jefferson as President, he named Albert Gallatin of Fayette County as his Secretary of the Treasury. Gallatin was a rich young man when he migrated to western Pennsylvania from Geneva, Switzerland, where he had graduated from Geneva University. Setting up a glass business at New Geneva in

Fayette County, he grew wealthy and served as a State legislator, Congressman, a member of Jefferson's cabinet, Minister to Great Britain and later in life, a leading New York banker. He served as Secretary of the Treasury from 1801 to 1813, longer than any other person. His home "Friendship Hill," in Fayette County is a handsome example of early western Pennsylvania estates and is a historical site visited by many people today.

New counties continued to be created. Often counties were set up for political reasons. People who lived in large counties continued to call for their counties to be broken up so they would be nearer to the court houses. Each county set up would have representation in the Legislature. In 1803 Indiana County was established followed by Cambria, Clearfield, Jefferson, McKean, Potter and Tioga in 1804. Bradford and Susquehanna came into being in 1810 and Schuylkill in 1811. Lehigh was set up in 1812, Lebanon, Columbia and Union in 1813 and Pike in 1814.

Simon Snyder, who was elected Governor in 1808, was the first inland Governor and the first from the laboring people. Earlier Governors were wealthy men from the Philadelphia area. Mifflin and McKean had received college educations while Snyder had only an elementary education. Snyder had been born in Lancaster of German parents, moved to York, and later was a mill and store owner at Selinsgrove along the upper Susquehanna. His election was another indication of the growth of democracy in the State

War of 1812 Threatens Pennsylvania

During Snyder's term, the United States became involved in the War of 1812. Although no British soldier set foot on the soil of Pennsylvania, the State played a major part in the war. A Pennsylvania regiment was at Baltimore when that city was attacked. When an invasion of northwestern Pennsylvania was threatened, 2,000 volunteers gathered at Meadville. Over 1,000 of these men helped in the invasion of Canada. The others were called to Erie to protect the building of a fleet to attack the British on the Great Lakes.

Oliver Hazard Perry directed Pennsylvania carpenters to build him eight small vessels. Using the nearby trees, the ships were quickly constructed and armed with guns hauled through the forests from Pittsburgh. With Pennsylvania crews, he sailed out to meet the British fleet in the Battle of Lake Erie in 1813. There on September 10, 1813, the American ships with 34 guns defeated the British fleet with 70 guns. The British lost 200 killed and 200 wounded to the 27 dead and 96 wounded on the American side. Perry's report "We have met the enemy and they are ours," became famous throughout the country, and the Pennsylvania Legislature voted him a gold medal.

General Jacob Brown of Pennsylvania led the American troops in their Canadian invasion. Commodore Stephen Decatur, Captain James Biddle and Captain Charles Stewart were naval heroes of the war from Pennsylvania. Captain Stewart commanded the famed ship, Constitution better known as "Old Ironsides."

Stephen Girard, a Philadelphia ship owner and banker, performed a great service to his country during the war. The government had tried to sell $5,000,000 worth of bonds to finance operations. Only $200,000 was subscribed. Girard, who had amassed the greatest fortune of his day, bought the remaining bonds and practically financed the entire war. When he died, he willed his fortune to set up a school to educate orphaned boys. The Girard Bank of Philadelphia is still among the leading banks of America today.

Political Changes Introduced

When William Findlay was nominated for Governor in 1817 by the Democrats, a new system was used. Up to this time all candidates were selected by the members of the party in the Legislature. In 1817 the Democrats held a special nominating convention to select their candidate. Under the convention system, even those counties with no party members in the Assembly could have a voice in choosing candidates. This method of using conventions to choose candidates was known as the Pennsylvania Plan and before long was used throughout the country. The President of the United States is still nominated in this manner.

In 1819 occurred the first real business panic in Pennsylvania. Banks failed. People who had their money saved in them lost it. Unemployment was high. The cause seemed to be the reaction from the War of 1812. In the election of 1820 the Federalist candidate,

Joseph Hiester, was elected only by a small margin. Since this time voters often have blamed poor economic conditions on the party in power. The Democrats seemed to think that a Pennsylvania German candidate was the best bet, and their candidates, Shulze and Wolf, were able to win the next two elections.

Free Public Schools Are Established

When Governor George Wolf was elected in 1829 he was determined to introduce a State system of public education. Over half of the children of the State never attended school. Most other northern states had public education systems for all children. Massachusetts had free education for all even before Pennsylvania was founded. In 1834 only the children of those who declared themselves paupers were to be given free education. Most of the schools in the State were conducted by religious groups. Other private schools were operated for the children of those who could afford to pay the fees. A Society for the Promotion of Public Schools had been founded in 1827 in Philadelphia but the cause needed political support.

Governor Wolf had been a school teacher. He insisted that all children should have the right to an education. He was aided by Senator Samuel Breck of Philadelphia who had been educated in the public schools of New England. Breck headed a special committee that gathered the facts and sponsored a bill in the General Assembly. In 1834 the bill became a law with hardly an opposing vote. However, when the members of the Legislature went home, many were met by angry opponents of the public schools. Some opposed the new school taxes, some opposed teaching the poor at public expense, and some opposed their children being required by law to attend school at all. Mennonites, Quakers, Reformed, Lutherans and Catholics had schools of their own and therefore did not feel the need for a public school system.

Throughout the State, in the election of 1835, men were elected or defeated according to how they stood on public education. Governor Wolf was defeated. Senators quickly returned to vote for the repeal of the free school law. The House of Representatives was more evenly divided. City groups were for the bill, religious groups opposed it if they had schools. Country districts with no schools

Pioneer schoolhouses were usually simple log buildings. The one pictured here was the first school in Clearfield County, built near Curwensville in 1803.

supported the bill, and northern Pennsylvania districts settled by New Englanders were heartily for it. The bill seemed doomed to defeat when Thaddeus Stevens of Gettysburg spoke fervently for the bill and thus saved the day. His speech swayed enough votes to keep the law from being repealed. Many public schools throughout the State have been named in his honor.

The number of public schools grew rapidly. Some were log, some brick, some stone and some clapboard. Most were one-roomed but all children were given a chance for an education. But there was a shortage of teachers. Philadelphia set up its own teacher training school and other cities followed. Beginning in 1855 the State began to support normal schools that later were to become the 14 State teachers' colleges of Pennsylvania. Millersville was the first, started in 1854. The position of county superintendent of schools was first set up in 1854. Thomas Burrowes and Andrew Curtin were the first heads of the "Common Schools," public schools, of the State.

Pennsylvania had no state colleges, but gave aid to the University of Pennsylvania during the Revolution and to Dickinson College beginning with the end of the Revolution. Later aid was given to Jefferson College at Canonsburg, Washington College at

Washington, Madison College at Uniontown, Western University of Pennsylvania (today's University of Pittsburgh) at Pittsburgh, Franklin College at Lancaster, Marshall College at Mercersburg, Allegheny College at Meadville, Lafayette College at Easton and Pennsylvania College at Gettysburg. Aid was also given to academies in practically every county until public high schools were set up beginning with Central High School in Philadelphia in 1838. In 1855 The Farmer's High School was founded in Centre County. It was later to become The Pennsylvania State University.

Anti-Masonry and a Third Constitution

In 1827 an incident in New York caused political troubles in Pennsylvania. A man had supposedly threatened to disclose the secrets of the Masonic fraternity. This man was killed and a group developed called the Anti-Masons. they advocated the outlawing of secret societies. The movement spread into Pennsylvania, Lancaster County especially. Scheming politicians saw a chance to use the organization to fight the Democrats. In 1832 Amos Ellman of Lancaster ran for Vice President of the United States for the Anti-Masonry Party against the Democrats. The Anti-Masonic issue together with the school issue in 1835 helped Joseph Ritner defeat the Democatic candidate for Governor, George Wolf. But no action was ever taken to outlaw the Masons.

In 1835 the people of Pennsylvania also voted by a small majority to write a new Constitution for the State. The 1790 document had been criticized as giving too much power to the Governor. The convention met in Harrisburg on May 2, 1837. The Democrats who wanted the change found that they were outnumbered by the Whigs and Anti-Masons. Little change was made except to cut the Governor's appointing power. Many jobs were made elective. The Governor was limited to two terms in each nine years. Judges of the Supreme Court were to serve for 15 years instead of for life. State Senators were to be elected for three years instead of four. But a backward step was taken by limiting the right to vote to white men. In the election of 1838, the Constitution was adopted 119,228 to 116,070. It was the first time that the voters had a chance to accept or reject a new Constitution.

An anti-Catholic riot led to this burning of a Catholic Church in Philadelphia in 1844. How does this scene differ from American ideals?

The election of 1838 resulted in one of the most sensational Assembly meetings. David R. Porter, Democratic candidate for Governor from Huntingdon County, won over Joseph Ritner, Anti-Mason, by 5,540 votes. The Anti-Masons refused to agree on the count. They also disputed the election of certain members of the General Assembly from Philadelphia. It was claimed that Anti-Masons had won the seats. When the Assembly met, both Democrats and Anti-Masons tried to organize the Legislature. A riot resulted among the members. Governor Ritner's term had not yet expired, so he called out the militia to enforce order. The guns of the soldiers were loaded with buckshot, and the incident is known as the Buckshot War. When the Whig members of the Legislature voted with the Democrats, the Anti-Masons were put out of power in the state for all time.

Political Turmoil Grips the State

During the administration of Governor Porter (1839-1845) another political party founded upon prejudice came into being. Known as Native Americans, a number of prejudiced people tried to oppose the influx of foreign-born peoples. In part, the prejudices arose due to the lack of jobs. Cheap labor from abroad, it was claimed, kept "Native Americans" off the payrolls of industry. Since many of the immigrants were German and Irish Catholics, religious prejudice entered the picture. Problems arose over the reading of the King James version of the Bible in public schools. In Philadelphia bitter feeling between Native Americans and Catholics finally flared into open riots. In 1844 a number of persons on both sides of the dispute were killed. Several Catholic Churches were set afire. The State militia was sent into action, and two of the militiamen were killed before riots subsided. As in the case of the Anti-Masons, prejudice was used by scheming men.

The Whig party mentioned above ardently opposed the political ideas of President Andrew Jackson and his many back-country followers. In 1840 the Whigs held their national convention at the Zion Lutheran Church in Harrisburg to nominate William Henry Harrison for President. It was a good political move, for Pennsylvania voted for him that fall. The Democrats, however, managed to hold on to the governorship of the State until 1848. Governor Francis Schunk had only served a few months of his second term when he resigned, July 9, 1848. He died 11 days later. William F. Johnson, a Whig from Armstrong County, who was President pro tempore of the State Senate, acted as Governor in accordance with the law at that time. He was elected to the position for a full term in November of that year by a margin of only 297 votes over the Democrat, Morris Longstreth.

During the administration of Governor Shunk the Mexican War was fought. Many Pennsylvanians did not approve of this war, but in spite of this the State in general supported it. The Vice President of the United States during the war was George Mifflin Dallas of Pennsylvania. He was the only Pennsylvanian ever to hold that office. James Buchanan of Lancaster was Secretary of State for the nation at that time. Pennsylvania sent nine regiments to the war when only six were called for in 1846. When General Winfield Scott invaded Mexico, two regiments of Pennsylvanians were there to help defeat the Mexicans.

Buchanan Is Elected President

Pennsylvania was important in national politics throughout the period before the Civil War. During that time every candidate for

President who carried Pennsylvania also won in the national elections. In 1856 the new Republican Party met in Philadelphia to nominate their candidate. The Democrats then, to assure the vote of Pennsylvania, nominated James Buchanan of Lancaster. Buchanan was the first man elected to the presidency from Pennsylvania. He had been a State Assemblymen for two years, a Congressman for ten years, a United States Senator for eleven years, Secretary of State four years and Minister to Great Britain before being elected President. Details of his actions as President are in the next chapter.

FARMING REMAINS THE MAJOR OCCUPATION

Farming was the main occupation of the residents of Pennsylvania until after the Civil War. Over half of the people were farmers. Because of that fact Pennsylvania had what is known as an agricultural economy. Many people living in towns also kept a cow or two and had a garden to raise vegetables. Mill owners and iron furnace workmen were usually farmers as well.

Following the Revolutionary War, more and more tradesmen moved inland. Small towns soon had their own carpenters, wagon makers, cabinet and chairmakers, cobblers, tailors and printers. Most of these tradesmen did their work in their homes or small shops. Often they received country produce in return for their wares. General stores continued to be the source of most manufactured goods for the farmers.

During the summer farmers took their fresh vegetables, fruits and meat into the larger cities where the residents did not raise their own food. Farmers' markets were to be found in all towns of any size. There townspeople could buy directly from the farmer. This gave the farmers all the profit possible. When the farmer lived inland, he had to ship his products to market through agents. The agent bought farm produce and hauled it to the nearest town where there was a market for it. Since there was no refrigeration, agents bought cattle and sheep and hired drovers to take them to market in the East. The drover rode through the countryside on horseback buying flocks and herds from farmers and taking them to the city to be butchered and sold.

New Farm Methods Improve Crops

The greatest export crop of Pennsylvania was wheat. Until about 1840 Pennsylvania led the nation in wheat production, but by 1860 it had dropped to fifth. Corn, oats, rye, barley, potatoes and hay were also grown in great quantities. However, a new movement to prohibit the sale of whiskey cut the production of rye. Fruit was not grown in great quantities at this time, but in 1827 the Pennsylvania Horticultural Society was organized and the next year held the first public exhibition of fruit in the United States.

Pennsylvania farmers made improvements to increase yields of farm crops. Joseph and Robert Smith of Berks County introduced an iron plow in 1800, but it was not until 1820 that such plows were in general use. Richard Peters of Philadelphia invented a horse drawn corn drill in 1819, and such machines were in general use by 1850. By 1840 a mechanical mower had generally replaced the scythe. McCormick's reaper, invented in 1834, came into general use by 1840. Steam tractors appeared in Lancaster County by 1858, and a few of the most prosperous farms had them by 1860. By 1850 wheat drills were in use, and corn shelling machines relieved the children of that job.

Pennsylvania farmers, like those elsewhere at that time, were slow to realize that constant sowing of a field to one crop reduced the harvest. However, the Pennsylvania German farmers introduced what is called crop rotation. They sowed a different crop—corn, oats, wheat and clover—on each field over a four-year period. They also fertilized their fields with lime, gypsum and farm manure.

These advances were made chiefly in the southeastern part of the state. In the northcentral part of the State frontier methods of farming were still practiced. A farmer there described life as follows: "It was lonesome for several years. People would move in, stay a short time and move away again....The few seeds that I planted the first year yielded little produce. We raised some halfgrown potatoes, some turnips, and some soft corn with which we made out to live until the next spring....During the three months it snowed 70 days.

We wore out all our shoes the first year. We had no way to get more, no money, nothing to sell, and but little to eat...and were in dreadful distress for the want of the necessities of life. After a while our clothes were worn Our. Our family increased and the children were nearly naked. I had a broken slate, I sold that and bought two fawn skins, of which my wife made a petticoat for Mary; and Mary wore the petticoat until she outgrew it; then Rhoda took it; till she outgrew it; then Susan had it; till she outgrew it; then it fell to Abigail, and she wore it out."

Harmonists Experiment in Community Living

Many unusual religious groups came to Pennsylvania to establish closely-knit community experiments. One of the most interesting of these came into the State in 1803 from Germany under the leadership of George Rapp. Calling themselves Harmonists, they believed in sharing their property and the products of their labor equally with each other according to each one's needs. They moved to the fertile Connequenessing Valley of Butler County and purchased 5,000 acres. The 750 members of the community set up a town called Harmony. Within two years they grew an annual surplus of 6,000 bushels of grain and 300,000 gallons of whiskey for sale. By 1815 they prospered to the extent that they wanted more land. What they bought for $20,000, they sold for $100,000 and moved to the State of Indiana.

In 1823 they returned to Beaver County where they established the community of Economy, now Ambridge. Through fine farming, manufacturing cotton, wool, and silk cloth, making wine, and dealing in lumber and oil, the group grew wealthy. They practiced Christian communism in accordance with the practice of the early church in Jerusalem as recorded in the "Books of Acts." All worked for the community, crops and money belonged to the community, and all were clothed and fed from the central warehouse. Most of them believed that married life should be avoided, so they had few children. New members came from outside converts. In 1831 a German adventurer settled among them. He talked many of the young people into leaving the colony and taking their share of the wealth. As the majority who remained grew older they found it

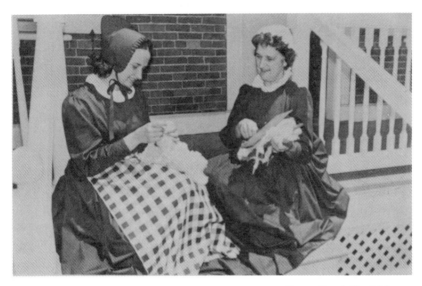

Beaver County Tourist Agency

Women at the Harmony Society in Beaver County reenact "carding" wool to be made into cloth. The religious community prospered in the early nineteenth century.

harder to keep things going. By 1890 the group was reduced to 200 in number, finally the society was dissolved shortly after 1900.

ECONOMIC GROWTH ADVANCES TRANSPORTATION

Even a farming community needed roads to get crops to market. Most of the surplus had to be hauled to Pittsburgh or Philadelphia. From Philadelphia crops were shipped out by ocean sailing vessels; from Pittsburgh surplus produce was shipped down the Ohio in flatboats, keelboats or rafts.

Turnpike Companies Improve Roads

The first real paved road was the Lancaster Pike which was built 1792-1794. William Bingham of Philadelphia raised $465,000 to finance the building of the road from Philadelphia to Lancaster. The road was paved with crushed limestone on top. This stone surfaced construction was called Macadam after the inventor Macadam of

Scotland. To pay for the road, the users were charged tolls. Every 10 miles a toll house was erected with a gate in the form of a long shaft known as a pike, across the road. To open the "pike" cost a wagoner 25 cents. This turning the pike gave the road the name of turnpike, often shortened to pike. Through collection of a few cents for every horse and rider, and 25 cents for every stagecoach, the road soon paid for itself. Up to 100 Conestoga wagons a day traveled to Philadelphia from Lancaster. Stagecoaches carried passengers over the route in twelve hours for $3.50.

The success of the Lancaster Pike resulted in the chartering of 220 additional turnpike companies by the State. Over 3,000 miles of such roads were planned. Philadelphia was connected with Pittsburgh by two such roads. One followed the Juniata Valley, the other followed the old Forbes Road through Chambersburg and Bedford. Other roads connected Erie and Pittsburgh and Erie and Philadelphia. As might be expected, few of these roads made profits like the original Lancaster Turnpike. A toll road needed constant traffic, and few areas produced the amount of freight exchanged between the fine farms of Lancaster County and the trading center of Philadelphia.

In 1806 the Federal government authorized the building of the National Road from Cumberland, Maryland, to the Ohio River. Albert Gallatin, who was Secretary of the Treasury, arranged for the road to run through his home county of Fayette. Construction of the roads reached Uniontown in 1817, and was continued through Washington to Wheeling in 1820. It was from forty to eighty feet wide. At Addison in Somerset County, an old toll house still stands along the modern concrete Route 40 that follows the same route. At first the roads followed the rivers. Streams were generally crossed at a shallow ford. At the larger rivers, ferries carried the traveler across for a toll charge. Later bridges gradually replaced ferries on the most traveled routes. The first bridge was built over the Schuylkill at Philadelphia in 1817. At Pittsburgh a bridge was completed over the Monongahela in 1818 and another over the Allegheny in 1820. One had been built over the Beaver at New Brighton in 1815. The Schuylkill Bridge was the first of wire suspension design; the others were wooden covered bridges. An iron chain bridge was built across the Jacobs Creek in Fayette County in

1801 by William Findley. The chain was made from inch-square links five feet long. All bridges were built by companies or individuals who collected tolls to pay for them.

Water Transportation Develops

Waterways were still considered the best means of transport whenever possible. Rafts, flatboats and keelboats were used on the rivers that were deep enough to float their cargoes. These, however, could not be handled easily in upstream travel. So as early as 1787 John Fitch of Bucks County built a paddle boat driven by a steam engine, and three years later he was operating a steamboat on the Delaware between Philadelphia and Burlington, New Jersey. Robert Fulton of Lancaster County developed the first commercially successful steamboat which he operated on the Hudson River in New York in 1807. By 1811 Nicholas Roosevelt had gone to Pittsburgh to build the New Orleans, the first steam boat on western waters. In 1814 the Enterprise carried guns from Pittsburgh to General Jackson at New Orleans. Steamboats caused great competition between Wheeling, Pittsburgh and Brownsville for the trade to the west. Wheeling built a low bridge across the Ohio to shut off traffic to the upriver in 1855. Pittsburgh did the same thing to keep Monongahela River traffic from the Ohio.

Steamboats, however, did not solve the transportation problems on rivers for the Allegheny or Monongahela were too shallow in summer. The Susquehanna was too shallow in all seasons for steamboats, and the Delaware had rapids at Trenton and above. To overcome these difficulties, a system of canals was designed along rivers. Perhaps the first canal in Pennsylvania was dedicated in 1797 on the western side of the Susquehanna at York Haven. It was designed to connect Lancaster and York. Dams were built right in the rivers to provide enough slack water to permit boats to navigate on the river itself where possible, and to fill canal locks at the side where the river was too shallow. This system is called a slack water canal.

A slack water canal on the Schuylkill allowed boats to move as far up river as Port Carbon in Schuylkill County. It was a huge financial success because it carried anthracite coal to Philadelphia.

Robert Fulton's successful steamboat of 1807 seemed a fearful thing to crews of sailing ships.

In 1827 the Union Canal Company finished a canal that connected the Schuylkill at Reading with the Susquehanna at Middletown. This union canal was a ditch dug to connect two streams. It got its water from the streams and used a system of locks. The Lehigh Coal and Navigation Company built a canal up the Lehigh to Stoddartsville between 1827 and 1838. The Delaware and Hudson Company built a canal across New Jersey which was extended to Honesdale in 1828.

State-owned Canal System Spreads Across Pennsylvania

Meanwhile, New York City was beginning to take away the western trade from Philadelphia. When news reached Harrisburg of the Erie Canal's being built, Pennsylvania decided that a competing canal would have to be built. In April 1825 a Board of Canal Commissioners was set up by the State to "construct navigable communications between the eastern and western waters of the

KEYSTONE OF THE NATION

state and Lake Erie." The following fourth of July work got under way on a canal north and west from Columbia along the Susquehanna River. The canal was a ditch dug along the river with water diverted into the ditch to float the boats. At Clark's Ferry, a bridge was built over the Susquehanna to carry the canal across to the west shore where it followed the Juniata to Hollidaysburg in Blair County. Work also began at the Pittsburgh end following the Allegheny to the north to the Kiskiminetas. There the Allegheny was bridged and the canal followed the Kiskiminetas and Conemaugh Rivers to Johnstown.

But there still remained the 36 miles separating Hollidaysburg from Johnstown where the Allegheny Mountain stood like a huge obstacle. To get over the mountain a system of inclined planes was constructed. Thus when the boats arrived at Hollidaysburg by water, they were then pulled up on railcars over the mountains to Johnstown. At one time it took 12 stationary steam engines and 12 teams of horses, and in later years 9 locomotives, to get one boat over the mountain.

By 1834 it was possible for a person to take a canal boat from Philadelphia to Pittsburgh. The route became quite popular and many visitors came just to experience riding over a mountain in a boat. Charles Dickens, the famous novelists of England, described his journey over the great Pennsylvania Canal in a book called

Pennsylvania's canals moved freight slowly but played a very important part in the development of the West.

American Notes. Trade was good, but soon it was discovered that the six-inch ropes used for pulling boats up the mountains rapidly wore out. This led John Roebling of Saxonburg to set up a wire cable plant in his little Butler County farming community. Cable then replaced the old rope. Roebling and his son Washington became the most famous builders of wire suspension bridges of their day. Their Brooklyn Bridge still stands.

Canals followed just about every river in the State. Canals along the Susquehanna followed the north branch to the New York border, and the west branch to Clinton County. A special branch led to Bellefonte to carry the iron from its furnaces. Along the Delaware the canal flowed from Easton to Bristol. Others followed the Beaver and Shenango to Erie, together with the French Creek feeder. Canals, like the turnpikes before them, were often built where not needed for political reasons. Pennsylvania owned more canal mileage than any other state.

At the beginning of the canal-building period the canals were owned and operated by private companies. But under Governors Shulze and Wolf the State itself entered the canal-building business.

Over a period of 30 years $101,611,234 was spent by the state on canals together with state-owned railroads. The financial burden of supporting this vast transportation system proved too heavy. Flood damage and competition from the rapidly spreading network of railroads put the state canals out of business between 1843 and 1858. The main line of the canals was sold to the Pennsylvania Railroad and the remainder of the state canal system was bought by

The famous Portage Railroad lifted canal boats over the Alleghenies on a series of inclined planes.

the Philadelphia and Erie. Canals have been criticized as a waste of money by the state. It is true that the waterways did not make a profit. The purpose was to provide transportation by water and they did that. Thousands of Pennsylvanians were employed in the building and operating of the canals. Numerous immigrants traveled westward over the canals. Untold tons of materials moved over the waterways that would have mired many wagons in the mud. Canals served a useful purpose when no other means of transportation could have done so well.

Railroads Displace Canals

While horses were slowly towing the canal boats throughout the state, men were at work to find ways of reducing the time and expense of transporting freight and passengers. A faster and cheaper means of transportation appeared with the coming of the railroad. The first railroads were built with board rails, and wagons were pulled over them by horses. Then an iron band was added on top of the rails, with the rails nailed to ties.

Pennsylvania's first railway, and one of the earliest in the world, was a short line built in Delaware County in 1809. In 1818 the Bear Creek Furnace in Armstrong County used a railroad to carry materials to the iron furnace. In 1827 the Mauch Chunk Railroad connected a coal mine with the Lehigh River. The mine cars operated down the hill by gravity over wooden rails. The empty cars were pulled up by donkeys, later "donkey" engines. A steam locomotive was first used on the Carbondale-Honesdale line of the Delaware and Hudson Canal Company. The Stourbridge Lion, a locomotive imported from England in 1829 and the first locomotive to be used in America, proved too heavy for the rails. Phineas Davis of York built a steam locomotive for the Baltimore and Ohio in 1831. A railroad was opened in June, 1832, between Philadelphia and Germantown using horse-drawn cars. In November of the same year a Philadelphia watch maker, Matthias Baldwin, placed his steam locomotive, Old Ironsides, into operation on the line. Old Ironsides was capable of 28 miles per hour. In 1834 the State government attempted to open up a railroad between Philadelphia and Columbia operated on the same principle as a highway. Rails were laid by the State and anyone could run his cars, pulled by his own horses, over the tracks.

Early railroads had locomotives and cars built almost completely of wood. In 1834 Baldwin's locomotive used on the Portage Railroad had wooden drive wheels, wooden boiler, and burned wood for fuel. The first iron rails to be made in Pennsylvania were made at the Great Western Works at Bradys Bend in Armstrong County in 1841. Danville in Montour County in 1845 made the first "T" iron rails.

The Philadelphia and Reading Railroad was chartered in 1833, and it connected the two cities by 1839. The Harrisburg, Portsmouth, Mt. Joy, and Lancaster was chartered in 1833. By 1837 the Cumberland Valley line was operating between Harrisburg and Chambersburg. This line ran a car with four sleeping sections in which there were three bunks each. Riders furnished their own bed linens and could ride on America's first sleeping car in 1839. The Pennsylvania Railroad was chartered in 1846. It first ran from Harrisburg to Pittsburgh in 1854. It bought the state-owned

Pennsylvania Historical and Museum Commission
The funnel stacked engine is pulling wooden cars around the hoseshoe curve, an engineering marvel of its day, to conquer the Allegheny Mountain.

Philadelphia-Columbia line and the Portage Railroad over the Alleghenies in 1857.

Railroads did not meet with a happy reception everywhere. Farmers feared they would raise their taxes and ruin their markets. Stagecoach companies and wagoners who were engaged in overland transportation feared the loss of their businesses. Road travel did fall to a point where the intercity roads were almost completely neglected. Farmers found that midwest wheat was shipped in cheaply by rail. But as a whole the railroads brought greater wealth to the state. New communities such as Altoona, 1849, and Susquehanna, 1846, were built by railroad companies. Other cities grew as division points such as Harrisburg, Pittsburgh, Easton, Allentown, Scranton, Erie and New Castle. By 1860 Pennsylvania had 2,598 miles of railroad track, more than any other State in the United States. The Baldwin Locomotive Works in Philadelphia was making over three-fourths of all American locomotives.

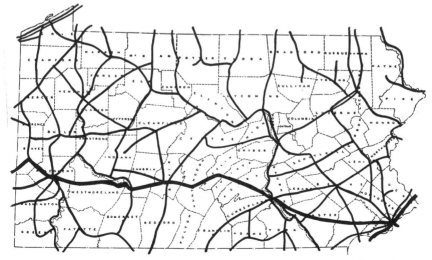

Laura Cornell

Railroads were built in every county but one. Do you see which it is? The Pennsylvania, Reading, New York Central, Lehigh Valley, and Baltimore and Ohio were the biggest operators.

PENNSYLVANIA BECOMES AN INDUSTRIAL CENTER

Anthracite Coal Starts an Industrial Boom

One of the most important factors affecting the growth of Pennsylvania in this period was the discovery of coal. Anthracite coal had been used in Europe but few Americans knew of its use. As early as 1770 a blacksmith named Obadiah Gore used anthracite coal to heat his forge. Various attempts were made to sell anthracite in Philadelphia, but few people would believe that it would burn. Colonel George Shoemaker had nine wagon loads of anthracite hauled to Philadelphia from Pottsville in 1812. When he arrived there with his coal, only one load could be sold. The rest was used for stone-surfacing a street.

Slowly, as people learned to use a draft to get more air to the fire, the use of anthracite grew. In 1818 the Lehigh Coal Company was organized and set up its own navigation system. It shipped 365 tons of coal to Philadelphia in 1820. About 4,000 tons were mined in 1820. By 1825 a great rush came to the area as thousands of people moved in to take up coal mining. The anthracite region in the Schuylkill, Lehigh and Susquehanna's north branch valleys, then a quiet farming region, suddenly became the most thickly settled area in the State. Scranton was laid out in 1840 and was soon a large city. Thousands of Irish came to Pennsylvania in the 1840s in time to take up many of the mining jobs that opened at that time. The Reading Railroad bought up coal lands and became a great producer and hauler. The Lehigh Valley Railroad was chartered in 1846 and its leading train took the name of Black Diamond. By 1846 there were over 7,000,000 tons of anthracite mined, and by 1860, 11,000,000 tons were being used for heating homes and factories, and producing steam for railroads, ships and machinery.

Bituminous Coal Aids Western Pennsylvania

Bituminous coal was found as early as 1759 in Fayette County by Colonel James Burd. In 1784 the coal of Mt. Washington, opposite Fort Pitt, was mined for use in making glass. By 1800 coal became a major industry around Pittsburgh, and in 1803 the first coal was shipped down the Ohio. Coal from the mine of William Boyd was floated down the Susquehanna from Clearfield County as early as 1804. That coal was sold in Lancaster County and some as far south as Baltimore. In 1830 deposits of bituminous coal were found in Tioga County, and in 1856 the Broadtop coal fields were opened. In 1835 the first coke was used in Huntingdon County by William Firmstone to make pig iron. In 1841 the coke industry was firmly established by McCormick and Campbell in Connellsville.

The coal fields of Pennsylvania were producing 3,000,000 tons of bituminous coal by 1860, but transportation difficulties held back their development. Shipping coal over the mountains was too expensive. Some was shipped down stream but the use of coal in western Pennsylvania for iron making was just getting underway in 1860. By then Pittsburgh was taking on the name of the "Smoky City" from burning soft coal in its homes and factories.

Iron Industry Moves Westward

By 1790 Pennsylvania was already producing over half of the iron in the United States. Most of it was produced in limited quantities. Modest communities grew up around such small-scale plantations. There is a small amount of iron ore in most parts of the state. The Cornwall furnace of Lebanon County was perhaps the largest operation in the state. It produced more iron than it sold in the years prior to the Civil War and had a huge surplus ready for use in that war. The mine at Cornwall remained the largest in the state.

Lehigh Valley Railroad

The Black Diamond Express was "the handsomest train in the world" as it appeared at its inauguration in 1896 for the Lehigh Valley's 50th anniversary.

A charcoal iron furnace of the finest type is illustrated. The charcoal and iron ore were poured in the top. Bellows were run by the water wheel. Finished iron was tapped from the bottom. Pig iron from such a furnace was sold to blacksmiths who fashioned it into numerous products.

By 1850 the iron industry had moved into the Juniata Valley. There were 48 furnaces, 42 forges and 8 rolling mills in the area of Huntingdon, Blair and Centre Counties. The early iron furnaces burned charcoal and limestone to smelt the iron ore. Forests were near at hand and wood was cheap. However, great amounts of charcoal were used, and soon it had to be hauled great distances. Limestone was available nearly everywhere. An example of the activity of one of these iron operations may be seen in the Bradys Bend Iron Company in Armstrong County. It was set up in 1839 and by 1845 had 500 families working at its mill. The company owned 6,000 acres of land from which to get its ore, wood and coal. It was one of the greatest plants of that time. By 1860 over half of the ore mined in America came from Pennsylvania. Slowly, more of the iron mills were being located in the Pittsburgh area as charcoal gave way to the use of coke.

Central Pennsylvania Thrives on Lumber Industry

The lumber industry, so necessary to the development of the state since its beginning, became more centralized by 1840. Local supplies of lumber became scarce in settled parts of the State, as farmers burned the virgin timber to make way for farms, and iron plantations cut down vast areas to feed their furnaces. Thus lumber had to be shipped in from the unsettled part of the state. Homes, wagons, barns, tools and stores were still built of wood, and as the population was growing so fast more lumber was needed. The part of the state least settled had the most wood, and so the northcentral part of the state became the greatest lumber producing area about 1840. Lumber camps were built, and hundreds of cutters were sent into Clearfield, Clinton, Potter, Tioga and Lycoming Counties. As men cut the trees, horses dragged the logs to the nearest streams. In the spring the floods carried them downstream to the cities below. Williamsport suddenly became the largest lumbering city in the United States. Here many mills and factories used the lumber to make numerous wood products. In 1846 a charter was given to a company to place a system of piers in the Susquehanna River at Williamsport. The piers were connected with logs bolted together to collect logs. Used for the first time in 1849-1850 over 300,000,000 feet of lumber were cut from logs collected. Individual logs were branded to tell to which company they belonged. By 1860 Pennsylvania was the greatest lumber produc-

Pennsylvania Historical and Museum Commission
Lumbering became a big industry even before the Civil War as the populated areas soon had to import lumber from the northern parts of the State.

ing State in the Union.

Great changes were in the making for Pennsylvania. Coal mining had crowded farming out of the anthracite region. Coal was rapidly becoming a major occupation in southwestern counties. Pennsylvania's milling industry was losing out to the city of Buffalo, but the iron industry was becoming stronger. The railroads of the state were tying together the cities and agricultural regions. Railroads were valuable in providing the necessary transportation to transform Pennsylvania into a great and powerful industrial state.

REVIEW QUESTIONS

1. Why did the northwestern portion of the State develop slowly before 1800? Why is the northcentral section not greatly populated today?

2. Give the reasons why Pennsylvania paid her Revolutionary War soldiers in land?

3. The removal of both the state and national capitals within a year was a blow to Philadelphia. Why were they removed?

4. What is meant by "The Athens of America"?

5. What was the "Hot-Water Rebellion"?

6. Give as many reasons as you can for the creation of new counties.

7. Who defeated Findlay for Governor in 1820? What significance does this question have?

8. What did the Free School Act of 1834 have to do with the defeat of George Wolf for Governor?

9. What changes were made in the new Constitution of 1838?

10. Name the President and Vice President elected from Pennsylvania in this period.

11. What was the main occupation of Pennsylvanians until the Civil War?

12. What new inventions aided the farmer in Pennsylvania?

13. Why was water still the best means of transportation in Pennsylvania before 1840?

14. How did the railroads meet the problem of transportation in Pennsylvania.

15. How did the discovery of coal help to change Pennsylvania from an agricultural to an industrial leader?

Do You Know the Meaning of or Can You Identify the Following Words or Phrases? Write sentences to prove it.

1. rural
2. Pennsylvania Plan
3. Free School Act
4. prejudice
5. crop rotation
6. panic
7. turnpike
8. Whiskey Rebellion
9. coke
10. Phineas Davis
11. Arthur St. Clair
12. Rembrandt Peale
13. Albert Gallatin
14. Oliver H. Perry
15. Stephen Girard
16. Thaddeus Stevens
17. Farmers' High School
18. Cumberland Road
19. Robert Fulton
20. John Roebling

Maps to Help Us Learn

1. Trace on your outline map:
    a. The Lancaster Pike
    b. The two roads which connected Philadelphia and Pittsburgh
    c. The National Road in Pennsylvania.
    d. The Schuylkill Canal.
    e. The Union Canal.
    f. The Pennsylvania Canal.
    g. The Carbondale-Honesdale Line.
    h. The Philadelphia and Reading Railroad.
    i. The Pennsylvania Railroad.
2. Show on your map the products of the farms of Pennsylvania. This can be done by writing the names of the products on the map or by drawing or pasting small pictures on the map. Place circles around those in which Pennsylvania leads the nation.

What Do You Think? Use the knowledge gained thus far to comment on the following statements:

1. Due to the tax on whiskey in Western Pennsylvania the farmers had the same grievances against the United States government as the colonies had against England.
2. Notice on a map of Pennsylvania the difference in area of the counties. These should be equal in size.

3. The construction of public works should be entirely in the hands of the State government.

4. The large families with ten to fourteen children in the 18th and 19th centuries were a great help to the community and nation.

5. The Erie Canal in New York was responsible for the downfall of Philadelphia as the leading port on the Atlantic seaboard.

ACTIVITIES
(Individual, committee or class project and class reports)

1. Plan a panel discussion on this subject: "Pennsylvania did its share as an agricultural leader; it has been a leader in industry; it seems as though it could be practically a self-sufficient state."

2. A crowd of men in western Pennsylvania is angrily confronting a group of men come to collect the whiskey tax. One of the men makes a speech urging war. Another says he will not fight against the government. Dramatize the scene.

3. Make a chart of all the political parties functioning in Pennsylvania during this period. Describe their origins, purposes and ideas, as well as your own judgment of them.

4. Give the impression of a farmer when he saw his first railroad train in operation.

5. Describe the trip of George Shoemaker to Philadelphia with his loads of coal and the results.

6. Make a working model of a canal boat and a canal lock. Then demonstrate to the class.

7. Locate the speech of Thaddeus Stevens in defense of the Free School Act. After practice, try to deliver the address as eloquently as Thaddeus Stevens might have done.

8. Locate the first public elementary, junior high and senior high school in your community. If possible find the dates, number of pupils and teachers.

9. Sketch or photograph any historic inns or taverns in your community. Locate any of the older homes in the area and describe their history.

10. Write a theme on the subject: "The Public School Is Necessary in a Democracy."

READING MATERIALS

Alexander, Edwin P., *On the Main Line: The Pennsylvania Railroad in the 19th Century*, New York, Clarkson N. Potter, 1971.
American Heritage, *The Erie Canal*, American Heritage, 1964.
Baldwin, Leland, *The Keelboat Age on Western Waters*, University of Pittsburgh Press, 1941.
Binder, Frederic Moore, *Coal Age Empire and the Utilization to 1860*, Harrisburg, Pennsylvania Historical and Museum Commission, 1974.
Drago, Harry Sinclair, *Canal Days in America*, New York, Clarkson N. Potter, 1972.
The Fight for Free Schools in Pennsylvania, Historic Leaflet, No. 6, Pennsylvania Historical and Museum Commission 19S3.
Frost, J. A., *Life on the Upper Susquehanna, i783-1860*, King's Crown Press, 1951.
Garbedian, H. G., *George Westinghouse: Fabulous Inventor*, Dodd, 1943.
Harpster, lohn W., *Pen Pictures of Early Western Pennsylvania*, University of Pittsburgh Press, 1938.
Hunter, L. C., and B. J., *Steamboats on Western Waters*, Harvard University Press, 1949.
Long, Amos, *The Pennsylvania German Family Farm*, Pennsylvania German Society Publications, Vol. 6, BreinigsviUe: The Society, 1972.
"Lumbering," *Pennsylvania History*, October, 19S2.
Ole Bull's New Norway, Historic Pennsylvania Leaflet, No. 14, Pennsylvania Historical and Museum Commission, 19S3.
Old Economy, Third and Last Home of the Harmony Society, Pennsylvania Historical and Museum Commission, 19S2.
The Pennsylvania Canals, Historic Pennsylvania Leaflet, No. 1.
Stevens, S. K., ` Pennsylvania Farmer, 1951-52.

Pennsylvania Department of Commerce

General John F. Reynolds of Lancaster was killed the first day of the Battle of Gettysburg. A statue in his honor was erected on the spot of his death. At Gettysburg, the horses that have one foot off the ground indicate the rider was killed.

chapter IX

Saving the Union

As Pennsylvania entered the year 1860, few dreamed that a Civil War was about to break out in the United States. Pennsylvania, along with the South, had supported the Democratic Party. The Commonwealth had practically eliminated slavery, but most Pennsylvanians were willing to let the South take care of its own slave problems. For Pennsylvania, the major political difference with the South was over the question of a tariff to protect the rapidly growing industry of the North.

ABOLITION OF SLAVERY GAINS SUPPORT SLOWLY

Slavery had been an accepted institution in colonial Pennsylvania. Blacks were publicly offered for sale in many places. As early as 1688 the Mennonites of Germantown protested the institution of slavery. In 1758 the Quakers declared members should not hold slaves. In 1776 they declared all slaves held by Quakers should be set free. The Pennsylvania Abolition Society was founded in Philadelphia in 1776. In 1780 the Pennsylvania Assembly passed the law gradually abolishing slavery. In 1800 the Reformed Presbyterian Church forbade members to be slave holders. But as late as 1817, a black girl was auctioned off in Greensburg. In 1833 the first national convention of Abolitionists (American Anti-Slave Society) was held in Philadelphia. The delegates were determined to organize the attack against slavery and to arouse people against it.

At hundreds of meetings, Lucretia Mott preached against the evils of slavery.

The majority of the people were not aroused. Many Pennsylvanians felt that the Abolitionists were fanatics. Mobs in Philadelphia actually burned houses of blacks and drove them from their work. In 1836 the Abolitionists could not rent a meeting place in the city so they built their own building, Pennsylvania Hall. When it was dedicated in May, 1838, mob action broke out again. John Greenleaf Whittier was reading an anti-slavery poem as the mob hissed and threw stones through windows. The next night they broke into the building, broke off the gas light pipe and lit bonfires next to the building.

Although there were only 64 registered slaves in the state in 1840, in 1844 Pennsylvania voted for slave-owner Polk for President because he pledged higher tariffs. The Abolitionist candidate for Governor in 1847, F. J. Lemoyne of Washington, received only 1,861 votes. David Wilmot, a Bradford County Congressman, in 1848 offered his Wilmot Proviso to keep all lands taken from Mexico free from slavery. His proviso lost but Wilmot gained national fame.

Underground Railroad Sends Slaves to Freedom

Pennsylvania did have a law forbidding the sending of a black out of the state to enslave him. But one time when a black slave-woman was sent back to her master in Maryland, the case was carried to the Supreme Court. The Court in 1842 decided that the

Pennsylvania law was unconstitutional because Federal law of 1793 required that slaves be returned. The Court stated that the enforcement of the law was a Federal job. If an owner found his slave in Pennsylvania, he would need a Federal marshal to arrest the slave and return him to the South. In 1850 a new fugitive slave law forced slaves to be returned if recognized by the owner and two witnesses.

As early as 1838, a number of people, mostly Quakers, set up a series of "stations" to help the slaves to get to Canada and freedom. After 1850 it became known as the "Underground Railroad" because so many slaves disappeared near Columbia, Lancaster County, that some one said, "There must be an underground railroad here." In 1851 an Edward Gorsuch and son went into Christiana, Lancaster County, in search of his runaway slaves. He found them, but when he attempted to take them back, he was killed and his son wounded. A Quaker bystander was arrested by a Federal marshal for failing to help quell the riot, but no court would indict him. The South pointed to this as an example of lawlessness.

John Brown, one of the most fanatical Abolitionists in the country, migrated to Crawford County as a tanner in 1859. Later he moved to Chambersburg where he planned a raid on the army arsenal and armory at Harpers Ferry, West Virginia, in order to get arms to free southern slaves. He was later hanged for treason. When his body was shipped through Philadelphia, Abolitionists mourned but a mob hissed and groaned.

Republican Party Gains Support

In 1856 James Buchanan of Lancaster was elected to the Presidency by the Democrats. In his cabinet he had two Pennsylvanians. Jeremiah S. Black, of Somerset, served as Attorney General and later as Secretary of State, and Edwin M. Stanton of Pittsburgh, served as Attorney General following Black. Buchanan failed to keep the nation from splitting into two parts over the slavery issue.

Many Pennsylvanians began to desert the Democratic Party in favor of the newly formed Republican Party as early as 1856. Simon Cameron, formerly a Democrat, became the first Republican

Pennsylvania Dutch Tourist Bureau
United States President James Buchanan (1857-1861) was born in a log cabin in Franklin County but live in beautiful "Wheatland" in Lancaster when elected President. The home is open to the public today.

United States Senator from Pennsylvania in 1857. Thaddeus Stevens, who had been a Democrat, Anti-Mason and Whig, turned Republican in 1856. David Wilmot, Democrat, and Andrew Curtin, Whig, had joined Republican ranks also.

When the 1860 Republican Convention was held in Chicago, David Wilmot was the presiding officer. On the first ballot for President, Cameron was third behind Seward and Lincoln. Cameron then threw his support to Lincoln in return for a Cabinet post.

In October, 1860, Andrew Gregg Curtin was elected Governor on the Republican ticket, and the next month Pennsylvania voted for Lincoln for President. A platform opposing the extension of slavery and supporting a high tariff to "protect" industry in the North made Pennsylvania a Republican State. Lincoln won in Pennsylvania by 90,000 votes, but the state was not in a quarrelsome mood. On December 13, 1860, seven days before South Carolina seceded from the Union, over 50,000 people gathered in Philadelphia's Independence Square where resolutions were adopted to the effect that "all denunciations of slavery as existing in the United States are inconsistent with the spirit of brotherhood and kindness."

President Lincoln did not take office until March 4, 1861, and the southern states began to retire from the Union in December, 1860. Buchanan, acting on advice from Secretary of State Jeremiah Black, did nothing about it. Buchanan's Secretary of War, John B. Floyd of Virginia, December 20, ordered 700 tons of guns and ammunition shipped from Lawrenceville to southern ports. This was the same day South Carolina seceded. Pittsburghers persuaded Judge Charles Shaler, law partner of the new Attorney General, Edwin Stanton, to stop the shipment. Mob action was imminent when Stanton wired an order to stop the loading of cannons on southbound steamboats.

Governor Curtin Acts to Save the Union

When Governor Curtin took office in January, 1861, he proclaimed Pennsylvania's peaceful intentions. "No one who knows the history of Pennsylvania and understands the feeling of her people," he said, "can justly charge us with hostility to our brethren in other states." However, Pennsylvania's new Governor also spoke out against the right of any state to secede from the United States. "It is the first duty of the national authorities to stay the progress of anarchy and enforce the laws, and Pennsylvania, with a united people, will give them an honest, faithful, and active support." There was no question of Pennsylvania's stand. There might be a willingness to compromise on the question of slavery but not on the question of secession.

On his way to Washington, Abraham Lincoln stopped in Pittsburgh, Harrisburg and Philadelphia to greet the people and make speeches. Pennsylvania was really on the border of the South. If Lincoln could not keep the support of Pennsylvania, he could not expect to keep the country together. He met with Governor Curtin in Harrisburg and visited Independence Hall in Philadelphia. When Lincoln took office, he named Simon Cameron as Secretary of War. Galusha A. Grow of Bradford County was Speaker of the United States House of Representatives in 1861-1863.

After South Carolina fired on Fort Sumter, April 12, Lincoln called for 14,000 troops to be raised in Pennsylvania. Six days later, 530 men from Pennsylvania's militia companies were on guard in Washington. These proud "First Defenders" included troops from Reading, Pottsville, Lewistown and Allentown. Instead of 14,000 men, 30,000 volunteered. Governor Curtin had the foresight to channel the overflow into the Pennsylvania Reserves, which set up a camp north of Harrisburg. At Camp Curtin men were prepared to be ready when called by the national government. When the Federal troops were defeated at Bull Run, the Pennsylvania Reserves were sent into action under Generals John Reynolds of Lancaster, George C. Meade of Philadelphia, and Edward O.C. Ord. A famed group were the "Bucktails" of McKean and Cameron Counties, who wore the tails of buck deer in their hats to give their uniforms distinction.

To unite the northern states more closely, Governor Curtin called a meeting in Altoona of all governors of the Union states for September 24-26, 1862. Governor Curtin was able to mobilize the thinking of the governors behind the Emancipation Proclamation of September. They drew up an address to the President that was to restore the failing morale of the North and unite the country in a firm determination to see the war through to victory.

PENNSYLVANIA BECOMES A BATTLEGROUND

Pennsylvania was an important key to the Union's defense. Its rail lines kept troops moving, but more important it supplied the army with needed materials. The Southerners found out that there were shoes, clothing and munitions stored in Chambersburg.

Confederates Invade Pennsylvania

On October 10, 1862, Confederate General J.E.B. Stuart led 1,800 horsemen without warning into the quiet town. The men cut telegraph lines and looted the warehouses. To haul off the goods, 1,200 horses had been taken from farms in the area. What they could not take was burned, together with the railroad station. The next day, Stuart was back in Confederate territory with his loot without a fight.

In June, 1863, General Robert E. Lee began a real invasion of the North. With a 75,000-man army he started up the Shenandoah Valley of Virginia. Great fear spread in Harrisburg, Pittsburgh and Philadelphia. Secretary of War Stanton warned that "Pittsburgh will certainly be the point aimed at by Stuart's raid, which may be duly expected. You should frankly inform the people of Pittsburgh that they must be at work." Factories shut down and 5,000 men began building fortifications. More than 30 forts, redoubts, and batteries ringed Pittsburgh and were guarded to the end of the war. At Harrisburg the great alarm caused the setting up of like defenses on the west shore. Fort Washington was erected in what is now Lemoyne. At Philadelphia, fortifications were erected to the south and west of the city.

On June 15, 1863, a detachment of cavalry rode into Greencastle, then on to Chambersburg. Horses and food were taken from the surrounding area. Less than two weeks later Carlisle was captured by the Confederates. Cumberland County people fled with their property across the Susquehanna. Some Confederate scouts appeared as far north as Mt. Union, along the Juniata. Troops occupied Gettysburg and York and moved to the Susquehanna at Wrightsville. Union troops burned the bridged and halted Confederate plans to cross the river. The people of York were forced to pay goods and cash valued at $35,000 to prevent damage to their town. On June 28 the Confederates moved to within three miles of Harrisburg, where they halted when commanded to return to Gettysburg. This was the most northern point reached by Confederate troops throughout the war.

Two days later, the first fighting took place at Hanover in York County where Stuart's cavalry came upon northern troops eating a luncheon provided by the citizens there. Union troops rode out of town and gave battle, and Stuart's troops retreated toward Gettysburg. About 50 men on each side were killed.

Battle of Gettysburg Turns the Tide

The Union forces of 97,000 men were under the command of

National Park Service
Gettysburg National Cemetery as dedicated by President Abraham Lincoln is pictured above. The dead were buried according to the states from which they came.

Gettysburg Battlefield looked like this to artist Adolf Dehn. Sightseers from all over the world come to see the most famous of all American battlefields.

Pennsylvania's General George G. Meade as they marched north on the east side of South Mountain from Maryland. General Reynolds of Lancaster was second in command and led the troops that arrived at Gettysburg on July 1. The first day's battle was on by eight o'clock in the morning. During that morning General Reynolds was killed, and his troops were forced back to the southeastern part of town until the main army arrived that night. General Winfield Scott Hancock of Norristown was placed in command. The next day the total forces of both armies were on hand, and a bloody encounter took place south of the town of Gettysburg. An important natural stronghold, known as Little Round Top, was taken with the aid of the Pennsylvania Bucktails. In the first two days of battle 20,000 northern troops were lost.

On the crucial third day, July 3, the greatest battle ever fought on American soil came to a climax. Over 100 artillery pieces on each side poured tons of shot, shell and shrapnel among their opponents. For two hours trees, rocks, tombstones and houses were shattered. Thousands of men lay dying. When the Union guns got too hot to fire any longer, they ceased. The Confederates thought they had wrecked Union guns and unfolded their plan. Fifteen thousand men charged across an open field, led by General Pickett. The Union guns reopened their cannonade, and Pickett's charge ended with a hand to hand battle. Pickett's men were doomed when their chance of retreat were cut off by General Hancock's infantry.

On July 4, 1863, Lee began a sorrowful march back to Virginia. Over 28,000 of his troops were lost. The Union army had lost 23,000 men but had won the battle. Meade's men spent two days "succoring the wounded and burying the dead." The war was not over but the Confederates never recovered from this defeat. Gettysburg was the turning point of the war. It was also the greatest and bloodiest battle on American soil.

The people of Gettysburg used their homes, churches, colleges, seminary, schools, barns, halls and stables to care for the wounded. There was no Red Cross organization, so the townspeople became nurses, cooks, waiters and grave diggers. Local doctors cared for the maimed until aid was sent in from other towns. A great tent hospital, erected east of town, was used for four months before the men were moved to permanent hospitals.

The northern army that took part in the battle contained a great number of Pennsylvanians. There were 34,500 men defending their own state. Most of them were the original Pennsylvania Reserves, but one company was made up of local college students. Fifteen Pennsylvania generals took part in the battle, including the next Governor, General John W. Geary.

Lincoln Speaks at Gettysburg

Governor Curtin suggested to the Union states, whose men were killed at Gettysburg, that a cemetery should be set up for those killed there. Pennsylvania presented the land and each state gave its share in beautifying the cemetery. On November 19, 1863, the bodies were buried according to states. Edward Everett, America's leading orator, gave a patriotic two-hour speech before a crowd of 15,000 spectators. President Lincoln spoke only two minutes, to give one of the most famous addresses of America. The closing phrase, "That this nation, under God, shall have a new birth of freedom, and that government of the people, by the people, for the people, shall not perish from the earth," made it the literary classic of the war. An act of Congress created the Gettysburg National Military Park under the jurisdiction of the War Department in 1895. In 1933 the National Park Service assumed responsibility for the area.

Chambersburg Is Burned

One year after the Battle of Gettysburg, Pennsylvania was again invaded by the Confederates. With General McCausland in charge, 3,000 men surrounded Chambersburg on July 29, 1864. The next day McCausland demanded that the citizens pay $500,000 in greenbacks or $100,000 in gold or their town would be burned. Chambersburg citizens told him they could not and would not pay the ransom. The courthouse bell was rung for a meeting but no one came. Leading citizens were threatened with kidnapping but still no payment was made. Soldiers were ordered to burn the town. Homes were broken into and articles of value stolen. In a brief period the whole town burst into flames and citizens fled in panic. Three thou-

SAVING THE UNION

Chambersburg Chamber of Commerce
South Main Street in Chambersburg was burned by Southern soldiers in 1864 after the townspeople refused to meet a demand for gold.

sand people were left homeless and destitute. Chambersburg was the only northern town destroyed in the entire war. Citizens throughout the State sent relief, and a claim bureau of the state paid over three million dollars to southern Pennsylvania for losses in the war.

Behind the Lines of Battle

When the war did not seem to be going well, some opposition to it occasionally arose. The number of volunteers fell off so much by 1863 that soldiers were forcibly drafted for the first time in American history. However, religious objectors to war like the Quakers, Mennonites and Dunkers were exempted from the draft by the payment of $300. The law also allowed the hiring of substitutes, and the more wealthy sometimes paid $700 to $1,200 for a replacement. Many men of Schuylkill, Columbia, Luzerne and Lackawanna Counties refused to be drafted. Philadelphia and Pittsburgh had similar problems at times. But most of the 362,284 Pennsylvanians who were in the Army were volunteers. Over

14,000 joined the Navy and Marines. Pennsylvania always provided more than her quota of men, and they served well. Pennsylvania coal miners in the Union Army constructed a shaft under a hill of Confederates in the siege of Petersburg, Virginia, in 1864, to make it possible to blow up a whole regiment of Confederates.

In the government, President Lincoln included Simon Cameron as Secretary of War. Cameron was later replaced by Edwin M. Stanton of Pittsburgh. Thomas A. Scott of the Pennsylvania Railroad Company headed all rail operations for troops as Assistant Secretary of War. Andrew Carnegie organized the telegraph lines. Jay Cooke of Philadelphia was the "Financier of the Union." His banks sold the bonds of the government to finance the war. For the first time advertising was used and bonds sold to people of all classes. Formerly, only the wealthy bought bonds. During the war Governor Curtin was re-elected in 1863, and Lincoln carried the State over the Democratic candidate from Philadelphia, General George McClellan.

During the war the economic situation of the state improved greatly. When the war began, the state was a half million dollars in debt, and at the end there was a two million dollar surplus. Farmers

The many thriving iron works of Pennsylvania helped bring victory for the North in the Civil War. This one is located on the Lehigh River at Catasauqua.

prospered from the sale of crops. Factories worked at full force. There were six new ironworks erected in Pittsburgh during the war to establish the city as the nation's iron and steel center. Coal mining made great gains in production and sales. Textile factories turned out huge amounts of clothing for soldiers. New rail lines were laid and old ones rebuilt. The rail traffic in the state was the greatest in the Union.

Pennsylvania's contribution to the Union in the way of war supplies was almost beyond the imagination of the time. Munitions, clothing, canned foods, tents, blankets and coal were sent to the army. From Pittsburgh's Fort Pitt Foundry came the 15-inch rifled cannon which was the world's largest at that time. By the end of the war a 2-inch cannon was produced. River boats from Pittsburgh were used for attacking cities along the Mississippi. The Cramp Ship Yards in Philadelphia built many navy vessels. Butterfield and Company, and Sharpe and Rankin of Philadelphia produced cannons, rifles and war supplies in vast amounts.

The Republican Party had promised higher tariffs to protect industry. Each meeting of Congress raised the tariff more during the war. Furthermore, the government said that anything that could be bought in America was not to be imported for the war. These laws helped to build the industries of Pennsylvania. The prices charged by the companies were often high and profits great. This helped to create the great wealth of the state. Many huge fortunes were made because of the war. However, the contributions of these mills, factories and mines, together with the great volunteer army of the state, were of such magnitude that the people of Pennsylvania ever since have been justly proud of their record in preserving the Union.

Stephen Foster's Music Helps Heal Feelings

Before the Civil War, throughout it, and to this day Pennsylvanians were better able to understand southern life through the music of Stephen Collins Foster of Pittsburgh. His songs, based on southern melodies, were sung everywhere.

Born in the Pittsburgh suburb of Lawrenceville, Stephen wrote his first song, "The Tioga Waltz," when he was a student at the Athens Academy at the age of sixteen. Later, as he worked along the Ohio River, he picked up ideas for his songs "Suwanee River," "My Old Kentucky Home," "Old Black Joe," "Oh Susanna" and "Jeanie with the Light Brown Hair."

Stephen Foster died at the age of 38 in 1864 but his music has survived in popularity. A collection of his works is now in a memorial in Pittsburgh.

REVIEW QUESTIONS

1. Outline the actions taken against slavery in Pennsylvania before 1860.
2. What difference was there in the attitudes of President Buchanan and Lincoln toward the problem raised by secession?
3. What part did Governor Curtin play in the success of the Emancipation Proclamation?
4. Why did Lincoln need the support of Pennsylvania in the early stages of secession?
5. Why did Pennsylvania support the Republican Party?
6. What did the Confederate armies hope to gain by invading Pennsylvania.
7. What was the importance of the Battle of Gettysburg?
8. Describe the raids of Chambersburg.
9. What is meant by "raising the tariff"?
10. Explain how our state government with a half million dollars debt could have a surplus at the end of the war.

Do you know the meaning of or can you identify? Write a sentence containing the following words or phrases:

1. secession
2. George Meade
3. Abolitionists
4. Jay Cooke
5. tariff
6. Cabinet
7. "Bucktails"
8. draft dodger
9. Republican
10. Edwin Stanton
11. Pennsylvania Reserves
12. Underground Railroad
13. Andrew Curtin
14. "First Defenders"
15. General Reynolds

SAVING THE UNION

Maps to Help Us Learn

1. Draw a map of the United States. Indicate by one color the Confederate States, by another color the Union States, and by still another color the Border States.

2. On an outline map of Pennsylvania, note and fill in the places mentioned in the text relating to the Civil War. Then trace the routes of the armies through Pennsylvania.

3. On an outline map of Pennsylvania locate stations of the "Underground Railroad," and then trace several likely routes across Pennsylvania.

What Do You Think? Use the knowledge gained thus far to discuss the following statements:

1. A law that permitted a person who was called into military service to hire another to take his place was fair and reasonable.

2. Instead of using human slaves today, we have become slaves of machines which is just as bad, and the end will be the same.

3. Pennsylvania cared more for the preservation of the Union than for the destruction of slavery.

ACTIVITIES
(Individual, committee or class projects and class reports)

1. Write two editorials on the death of John Brown, one for a pro-slavery and one for anti-slavery newspaper.

2. Imagine that you are a member of a Pennsylvania family that has been facing a very serious problem for several days. One evening your father announces that he will join the Union forces, and your eldest brother that he will join the Confederate forces. Describe the parting and the conversation that took place.

3. Write an editorial that an Abolitionist or Pennsylvanian might have written to a newspaper after the Emancipation Proclamation.

4. Read an account of Pickett's Charge and describe it to the class using the blackboard.

5. Draw a cartoon or poster to illustrate the two words "Underground Railroad."

6. Have one student give the Gettysburg Address. Then another student should relate the story of how President Lincoln came to be at Gettysburg on that occasion.

7. Try to draw a cartoon showing what some of the former slaves thought freedom meant.

8. Give a report on Pennsylvanians who were in Lincoln's Cabinet.

9. After thorough research and study, report on the contributions of Pennsylvania to the North in the Civil War.

10. If your locality was the scene of any Civil War event, find the facts from your Historical Society and report to the class.

READING MATERIALS

Barton, W.E., *Lincoln at Gettysburg,* Bobbs-Merill, 1930.
Benet, Stephen Vincent, *John Brown's Body,* Doubleday, 1929.
Binder, Frederick M., *Pennsylvania Negro Regiments in the Civil War,* Journal of Negro History, XXXVII, Oct., 1952, 383-417.
Brigace, W. J., *Jeremiah Sullivan Black,* University of Pennsylvania, 1934.
Duff, James H., *"David Wilmot, Statesman and Political Leader,"* Pennsylvania History, Vol. 12, 1946.
Grimm, H. L. and Roy, P. L., *Human Interest Stories of the Three Days' Battles at Gettysburg,* Times and News Publishing Co., 1927.
Kantor, MacKinlay, Gettysburg, Random House, 1952.
Klein, F. S., "Wheatland," *American Heritage,* Spring, 19S4.
Levin, B., "Pennsylvania and the Civil War," *Pennsylvania History,* Vol. 10, 1943.
Ludwig, Charles, *Levi Coffin and the Underground Railroad,* Scottdale, Pennsylvania Herald Press, 1975.
Shankman, Arnold Michael, *Conflict in the Old Keystone: Anti-war Sentiment in Pennsylvania, 1860-65,* Dissertation, Emory University, 1972.
Stevens, S. K., *Lincoln and Pennsylvania,* Pennsylvania Historical and Museum Commission.
Swetnam, George, *Pittsylvania Country,* Duell, Sloan, and Pearce, 1951.
Thaddeus Stevens: *Champion of Freedom,* Historic Pennsylvania Leaflet, No. 7.
Tucker, Glenn, *High Tide at Gettysburg: The Campaign in Pennsylvania,* Dayton Ohio, Press of Morningside Bookshop, 1973 [Reprint].
Turner, E. R., "The Underground Railroad in Pennsylvania," *Pennsylvania Magazine of History and Biography,* Vol. 36, 1912.
Weber, T., *Northern Railroads in the Civil War, 1861-65,* Kings Crown Press, 1952.

chapter X

The Age of Big Business

Following the Civil War Pennsylvania made the most remarkable advance in industry and wealth in history. From an agricultural state Pennsylvania was transformed into the greatest industrial center in America. In politics the Republican Party controlled the scene through the end of the century. Waves of immigrants moved into the rapidly growing cities. The wealth created by new industries permitted Pennsylvanians to live in a manner unsurpassed anywhere in America.

As noted in the previous chapter, the Republican Party gained power in Pennsylvania in 1860. Following the war, the party continued to hold the major offices. In the United States Congress, Thaddeus Stevens of Lancaster County fought for impeachment of President Johnson for not carrying out his party's stern demands against the South.

A succession of Civil War heroes were elected Governors after the War. All were men of good character, though not particularly well trained for the job. All of them were Republicans until 1883. John W. Geary of Westmoreland County, elected in 1869, was a hero of Gettysburg. John F. Hartranft, Governor from 1873 to 1879, from Montgomery County, was a gallant general of six major battles. Henry M. Hoyt of Luzerne County, who served for the next four years, was also a general.

The high level of prosperity that followed the war brought much money into the State treasury. Thus taxes could be removed from cattle and farm implements and no longer collected on each ton of railroad freight. In 1882 further tax reductions were made. Real estate taxes were now collected only by local governments. Except for the personal property tax, no direct taxes were any longer paid to the state. Taxes were shifted to corporations. Since the majority of the people were not paying taxes to the state, they lost much of their former interest in how the money was spent, and hence the interest in state government declined. The income of the state increased constantly so that the state debt was systematically reduced.

POLITICAL BOSSES CONTROL THE STATE

Although the Governors were above reproach, some of the men in politics in the last half of the 19th century have been severely criticized. Simon Cameron, who gained a lot of political power during the Civil War, was the first of a long line of so-called political bosses in Pennsylvania. Since United States Senators were chosen by the State Legislature at that time, Cameron was able to have himself elected Senator in 1867 by controlling votes in the Legislature. When he resigned in 1877, he had his son Donald Cameron elected in his place. Donald Cameron served until 1897. For 30 years either the father or the son was one of the United

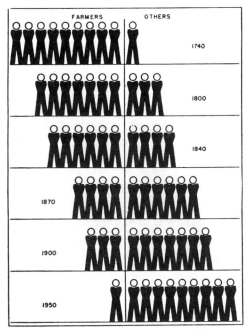

Farmers outnumbered all others in 1740, but as Pennsylvania grew, the emphasis shifted. Ever since 1870, Pennsylvania has been predominately industrial.

THE AGE OF BIG BUSINESS

States Senators from Pennsylvania. From 1887 to 1904 Matthew Stanley Quay filled the other Senate seat.

These men, as bosses of the Republican Party, controlled the government of the State of Pennsylvania. Each person who got a political job had to donate two% of his salary to the party. Corporations and businessmen donated large sums to the party also. In return for such support these men, Simon and Donald Cameron, and later Matthew Quay, pretty much decided who got political jobs. They also protected business by favorable legislation. Since postwar prosperity kept taxes down, they were also able to keep the average voter satisfied.

It should be pointed out that these men were giving the people in general the type of government they wanted. The state did not interfere with farmers or businessmen. In Congress the Senators voted for higher and higher tariffs to help Pennsylvania's new industries grow in size and wealth. By creating powerful organizations or political "machines" in the big cities, party bosses could control vast blocs of votes. This intensive kind of political organization spred even to the remote counties.

Fourth Constitution Is Adopted

However, some dissatisfaction with this state of affairs began to appear. At times there was talk that members of the Legislature took money to vote a certain way on various bills. Jeremiah Black, former United States Attorney General said, "The fact cannot be questioned that our Legislature is and has been utterly corrupt." Cries of corruption in state government increased. As early as 1850 the Constitution had been amended so that State Supreme Court Judges would be elected rather than appointed, to keep them free of control. Some people thought that the Legislature should not be allowed to make special laws for groups or localities. Between 1866 and 1872 there were 8,755 special laws passed and only 875 general laws. Finally in October, 1872, the people of the state voted 5 to 1 in favor of a state Constitutional Convention to correct the faults of the old one.

On November 12, 1872, 133 delegates assembled in. Harrisburg to draft the new Constitution. In January they met in Philadelphia to finish their job which took until November 3, 1873. To make the

Legislature less subject to boss control, the number of State Senators was increased to 50 and the number in the House of Representatives to 200. Four sections of the new Constitution dealt specifically with bribery and its punishment. To ward off raids on the State treasury, even the manner of giving contracts was defined. The Legislature was forbidden to pass special laws of many sorts, such as the one that made Bloomsburg the only "town" in the state. The Assembly was to meet only every two years thereafter.

The Governor was given the responsibility of appointing most of his own Cabinet. The Treasurer, Auditor General, and Secretary of Internal Affairs were exceptions and to be elected by the people. The Department of Internal Affairs was set up to keep an accounting of land, mineral resources and business organizations. Railroads were required to report to the Department of Internal Affairs. For the first time, the position of Lieutenant Governor, that corresponds to the office of that of Vice President in the national government, was established. The Governor's term was lengthened from three to four years, but he was forbidden to succeed himself. A special power given the Governor allowed him to veto parts of an appropriation bill while permitting the rest of the bill to become law. For example, it became possible for him to veto $50,000 of $100,000 voted for an item. State debt was limited so that it could not exceed $1,000,000.

Supreme Court members were to be elected for 21 years rather than the former 15 years. Some years later, 1895, the State Superior Court of seven members was set up to relieve the Supreme Court of part of its work. The Superior Court was to hear appeals involving less than $1,000. This was later increased to $2,500.

Blacks were no longer denied the right to vote. Aid to church-owned schools and colleges was forbidden. Up to this time aid had been given Washington, Jefferson, Madison, Franklin, Marshall, Lafayette, Gettysburg, Allegheny, and Dickinson Colleges and numerous academies.

Although amended several times, this constitution remained in force until 1968. At that time a limited Constitutional Convention was held, and the revised document is now known as the Constitution of 1968. (Chapter XVI describes the state government under the terms of this document.)

Depression Creates Labor Disputes

The prosperity that followed the Civil War ended in 1873, with the failure of the great banking house of Jay Cooke and Company of Philadelphia. Since the bank had a large part in American industrial expansion, its bankruptcy caused numerous other banks and businesses to fail. As business got bad, railroads cut rates to keep their business. Wages were then cut also to the extent that the New York and Erie Railroad workmen went on strike in 1874. Violence broke out and the State militia was sent in to restore order. In 1877 further wage reductions prompted the Baltimore and Ohio workers to strike. Soon the strike spread all over Pennsylvania. At Scranton, Wilkes-Barre, Reading and Pittsburgh workers burned railroad property and stopped trains. The Pennsylvania Railroad, to save money, ran trains with two engines and as few workmen as possible.

At Pittsburgh the railroad workers refused to run trains without full crews. When non-union men tried to run the engines, workmen seized the yards. Local police and militia stood by as the strikers burned 14 buildings, a railroad hotel, a station, 126 locomotives and 1,600 wooden cars. Over 4,000 State and 600 Federal troops were sent in to restore order. Railroad cars had been broken into and looted by some who came to the aid of the strikers. Over three million dollars damage was done.

Strikes had become common by the 1870s and usually ended with violence and the calling of state troops to maintain order. In 1871 a "Sawdust War" broke out in Williamsport when sawmill workers struck for higher pay. In 1875, Luzerne County anthracite miners struck for six months. This "Long Strike" resulted in numerous acts of violence at the hands of the Molly Maguries.

The Molly Maguires was an organization developed to protect miners of the anthracite region. During the Civil War members refused to be drafted or join the army. They later began using violence against mine owners and foremen. If they felt a mine owner or foreman was unfair, he was mysteriously injured or killed. Many of the mines were owned by the Philadelphia and Reading

A meeting of the "Mollies" in the hard coal regions usually was a secret affair to plan methods of gaining what they wanted.

Company. This company at last hired Pinkerton detective James McParlan to collect evidence against the ringleaders. He worked his way into the organization and later gave evidence to send 15 "Mollies" to their death in 1876. Many more were sent to prison.

Public opinion in these years generally opposed the new efforts of laborers to organize into unions so that they could bargain better with employers. Workmen were forced to take the wages offered. Working conditions, however, were so bad generally that the unions gradually gained some power. In 1878 when Governor Hartranft gave his final message to the Assembly, he called for the use of arbitration and conciliation as better methods of ending labor disputes than using troops.

THE POLITICAL WATERS ARE TROUBLED

Governor Henry M. Hoyt was elected in 1879 with the aid of the Cameron-Quay machine. He named Matthew Quay as Secretary of the Commonwealth. Hoyt, however, resisted the dictates of Quay, and by 1882 the Governor tried to fight the Cameron-Quay group. When the Republican machine insisted on nominating General James Beaver for Governor, Hoyt and other independents held a convention of their own. "Instead of the insolence, the proscription and tyranny of the bosses and machine rulers," they proclaimed, "we demand the free and conscientious exercise of private judgment in political affairs, and the faithful discharge by those who assume representative trust of the express will of the people." The Independent Republicans nominated Senator John Stewart of Franklin County.

A Democratic Governor Is Elected

The Democrats then saw their chance. For the first time since the Civil War they won the governorship. They nominated Robert E. Pattison, a 32-year old Philadelphian who was highly intelligent, honest and very able. With Stewart drawing many votes, Pattison won over Beaver by 40,202 votes. With Pattison the Democrats elected the Lieutenant Governor, a Supreme Court member, the Secretary of Internal Affairs and a Congressman-at-large. They thus gained control of the State government.

Governor Pattison was determined to improve the quality of state government. He introduced economical and efficient methods of administration and was popular with the people. However, the Assembly adjourned without making its reapportionments of districts for electing members of Congress, courts and the Assembly. Pattison recalled them the next day for a special session June 7, 1883. The Assembly met for six months and still did not do the job. The members of the Senate wanted it done to help Republicans. The House Democrats wanted to set up districts to help their party. The cost of the useless session provoked a great deal of criticism. While the average workman got a dollar a day, the assemblymen drew $10 a day and thus spent half a million dollars for nothing. When the Assembly met in 1885, they set the salaries for members at $1,500 per session and $500 for extra sessions to cut costs.

In 1886 Pattison could not run again for Governor because of the constitutional prohibition against reelection, so the Democrats supported his Lieutenant Governor, Chauncy F. Black. The Republicans backed the Quay candidate, General James A. Beaver of Bellefonte, who had lost a leg in the Civil War. This time Beaver won the election, and Quay was acknowledged as the Republican leader. He had been elected to the United States Senate, the job he held until his death in 1904.

During Beaver's term two great natural disasters hit sections of

238 OUR PENNSYLVANIA HERITAGE

Pennsylvania. In March of 1888 high winds and snow cut off travel for a week in eastern Pennsylvania. Telegraph poles were down, shipping destroyed and railroads blocked. This has since been known as the "Great Blizzard of 1888."

Disaster Hits Johnstown

The greatest disaster of the century in loss of life was the Johnstown Flood of May 31, 1889. Rains had fallen for days. Rivers and streams had overflowed throughout the State. A dam on the South Fork of the Conemaugh River broke from the weight of the swollen waters. Whistles were blown, telegraph messages sent, and a horseman raced to give the alarm to the city down the valley through Mineral Point, Conemaugh, Franklin and Woodvale to Johnstown. There the swollen river drowned 2,200 people and did $25,000,000 worth of property damage. Many houses up the valley had been pushed from their foundations and washed down stream. At Johnstown they were caught behind a stone railroad bridge. Those who were on the houses thought they were safe, but oil on the water ignited and set the wooden homes aflame. Many more died from the flames.

Governor Beaver set up a Flood Relief Commission. Over three

Pennsylvania Historical Society
The Johnstown Flood caused tremendous loss of life and property.

THE AGE OF BIG BUSINESS   239

million dollars from all over the world were contributed to the victims. Adjutant General Daniel Hastings was sent to preserve order. Clara Barton, founder of the American Red Cross, was on hand to aid the State Board of Health. She set up the first disaster relief that was conducted by the Red Cross. For many decades Johnstown was remembered as "The Flood City."

Prohibition Gains Support

For some time agitation for limiting the use of alcoholic drinks in the state had been increasing. In 1885 the Assembly passed a law requiring all schools to teach the effects of alcoholic drinks, stimulants, and narcotics. In 1887 and 1889 the Legislature passed a proposed constitutional amendment to outlaw the manufacture or sale of alcoholic beverages. The public voted against the amendment, but increasing numbers believed that some control of the saloon was necessary.

The new Prohibition Party had candidates for Governor in every election from 1872 until today. In the election of 1898 the Prohibition candidate, Silas C. Swallow, gained 132,931 votes which was the highest vote ever recorded by a Prohibition candidate.

Pattison Proposed Election Reforms

Following the work he had done at Johnstown in flood relief, Adjutant General Daniel Hastings tried for the Governorship in 1890. He did not receive the nomination since Quay decided to support George W. Delamater. The Democrats grabbed the chance and nominated Robert E. Pattison for a second term. By a close vote Pattison became the first Governor to be elected to a second term under the 1873 Constitution. However, the Lieutenant Governor and both houses of the Legislature were Republican. Pattison called for election and ballot reforms, personal registration and regulation of money spent by candidates for elections.

On June 19, 1891, the Australian ballot system was put into law in Pennsylvania. Many politicians opposed it saying no person should be ashamed to vote in public. However, the public demanded a secret ballot. From then on a man could not be intimidated in his voting. Previously he marked his ballot in public or used one given him by the political party. Now he used a ballot printed by the government and voted in the privacy of a voting booth.

The Banking Department of the State was set up in 1891 to supervise the banks of the Commonwealth. For the first time bank deposits were closely supervised to see that they were maintained safely and according to law. Before this time banks made bad loans and lost the money of their depositors. In times of poor business, banks often failed.

Rural Improvements Begin Under Hastings

Republican Daniel H. Hastings of Bellefonte was elected governor in 1894 over William M. Singerly, by the largest majority in the state's history. Hastings was a handsome teacher and lawyer, and a fine speaker. During his administration, the State Department of Agriculture was created in 1895. Two years later the new department began to buy up abandoned lands for forests. Some 55,000 acres of woodland were purchased in the mountain areas of the state. Lands which were held for non-payment of taxes were bought to build up timber reserves. Joseph T. Rothrock, University of Pennsylvania botanist, was a leader in this important move to conserve our forest resources that were, until then, rapidly disappearing.

Farmers of the state were the first to get rural free delivery (RFD) of mail. The United States Post Office Department set up the first routes at New Stanton, Westmoreland County, and Roffsdale, Lancaster County. The great improvement it meant to farm life, having mail delivered every day to the farm rather than having to go to town for it, can hardly be imagined today.

State Capitol Burns

Shortly after midday, February 2, 1897, the State Capitol caught fire and quickly burned to the ground. Some important books and records were lost. The old Capitol had been built in 1819 and had witnessed the inauguration of sixteen governors and, the visits of

THE AGE OF BIG BUSINESS 241

six presidents. The Legislature moved its meeting to the Grace Methodist Episcopal Church of Harrisburg for the remainder of the session. A stormy effort was made to move the capital back to Philadelphia where Independence Hall was still standing. It was decided to rebuild on the old location in Harrisburg. A temporary fireproof building was ready for the next Legislature.

When the Spanish-American War broke out on April 20, 1898, Pennsylvania was called upon to supply 10,000 troops. Volunteers from the State National Guard filled the quota immediately. A month later a quota of over 6,000 more men was sent to Manila where it helped capture the Philippine Islands first from the Spanish and then from the natives. The Sixteenth and Fourth regiments were sent to Puerto Rico. The other troops did not leave the country.

Quay Keeps Political Controls

Before the end of the century another attempt was made to take control of the Republican Party away from the Quay machine. John Wanamaker, the great Philadelphia merchant, used his wealth to fight Quay. Wanamaker had been Postmaster General under President Harrison, 1889-1893. He decided to run for United States Senator in 1896 but was defeated by Boies Penrose. Penrose of Philadelphia helped Quay and remained as Senator until his death in 1921. Wanamaker then tried for the governorship. He told the people, "Quay has so directed legislation that the privileges of corporations are well nigh absolute, while their interests have been so well protected that an unjust proportion of taxation falls upon the people." Wanamaker withdrew from the race in favor of an independent candidate. However, the Quay candidate, William A. Stone of Pittsburgh, won in the nominating convention. The Democratic candidate, George A. Jenks, was defeated in the fall election, thus keeping Quay in control. Despite Wanamaker's charge that "Laws are made by one man and largely administered by the same individual," Quay was elected Senator over Wanamaker in 1901.

So in politics from 1860 to 1900 the political machine of Cameron and Quay maintained political control. When Quay's leadership was fought, the Republicans lost. Most Pennsylvanians disliked machine government but they accepted it because thus far no effective means of combating its organization had been found.

BIG BUSINESS DOMINATES PENNSYLVANIA

There was no question that the growth of industry and wealth during the period 1860-1900 exceeded all previous bounds. The greatest industries of the period were steel, oil and coal mining.

Before the Civil War very little steel had been made in America. Pennsylvania produced three-fourths of the supply in 1860. By 1860 coal had replaced charcoal as fuel, and for this reason the steel industry moved into the coal districts of Pittsburgh and Johnstown, though at Bethlehem and other cities near a supply of coal the steel industry continued to grow. In each of these cities independent companies grew and prospered. These companies were usually run directly by the men who owned them. The growth of the huge steel companies is best illustrated by the story of Andrew Carnegie.

Carnegie Builds a Steel Empire

Andrew Carnegie was born in Scotland in 1835 and came to America with his parents in 1848. The family settled in Allegheny, now part of Pittsburgh, where Carnegie went to work in a bobbin factory for $1.20 per week. He soon became a messenger boy, telegrapher and railroad official. In the Civil War he helped organize the northern telegraphic system and invested some money in an iron works in Pittsburgh. By the end of the Civil War, he was already rich from iron and oil investments. After the war he decided that the future was in steel. A new mill was built in Braddock's Field in 1873 and Carnegie placed Captain Bill Jones, whom he hired away from Johnstown mills, in charge. Using the Bessemer process, the mill out-produced any in America. Jones was paid $25,000 a year, as much as the President of the United States at that time. In 1888 Carnegie opened a mill at nearby Homestead using the open hearth process. Charles M. Schwab was hired to run the new plant and it prospered also.

To supply these operations, Carnegie needed coal and coke.

THE AGE OF BIG BUSINESS

Gimbel Pennsylvania Art Collection

The steel industry in Pennsylvania requires enormous machinery and many thousands of workmen. Most steel companies, therefore, are large corporations.

Henry Clay Frick of Broad Ford, Fayette County, had begun a coke company when he was only 21 years old. He soon owned four-fifths of all the coke ovens in America, with their center of production in Fayette and Westmoreland Counties. Frick became a partner with Carnegie and became manager of the Carnegie Mills in 1889.

When he needed a railroad to haul his ore from Lake Erie, he bought the Pittsburgh, Shenango and Lake Erie Railroad. Renaming it the Bessemer and Lake Erie, he hauled his own ore and limestone south and his steel north. When he feuded with the Pennsylvania Railroad in 1883, he started his own South Penn line from Pittsburgh to Reading. It was never finished but the roadbed and tunnels were one day to become part of the Pennsylvania Turnpike.

Carnegie controlled his money well so that in time of depression he was able to build his new plants at low cost. In prosperous times he prospered more. He advocated that wealthy men should distribute surplus funds to institutions and organizations of public welfare. In 1901 he sold his holdings to the United States Steel Corporation for $492,000,000. He then spent the remainder of his life giving away $350,000,000. Some of these gifts were to public libraries, colleges, churches, Carnegie Institute of Technology, Carnegie Institution of Washington, Hero Funds, The Carnegie Endowment for International Peace and the Carnegie Corporation of New York.

Other steel companies were built up in the same period. The Bethlehem Iron Company became the second largest steel producer, as it took over the Cambria Iron Company, the largest in the country in 1865, at Johnstown and the Pennsylvania Steel Company at Steelton. The Jones and Laughlin Steel Corporation of Pittsburgh was another large producer.

Oil Becomes Big Business

Oil as an industry got its first big push just prior to the Civil War. Indians had shown oil to early travelers in Venango County. It was known to be good for burning in lamps but was too expensive and scarce. Samuel Kier hit oil by accident when drilling for salt at Natrona in 1847. He sold some, but the supply was small. However the demand for kerosene was greatly increasing for use in lamps, so a New England group organized the Pennsylvania Rock Oil Company and hired Edward L. Drake to drill a well near Titusville. In August, 1859, oil was struck at 69.5 feet. The well produced 40 barrels a day, more oil than was ever seen from one source. Oil was worth over a dollar a gallon, or $31.50 a barrel. Men rushed to the scene in great numbers. A forest plot became Pithole City with 15,000 people in 1864, but the great oil boom faded and in 1870 it was gone. Men resorted to all kinds of trickery, even murder, to get leases. They burned rivals' derricks and tanks and stole oil shipments. Farmers grew rich by selling oil rights to their lands.

By 1864 the oil trade in Pittsburgh had become a $15,000,000 business. First, oil was hauled to rivers by horses, later by rail, and finally a wooden pipe line was laid. One family, the Tarbells of Titusville, grew wealthy making wooden barrels. Ida Tarbell, a

Pennsylvania Department of Commerce
Colonel Drake's famous oil well derrick has been reconstructed near Titusville in recent years.

daughter of this family, later wrote, among other brilliant studies of industry, a history of the Standard Oil Company telling of the growth of the industry. The oil and gas industry spread from Titusville to Venango, Warren, Butler, Armstrong, Allegheny, Beaver, Clarion, Elk, Forest, Greene, Jefferson, Lawrence, McKean, Mercer, Potter, Tioga and Washington Counties. By 1891 the oil industry of the world centered in Warren, Venango and McKean Counties with 31,000,000 barrels a year being produced.

Pennsylvania oil production eventually came to be dominated by the Standard Oil Company, so Pennsylvanians went elsewhere to seek oil riches. In 1886 Joseph Pew of Mercer set up an oil company in Ohio. He later moved it to the Texas fields and brought the oil to Pennsylvania for refining. His Sun Company is one of the nation's leading energy corporations. W.L. Mellon, a Pittsburgh banker, got into the Texas oil business near the turn of the century and formed the Gulf Oil Corporation. By 1900 the oil industry was no longer centered in Pennsylvania.

New Industries Create New Products

George Westinghouse was another Pennsylvanian who grew to fame and fortune in this period. He moved to Pittsburgh from New York State in 1868. At the age of twenty he invented the air brake for railroads. Up to that time trains were stopped with hand brakes on each car. By 1872 his invention was used throughout the world. His later inventions gained hundreds of additional patents for him. He invented railroad signals and formed the Union Switch and Signal Company. He set up the first natural gas company in western Pennsylvania after hitting a large well near Murrysville. In 1886 he developed alternating current electric lighting. That year he lit the town of Lawrenceville with 400 street lights. In 1890 he developed an electric motor; in 1895 he put in generators at Niagara Falls; in 1898 he developed a steam generator of electricity, and still later built a steel rolling mill and developed an electric railroad locomotive.

In Pittsburgh the first aluminum mill of America was established. A young Ohioan, Charles Martin Hall, discovered a cheap method of producing aluminum to reduce the price of the metal from $2.00 to 75 cents a pound by 1873. With the aid of Captain Alfred Hunt, the Pittsburgh Reduction Laboratory was set up in 1888. With the aid of the Mellon Bank a plant was built at New Kensington in 1891. By 1907 the company became the Aluminum Company of America. Shiny light pots and pans soon replaced the cast iron tea kettles, pans and skillets through America. Soon numerous new uses were found and the price was cut to 20 cents a pound.

Unsightly limestone that was not good enough to use for building stone was found valuable for making cement in 1870. David Saylor ground some rocks into a powder, heated it, and thus discovered American Portland cement. He began operations at Coplay in 1871. This type of cement was necessary for building and until his time had to be imported. The Lehigh Valley became the leading cement producing area of the country. Portland cement was also made at Wampum, Lawrence County, by 1875.

THE AGE OF BIG BUSINESS

The Railroad Network Expands

Heavy transportation demands of the Civil War led to a rapid expansion of Pennsylvania's railroads. By 1874 there were 8,960 miles of track, and in 1900 there were 25,000 miles, the distance around the world. Three hundred companies operated in the state by 1900. The Pennsylvania Railroad replaced all wooden bridges with stone or steel ones on its line from Harrisburg to Pittsburgh, and new yards were built at Conway and Pitcairn. Steam heated cars were introduced and dining cars were in operation by 1897. Open platforms were replaced with vestibules, and by 1887 the luxury Chicago Limited had electric lights.

John C. Brill's horse car company in Philadelphia, which sold cars all over America, introduced one of America's first electric lines in 1886. By 1900 electric street cars were in operation throughout the country using Brill cars. The Baldwin Locomotive Works continued to turn out the majority of America's steam locomotives. Carnegie's Keystone Bridge Company made the first pressed steel railroad cars in 1895. Four years later the American Car and Foundry Company was formed in Berwick to manufacture cars and equipment. John Hansen and "Diamond Jim" Brady set up the Standard Steel Car Company in Butler in 1902.

Railroad lines were extended to practically every town in the state. Smaller lines were absorbed into the larger ones until by 1900, the Pennsylvania Railroad had working agreements with the Allegheny Valley, The Philadelphia and Erie, The Philadelphia, Wilmington and Baltimore, and The Pittsburgh, Fort Wayne and Chicago lines. The Reading lines extended through the hard coal fields. The Lehigh Valley carried the coal and steel from its river valley to New York. The Buffalo, Rochester and Pittsburgh spread through western Pennsylvania.

Big Business Leads to New Immigration

The methods and influence of big business penetrated everywhere. John Wanamaker bought an abandoned freight depot to set up in Philadelphia the world's largest dry goods store in 1876. This "grand depot" was the beginning of the department store in America. For the first time almost anything could be bought under one roof. In 1879 Frank W. Woolworth opened his store in Lancaster that was the beginning of a vast chain of "five and dime" stores. This first store sold only articles costing 10 cents or less.

New manufacturing industries appeared in practically every community of the State. By 1900 there were more big industries in the Commonwealth than in any other state. As the industries grew, greater amounts of capital funds were needed. Banks and bank owners often helped to finance new ventures and often took stock in the businesses. More and more machinery was introduced. More and more workers were needed to fill the jobs in the mills. Farmers' children went to the cities to work, but still there were not enough workmen.

In order to get more workers, a manufacturing or mining company often sent agents to Europe to get them. The wages of America often appealed to the poorer Europeans. Until 1890 most of those who came were Irish and German. In that year there were 5,258,000 people in the state of whom 731,000 were foreign born. After 1890 most of the new workers came from Italy, Poland, Russia, Czechoslovakia, Austria, Hungary, Lithuania and Yugoslavia. These people were the workers who mined the coal, laid the railroad tracks, made the steel and built the many new industrial plants and office buildings. Although the level of wages slowly increased, there were times when workers did not receive wages high enough to enable them to live decently. Prior to the Civil War, most workmen could afford to quit jobs if they did not like them. Now, however, there were times when there were more workmen than jobs, and so quitting did not solve the individual worker's problem. To improve his living and working conditions, he depended more and more on uniting with his fellow workmen in strikes and union activity.

Among the steel workers a union called the Amalgamated Association of Iron, Steel and Tin Workers had been successful in working with the Carnegie Steel Company. Their three year agreement as to wages ran out July 1, 1892. Carnegie was out of the country and Henry C. Frick was in charge of the company. Frick announced he would cut all wages and a strike resulted. Three hundred Pinkerton detectives were hired to protect the mills at Homestead. A fight followed with three Pinkertons and seven

Homestead men killed. Eight thousand National Guardsmen were sent in for three months to protect imported non-union workers. Public opinion seemed to favor the union until July 23, when a Russian anarchist, Alexander Berkman, who had no direct connection with the workers, wounded Frick. This single act destroyed the union's support.

In April of 1891 a coal mine strike at Frick's Moorhead, Westmoreland County, mine resulted in 11 strikers being killed and 75 wounded. A coal strike at Hazleton in 1897 was a clash between sheriff's deputies and strikers with 20 strikers killed and 50 wounded.

By 1900 most Pennsylvanians agreed that craft labor unions were worthwhile. This type of union is made up of those who perform skilled jobs. In 1887 these workmen organized The American Federation of Labor at Pittsburgh. The AFL would not allow unskilled factory workers to join their union. The unskilled factory workers and the coal miners, many of them uneducated immigrants, found no way to improve their conditions. Public opinion opposed their organizations and their strikes continued to be put down by force.

PENNSYLVANIA EVALUATES 100 YEARS

At Philadelphia in 1876 a celebration was held to commemorate the 100th anniversary of the Declaration of Independence. This world's fair attracted many visitors to see the latest in American advances in science. The telephone of Alexander Graham Bell was a great attraction. New electrical inventions amazed the thousands of visitors. Europeans greatly admired the American advances in invention and industry but in general felt that America was greatly lacking in culture.

Since America had spent so much of its energy in business and industrial expansion, it is understandable why her fine arts had not prospered. And yet during this century men like Thomas Eakins of Philadelphia were painting great pictures that today are regarded as masterpieces. The paintings of Mary Cassatt of Pittsburgh rivaled those of current Europeans. William Glackens of Philadelphia and

George Luks from Williamsport painted the poor and the children of Pennsylvania in a style that brought them lasting honors.

In literature, Bayard Taylor of Kennett Square, one of the first of America's world travelers, wrote many popular and interesting novels, travel books, and poems, and his translation of Goethe's Faust is known throughout the English-speaking world. Frank Stockton of Philadelphia was one of the most gifted short story writers in America. The Ladies' Home Journal and The Saturday Evening Post, published in Philadelphia, were the most widely read magazines in America.

Education improved greatly. In 1895 all children between the ages of eight and thirteen attended school. Free textbooks had been provided in 1893. Every district was allowed a high school in 1895. To provide teachers, the state took over 12 normal schools. Twenty new colleges were set up by private organizations in the same period. The great fortune-makers of Pennsylvania gave huge grants of money to help colleges. Carnegie gave to Carnegie Institute of Technology, Ario Pardee to Lafayette College, Asa Packer to Lehigh, Joseph Wharton and C.C. Harrison to Pennsylvania, William Thaw to Pittsburgh, Joseph Taylor to Bryn Mawr, A.J. Drexel to Drexel Institute, Charles Schwab to St. Francis, and A.L. Thiel to Thiel College.

Pennsylvania had seen radical changes between the Civil War and 1900. Now most people were non-farmers. Cities had grown rapidly with Philadelphia reaching the million mark. The population of the state had grown from 2,906,215 in 1860 to 6,332,116 in 1900. Railroads had displaced the canals as the major means of travel. Roads fell into disrepair. Steel, oil, coal and manufacturing became the major industries. The Republican Party controlled the politics of the State with the exception of the two elections of Pattison. In every Presidential election during the period, Pennsylvania voted Republican. Beginning in 1890 a new wave of immigration changed the complexion of Pennsylvania. To fill the jobs in the factories and mines, thousands of Italians, Poles, Russians and Slavic peoples entered the state, and large Catholic and Jewish communities flourished in the cities. Wages and living conditions slowly improved, and the means of getting an education was com-

THE AGE OF BIG BUSINESS

ing within the reach of all, as public high schools appeared in practically every town.

REVIEW QUESTIONS

1. What is a political "boss"? Who were the leading party bosses in Pennsylvania during the period under study?
2. What governmental changes were made in the fourth State Constitution?
3. What effect did the failure of Jay Cooke and Company have on Pennsylvania?
4. What was the purpose of the Molly Maguires? How were they broken up?
5. The Republicans helped Pattison become Governor in 1883. How?
6. What are the advantages of the Australian ballot system?
7. How did the RFD improve the life on the farm?
8. Describe the discovery of oil in Pennsylvania?
9. The genius of George Westinghouse made railroad travel safer and brought improvements in electric power. Explain how?
10. What European countries furnished most of Pennsylvania's immigrants in the later decades of the 19th century?
11. What improvements were made in our public school system during this period?
12. Name the Governors during this period with a few pertinent statements about each administration.

Do you know the meaning of or can your identify? Write a sentence containing the following words or phrases, showing their relation to Pennsylvania:

1. Clara Barton
2. prohibition
3. RFD
4. Edwin Drake
5. John Wanamaker
6. coke
7. kerosene
8. immigrant
9. A. F. of L.
10. Johnstown Flood
11. Australian ballot
12. standard of living

13. "big business" 15. normal school
14. department store

Maps to Help Us Learn

1. On a map of Pennsylvania show by various colors the original deposits of coal, oil and iron that were found in Pennsylvania.

2. On a map of Pennsylvania, dot the entrance points of the immigrants. Then use different colored lines to indicate where they traveled and settled down in Pennsylvania. Use more than one line of the same color if necessary.

What Do You Think? Use the knowledge gained thus far to discuss the following:

1. Any person who holds a political job should be willing to donate two% of his salary to his party.

2. Pennsylvania would suffer severely if all tariffs were removed.

3. The State of Pennsylvania has benefited much by becoming the home of so many different nationalities.

4. The strike is a better method than making laws for improving working conditions.

5. The increase of leisure time won by the unions has aided the development of American culture.

ACTIVITIES
(Individual, committee or class projects and class reports)

1. Make a list of industries in your own community. Would they be considered "Big Business?" Discuss with the class.

2. Make a scrap-book illustrating the work of Pennsylvania painters of the past one hundred years.

3. List as many things as possible to show how Andrew Carnegie aided in the cultural development in Pennsylvania.

4. Use the survey made in Chapter III or make a new one to analyze the make-up of the population of your community in relation to nationality groups coming here since 1900.

5. If you live in an area which is threatened by flooding, find out

THE AGE OF BIG BUSINESS

what problems are involved and what is being done to alleviate the situation.

6. Plan a panel on the topic, "The worker today has more opportunities to deal with the employer than during the 19th century." Use community leaders if available or several classmates as a panel.

7. Make a graph showing the increase of population in the period 1800 1900.

8. Draw posters advertising the 100th anniversary of the Declaration of Independence.

9. Construct a model of any invention made in this period.

READING MATERIALS

Aurand, Harold W., *From the Molly Maguires to the United Mine Workers; the Social Ecology of an Industrial Nation, 1869-1897,* Philadelphia, Temple University Press, 1971.

Burgoyne, Arthur G., *Homestead; a Complete History of the Struggle Between the Carnegie Steel Company and the Amalgamated Association of Iron and Steel Workers,* July 1892, New York, Augustus Kelley, 1971 (Reprint)

Carr, C. C., *Alcoa, An American Enterprise,* Rinehart, 1952.

Coleman, J. W., *Labor Disturbances in Pennsylvania, 1850-1880,* Catholic University of America, 1936.

Daniels, Belden L., *Pennsylvania; Birthplace of Banking in America,* Harrisburg, Pennsylvania Bankers Association, 1976.

Darrah, William Culp, *Pithole, the Vanished City: A Story of the Early Days of the Petroleum Industry,* Gettysburg, Pennsylvania, The Author, 1972, (Address: R.D. 1, Gettysburg, Pennsylvania, 17325.)

Department of Education, *American Diversity,* Harrisburg, Pa., 1973.

Dolson, Hildegarde, *Disaster of Johnstown: The Great Flood,* Random House, 1965.

Evans, H. O., *Iron Pioneer,* Henry W. Oliver, Dutton, 1942.

Giddens, P. H., *Early Days of Oil, Pictorial History of the Beginning of the Industry in Pennsylvania,* Princeton University Press, 1948.

Holbrook, Stewart, *Iron Brew: A Century of American Ore and Steel,* MacMillan, 1939.

Korson, George, *Coal Dust on the Fiddle,* University of Pennsylvania Press, 1943.

Livesay, Harold C., *Andrew Carnegie and the Rise of Big Business,* Boston, Little, Brown and Company, 1975.

Martens, Charles D., *The Oil City: A History,* Oil City, First Seneca Bank and Trust Company, 1971.

Stevens, S. K., *Pennsylvania, Titan of Industry,* Lewis Historical Publishing Company, 1948.

The Story of Colonel Drake, (Picture booklet), Quaker State Oil Refinery Corporation, Oil City, Pa.

Swetnam, George, *Pittsylvania Country,* Duell, Sloan, and Pearce, 1951.

Tincom, H. M., *John White Geary,* University of Pennsylvania Press, 1940.

254 OUR PENNSYLVANIA HERITAGE

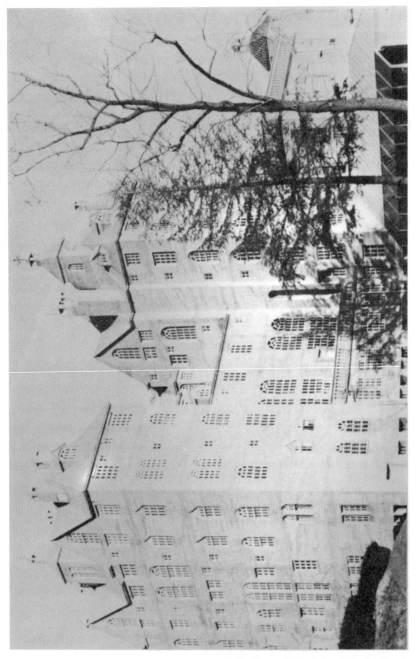

Bucks County Historical and Tourist Board

One of the world's most interesting and unusual buildings is the Mercer Museum in Doylestown, Bucks County. This "cassconcrete extravaganza" built to house Dr. Henry Mercer's collections of early Americana. Dr. Mercer's pottery company made the tiles for the floor and dome of the new State Capitol.

chapter XI

Entering the 20th Century

As Pennsylvania entered the twentieth century, industry was booming and living conditions steadily improved. Political parties slowly permitted more democratic measures and invited participation in party affairs. By 1898 a black was elected to the Assembly. New departments of government began to widen the scope of state services. A new era of transportation, education, recreation and communication began. Mud roads, one room schools, "magic" lantern slides and party line telephones were modern for the day.

NEW PROBLEMS ENTER WITH NEW CENTURY

Trouble in the hard coal fields broke out again in May, 1902. The miners had organized into the United Mine Workers with John Mitchell of Scranton as president. Plans were carefully laid and demands were presented to the mine owners. The union asked for a 20% raise in pay, reduction of the work day from ten to nine hours and recognition of the union. The companies refused to negotiate and the strike began May 9, 1902. Over 150,000 miners were idle for five months. Members of the union in the soft coal areas sent in $2,000,000 to aid the men. A real deadlock developed but the miners remained orderly. Almost 9,000 or 92% of the National Guard was sent to the scene but the mines remained closed.

As October and cold weather approached and people clamored for coal, President Theodore Roosevelt demanded a fair settlement. A national coal commission studied the demands, and the miners then got a 10% raise and a nine-hour day. Although demands for union recognition were refused, the settlement was a great victory for the union. It marked also the first national intervention in a coal strike. John Mitchell became honored among his men. In 1916 the work day was cut to eight hours, with a 10% raise and union recognition. In 1923 a further 10% raise was gained.

Further improvements in laboring conditions were made. A child labor law was adopted to limit the use of children in industry. A workmen's compensation law provided for accident insurance on employees.

New Capitol Symbol of Pride

Quay, with his lieutenant, Penrose, continued to dictate to the governors of the state. In 1902 young Republicans chose John Elkin of Indiana as their candidate for Governor. Quay demanded they accept Judge Samuel Pennypacker of Philadelphia. Quay knew he had to have a strong candidate to defeat Robert Pattison who had twice defeated the Republicans. Quay was right. He got the support of the Elkin's faction by naming him to the State Supreme Court and Judge Pennypacker was elected.

Pennsylvania's new capitol building was completed October 4, 1906, with Theodore Roosevelt as the main speaker at the dedication. He was extremely popular with Pennsylvanians and 50,000 spectators attended the ceremonies. The capitol building was one of the finest in the country. With 475 rooms, its circumference is over one-half mile and it covers two acres. Flanking the main entrance are two groups of statuary, Work and Fraternity and Burden of Life sculptured by George Grey Barnard of Philadelphia. The first floor has a tile pavement uniquely laid under the direction of Henry Mercer of Doylestown. The multicolored tile pictures 400 views of birds, animals, industry, occupations and transportation of Pennsylvania. Viewed from above, it looks like a fine carpet. Murals were painted throughout the capitol by Edwin Austin Abbey and Violet Oakley to picture the fine historic past of the state.

ENTERING THE 20TH CENTURY

Historical and Museum Commission

The "State House" above was used for the capitol in Harrisburg until it burned February 2, 1897.

Pennsylvania Department of Commerce

The modern capitol building in Harrisburg is surrounded by administrative buildings. The round building is the William Penn Memorial Museum and the tall buildings house the Transportation and Health and Welfare Departments.

Increase of Autos Demands Better Roads

Roads throughout the state had been for some time in terrible condition, so anyone wishing to go any distance used the railroads. Since 1836 roads had been under the control of local township officials. Road supervisors were elected and could tax property owners to keep roads in shape. If an owner wished, he could work off his tax at $1.50 a day. Few roads were usable year around. When in the 1890s bicycling became popular, a few roads were smoothed but soon the craze passed. The coming of the automobile brought a demand for better roads. Rural mailmen and school leaders who traveled over country roads joined the cry for improvement.

The Sproul-Roberts Act of 1903 created a State Highway Department and set up $6,500,000 for counties to distribute for road improvement. In two years only 105 miles of good roads were to be found in the whole state. That year the first auto license fees were charged and license plates issued.

With increased demand for better roads in 1911 the state began a complete survey of all roads. Provision was made for the state to take over 8,835 miles of roads which were to be made "smooth, firm, and convenient to travel." Some of the old toll roads still in use were to be bought by the state.

The early auto industry, now headquartered heavily in Detroit, made something of a beginning in Pennsylvania. In 1900 there were 75 automobiles manufactured in Pennsylvania, while the country as a whole turned out less than 300. Electric automobiles were made in Philadelphia in 1895. Charles Duryea road-tested his famous hill-climbing autos at Reading's famous Mt. Penn between 1900 and 1907. The Autocar Company of Ardmore introduced the drive shaft that made possible rear wheel drive in 1901, and made other improvements in auto mechanics. Wagon shops and railroad manufacturers turned to making cars. Chadwick, Dragon, Pullman, Matheson, Reading and Standard were made in Pennsylvania. These cars cost over $2,000. The tires for cars cost $40, but they wore out in about five hundred miles. The Standard Truck was made in 1906 by the Standard Steel Railroad Company in New Castle. The Standard Eight automobile was made in Butler from 1916 to 1921.

Election Reform Challenges Machine Politics

To cut down election frauds, a 1906 special session of the Assembly passed election reform bills. For years voters could demand the right to vote wherever they happened to be on election day. In this way party "hacks" sometimes voted twice or more in moving from district to district. In Philadelphia 80,000 padded votes were found in one year. The Municipal Reform League was instrumental in demanding a change. A new law was passed requiring all voters in cities to register age, residence, and personal appearance to cut down floating and extra votes. A second reform instituted the popular primary for nomination for state offices. The party convention nomination plan had been used since 1817. Many people felt that if the voters as a whole nominated the candidates, "bosses" could not dictate to the nominees. Since 1906 party members vote on candidates for nomination in the spring, and the winner is the party candidate for office in the fall. Party leaders still get together and "advise" that a certain person be nominated by the party in the primary election, though voters make the final choice. A third reform was the introduction of civil service into Philadelphia and Pittsburgh municipal offices. Up to this time all job-holders, even typists, were appointed and discharged according to political requests. Since 1906, many city jobs have been made permanent and free from political pressure. It should be noted, however that the thousands of state jobs were still distributed according to the "spoils system."

Penrose Follows Quay as Boss

Matthew Stanley Quay, Republican boss of Pennsylvania, died in 1904. His power in the Republican Party fell to Boies Penrose of Philadelphia, the junior United States Senator from Pennsylvania. Penrose had been in the State Legislature for 12 years and had been in the United States Senate since 1897. He was a rich, brilliant lawyer and politician. He was an ardent champion of the protective tariff, and big business supported his rule of the party. He distributed the big contributions of business to the party. Although he did not want or need money for himself, he loved political power, and ran the Republican Party until his death in 1921.

Philander C. Knox of Pittsburgh was appointed to take the vacancy in the Senate occasioned by Quay's death. Knox had been Attorney General of the United States from 1901 to 1904. He served as a United States Senator until 1909, when he resigned to become Secretary of State where he served until 1913. In 1916 he was returned to the Senate where he remained until his death in 1921. He was a strong supporter of high tariff and big business, and served as a lawyer for Carnegie during the Homestead Strike.

Capitol Fraud Uncovered

Near the end of Pennypacker's term a Republican Party split in Philadelphia resulted in the election of William H. Berry, a Democrat, as State Treasurer. In May, 1906, Berry announced that the building of the new capitol building had cost $4,000,000, but to furnish and equip it cost $13,000,000. In his own office he found that the state was charged $15,500 for panelling when its actual cost was only $1,800. Fraud and illegal overcharges were found in all parts of the building.

Despite the fraud charges Republican Edwin S. Stuart of Philadelphia won the Governship in 1906 by promising a complete investigation. Senator John Fisher investigated the charges and found there had been intentional cheating with false certificates and invoices. Architect Joseph Houston and contractor John Sanderson, along with the former State Treasurer and State Auditor General and 10 others, were found guilty in 1908. One and a half million dollars was returned to the state, but $4,000,000 was lost. Few of the men, however, served prison sentences. The whole affair made the most startling political scandal in the state's history.

Political corruption also infected our cities during this period. Municipal misrule in Philadelphia became notorious. In Pittsburgh in 1908 seven city councilmen were arrested for bribery, and over 80 persons were indicted for bribery, perjury and other crimes. Pittsburgh, by the way, expanded its population greatly by absorbing Allegheny City, now North Side, in 1907. Combining the two cities raised the population from 321,000 in 1900 to 533,000 by 1910.

THE STATE TAKES ON NEW DUTIES

Many dissatisfied voters decided to support William H. Berry for Governor in 1910. However, he ran on the Keystone ticket when the Democrats nominated another candidate. John K. Tener, an Irish immigrant of Pittsburgh, managed to gain a plurality to keep the Republicans in power. Tener, who had played big league baseball for some years, served as president of the National League for three years after his term as Governor.

For the first time since the Civil War Pennsylvania did not vote for a Republican candidate for President in 1912. At that time Theodore Roosevelt had broken with the Republicans and ran as an independent candidate. In Pennsylvania as the Washington Bull Moose Progressive candidate, he received 444,894 votes to gain 38 electoral votes. Roosevelt was always popular in Pennsylvania. His action in the coal strike endeared him to workmen. At the same time he saw the value of corporations and big business. He was progressive in a popular way. He and the Republican W. H. Taft were defeated by Democrat Woodrow Wilson. Woodrow Wilson chose William B. Wilson of Blossburg to be the first United States Secretary of Labor in 1913.

Congress passed the 17th Amendment to the United States Constitution and submitted it to the states in 1913. Pennsylvania was the 35th of the necessary 36 states to ratify it into being May 31, 1913. Before this, all United States Senators were elected by a vote of the Legislature. Now they were to be directly elected by the voters. When popular election of Senators was first held in 1914, Penrose was able to win reelection to the Senate.

State Police Established

Pennsylvania Mounted Police or "State Constabulary" was set up May 2, 1905, with 228 men. Divided into four districts with headquarters at Greensburg, Punxsutawney, Wyoming and Reading, details of two to six men were placed in each county. By this means the state hoped to reduce the calls for state militia and to patrol areas with no regular police. The new State Police did not

Pennsylvania's first State Police rode horseback and wore hats like the famous English bobbies.

interfere with local officials. They entered into a disturbance only on call from local officials. The first year only 694 arrests were made. The men were often called to patrol strike areas and to arrest criminals. By 1927 their numbers increased to 300 and by 1930 to 410. These men were not highway patrolmen but criminal detectors like the Canadian Mounted Police. Their efficiency and organization won for them a high national reputation that continues to this day.

Conservation Begins

For some time special pleas had been made for state protection of our dwindling natural resources. Many streams and rivers in the state were so badly polluted that fish could not live in them. Killing of game was getting out of hand. At last in 1901 non-residents were required to have hunting licenses, and four years later the first game refuge was set up. By 1913 hunting licenses were required of all hunters. The same year hunting seasons were defined to protect the game. Water resources were taken under control of the state too.

ENTERING THE 20TH CENTURY

From this time, no one could alter the flow of any stream without the approval of the state.

Ever since the disaster at Johnstown proposals for flood control were made but no effective action was taken. In September 1911 another flood disaster occurred at Austin in Potter County when a poorly constructed power dam across the narrow valley broke after heavy rains fell. Residents were partially warned but over 100 lives were lost and five million dollars damage done.

State Begins Regulating Schools and Businesses

Schools of the state multiplied rapidly, and so it was necessary to combine all the laws pertaining to education. This law, passed in 1911, was called the School Code. It tried to make schools uniformly better. School districts were classified according to population. A State Board of Education of six men was formed to oversee the system. For the first time the powers of the state, counties, and local districts were defined. Qualifications for being a teacher were set up and a minimum salary provided. All schools were to operate

Before the 1930s thousands of Pennsylvania children still attended one-room schoolhouses, and many still did in the early 1960s.

six months a year and Saturday sessions were forbidden. By this time, practically every district either had a high school or provided for students to go to a neighboring one.

The growing power of big business also called for regulation. In 1913 the Public Service Commission, now known as the Public Utility Commission, was formed to regulate public utilities. Further regulation of industry was provided for by the establishment of the Department of Labor and Industry.

World War I Breaks Out

Martin G. Brumbaugh, a prominent educator, became Governor in 1915 and served throughout the hectic days of World War I. Brumbaugh's leadership at this time was important because he was a member of the Church of the Brethren which opposed war as contrary to the teachings of Christ. In 1916 the Pennsylvania National Guard was called to protect the Mexican Border. A year later war was declared against Germany on April 6, 1917. Pennsylvanians made up the 28th Division and were ordered to Camp Hancock, Georgia, and then to France. Some 370,000 Pennsylvanians were in the armed forces during the great war. Pennsylvania's troops distinguished themselves at the battles of Saint Mihiel and the Argonne Forest. Battlefield markers have been erected to Pennsylvania dead on various fields in France.

Two Pennsylvania generals, Tasker H. Bliss of Lewisburg and Peyton C. March of Easton served as chiefs-of-staff during the war. They served as members of the Supreme War Council of the Allies together with leading European officers. General Bliss served also on the American Commission to negotiate peace at Paris, 1918-1919.

Pennsylvanians responded well to the call for civilian aid. Liberty bonds in excess of two billion dollars were bought. Over sixty million dollars were donated to the Red Cross, Y.M.C.A. and Knights of Columbus for work with the troops. Factories worked night and day turning out needed materials of war. War contracts were filled by more than 2,000 Pennsylvania businesses to supply everything from war vessels to shoe strings. William Atterbury president of the Pennsylvania Railroad, was called upon to be director general of all American transportation during the war. The

Federal government took over all railroads and he directed them. More coal was mined in 1917 than in any other year in the history of Pennsylvania.

Many people held in suspicion the large portion of Pennsylvania's population who were Americans of German ancestry. A number of these Pennsylvania Germans belonged to churches that opposed war on religious grounds, and some were imprisoned for refusing to bear arms. Some of the older German-Americans still held their homeland dear. Much hardship was endured by these groups. Prior to this time many schools in Pennsylvania German areas used the German language. Beginning in 1921, all public schools were required to use the English language.

Sproul Expands State Services

William C. Sproul, who had been a State Senator from Chester for 22 years, became Governor in 1919. He had always been a spokesman for better highways. During his administration the roads were classified into those which came under state or local control, and state highway districts were set up as we have them today. A system of numbered routes was established from border to border. A fifty-million dollar bond issue started in 1918 began a large-scale paving program throughout the State. By 1921, 72% of Pennsylvania's farmers had automobiles and were in need of good farm-to-market roads.

Educational advances were consolidated in the Edmonds Act of 1921. The school term was lengthened to eight months in rural areas and nine in towns over 5,000 population. Qualifications and salaries of teachers were raised by giving the state power to issue teacher certificates. To get more teachers, free tuition was provided at normal schools. ALL elementary courses were standardized.

Two Federal constitutional amendments respectively outlawed the manufacture, sale and transportation of alcoholic beverages in 1919 and gave women the right to vote in 1920. Pennsylvania was slow in adopting prohibition and did not approve it until February 26, 1919, 28 days after it was already a part of the Constitution. Pennsylvania was the eighth state to approve, June 27, 1919, women's right to vote.

A short-lived depression hit Pennsylvania in 1919-1920 and helped to bring about the establishing of another state department. A new Welfare Department was organized "to take over loosely joined boards and commissions in charge of penal, charitable, and philanthropic institutions of the state."

Penrose's Death Ends Era

Political power in Pennsylvania became disorganized in 1921 when both United States Senators Knox and Penrose died. William E. Crow was named to Knox's place and then he died, too. David A. Reed of Pittsburgh and George Wharton Pepper of Philadelphia were named to the offices by Governor Sproul. But who was now to be the political leader? Joseph Grundy of Bucks County and W. L. Mellon of Pittsburgh tried to gain control, but neither attained the power of Penrose, Quay or Cameron.

An important figure in Pennsylvania and American history in this era was Andrew Mellon of Pittsburgh. He and his brother expanded their father's banking business to become one of the richest families in America. In 1907 the family began the Gulf Oil Company that grew to become the third largest oil company in America. Their Pressed Steel Car Company prospered. Large investments in aluminum produced the Aluminum Company of America, widely known simply as ALCOA. With holdings in coal, coke, chemicals, glass and paint companies the family was a powerful force in building Pittsburgh. President Harding appointed Andrew Mellon as Secretary of the Treasury, and he served in that position for 12 years. Taxes were reduced and government income increased during his period of service under three Presidents.

PINCHOT INTRODUCES REFORMS

The widening east-west split in the Republican Party became more noticeable in 1922 when the organization's candidate for Governor, George Alter of Springdale, was defeated in the primary by Gifford Pinchot of Milford. Pinchot was not a party regular but a wealthy, idealistic reformer who was an expert politician. He had become the first professional forester in America. He had served

ENTERING THE 20TH CENTURY

Theodore Roosevelt and Taft as a conservationist. As Governor he enlarged State forest preserves with a $25,000,000 bond issue and expanded conservation by use of convict labor. A new fish and game code was adopted.

Pinchot was a great organizer. He reorganized the executive branch of the government in what is known as the Administrative Code of 1923. Twelve departments were formed to be headed by men appointed by the Governor. Each man was responsible to the Governor and outlined his needs in detail so that a sound budget could be adopted. For the first time a detailed state budget was presented to the Legislature in 1925. It was adopted almost without change. A planning board was also set up to look ahead to future needs.

An ardent believer in Prohibition, Pinchot got the Assembly to pass the Snyder Act in 1923 to outlaw saloons and provide for the punishment of violators of Prohibition. However, the assemblymen refused to give any money to enforce the law, but this did not stop the Governor. He used money donated by the Women's Christian Temperance Union (WCTU) to hire agents to stop illegal manufacture and sale of alcoholic drinks.

A state debt of $20,000,000 vanished with Pinchot's expert handling of finances. Using a pay-as-you-go system for the first time, no new general taxes were needed. Roads got the revenue from the first gasoline tax levied in 1921. To aid investors, a so called Blue Sky law regulated sales of securities. In conjunction with Federal legislation, an old age public assistance plan was adopted.

Another fight developed for control of the Republican Party in 1926. Mellon and Grundy came to terms, but William Vare of Philadelphia and Pinchot went their own ways. With a well-oiled political machine in Philadelphia, Vare set up his own candidate for Governor and ran for the United States Senate himself. Pinchot also ran for Senator against the "organization" candidate George Wharton Pepper, the Philadelphia lawyer. To get elected to a $10,000 Senate job, the three men admitted spending $1,482,511. William Vare won the primary and general elections, but the United States Senate refused to seat him because of the methods he used to get elected. John Fisher, an Indiana County Republican organization man who had conducted the capitol investigation in 1907, came through with the greatest majority in Pennsylvania history: a vote of 1,102,600 to 365,000 over Eugene C. Bonniwell for Governor.

Governor Fisher Introduces More State Services

The work of the state government expanded rapidly under Governor Fisher, and at the same time election methods were improved. The Davis-Harris Act provided for the use of automatic voting machines, which, by 1935, were used by over 60% of the voters in the state. More efforts were made to guarantee honest elections by limiting political activity at the polls and requiring stricter registration.

Fisher insisted on stricter financial management. He had seen how the capitol fraud happened. In 1929 he transferred all state collections to a new Department of Revenue. Over 300 collection agencies and funds were reduced to seven. From that time on state finances were divided into the General, Highway, Farm Show, Banking, Fish, Game, and Milk Control funds. All institutions were required to turn all funds over to the Department of Revenue. All spending was to be channeled through the State Treasury and checked by the Auditor General. All state-owned buildings costing over $4,000 were to be planned and supervised under the direction of the new Department of Property and Supplies.

Pennsylvania was enjoying great prosperity during the 1920s, and the state was richer than ever. When the tax on gasoline was raised to three cents a gallon, the biggest pay-as-you-go paving program in history got under way. Without borrowing money 4,000 miles of new roads were laid and 1,000 miles resurfaced. All borough and city streets that connected state highways were taken over. These were the major concrete roads that formed the primary routes. The last toll road in the state, connecting Lancaster and New Holland, was purchased and freed in 1930. To insure more safety on the highway, the safety inspection of automobiles was put into effect.

Being interested in history, Governor Fisher had the state Historical Commission draw up signs telling the name and origin of each community in the state. These signs were erected along highways leading into the towns.

Governor Fisher became widely known as "The Builder." The last two years of his administration marked the greatest state building program in our history. From current funds were built a new prison at Graterford, 30% more mental hospital buildings, armories, 31 new buildings for State Teachers Colleges, a tuberculosis sanatorium, and the huge Farm Show Building. At Penn State more money was spent on buildings than had been spent in its whole 75-year history. The Governor turned over keys to 12 new major and many minor buildings when the college (now a university) celebrated is diamond jubilee. Almost a half million acres were added to the State forests including the famous Cook Forest's 6,000 acres.

Overproduction and Strike Hit Coal Industry

With most of the state enjoying prosperity, the coal regions gave warning of dire days ahead. Since 1920 great wage gains had been made by miners under the direction of John L. Lewis. However, too much coal was being mined. Then non-union mines in West Virginia began to undersell the Pennsylvania coal companies. To keep from closing the mines, some owners sold out to "straw men" and then reopened as non-union at lower wages. In 1925 the Pittsburgh Coal Company cut wages 33% in violation of their contract with the union. Two years later another wage cut was announced with the notice, "We regret that owing to a fall in the market price of coal, it is necessary to cut wages." Even non-union mines cut wages. When the union's contract expired on April 1, 1927, all owners cut wages and declared their mines non-union. A strike was immediately called in bituminous mines throughout the northern United States, and 100,000 miners were out of work in Pennsylvania.

When companies imported miners from the South, violence followed. Miners living in company houses were evicted. In some cases furniture was kept for back rent. The strike dragged on through the winter. Congressional investigators went to the scene to see "men, women, and children living in hovels," which were often built of cardboard. Governor Fisher called for Federal intervention as in the 1902 strike but President Coolidge refused. After 15 months of unsuccessful striking, the men were advised by John L. Lewis to get the best local contract they could. Lewis and the United Mine Workers were forced to admit defeat.

At a time when America was enjoying one of its most prosperous eras, Pennsylvania miners were living on wages which, according to Governor Fisher, "in some instances figures below that which will permit a proper standard of living." Too many mines had been opened during World War I, and too many men tried to make a living at coal mining. Southern miners took lower wages and forced prices down everywhere. From this time on West Virginia produced more bituminous coal than Pennsylvania.

Overproduction and poor working conditions in the mines might have served a warning, for in 1929 the stock market crash started a severe depression that hit all industries. Soon hundreds of thousands were out of work through no fault of their own. Luckily for Pennsylvania a great building program was underway. Many men were hired to work on roads and buildings. When the Fisher term ended in 1931, the Governor was able to report a huge $28,900,000 surplus for use in the next administration.

PENNSYLVANIA TAKES UP NEW WAYS

Change seems to have been the order of the day in the first three decades of the twentieth century. In this period ideas changed, and government took on more and more jobs. Women became freer in action and dress. Boss rule declined and the people gained more power. Wealth grew, but too many people bought too much on installment plans. Many Pennsylvanians did not realize that change required long and careful preparation.

Pennsylvania artists seemed to have followed the pattern of the era. Writers of the state were highly popular. Owen Wister's *Virginian* was 1902s best seller and the first great cowboy story. Kate Douglas Wiggin's *Rebecca of Sunnybrook Farm* was best seller in 1903. Mary Robert Rinehart's *The Circular Staircase* was a best seller in 1908. Henry Van Dyke's *The Other Wise Man* became one of the most beloved stories of the time. Charles Wakefield

Cadman produced the most popular Indian music of all time with his "From the Land of the Sky Blue Water." Stephen Vincent Benet won a large following with his "John Brown's Body" and the popular "The Devil and Daniel Webster".

New changes in communications brought all America into a more closely-knit unit. The greatest impact on American life in this period was probably made by the introduction of the home radio. Dr. Frank Conrad of the Westinghouse Corporation in Pittsburgh was the first to develop radio commercially. The Westinghouse radio station KDKA began commercial broadcasts on November 2, 1920. KDKA was also the first to broadcast recorded music, news, religious services and professional baseball. Radio proved a new world of entertainment for all. It especially was welcomed by the rural population. By 1952 Pennsylvania had 161 radio stations. Atwater Kent of Philadelphia was an inventor and manufacturer of note in this period. Philco in Philadelphia and Westinghouse in Pittsburgh were producing fine radio sets.

Moving picture productions also greatly influenced the lives of Pennsylvanians. As early as 1861 Coleman Sellers had invented the paddle wheel type of movie in Philadelphia. Picture cards were attached to a wheel that when turned showed the action. In 1878 Edward Muybridge of Philadelphia used a series of cameras to get action prints that he showed through his projector for one of the first movies. A moving picture studio was set up in Philadelphia in 1898. Most early movies were shown along with a stage show. In 1905, in Pittsburgh, the first theatre exclusively for movies was opened. This "Nickelodeon" presented in 20 minutes The Great Train Robbery. From this beginning the owner, John Harris, set up a large chain of theatres in western Pennsylvania. The Warner Brothers opened a theatre for showing movies in New Castle in 1904. They soon went to Hollywood to produce their own movies. Movies influenced styles of dress, manners and social values.

Air travel had gripped the imagination of men for ages. Gasfilled balloons were made in Pennsylvania for the Union army observation corps in the Civil War. A gasoline powered balloon was built by Caesar Spiegler in Lancaster in 1878. Samuel P. Langley of Pittsburgh built a pilotless steam powered plane that flew 4,300 feet in 1896. As secretary of the Smithsonian Institute in

Washington, he helped develop a piloted gasoline engine plane that was tried December 8, 1903, but proved defective. Nine days later the Wright brothers were to gain fame for their first successful plane. Airplanes increased in use and commercial airlines developed. In 1927 the State Aeronautics Commission was set up to control airplane travel in the State. In 1928, Harold F. Pitcairn introduced the autogyro type of airplane to America, when he built his plant at Philadelphia. By 1933 there were over one hundred airports in the State.

REVIEW QUESTIONS

1. What was the purpose of the coal strike of 1902 and what did it accomplish?

2. Describe the work of the artists who were responsible for making our Capitol building one of the finest in the country.

3. What is meant by reform? List some of the efforts made at "reform" during this period.

4. What was the worst example of political fraud in this period? Does this reflect on our democratic system?

5. What made President Theodore Roosevelt so popular in Pennsylvania?

6. What was Pennsylvania's contribution in manpower and resources in World War I?

7. What is the importance of the Edmonds Act today?

8. What reason could you give for calling Gifford Pinchot a progressive?

9. What historical contribution did Governor Fisher make to our local communities?

1.0. Name the three amendments added to our national Constitution during this period and their effect on Pennsylvania.

Do you know the meaning of or can you identify? Write a sentence containing the following words or phrases, showing their relation to Pennsylvania:

1. union
2. State Constabulary
3. John Mitchell
4. Sproul-Roberts Act

ENTERING THE 20TH CENTURY 273

5. KDKA
6. mural
7. fraud
8. budget
9. WCTU
10. non-union
11. Violet Oakley
12. 28th Division
13. John L. Lewis
14. Charles W. Cadman
15. Stephen Vincent Benet

Maps to Help Us Learn

1. On an outline map of Pennsylvania mark by symbols the heaviest concentration of coal miners and other industrial working men during this period. Now in case of a miner's strike, answer these questions:
a. What% of Pennsylvania workmen would be idle?
b. What would happen to the economy in these areas?
c. What would happen to the economy in Pennsylvania as a whole?
d. Can Pennsylvania afford the loss resulting from the strike?
e. Should the quarrel be arbitrated?

What Do You Think? Use the knowledge gained thus far to discuss the following:

1. Is it possible to make governmental improvements under machine politics?
2. Is it possible for a party machine to dominate voters who are educated?
3. Taxes paid on gasoline should be used only for highway repair and construction.
4. Much good education comes through the use of movies.
5. Do you think the national government should intervene in strikes as it did in the coal strikes in Pennsylvania?

ACTIVITIES
(Individual, committee or class projects and class reports)

1. Read a book written by a Pennsylvanian during this period. Report on the author and summarize the book.
2. Make a cartoon depicting the capitol graft scandal.

3. Draw a poster which shows your ideas of a political boss.

4. Make a list of Pennsylvania writers of the last 100 years.

5. Find the names of some of the largest national unions functioning in Pennsylvania. Then write a short history about one of them.

6. Hold a panel discussion on the advisability of dissolving the State Police in favor of the local police.

7. Name the Governors during this period. Now pick one or two that you think are outstanding and tell why you think so.

8. Dramatize the impact of the first radio broadcast on Pennsylvania's rural population.

9. In chart form show Pennsylvania's contribution to air transportation.

10. By using cross-section models demonstrate how roads were built in 1836 and how they are built today.

READING MATERIALS

Atland, Millard, The Pennsylvania Citizen, Penns Valley Publishers, 1964.

Blackson, Charles C., Pennsylvania: Black History, ed. by Louise D. Stone, Philadelphia, Portfolio Associates, 1975.

Bubb, Fred, Endless Mountains Areas Sees No End to Future Crowth and Prosperity, Pennsylvania Forests 63:68, 71, September 1973.

Carson, H. L., "Life and Services of Samuel W. Pennypacker," Pennsylvania Magazine of History and Biography, Vol. 41, 1917.

Clepper, H., "Rise of the Forest Conservation Movement in Pennsylvania," Pennsylvania History, Vol. 12, 1946.

Davenport, Walter, Powerand Glory, The Life of Boies Penrose, Putnam, 1931.

Development of the Highway System of Pennsylvania, Department of Highways, 1932.

Dunaway, W. F., A History of Pennsylvania, Prentice-Hall, 1935.

Harrisburg, Pennsylvania's Capitol City, Historic Pennsylvania Leaflet, Historical and Museum Commission, 1953.

Pennsylvania Capitol Buildings, Commonwealth of Pennsylvania, 1949.

Shallo, Jeremiah Patrick, Private Police, with Special Reference to Pennsylvania, Montclair, New Jersey, Patterson Smith, 1972 (Reprint).

Stevens, S. K., "Pennsylvania Governors," Pennsylvania Farmer, 1951-1952.

Taylor, William S., Development of the Professional Education of Teachers in Pennsylvama, Lippincott, 1924.

Vare, W. S., My Forty Years in Politics, Ronald Swain Company, 1933.

Voigt, Williams, The Susquehanna Compact, Guardian of the River's Future, New Brunswick, Rutgers University Press, 1972.

chapter XII

The Later Decades

Beginning in 1929, Pennsylvania suffered greatly as the depression forced industries to close, and hundreds of thousands of men and women lost their jobs. Businesses by the hundreds failed. Gifford Pinchot, who had been popular with the voters in his first term, was re-elected in 1930. He promised lower taxes, better roads, cheaper rates from utilities and better protection for workers. Again he had to fight the Republican organization to win. The Democratic candidate announced he favored ending Prohibition and came close to winning the election. For the first time in history the Communist Party ran a candidate who received 5,000 of the 2,000,000 votes cast.

DEPRESSION HITS HARD

Economic conditions throughout the nation grew worse in 1931. Banks failed because people rushed to draw out their savings at a time when their money was out on loans. Factories were closed from lack of market for their products. When Pinchot took office there were already close to a million unemployed. Soon one of every four workmen of the State was out of work. It was the worst depression in American history. Pennsylvania was hit extra hard because one-tenth of all the unemployed in the nation lived in the Commonwealth.

In 1931 the Bankers Trust Company of Philadelphia closed. One fifth of all the families in Philadelphia had their deposits in that bank. By October of that year 40 more banks closed. Governor Pinchot declared a bank holiday March 4, 1933, when 147 banks had closed. This kept persons from taking money from Pennsylvania banks. Also banks were given a chance to convince the people of their safeness. Slowly most of the banks reopened, but some people never got all their money back.

The State Provides Relief

When economic conditions did not improve, a special legislative session was called for November 9, 1931. Governor Pinchot explained that the old system of caring for the poor was outdated. At that time all destitute were cared for by poor boards in the counties and local units and by local charities. The job was now too big for local agencies to handle. The Talbot Act provided $10,000,000 to be distributed through the local poor boards of the state. When one realizes that the number needing assistance had reached over a million, the $10,000,000 was of little help. Some persons questioned the legality of using state funds for relief of the poor. But the Pennsylvania Supreme Court ruled, "To hold that the state cannot or must not aid its poor would strip the state of a means of self-preservation and might conceive untold hardships and difficulties for the future."

A state Emergency Relief Board was set up by a second special Legislature in 1932 to supervise aid to the unemployed. Money was still given through local boards, according to unemployment. Some unemployed were hired to work on state highways. To get the money an Emergency Relief Sales Tax Act was passed. One percent of the gross income from sales was paid to the state, but it was not collected directly from the consumer as was the sales tax beginning in 1953.

The number of people receiving state aid grew from 676,000 in September, 1932, to 1,988,000 in May, 1933. In March of 1933 over 37% of all workers were unable to gain employment. Aid to these people came first in the form of a food check that could be exchanged for a stated amount of food at any store. In the winter of 1932 free fuel and shoes were added. Seeds, medicine, surplus foods, clothing and rent were later given. Beginning in the winter of 1934 the money was given directly to the families to buy what they needed. By that time relief was costing the state $10,000,000 a month. However, the most a family could receive was $35 per month.

Veterans of World War I and the Spanish-American War received a cash bonus from the state after the election of 1933. Pennsylvania voters approved a $50,000,000 bond sale to give the men an average of $139.60 each. This not only served as a reward to the men but also put more money in circulation.

Strikers Gain Protection

Since the Civil War private police hired by the coal and iron industries had been used to protect property of the companies. These men were often unlawfully brutal, especially toward the new immigrants. In 1929 two coal and iron police had beaten a miner to death near Pittsburgh. The Legislature, under Governor Fisher, restricted the use of such police with the Mansfield Bill of 1929. Governor Pinchot called for total abolition of private policemen. The Assembly refused to pass his bill, but the Governor simply refused to give police commissions and thus killed the private police forces.

In 1933 there were 629 labor strikes for higher wages, better conditions and union recognition. That summer the miners of Fayette County struck and demanded union recognition. Governor Pinchot sent Erie National Guard troops to Brownsville on July 29 for two weeks. For the first time in American history, troops were sent to protect the strikers. All violence was stopped and the strike ended in an amicable agreement.

In October of the same year 150,000 textile workers in 10,000 plants throughout the State struck. Women and children, textile workers, had been working 50 to 54 hours a week for as little as one to three dollars a week. In many of these "sweat-shops" workers were forced to take sewing home to keep up their work. At that time the Pennsylvania Legislature ratified the Child Labor Amendment to the United States Constitution to restrict children under 18 from working throughout the country. However, the necessary 38 states have not ratified the proposal in over fifty years.

Pennsylvania Department of Transportation

Automobiles made Pennsylvanians realize that roads which served horses and wagons would have to be paved for twentieth century travel. The 1910 road above was in Adams County.

Pennsylvania Department of Transportation

Blacktop toads like this one in Monroe County were built throughout the State under Governor Pinchot to provide work for unemployed and "get the farmer out of the mud."

Farmers Get Out of the Mud

"Get the farmer out of the mud" was a Pinchot campaign slogan. Most of the main highways had been hard-topped during the Fisher Administration, so rural roads were next. Actually two purposes were served in the road building program. Improved transportation resulted and employment was provided for thousands of men. In 1929 there were 8,000 highway workmen, in 1934 there were 80,000. Much money from the Federal government was donated to the state in this period. In 1933 a $50,000,000 road bond issue was approved by the voters of the state.

Over 10,000 miles of secondary, farm-to-market roads were built. These were of crushed stone surfaced with inexpensive bituminous asphalt. These roads were good in all seasons of the year and cheap to maintain. In appreciation of these roads, many people continued to call these black-topped highways "Pinchot roads." In addition to improving the state roads, the State Highway Department temporarily took over thousands of miles of township roads. By using Federal and state funds to improve these township roads, thousands of otherwise unemployed men were given work. Twenty thousand miles of township roads and 1,000 miles of borough and city streets were added permanently to the state system. Six hundred miles of road from abandoned turnpikes were also added. By 1935 Pinchot's administration had taken over 35,000 miles of highways, double the mileage of state roads in 1931.

More road-building and conservation work was undertaken by the Federal government which set up 94 Civilian Conservation Corps camps in the state. The CCC in Pennsylvania was made up of 16,000 young men, 18-25 years of age, who planted more than 7,000,000 trees and built 1,350 miles of roads and over 3,000 miles of trails through our forests areas. Fine recreation dams were built in 21 areas that have since been popular state parks. Over a thousand fish dams were also built. In January 1934 the 17,000 acre Pymatuning reservoir was completed. It reduced floods and provided water and recreation for the northwestern part of the state.

State Takes Over Liquor Sales

The election of Franklin Roosevelt as President in 1932 was followed by the national repeal of prohibition in 1933. Pennsylvania was the 35th of the necessary 36 states to approve its repeal. However, Governor Pinchot always opposed the liquor industry, and prohibitionists had given him their votes in the 1930 election. On the basis of that support a special Liquor Control Act was passed that provided that all liquor and wines had to be sold in state-owned stores. Some states allow grocery, drug or other stores to handle the sales. But in Pennsylvania strict regulations were set up to enforce the lawful selling of alcoholic beverages. No sales room can be within 300 feet of any church, school, hospital or playground. One fifth of the boroughs and a third of the townships still forbid the sale of alcoholic beverages in their municipalities.

THE LITTLE NEW DEAL

Hard Times Put Democrats in Power

Gifford Pinchot was one of the most active Governors in Pennsylvania history. However, despite the fine work of his administration, economic conditions in the state were still poor at the end of his term. Few new homes had been built. Over one-third of all families renting houses shared them with others. One-third of the homes were still without electricity. Employment had dropped 31% in four years. Store sales were cut almost by half. Many small, individually-owned stores went out of business, as "chain" stores now controlled 34% of the retail business with fewer store units.

Democrats took control of Pennsylvania in 1935 after the election of George H. Earle of Montgomery County. He was the first Democrat elected Governor in forty years and only the second since the Civil War. Joseph Guffey of Pittsburgh was elected the first Democratic United States Senator from Pennsylvania in over 75 years. When Franklin Roosevelt ran for a second term as President in 1936 he was to be the first Democratic candidate to receive Pennsylvania's electoral vote since James Buchanan in 1856. The Roosevelt administration brought about rapid political, social and economic changes that were known as "The New Deal." The ad-

THE LATER DECADES

Gimbel Pennsylvania Art Collection

This stark painting of the Mt. Washington section of Pittsburgh reminds us of the grim bleakness that came to many industrial areas during the depression.

ministration of George Earle came to be called "The Little New Deal."

State Takes Action on Relief and Labor Problems

Unemployment and suffering continued to plague the state. Aid to the needy was consolidated into a new Department of Public Assistance which set up unpaid County Boards of Assistance to be responsible for local administration of aid. Employees of the department were hired on a merit system to keep their jobs free from political pressure. The Department of Public Assistance gave financial aid to the aged, widows, children and the blind. When possible, jobs were created for the unemployed through the Federal Works Progress Administration. Most of this type of hiring was for highway work. It reached its peak in 1938 when 140,000 men were working on Pennsylvania roads. When the W.P.A. was abandoned in 1943, only 2,000 were so employed.

Labor legislation was enacted to give workmen better conditions and to control the great powers of large corporations. These laws established improved labor relations, a minimum wage for women and children, unemployment compensation and abolished sweat shops and home work. The use of private police and anti-labor injunctions was also restricted. State Police were withheld from all strikes except to maintain order.

Labor unions grew very strong with the aid of Federal and State laws that required collective bargaining between workers and employers whenever requested by the workers. To gain union recognition in steel plants at Johnstown, a serious strike developed in 1937. Governor Earle refused to send State Police or National Guard troops to guard non-union workers. He ordered the plant closed until a settlement was reached. At the Hershey Chocolate Corporation, a sit-down strike developed with workers refusing to leave the plant. In this way they hoped to keep others from taking their jobs while a settlement was being reached. The sit-down strike method was later outlawed, but strong unions developed in practically all industries under the leadership of the new Congress of Industrial Organizations (CIO). Few strikes since this period have resulted in violence.

The Pennsylvania State Police and The Highway Patrol were merged into one unit called the Pennsylvania State Motor Police in 1937. State Police had done the criminal detection, whereas the Patrol's work had been confined to checking highway traffic on their bright red motorcycles. To be classified as patrolmen was a blow to State Police pride, so in 1943 the name was changed back to the Pennsylvania State Police. The patrolmen had reason to be proud also, for between 1935 and 1939 highway deaths in Pennsylvania had been reduced 40%.

An important school law adopted by Earle's administration established what is called teacher tenure. For many years teachers had felt insecure because they did not know until school time whether or not they had been rehired. Sometimes they were fired for political or other reasons not related to school work. Women were sometimes dismissed simply because they got married. It was a common practice to force teachers to give part of their salary back to keep their jobs during the depression. Since the tenure act of 1937, a teacher has two years in which to prove his worth. Thereafter, he can be dismissed only for a few serious charges.

Floods Cause Huge Damage

In March, 1936, heavy snows melted, and five inches of rain fell in one day to create one of the most terrible floods in the history of the Allegheny, Monongahela, Conemaugh, Ohio and Susquehanna Valleys. Property damage totaled close to a half billion dollars and almost 200 people died. Over 400,000 people were left homeless. Pittsburgh considers 25 feet of water in its rivers as flood stage, but on March 28 the level rose to 46.4 feet. Farther down along the Ohio damage was even worse. Over 200 towns in the state were partially flooded. Over 275 highway bridges had to be replaced. Beginning in 1937 the United States Army Engineers began flood control work in the Ohio River drainage area.

Public Authorities Extend Government Services

The State Constitution prohibited the state from going into debt more than one million dollars. It also restricted the borrowing power of local governments. But the rapidly expanding work program made necessary by the depression required large amounts of money. To get around the debt limits imposed by the Constitution,

United States Army Corps of Engineers

Following the disastrous floods of 1936, flood control dams were built in western Pennsylvania. The Conemaugh Dam, above, was the largest. It can hold almost 100 billion gallons of water. It was completed in 1953.

a new kind of government unit was created. These are called authorities, and they could borrow money to finance the building of public works and facilities which are then rented to the parent government to pay off the loan. In this way the government met the public needs but legally was not in debt. The General State Authority built buildings for the state. Municipal authorities constructed various kinds of public facilities for local communities. Housing authorities built public housing properties. By adding their share to public projects, state and local governments could thus get Federal gifts of money through the Public Works Administration. Many people were employed on these projects who might not otherwise have had jobs.

An example of this type of project was the Pennsylvania Turnpike Commission, set up to build a toll highway across the State. The Federal government contributed $26,000,000 to the project. The Commission, created by the state, then sold millions of dollars worth of bonds. Walter A. Jones of Pittsburgh gets credit for having brought the idea to reality. A 160-mile, four-lane, controlled access, all weather highway from Irwin near Pittsburgh to Middlesex near Harrisburg was begun in October 1938. It used the old right-of-way of the old unfinished South Penn Railroad. By using the old tunnels and moving huge quantities of earth, the superhighway was built with no more than a three% grade. The "dream highway" was finished within two years and opened for traffic October 1, 1940. By charging a toll the road was to pay for itself.

The success of the turnpike highway caused extensions to be laid west to the Ohio border, and east to the Delaware River and north to Scranton. Other states have copied the system and it became possible to travel from New York to Chicago by superhighways built by the turnpike commissions.

Progress was made in other fields of transportation as well. In 1934 the Budd Company of Philadelphia produced the first diesel streamliner, *The Zephyr*. Electric railroading replaced coal-burning locomotives on the Pennsylvania Railroad from Philadelphia to New York in 1933. By 1938 electric trains used 2,000 miles of track as far west as Harrisburg. The giant Safe Harbor Dam completed in 1934 across the Susquehanna provided part of the power for run-

Pennsylvania Turnpike Commission

Beginning with abandoned tunnels of an unfinished railroad, America's first super highway was to follow.

The old railroad tunnel was improved to use as a two lane highway tunnel and then duplicated for dual tunnels.

Pennsylvania Turnpike Commission

Pennsylvania Turnpike Commission

Linking the East to the West is an important role played by Pennsylvania's Turnpike.

ning the trains. Electric passenger trains averaged 70 miles per hour in southeastern Pennsylvania scheduled runs.

More Services Demand More Taxes

Along with the expansion of state activities in aid for the needy, the State began to take over the care of all mentally disabled persons. By an act of 1938 all buildings, property and equipment of local and county mental institutions were transferred to the state. The expense of maintaining and expanding these mental hospitals had proved too great for local governments.

Providing adequate milk at a price whereby farmers could make a fair profit, had been a problem for many years. In 1933 Governor Pinchot established a temporary Milk Control Commission. Governor Earle strengthened the law to stop milk price cuts which reduced the price paid the farmer. The Commission set the price to assure adequate returns to the dairy farmer. By this act farm income increased. Numerous suits were filed to declare the law unconstitutional. Courts upheld the law and the Commission continued to control the price of milk.

In order to pay for all these extended services by the state, numerous new taxes were introduced. Cigarettes and liquor were taxed. Gasoline taxes were increased. Corporation income and loans were taxed. To bring the small individually-owned businesses into a stronger position to compete, a graduated tax was placed on all chain stores and theatres. Under this tax law, the more stores a firm owned, the greater the tax. A graduated income tax for individuals was approved by the Assembly also. Both of these graduated taxes were ruled unconstitutional by the State Supreme Court. Graduated taxes violate "Article 8, Section 1," of the State Constitution which provides, "All taxes shall be uniform."

Election laws were all combined into the Election Code and personal registration was provided in all districts. Until this time, personal registration of voters was required only in cities. In boroughs and townships registry assessors prepared lists of voters. Then a person had to register personally in his district to vote. If he failed to vote every two years, he had to re-register. Watchers from each party check to see that each person votes only once.

The Political Balance Shifts Again

Governor Earle's administration had been filled with lively disagreements in the Legislature when the Republicans kept control of the Senate in 1935. In 1937 the Democrats got control of both houses, but many of the more important laws passed were declared unconstitutional. The Supreme Court did not think the graduated income tax and setting maximum hours of work were within the constitutional rights of the Legislature. By 1938 trouble brewed within the executive branch. Attorney General Charles Margiotti claimed that some members of the administration were corrupt and guilty of misconduct in office. Margiotti was dismissed, but he presented his charges to the Republican district attorney of Dauphin County in which the capital is located.

Charges were filed against Governor Earle and 14 of his officials. Since 1938 was an election year, much political maneuvering took place. Democrats tried to stop the investigation. Republicans wanted to do everything possible to embarrass the Democrats. A grand jury conducted an investigation and reported before the election that the charges were unfounded. Great harm was done to the reputation of the Earle administration, but one cannot deny that many gains were made in social, labor and economic legislation during this period.

Superior Court Judge Arthur H. James of Luzerne County, an ex-coal miner and Lieutenant Governor, 1927-1931, was nominated by the Republicans in 1938. Gifford Pinchot made a determined bid for his third term but was unsuccessful. Factions within the Democratic Party fought among themselves and the Republicans returned to power. Governor Earle was a candidate for United States Senator James J. Davis' position but was unsuccessful.

Governor James pledged restoration of jobs in private industry to replace WPA employment. "Rule by the overlords of labor" was to stop. Practically one of every five persons in the state was still being supported by the government. A new Department of Commerce was formed to attract and expand private industry. But widespread unemployment continued until the beginning of World War II in 1939.

Since the beginning of the depression "bootleg" coal mining had been going on in the southern anthracite coal fields. When many company mines shut down operations, the unemployed miners leased land and took the coal found under it. Usually the coal was owned by some company. Company police were forbidden to trespass on the top of the land which was leased to the miners. If arrested for stealing the coal, the miners were found not guilty by friendly juries. The coal was sold at low prices and kept the price of commercially mined coal down also. Over 10,000 men were engaged in this bootlegging in 1941 in 3,000 mines. With the improvement of the coal business, the practice declined, but as late as 1947 some 2,500 men were still digging bootleg coal.

DEPRESSION VANISHES IN A SECOND WORLD WAR

By the summer of 1939, war in Europe was becoming a reality. That summer Pennsylvania's National Guard troops had a special mobilization at Manassas, Virginia. The following fall the Federal government called the Pennsylvania men into full-time duty at Indiantown Gap, and the camp became a regular army post. A wartime draft was set up the same year. When the Japanese struck Pearl Harbor in Hawaii on December 7, 1941, thousands of Pennsylvanians were already in uniform. By the end of the war 1,170,000 men and women from Pennsylvania had joined the armed forces. Over 33,000 Pennsylvanians lost their lives in the war.

Pennsylvanians on Many Fronts

Fighting men from Pennsylvania served in the 28th Division which was sent to England in 1943 and invaded France on July 22, 1944. Paris was occupied by the "Keystone Division". They drove the Nazis across France, Belgium, Luxembourg and back into Germany. The "Keystone Division" was the first American unit in Germany. In the desperate attack by the Germans at the Battle of the Bulge, nine divisions hit the Pennsylvanians who were supposed to be resting. By holding out as long as possible the men played a large part in bringing the war to a victorious end. With the conclusion of the war in Europe, the division was returned to Indiantown Gap and deactivated in 1945. The following year it became the Pennsylvania National Guard again. The Germans nicknamed this division the "Bloody Bucket Division" because of the red keystone patch worn on their uniforms.

Volunteers and drafted men were active on all fronts of the war. Pennsylvania men earned more Congressional Medals of Honor than men from any other state. Thirty-two won the nation's highest honor as compared to New York's 30 and Texas's 26. Corporal Charles "Commando" Kelly of Pittsburgh was honored for knocking out machine gun nests and killing 40 snipers in Italy. Pfc. Alton W. Knappenberger of Spring Mount held back two companies, 300 men, single handedly on the Anzio bench head in Italy. Marine Corporal Anthony P. Damato of Shenandoah smothered a Japanese hand grenade with his body to save the lives of his companions.

Over a hundred Army and Air Corps generals came from Pennsylvania. Chief of Staff of the entire army was five-star General George C. Marshall of Uniontown. President Truman said, "He takes his place at the head of the great commanders of history." General Marshall later served as the United States Secretary of State and as Secretary of Defense. His Marshall Plan has been given credit for saving many nations in Europe from depression and communism.

Other leaders in the war from Pennsylvania were General Joseph McNarney of Emporium, who was to follow General Eisenhower as head of the German Occupation. General Henry H. Arnold of Gladwyne headed the Army Air Corps throughout the war. After the war he turned the command over to General Carl Spaatz of Boyertown who had headed the air forces in Europe during the war. Colonel Francis Gabreski of Oil City shot down more enemy planes than any other pilot. Admiral Harold R. Stark of Wilkes-Barre was Chief of Naval Operations at the beginning of the war and later headed the Allied fleets in Europe.

Forty naval and military posts were in operation in Pennsylvania during the war. Indiantown Gap was used to train hundreds of thousands of men. Camp Reynolds, Mercer County, was set up in 1942 and at the end of the war was used as a prisoner-of-war camp. New Cumberland Reception Center inducted over half a million civil-

290 OUR PENNSYLVANIA HERITAGE

ians into military life. Middletown Air Depot serviced the entire eastern seaboard with airplane parts. Carlisle Barracks was a medical center, and Harrisburg Academy became an intelligence school. Ordinance depots at Letterkenny, Cressona, Williamsport, Meadville and Danville stored munitions. Thirty-eight colleges trained soldiers and sailors in various fields of study.

Civilians Produce for War

On the home front Pennsylvania organized civilians to be ready for all types of emergencies. Before the United States entered the war in 1941, state, county and local councils of defense were established. Over half a million citizens served as air raid wardens, auxiliary police and firemen and in emergency units of all types. Victory gardens were planted by hundreds of thousands of Pennsylvanians to grow needed food. Salvage drives were made to collect needed rubber, aluminum, steel and other products. Ration boards were established to maintain a fair distribution of meat,

Pennsylvania in World War II was called "The Arsenal of Democracy" because it supplied so many materials of war. This scene at Reading show molten steel being poured into molds for fashioning into the "sinews of war."

THE LATER DECADES

sugar, shoes, gasoline, tires and automobiles. Highways were patrolled to allow faster movement of military units, and schools gave up 20% of their typewriters to the armed forces. A Pennsylvania Reserve Defense Corps was kept ready to guard strategic places.

Unemployment ceased and a worker shortage took its place. Jobs for 2,500,000 workers were available by 1943. Farm workers were very scarce, and in some cases farmers' children were returned from the army to work. The State Department of Commerce organized a listing of all available factories, and over 13 billion dollars was spent on war contracts in the State. More coal was produced than at any other time since 1930. Cement production zoomed. Oil reached its highest production since 1897. More steel was produced in Pennsylvania than in Germany and Japan combined.

A 36-inch mortar to fire the world's heaviest projectile was produced by the Mesta Machine Company in Pittsburgh. The Frankford Arsenal developed and the Miller Printing Machine Company of Pittsburgh produced a recoilless rifle to fire 75mm. shells. A new improved torpedo was developed at Pymatuning Lake by the Westinghouse plant of Sharon. Many of these Westinghouse torpedoes sent Japanese ships to the bottom of the oceans. Jeeps were developed by the Bantam Automobile Company of Butler. Sylvania Electric, with plants throughout the State, developed and produced the highly secret VT fuse which exploded shells near a target. Hershey Chocolate Company developed and produced an emergency chocolate food.

Philadelphia's navy yards produced 50 large warships including three of the world's largest battleships and four huge aircraft carriers. At one time 70,000 workers were engaged in work at the yards. Pittsburgh, Ambridge and Erie produced 385 ocean-going landing crafts. One-third of the nation's tank ships were produced at the Chester yards. Pennsylvania's Farm Show Building at Harrisburg was converted into an aeronautics school that graduated 12,000 students. Later it became an airplane engine overhaul plant.

Major General Edward Martin of Washington County was elected Governor of Pennsylvania in 1942. He had held many offices in the state and was commander of the 28th Division when war broke

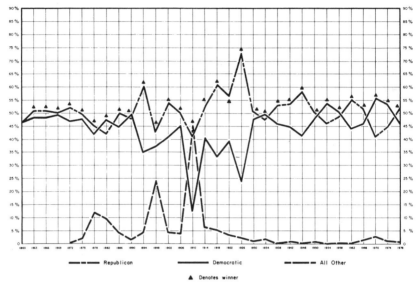

Percentage of votes cast by party: 1860-1978 (Gubernational Election)
Courtesy of Pennsylvania Department of Commerce

out. Because of the war, many state governmental activities were curtailed or eliminated. As in the Civil War, the State debt was substantially reduced. Obligations were cut from 124 million dollars to 44 million. In 1944, Pennsylvania soldiers were given the right to vote by mail. Previously, polling places for soldiers had to be set up in their military units. The majority of Pennsylvania's votes went for Franklin D. Roosevelt who began his fourth term as President.

POSTWAR PERIOD BRINGS CHANGES AND NEW PROBLEMS

Post war planning had been underway since 1943, when a commission was established. Natural resources, agriculture, stream pollution and transportation were studied. Many counties and cities throughout the State did the same thing. Allegheny County's Conference on Community Development and the Beaver County

Planning and Zoning Commission set their sights on the future.

As the war drew to a close in 1945, a State Soil Conservation Commission began work at controlling soil erosion to stop the washing away of valuable top soil from farms. Large war crops and little fertilizer had damaged the same fields that had also been neglected in depression years. During the war much coal had been hastily stripped in areas where it was near the surface. Great waste piles and deep water holes were often left when the coal was gone. The Bituminous Coal Stripping Act of 1945 required that in the future all stripped areas were to be filled in and leveled to their original contours. Later the same law was applied to the anthracite areas. Some operators not only returned the land to use but planted trees as well. To improve the conditions of our streams and rivers, mining companies and industries were prohibited from dumping any pollution or wastes into streams.

Conservation of human resources was also undertaken. War medical examinations indicated that many Pennsylvanians had not had proper medical care. Beginning in 1945, school children were to be given dental and medical examinations every two years. Those who needed free treatment were to get it. Over half the children examined the first year were in need of medical attention. This was more pronounced in the larger cities. When the Federal government offered aid for hot school lunches, the program was begun in Pennsylvania schools in 1946.

Increased automobile accidents and resulting costs brought about the passage of a law requiring car owners to prove their financial responsibility. Beginning in 1947 all automobile owners had to have liability insurance or post a bond when involved in an accident. The Pennsylvania State Police were steadily increased in number from the original 228 to over 3,000. Beginning 1946, their work was aided by the use of three-way radio service in the patrol cars.

Politics Since World War II

Neither major party has been able to dominate during the war period. Republican's held the governor's office from 1946 to 1954—with Governors Martin, Duff and Fine. Democrat Leader

and Lawrence held the Governorship from 1954 to 1962. Then followed Republicans William W. Scranton and Raymond P. Shafer. Democrat Milton J. Shapp, chosen in 1970, and again in 1974, was the first Governor in recent times who was eligible to succeed himself for a second term. Republican Richard Thornburgh was elected Governor in 1978 and 1982. Democrat Robert Casey won in 1986 and 1990. Republican Thomas J. Ridge won in 1994. Governor Ridge resigned October 5, 2001, as he was appointed to be Director of Homeland Security by President George W. Bush. Lieutenant Governor Mark Schweiker is the Acting Governor serving until a new Governor is inaugurated in 2003.

The same bipartisan trend was evident in the choice of United States Representatives and Senators. Republican Edward Martin, defeating Senator Guffey in 1946, was the first Governor to become United States Senator since 1855. After serving two terms, he was succeeded by James H. Duff. Democrat Joseph S. Clark, elected in 1958, served two terms. Republican Hugh Scott, elected to the second senatorial post in 1958, served as Minority Leader when he retired in 1976. Republican John Heinz served from 1977-1992. Democrat Harris Wolford, 1992-1994, and Republican Richard Santorum in 1996. Republican Richard Schweiker defeated Senator Clark in 1968 and Republican Arlen Spector was elected in 1980. Meanwhile, the Pennsylvania delegation in the United States House of Representatives has been about evenly divided between Democrats and Republicans.

Bipartisanship was also the rule at the local level, although numerous areas adhered to one-party rule. The tendency was for the larger cities to prefer Democrats and the smaller ones, especially suburbs of large cities and rural areas, to prefer Republicans. Republicans tended in a conservative direction, with Democrats taking a more liberal stance, although the differences were seldom sharp or extreme.

In presidential elections, Pennsylvanians preferred Republican Eisenhower in 1952 and 1956; then Democrats Kennedy in 1960, Johnson in 1964, and Humphrey in 1968. In 1972 Pennsylvanians voted for Republican Nixon, in 1976 for Democrat Carter, for Republicans Reagan in 1980 and 1984, Bush in 1988 and Democrat Clinton in 1992.

Loss of National Power

The population of Pennsylvania grew at a slower rate than many of the sun-belt states after 1940. First California, then Texas and Florida surpassed Pennsylvania in population. The 1990 census showed Pennsylvania with less than 0.1 percent population growth.

In 1950 Pennsylvania had its representation in the United States Congress reduced from 33 to 30. The 1960 census resulted in the representation being cut to 27 members, in 1970 to 25, 1980 to 23 and in 1990 to 21. Since 1920 the electoral vote had been reduced by 17. The number of Congress members from Pennsylvania was reduced from 36 to 19 by 2000. Pennsylvania's political power was reduced accordingly.

Social Changes

Many ideas that were time honored began to change in recent years. The idea that Sunday must be a day of quiet religious observance gave way following World War II. Previous to that time it was unlawful to have commercial dancing, motion pictures, athletic games, or sale of alcoholic beverages on Sunday. Betting on horse races or holding lotteries were criminal acts at any time.

One by one the laws were changed until by 1972 Pennsylvania had a state run lottery, betting on horse-racing and Sunday commercial entertainment. Most of the "blue" laws were repealed, but it was still illegal to sell many articles on Sunday until courts held all such laws void.

Rights of Youth and the Aged

The rights to vote, own property, get married and hold many offices were granted to citizens who reached the age of 18 years rather than the previous 21 years of age. Young persons were named to boards of trustees of State Colleges and Universities and were elected to public offices.

A Department of Aging was established in 1978 to advance the well being of older citizens. The department advocates individual and class rights and needs of older citizens and the adult handicapped. The percentage of citizens of Pennsylvania who are older than 50 years grew in recent years as people live longer and some younger persons move to other states for employment. Special laws were passed to protect the rights of the elderly.

Rights of Women

Pennsylvania had agreed in September 1972 to a proposed Federal constitutional amendment that "Equality of rights under the law shall not be denied or abridged because of the sex of the individual." The voters added those words to the State Constitution.

A woman had first been appointed to a State cabinet position in 1923 when Dr. Ellen Potter was named Secretary of Welfare. The first woman State Supreme Court justice was Anne X. Alpern, named by Governor Lawrence in 1961.

The first woman elected to the General Assembly was Mrs. Mabelle M. Kirkbridge of Montgomery County in 1921. In 1994 there were 19 women. Mrs. Flora Vare of Philadelphia was the first woman elected to the State Senate in 1925 to serve two years. Mrs. Jeannette Reibman of Northampton County was elected to a full term in the Senate in 1966 and six more times. There were four women senators in 1994.

The first woman to be elected to a state-wide position was Genevieve Blatt of Pittsburgh who was elected Secretary of Internal Affairs in 1952. . Grace Sloan of Clarion was elected State Treasurer in 1960, Auditor-general in 1964 and state Treasurer again in 1969 and 1973.

Women held hundreds of locally elected offices throughout the state.

Minority Group Citizens

The number of black citizens in Pennsylvania has pratically doubled since World War II. In 2000 there was one black citizen for every 10 white persons. Most of the blacks moved into Pennsylvania from southern United States to the cities of Philadelphia, Pittsburgh, Chester and Harrisburg.

In 2000 there were 12 black men and three black women serving in the House of Representatives. Two represented Pittsburgh and eleven were from Philadelphia. Leroy Irvis of Pittsburgh who served in the House beginning in 1959, was majority leader in 1969-1972, and was Speaker of the House in 1977 and 1983-1988. There were three black senators from Philadelphia by 1993, including the first black woman in 1984, and one in 2000.

Andrew Bradley was appointed as the first black cabinet member in 1957 and served as Secretary of Property and Supplies until 1963. Robert Nix has served as a Congressman from Philadelphia for 20 years beginning in 1958. Robert Nix, Junior, was elected to the State Supreme Court in 1971 and became Chief Justice.

C. DeLores Tucker of Philadelphia became the first black and woman Secretary of State in 1971.

Hispanics

A new minority group appeared in the 1970 census as over 40,000 Hispanics were found. Over half of this population was in Philadelphia with Pittsburgh, Bethlehem, Reading and Lancaster having significant settlements. A Council on Opportunity for the Spanish Speaking was set up in 1972. The Hispanics moved into cities as the more affluent whites and blacks moved out. By 2000 there were 394,088 Hispanics in Pennsylvania.

Movement from the Rural Areas

The number of citizens living on a farm economy decreased continually following World War II. Between 1960 and 1970 over 300,000 people left the rural areas. During the same period hundreds of thousands moved out of the large cities. This has resulted in more persons living in suburban areas. Both the rural areas and large cities found that much of their population was elderly and poor. Beginning in the 1970s there was a movement to selective rural areas within commuting distance to some urban areas.

Movement from Cities to Suburbs

As you noted in chapter one, hundreds of thousands of people have moved out of Philadelphia into neighboring counties. In 1990, the only cities that did not lose population were Allentown, Bethlehem, Coatesville, Easton and Lancaster. Some suburban communities were now bigger than cities. Not only have people moved from cities to suburbs, but many factories have made the same move. Because of this, people now move to the suburbs for better living and working conditions.

Employment

Pennsylvania had been known for generations as the state of great coal mines, huge steel mills, numerous farms and many factories. Transportation also was big business.

Following World War II, it became cheaper and cleaner for industry and railroads to switch from the use of coal to other fuels.

The new factory of the Eberhard Faber Company in Mountain Top, a suburb of Wilkes-Barre, is an example of the new industries built in Pennsylvania recently. The attractive factory manufactures millions of pencils for schools, business and consumer use. The factory was formerly in the New York City area.

Anthracite coal mining was most seriously affected. The number of coal miners in northeastern Pennsylvania was reduced by almost 100,000 men between 1927 and 1950. Between 1950 and 1970 another 62,000 reduction of work force took place in hard coal mining. By 1990 only 2,250 were so employed.

Soft, bituminous, coal mining saw the work force reduced from 131,000 in 1927 to 94,000 in 1950, to about 14,000 in 1990. Actually, the production of soft coal in 1990 was as great as in the 1960s, but the production per man was increased by the use of machines. The use of coal for steel and electric production increased but fewer men were needed. Many mining jobs were abolished as men reached the retirement age. But in the late 1970s new jobs were opening in soft coal fields in the states of Wyoming and Montana rather than Pennsylvania.

The Pennsylvania Department of Commerce, established in 1939 to attract industry, set up an Industrial Development Authority in 1956 to lend money to build factories to attract industry. As new factories were built, literally hundreds of thousands of new jobs were added. Between 1968 and 1972 over 1,200 new plants were built in Pennsylvania.

The same story was true as railroad employment decreased. The older workers retired and few new workers were employed. Truck lines, airlines, bus lines and automobile service agencies hired many young people, but often the jobs were in cities different from railroad centers. A former locomotive plant in Eddystone became a manufacturing plant for giant Boeing helicopters. Piper aircraft, made in Lock Haven, ceased operation. Volkswagen automobiles were made in New Stanton beginning in 1978, but the plant was converted to a Japanese TV tube factory.

Television and electronics, which were only dreams to most people before World War II, became the basis of employment for thousands of workers as RCA, GTE, and General Electric expanded some plants and built new ones in Pennsylvania. A small company founded in 1941 in Harrisburg as Aviation Marine Products, turned to electronics and by 1973 employed over 5,000 in plants throughout Central Pennsylvania. AMP now has plants throughout the United States and in twelve foreign countries. The fortune earned by Milton Shapp from his electronics companies helped him to be elected Governor in 1970.

Television stations were started by private corporations in each of the metropolitan areas. Millions of receiving sets brought about the need for performers, announcers, technicians, salesmen and repairmen. Thousands of new jobs were created. In 1968 the legislature set up a public television network with stations in Allentown, Bethlehem, Erie, Hershey, Philadelphia, Scranton, WilkesBarre, and University Park.

The steel industry was to be the largest factory employer in Pennsylvania. United States Steel is the largest single employer. Its headquarters are in a new sixty-four floor building in Pittsburgh, and it has plants throughout the state and nation. The change of the source of iron ore to Canada and South America caused United States Steel to build a huge plant in Bucks County along the Delaware River. Thousands of steel workers moved there as older plants were shut down elsewhere. Imports of Japanese and German steel had an adverse effect on Pennsylvania.

Farming became less desirable as a means of livelihood as equipment and labor became expensive. Small farms became uneconomic. Thousands of small farms were abandoned or merged into larger ones. Many became sites for housing developments. Farmers retired, moved, or went to work in town. Some marginal farm areas are part of the poverty area of Appalachia.

By 1990 there were areas that had lost their industries such as coal in parts of Fayette County, steel in Beaver County or the railroad in Altoona where unemployment was still high in the nineties. However, most people were employed at jobs that paid adequate wages. More women were employed. Blacks from the South and Hispanics moved into the cities to take up jobs that had been left by those who went into more skilled jobs.

The problem of matching the possible employees with jobs had been taken on somewhat by the state through several of its departments. In 1966 a Department of Community Affairs was established to help communities and their citizens solve such problems as housing, redevelopment and poverty.

The problem of changing a busy dangerous crossroad to a smooth interchange of Interstate Highways 83 and 283, U.S. Highway 322 and local streets costs the Transportation Department more than $10,000,000. This interchange near Harrisburg is exceeded only by the Schuylkill Expressway and the Penn Lincoln Parkway in traffic.

Changing State Government

More government to do more things has seemed to be the change in State Government since World War II. Many of the activities carried on by local or county governments had been taken over by the state. Many things that citizens used to do for themselves were now being done by the State Government.

Transportation

Prior to World War II most cities, boroughs and townships took care of their own streets and roads. In townships, if a taxpayer was short of cash he could work off his township or "road tax" by giving the township several days of physical labor. He would work for the township on days he felt he was not needed on his own farm.

As the township roads became part of the state system of highways, or later a part of the interstate system, the construction cost millions of dollars per mile and became a state responsibility. The roads were maintained from funds from gasoline taxes. As you would expect, the tax was raised several times during the period until it reached fourteen cents in 1983. The Federal government grants the state money to aid in building and maintaining interstate and the older highways designated as U.S. routes.

Railroads gradually lost most of their passenger business to private automobiles, buses and airplanes. In the 1970s, a railroad passenger train took seven hours to travel from Philadelphia to Pittsburgh. A private automobile or motor bus could make the trip by turnpike and expressway in less than six hours and a regular jetliner in less than an hour. The only long distant trains left were two east and west each day that crossed Pennsylvania as part of a national system that connected New York and Washington with Chicago. Philadelphia was served also by electric "metroliners" that connected New York and Washington. State subsidized commuter trains still served Philadelphia and Pittsburgh.

In 2000, most persons in Pennsylvania traveled by private automobile and those without automobiles used busses to reach their destinations.

The once rich Pennsylvania Railroad merged with the New York Central to become the Penn Central but by 1972 it was bankrupt. The Reading Railroad and the Lehigh Valley Railroads declared themselves bankrupt also. The lines were consolidated in a government owned organization called Conrail.

By 1972, 67 percent of the freight in Pennsylvania was carried by trucks, only 24 percent by rail, 8 percent by boat and less than 1 percent by airplane.

Between 1965 and 1970 the number of airline passengers boarding planes in Pennsylvania doubled so that over 6,000,000 persons used airline travel in 1970. Air freight tonnage also doubled.

The state realized that all transportation is affected by any segment so in 1970 the Department of Transportation (Penn DOT) was established to replace the Department of Highways. The development owned organization called Conrail, later sold to Norfolk Southern, Western and CSX.

Public Utilities

In 1937 the Public Utility Commission was created to provide citizens with reasonable rates and adequate service. The state enjoyed general growth and good services in telephones, water, natural gas and electricity. The demand for inexpensive and greater

Metropolitan Edison Company
Nuclear energy power plants for electricity came into use after World War II. The Three Mile Island plant near Middletown, pictured above, gained world wide attention in 1979 because of a near fatal mishap in the unit on the left.

supplies of electricity brought the approval of nuclear energy plants. There were three such plants in 1979. The one on Three Mile Island in the Susquehanna south of Harrisburg had an accident. Thousands of women and children within two miles of the plant evacuated because of fear of radiation exposure. The danger subsided and people returned. The plant remained closed for seven years. The undamaged unit resumed operation.

Public Welfare

Under Governor Earle in the 1930s the state had assumed the financing of all local mental hospitals. Since one of every 20 Pennsylvanians would be having to use such facilities one time or another it was necessary to expand the existing facilities and better care was provided. The costs soared and the number of patients increased until the last two decades as better treatment actually reduced the number of patients being institutionalized for mental illness. The state now subsidizes community resources offering inpatient and outpatient services close to home to reduce the need for institutions.

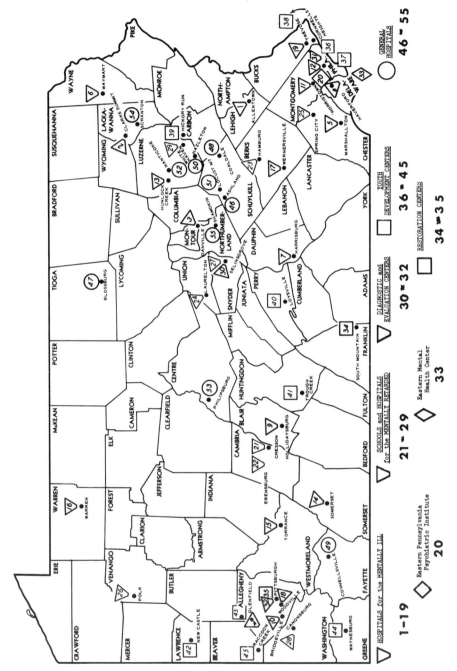

For decades counties had maintained "poor farms" to care for the financially distressed aged. As the number of persons living to old age grew and costs increased, the counties were burdened, but Federal social security gradually provided old age insurance. However, many farmers and self-employed had no social security and had to be cared for by the government. The state still worked through County Boards of Assistance to provide financial aid to those citizens over 65 years of age, children who have only one parent, blind persons, and the general needy. Often Federal money is supplied through the state to be dispensed through county boards. Apartments for the elderly are now being built in all communities.

As with the persons needing mental assistance, the state is trying to get older persons to be cared for in their own homes rather than in institutions. Orphan children are being placed with families rather than in government institutions.

In order to provide for medical assistance of citizens, the State Government built 10 general hospitals in regions where there were no hospital facilities to encourage good medical care. The state had subsidized all other hospitals since the early part of the century. Federal money has also been increased for this purpose. The state

Hunter, Caldwell & Campbell
Buchanan School is a new elementary buildiing in the Lewistown School District, Mifflin County.

has usually paid the fees of those hospitalized who have no private funds.

To reduce the need for hospital care and to provide better care for the needy, the State during the administration of Governor Scranton established Pennsy-care. This made it possible for more medical patients to be treated without being hospitalized. This program also helps those in need of medical treatment to stay in their own homes.

The idea of providing care for those in need because of financial difficulties, mental problems, health problems, or family problems caused the State to merge the old Department of Welfare and the Department of Public Assistance into a Department of Public Welfare in 1958.

Education

Many experts had predicted that the number of school children would be reduced during the 1940s. During World War II no new school buildings were built. College enrollments had declined.

Immediately following World War II, public schools were overcrowded, and the State moved immediately to help school districts to build needed buildings. Returning veterans married and the

The Pennsylvania State University's Old Main Building houses offices of the University that is the largest in the State in terms of the number of full-time students it enrolls.

Millersville University Photos
Millersville, founded as a normal school in 1859, is Pennsylvania's oldest State-owned University. The big library has replaced the attractive old one, now an executive building.

resulting children soon caused even more overcrowding. In 1947 the State School Building Authority was established to borrow the funds to build needed school buildings. The buildings were rented to the local districts for the number of years necessary to pay for the building. In 1949 the state agreed to pay part of the rent in reverse proportion to the wealth of the district. Building costs soared as more buildings were needed, but practically every school district built new high schools and several elementary schools.

Salaries for teachers, which are the greatest expense in running a school, were raised from a minimum mandate of $1,400 a year in 1947 to $2,400. New laws raised the minimum until it reached a $6,000 minimum in 1968. Thereafter, with the advent of the Public Employes Act, salaries are determined by negotiations.

Returning veterans of World War II caused colleges to overflow. As a move to provide more state aid, the fourteen State Teachers Colleges were expanded greatly from small institutions of several hundred students each to institutions with each having thousands of students. As programs were expanded the names were changed to State Colleges and in 1983 they became State Universities of the state system. State aid to the private institutions of Pennsylvania State University, University of Pittsburgh, Lincoln University and Temple University grew, and the State demanded greater control in return for lowering tuition for all students and paying high amounts of money for buildings and operating expenses. The four universities became known as state-related universities.

To provide good college education to more students, two year community colleges were begun under Governor Scranton.

The number of school districts was reduced from over 2,500 to less than 550 by a Lawrence administration law to cut administrative costs and improve education. The county school offices, headed by superintendents, were reduced to 29 intermediate units under Governor Shafer.

The great number of persons wishing to attend colleges brought pressure to have the state grant scholarships. Under Governor Lawrence in one year, $25,000 was given to State students. In 1989 about $120 million was given and $790 million lent to help hundreds of thousands of students. The Pennsylvania Higher Education Assistance Agency was established in 1963 to distribute the money.

The costs of elementary and secondary public schools, of which

Philadelphia Convention and Tourist Bureau
As part of the redevelopment of Pennsylvania in the period after World War II the beautiful Independence Mall was built by the State in Philadelphia. The large building is a new U.S. mint where coin money is made

the state pays about one half, and the costs of supporting institutions of higher learning and scholarships consume about half the state's General Fund revenues each year.

Improving Environment

Following World War II citizens demanded better living environment. Many people had thought that coal mines naturally produced sulfur drainage in streams. Steel mills produced dirt in the air. Chemical plants often killed plant life in their area, and in the late 1940s twenty-one persons died from fumes from a zinc plant in the Monongahela Valley. Almost all the cities of the state had some unsightly and often dangerous areas.

The City of Pittsburgh began a smoke abatement plan as early as 1946 and practically wiped out its infamous "smog," a combination of smoke and fog, by 1953. In 1949, the State General Assembly directed the Department of Health to study air pollution and its effect on health. In order to clean up streams, the state required communities to build sewage plants and gave financial aid for them to do so. Coal mines were sealed if abandoned. Operating mines were required to treat mine waters before turning the water into streams. Industrial plants were required to install equipment to stop pollution of the air, land and water.

As a move to make life more enjoyable in cities and elsewhere throughout the state, redevelopment plans were undertaken. The state paid part of the cost to clear blighted areas of the cities to rebuild them with taxpaying new buildings, businesses or homes. Often open areas were left to be parks such as Independence Mall in Philadelphia or Point Park in Pittsburgh. Many smaller cities and towns did the same thing with varying success.

New recreation areas were provided in state parks throughout the state. A plan was developed, under Governor Lawrence, called Project 70, to provide open space lands. Every one was to have a state park within 25 miles of his home. New recreation dams were erected to provide boating and bathing areas. Historic sites were improved.

Under Governor Shafer in 1971, a Department of Environmental Resources was established to be responsible for air, soil, minerals, forests, water and parks. This move consolidated the former

Departments of Mines, Internal Affairs, and Forests and Waters. Governor Ridge seperated the department into "Environmental Protection" and "Conservation and Natural Resources."

Who Pays for all This?

Citizens demanded and got more government services for welfare, education, transportation, environment, employment and practically every part of their lives. Who was to pay for it?

Until World War II the vast majority of taxes were paid by corporations from their income. The average citizen paid directly only if he used cigarettes or liquor which had direct taxes visible by the stamps on the packages. If corporations were taxed more, they might move to other states. Schools were supported locally by real estate taxes, but in some places real estate taxes were forcing people to move out of the district.

The first state tax to affect every taxpayer began in 1953. After the legislature met a record 355 days, it agreed to institute a one percent sales and use tax. This direct tax was on practically everything except life's three essentials: food, shelter and clothing. Later, the sales tax was raised under Governor Leader to three percent, Governor Scranton to five percent and Governor Shafer to six.

A sales tax affects the poor in many respects more than the rich. If a person makes more than he spends, he pays a lesser percent of sales tax than a poorer person. Several attempts to impose a state income tax were unsuccessful until 1972, when Governor Shapp needed more revenue to balance his budget. An attempt to institute a graduated income tax was found to be a violation of Article VIII of the State Constitution. A new law set the tax at two and three-tenths percent of all income. Persons who earn a few thousand dollars per year or persons earning a million dollars, each pays the same rate on a dollar earned.

In 1972 the state was able to pay all bills, but new taxes were needed by 1977.

Disastrous Floods of 1972 and 1977

A rain storm that started in the Caribbean area in late June of 1972 hit east central Pennsylvania with 12 inches of rain that caused the Susquehanna, Juniata, and Schuylkill Rivers and their

THE LATER DECADES

numerous branches to overflow in the worst flood in Pennsylvania history.

The dikes along the Susquehanna at Wilkes-Barre broke to allow the river to flow into downtown areas 18 feet above flood level. Numerous smaller towns and individual homes were also flooded from the New York border to Maryland.

Over 65,000 homes, 5,000 factories and businesses, 330 school buildings, and 23 colleges were damaged. Over 65,000 persons applied to the State and Federal government for disaster relief. Many farmers saw their crops destroyed. Even the Governor of Pennsylvania was forced to move out of his official home near the Susquehanna in Harrisburg.

Estimates of over two billion dollars damage were made, and more than 50 deaths resulted from the flooding. Thousands of employes were left without jobs temporarily, and in some cases factories did not reopen.

Sunbury, a river front community that built a concrete dike along the Susquehanna, was one community that escaped damage. The water came to within one inch of the top of the wall.

On July 19, 1977, the Johnstown area was flooded for the third time in a century. Almost 12 inches of rain fell in 10 hours. Six

Edward Hoffman - Capitol Films, Harrisburg

Even the home of Pennsylvania's Governor could not escape the 1972 flood.

dams broke causing the deaths of 73 people and over 200 million dollars of damage.

The floods caused long time damage to the lives, property and economics of the regions. Some factories closed and more jobs disappeared. Pennsylvania remained the nation's most flood prone state.

PENNSYLVANIA PREPARES FOR A NEW CENTURY

As Pennsylvania prepared for a new century, its citizens young and old have been made to realize that the present problems are continuing ones. As Governor Lawrence said in 1961, "Pennsylvania suffers from the fact that she grew up too soon. The towns, the streets, the factories... are not the kinds of towns, streets and factories which spell prosperity in the mid-20th century. We must make them so. The job is expensive. The job is difficult; and the job is ours."

Pennsylvania has great potential. It has location, natural resources, labor pool, transportation and communication facilities, power and scenic beauty. Our state has improved the education and the mental health of its citizens, built better highways and tried to increase the efficiency of the state government.

In 1976, Pennsylvania, along with the other 49 states, celebrated the bicentennial of the birth of the United States. Most Pennsylvanians looked proudly to the future. In 1981 Pennsylvania celebrated its three hundredth birthday.

As you complete this chronological history of Pennsylvania, it would be good at this time to repeat the words of William Penn. "Governments, like clocks, go from the motion men give them, and as governments are made and moved by men, so by them are they ruined too; wherefore governments rather depend upon men than men upon governments. Let men be good and the government cannot be bad."

In addition to knowing the history of its state, a good citizen needs to know and understand his community, local, state and national governments. We cannot hope to improve those things which we do not understand. Each of us must understand that there

THE LATER DECADES 313

is a new America every morning as we arise. We cannot hold back change. We must plan to live with change and to help guide the changes for the betterment of others and ourselves.

REVIEW QUESTIONS

1. How did the stock market crash in 1929 affect Pennsylvania?

2. What did Pennsylvania do to relieve unemployment and suffering during the harsh economic times of the 1930s?

3. What was meant by the slogan, "Get the farmers out of the mud"? Has the interstate highway system helped?

4. How did the ratification of the Twenty-First Amendment to the Federal Constitution affect the people of Pennsylvania?

5. Tell what kind of work was done by the CCC in Pennsylvania.

6. Why was there an increase in strength of labor unions since the 1930s?

7. How did the teacher tenure law provide for greater stability in the schools?

8. What is the General State Authority and what is the reason for its existence?

9. What are the advantages of a four-lane highway? Are there any disadvantages?

10. Identify some of the major military leaders of World War II who came from Pennsylvania and tell what role they played during the war years.

11. What organization in Pennsylvania has aided many thousands of college students either by loan or scholarship?

12. How did the industries of Pennsylvania meet the challenge of World War II?

13. What steps have been taken since 1920 in Pennsylvania to conserve our natural resources?

14. The State Public School Building Authority proved to be a boon to local school districts. Explain why.

15. Identify some of the lasting problems recent floods have brought to Pennsylvania.

Do you know the meaning of or can you identify? Write a sentence containing the following words or phrases, showing their relation to Pennsylvania:

1. depression
2. tercentenary
3. tenure
4. CIO
5. sales tax
6. authority
7. smog
8. Johnstown
9. George Earle
10. George C. Marshall
11. Dwight Eisenhower
12. William Scranton
13. bootleg mining
14. Public Utility Commission
15. William Scranton
16. PennDOT
17. Public Employe Law
18. lottery
19. community college

Maps to Help Us Learn

1. Draw an outline map of Pennsylvania and try to locate the military bases in Pennsylvania. Notice in what areas many were located.
2. On an outline map of Pennsylvania draw the original Turnpike with extensions. Then locate all the four-lane highways you can, the state forests, state parks and recreation areas.
3. On a map of Pennsylvania select a certain group of cities. Then show how suburban areas have grown around them by drawing a circle about the city proper and another large one to indicate the suburban dependents.

What Do You Think? Use the knowledge gained thus far to discuss the following:

1. Do you think it more difficult to be a good citizen today than it was in colonial Philadelphia?
2. "Collective bargaining" as used by labor has settled many labor disputes. But we must remember it can be misused.
3. Do you believe that the Governor should be given credit for prosperous times and blamed for hard times?
4. Conservation is one of the great problems of this State.
5. "Let men be good and the government can't be bad."

ACTIVITIES
(Individual, committee or class projects and class reports)

1. Draw a cartoon illustrating the slogan, "To lift the farmer out of the mud."
2. Draw a cartoon illustrating the repeal of prohibition in 1933.
3. Draw a poster in color and give it the title, "Heroes of World War II" in Pennsylvania.
4. Some students may have visited one or more of our state parks. Let them report on their visit. What did they find there and how did they enjoy themselves?
5. Make a report on what it means to a worker to be a member of a labor union.
6. Report to the class on the measures our state government has taken to conserve one of the following: soil, forests, water supply, fish and game, state parks.
7. Draw a poster calling the public to aid the clean streams program.
8. Write a composition on the revival of the coal industry in Pennsylvania.
9. Write a newspaper editorial taking a stand for or against the following statement: The state should provide television stations for educational purposes.
10. Prepare a "You Know Me" quiz for the class, using any of the important people in the text.
Sample: You know me. I am the first Democratic Governor to be elected in Pennsylvania since 1934. (Leader)

READING MATERIALS

Alexander, John K., et. al., *Philadelphia: 1776-2076, A Three Hundred Year View*, New York, Kennikat Press, 1975.

Beers, Paul B., *Profiles in Pennsylvania Sports*, Harrisburg, Stackpole Books, 1975.

Brown, Ira V., *The Negro in Pennsylvania History*, University Park Pennsylvania Historical Association, 1970.

Buni, Andrew, and Robert L. Vann *Politics and Black Journalism*, Pittsburgh, University of Pittsburgh Press, 1974.

Cochran, Thomas Childs, *Pennsylvania: A Bicentennial History*, New York, Norton, C. 1978.

Cox, Frederic, "The Three Mile Island Nuclear Station," nine articles by Cox et. al., *Pennsylvania Forests*, Fall, 1970.

Daniels, Belden L., *Pennsylvania, Birthplace of Banking in America*, Harrisburg, Pennsylvania Bankers Association, 1976.
Darden, Joe T., *Afro-Americans in Pittsburgh*, Lexington, Mass., Lexington Books, 1973.
Debates of the Pennsylvania Constitutional Convention, 1967-68, Harrisburg, Pa., Division of Documents, 1969.
Ershkowitz, Miriam and Joseph Zikmundi II, eds., *Black Politics in Philadelphia* New York, Basic Books, 1973.
Henry, J. T., *The Early and Later History of Petroleum, with Authentic Facts in Regard to its Development in Western Pennsylvania*, Library of Early American Business and Industry, 38, New York, A. M. Kelley, 1970, (Reprint)
Jones, W. G., *The New Forest*, Penns Valley Publishers.
Korson, G. G., *Pennsylvania Songs and Legends*, University of Pennsylvania Press, 1949.
Li, Hui-Lin, *Trees of Pennsylvania, The Atlantic States and the Lake States* Philadelphia, University of Pennsylvania Press, 1972.
McGeary, M. Nelson, *Pennsylvania Government in Action: Governor Leader's Administration*, Penns Valley Publishers, 1972.
Origin and Development of Public Assistance in Pennsylvania, Department of Public Assistance.
Parkhurst, Murial Taylor and others, *The Pennsylvania Story*, Philadelphia Franklin Publishing and Supply Co., 1970 (Reprint).
Pennsylvania Commission to Study and Evaluate the Consequence of the Incident at Three Mile Island, *Report of Governor*, Harrisburg, The Commission, 1980.
The Pennsylvania Manual, Commonwealth of Pennsylvania, each two years.
Pennsylvania State Association of Boroughs, *Guide for Labor Relations in the Public Sector in Pennsylvania*, by Arnold Addison, Harrisburg, The Association, 1972.
Pennsylvania Turnpike, Pennsylvania Turnpike Commission, Harrisburg.
The Peoples of Philadelphia, A History of Ethnic Groups and Lower Class Life, 1790-1940, ed. by Allen F. Davis and Mark H. Haller, Philadelphia, Temple University Press, 1973.
Shank, William H., *300 Years with the Pennsylvania Traveler*, York, American Canal and Transportation Center, 1977.
Smith, Reed M., *State Government in Transition*, University of Pennsylvania Press, 1961.
Stevens, S. K., and Schlegel, M. W., *Pennsylvania at War, 1941-1945*, Pennsylvania Historical and Museum Commission, 1946.
Voight, William Jr., *The Susquehanna Compact Guardian of the River's Future*, N. J. Rutgers University Press, 1972.
Wolf, Edwin II, *Philadelphia: Portrait of an American City*, Harrisburg, Stackpole Books, 1975. (A bicentennial history.)

chapter XIII

Living in Our Local Communities

Every person lives in a local community. This may be a large city like Philadelphia or Pittsburgh, a medium-sized city like Lancaster or New Castle, a borough like Bellefonte in Centre County or Hanover in York County, or a small village, or in the "country" on a farm. Those who live in the same community have interests in common because they live and work together. They are all interested in how well the factories or mines are working, the wages they are paid, the tax rates, the condition of the streets or roads and the price of food. No matter how different they are in race, religion or wealth they are cemented together by these common community concerns.

People who live in a community must have rules by which to live happily together. A community without rules or regulations is one without security or friendship. It is not a good place in which to live. People living there do not feel safe; there is fear in the air. They are indifferent or antagonistic to their neighbors.

Some rules are laid down by the local government in the form of city, borough or township ordinances. For example, dogs may not be allowed to run loose; boys and girls may not ride bicycles on the sidewalk; the speed limit for motor vehicles may be set at 35 miles per hour.

There are other rules and regulations that are not written but they are just as binding on the members of the community. They are called customs, sometimes "unwritten laws," and are accepted as hard and fast rules of behavior by most people. These customs may be centuries old, handed down from generation to generation. Most of the forms of politeness, which are signs of culture, have come down through the ages. The custom of helping neighbors in distress is equally old, but it is ever new and living to the people who give and who receive the needed assistance. Customs may be old but if they are good, they are always modern, too.

Persons who break rules and regulations generally get into trouble. If they break a local ordinance, they may be fined or even put into jail. If they break a state or national law, their punishment may be even heavier. When they disregard custom, they are looked upon as anti-social and may lose friends. Sometimes people break rules accidentally or out of ignorance, but if their hearts are in the right place, the community overlooks and forgives minor infractions. But a person who continually breaks the rules and flaunts the law usually finds himself on the wrong side of life and pays heavily for his disregard of the accepted pattern of community living.

One of the things that cements people of a community together is the opportunity of meeting friends, acquaintances, and fellow citizens face to face on the streets, in the homes, in the stores and factories. When people can talk about the same problems, when they can share the same fortune or danger together, they are a united community and are made stronger than if they go through the world alone. When there is a high degree of cooperation in a community, there is good community spirit. Members are loyal to each other and willing to help improve the community.

To define a community applicable to groups of people living in the same area under similar conditions would allow us to include families, neighborhoods, churches, schools, political parties, cities, counties, states, nations and the world as a whole. Each of us is the member of many communities, and we must adjust ourselves to the responsibility that we owe to each of them.

In this chapter we shall indicate the importance of the family, the church, and the school to the individuals, and how the individual in return is expected to contribute to his organizations.

THE FAMILY

A family is defined as a group of people closely related by birth, marriage, or adoption, living together in one household. All over the world the family is the primary unit of community life in which each person lives. When a child becomes an orphan, everyone tries in some way to help him become a part of another family.

Many persons fail to recognize the importance of the family in the life of every individual. The old saying that "as a twig may be bent so it grows" applies to family training of children. Adults are simply grown children behaving as they have been trained. Parents provide examples for children to follow, whether or not they plan it so. A child learns to follow orders from his parents and to abide by family rules. These become habits of behavior as the child grows older. In a family a child learns that he must cooperate in order to accomplish things. If he learns these things well in the home, he is ready for a satisfying community life.

Families teach their children things that are simply taken for granted later on. Few persons stop to think that they have learned their spoken language at home. The fact that practically every student speaks English is not questioned. It is only when we meet a child who has been brought up in a home where a foreign language is spoken that we realize children learn to speak as their parents do. The children of parents who speak poor English often speak the same way. Parents with accents or local ways of pronouncing words pass these things along to their children. Some Pennsylvanians say "poke" for paper bag and "redd up" for cleaning a room because their parents have used these expressions.

Families teach their children good or bad manners. We can always point out the children who have been taught to conduct themselves properly in public. The way we eat, sit, walk, dress and act is most often learned at home. But if a child finds that his family's ways of doing things differs from that of the majority around him, he may change in order to conform to the behavior of his friends. Yet the family influence remains the strongest. Through the years much of what we continue to do we were taught in early life.

Religion is usually a family affair. With a few exceptions, children attend the same churches as their parents. They accept the same religious ideas that they hear at home. The same is usually true of politics. Parents have a decisive influence over the selection of political party affiliation on the part of their children. Ideas of equality and tolerance are planted in the home. Schools do not teach racial and religious intolerance, yet many students have strong bias against some races and creeds. These attitudes were copied from those found at home.

The family throws the cloak of security over its members. The feeling that there is no need for fear comes in a stable and happy home. A child brought up in a family that provides understanding, happiness and security does not have to go elsewhere in search of those things.

The family fills other basic needs of its members such as food, shelter, clothing and companionship. In times of financial stress, members of a family tend to unite to reduce the cost of living.

In 1969, the average family of the United States consisted of 3.19 people compared to 3.37 in 1950. In Pennsylvania the average family is somewhat smaller. Even within the State, family averages are different. The counties along the northern border tend to have smaller families, while those in southwest Pennsylvania have the largest average families. Pike County averages 2.97 persons per family and Fulton County 3.81 to give the extremes.

Families that are broken by death, divorce, or separation lose many of the values that are needed for the proper raising of children. Governments, churches, and schools, as well as friends and members of the families, do everything possible to help in such cases. At one time orphanages and poor farms took care of most children separated from families, but today everything possible is done to keep families together.

Marriage is recognized by most churches as a religious ceremony of great significance. It is generally agreed that only under very serious circumstances should marriage be broken. The government, realizing the seriousness of marriage, has set up strict marriage laws. Even though a person is married in a church, he must abide by government regulations. Each state has its own laws on marriage. Every state requires a license for marriage which in Pennsylvania is issued by the Clerk of the Orphans' Court in the county. In Pennsylvania a couple must wait three days after they apply in order to get their marriage license. This discourages hasty marriages. Persons to be married must be over 18 years of age, but with parent's consent they may be as young as 16. In order to protect against transmission of disease, all persons to be married must be examined by a licensed physician.

Although a person may be required according to the regulations of his church to be married in the church, the Commonwealth of Pennsylvania recognizes marriages performed by a minister, priest, or rabbi; or by a judge, or district justice; or by a mayor of a city or borough. Religious societies, institutions and organizations are allowed to join members in marriage according to their rules and customs, but in all cases state regulations must be observed.

Once a family has been formed, the government, churches, schools and friends try in every way possible to keep the unit together. The governments have not always taken an active part in trying to keep families together. Until recent times, government was concerned only with the care of orphaned and dependent children, the aged and the needy. During the great depression of the 1930s, when millions of families needed financial assistance, the Federal Social Security program was established in cooperation with the states. In that period, the Commonwealth of Pennsylvania expanded its welfare program to give financial assistance to the aged, the blind, the disabled and the unemployed. The program provides for enforced insurance for all employed persons so that they will receive an annuity for their old age. Furthermore, the Commonwealth provides in some way for all people who cannot fend for themselves.

One of the most serious problems of the community is the broken home caused by the desertion by the mother or father. Churches teach that once a couple is married, they should remain together. Some churches forbid divorce for their members. A divorce disunites or dissolves a marriage. Divorce laws, like marriage laws, are made by the state. Pennsylvania requires that a person live in the state for at least a year before he may ask for a divorce. Even then the divorce is granted only after a court hearing before a common pleas judge, but is no longer for only serious causes.

The cooperation of all members of the family is needed to make a happy home. If children accept everything and give nothing in return, they have not done their part. The best members of a family are those who do the most for the others. Every young person should always be ready and willing to help.

A modern American writer said, "I cannot remember that either my father or mother ever took me solemnly into a room to tell me great moral truths about life. Being around them, seeing how they acted, hearing their informal words about people and things, seeing how they liked each other and did things for each other, we somehow got the feeling of what it meant to be decent human beings."

THE CHURCH

The major religions of the world are Brahmanism, Buddhism, Judaism, Christianity and Mohammedanism. In the United States the Christian and Jewish religions predominate. Christians are generally considered either Protestants or Catholics according to their rejection or acceptance of the Pope of Rome as their spiritual leader. Jews like Christians, have a belief in one God but do not accept Jesus Christ as the Son of God.

Without going into a study of specific beliefs, we must stress the great influence that religious groups have upon communities. Most religious groups in America believe in a life after death as a reward for righteous living. This faith in the future contributes to a worthy life in the present. In this manner an inspiration is provided for all to live better lives.

American governments have allowed people to choose their religions, and no one can be forced to join any church. The United States Constitution states, "Congress shall make no law respecting an establishment of religion, or prohibiting the free exercise thereof." In the present Constitution of Pennsylvania, freedom of religion is proclaimed as follows: "All men have a natural and indefeasible right to worship Almighty God according to the dictates of their own consciences, no man can of right be compelled to attend, erect or support any place of worship, or to maintain any ministry against his consent; no human authority can, in any case whatever, control or interfere with the rights of conscience, and no preference shall be given by law to any religious establishments or modes of worship."

Religions are recognized by governments, and they influence our every day lives. In the courts, witnesses are expected to swear on the Bible, but exceptions are made for Quakers and members of other religious groups that do not believe in taking oaths. Schools are not open on Sundays and religious holidays such as Easter, Good Friday, Christmas and Thanksgiving Day. The "Ten Commandments" of the Bible are accepted by Christians and Jews alike, and are reflected in the law in most states. All places of worship are tax exempt.

Since churches teach good morals, their influence has spread beyond their membership. Churches have taught their members to love their neighbors and thus have brought about the establishment of hospitals and homes for the aged and for orphans. Since most churches want their members to be well educated, practically every church denomination in Pennsylvania has a college for the preparation of its leaders, as well as for the general education of its members. Some churches also have established elementary and high schools for the education of their children.

THE SCHOOL

Education is the acquiring of knowledge, skills and attitudes. Education starts from the day that one is born and continues until he dies, but most people think of education as the learning that goes on when they are in school.

Schools were set up as substitutes for the long method of learning by experience. It has often been said that experience is a good teacher but it is an expensive one. Until 1834, except in Philadelphia, only those whose parents could afford to pay for their schooling were usually able to gain a formal education in Pennsylvania. It is now possible for a young Pennsylvanian to attend from kindergarten through twelfth grade at the expense of the school district.

The Federal government has little to do with the public schools. Each state conducts its schools in its own way. Although the schools throughout the United States are basically the same, there are really 52 different systems including the District of Columbia and Puerto Rico. In Pennsylvania, basic authority rests with the local school boards which are usually composed of members of the community elected for that purpose.

In Pennsylvania every child between the ages of eight and seventeen years of age is required to attend school until he is graduated from high school. This does not mean that one must attend a public school, although in many communities the public school is the only school. A public school is one operated by the government. Every public or non-public school must be kept open at least 180 days each year. In many communities there are parochial schools that are operated by religious groups. In many respects parochial schools are like public schools. They usually have classes in religion in addition to the regular required courses. Most of them are conducted by the Roman Catholic Church. There are also schools established by Mennonites, Amish, Baptists, Friends, Lutherans, and Hebrews. There has been a recent growth of small "Christian" schools.

Another type of school is the private school. A private school is one owned and operated by a person or corporation. These schools also must give certain courses required by the state but otherwise teach whatever subjects they choose. Some are day schools but others are boarding schools where the students stay for their meals and make their home for the whole school term. Some private schools are military schools and require that the students live by military rules and dress accordingly.

Most children in Pennsylvania attend public schools. In 1993 there were 334,114 children in non-public schools in this State but 1,717,613 in public schools. The state is divided into school districts which are grouped into 29 intermediate units for the purpose of sharing and coordinating services. The school board is elected by the voters in every district except in Philadelphia where it is appointed by the mayor. Supervising the schools of the State is the Secretary of Education, who is appointed by the Governor. In 1993 there were 501 school districts—1,900 fewer than in 1944. Districts were consolidated to improve, equalize, and expand educational opportunities, make better use of state aid and reduce costs. One purpose of schools is the education of the young people of the state to become good citizens. In order to accomplish this goal, the state prescribed certain courses that are to be taught in all schools: parochial, private and public. Examples of such prescribed courses are American and Pennsylvania history and government. The state also prescribed that all schools must teach in the English language, but otherwise the conduct of the schools is up to the local governing body.

School districts are separate governmental units in Pennsylvania. The school boards adopt local policies, levy taxes, and elect the persons who save the schools as teachers, administrators and superintendent. Every district school board has a vote to elect the executive director of the Intermediate Unit.

Although the local board elects the principals and teachers of the district, the state prescribes the requirements for becoming a teacher and sets the minimum salary that must be paid to a teacher. In return the state gives an annual grant of money to each school district according to a formula it has established to help districts in accordance with their needs.

Today there are more than 1,700,000 children in Pennsylvania public schools and over 100,000 teachers. Education is expensive; about half of the general funds of the state are spent for education. In addition, local taxes are levied by school boards on real estate, occupations, wages or individuals in order to meet the cost of schools.

Schools have advanced far ahead of the one-room type that taught the fundamental "reading, 'riting, and 'rithmetic," to our ancestors. Today hundreds of different courses are taught to meet the challenge of modern life. Reading, writing and arithmetic are still taught, but so also are agriculture, business, mining, machine shop, radio, safe driving and many other subjects our fathers never even heard of. More of the school districts have separate vocational-technical high schools for those students who wish to learn more technical subjects. In keeping with the definition of education as the acquiring of knowledge, skills and attitudes, a student can learn about more subjects than ever before. Today with such varied courses a student, with the help of his parents and school officials, should choose his future courses wisely. It is not too soon for junior high students to begin laying their plans for senior high school courses.

If one is going to college, he should realize that many colleges have requirements as to studies that should have been passed in high school. It is best to know about these in plenty of time. Many schools now give aptitude tests to help students understand their strong and weak points. More and more schools are now providing guidance service through the teachers or the guidance directors to help students prepare for their future careers.

Today high schools provide numerous services for the education of their students. The regular academic classes provide the basic courses that teach the student the skills and understanding that help make him a better citizen and prepare him for higher education. The school library provides reading matter on many subjects. Young people should realize that the libraries of our communities provide a storehouse of information even after we are out of school.

Beyond academic knowledge, the high schools today provide more and more training in the fine arts. Students now receive training in dramatics, painting, sculpturing, playing musical instruments, singing and dancing.

Some students are educated in Vocational-technical schools for making clothing, foods, plastics, wood, metal, becoming skillful with electronics, automobile mechanics, farming, aviation, printing and similar pursuits. Many schools teach students to be office workers. Many schools are conducting night schools. Adults may take a variety of courses there.

Extracurricular activities of the modern high school are designed to allow the young person to develop many talents and to learn how to get along with his fellow schoolmates. When we elect our schoolmates to be school or club officers, we are practicing democratic procedures which will be used in civic affairs in later years.

Many students upon graduation from high school go to college. A college is a school of higher learning that is designed to give further general or specific education. When a group of colleges, teaching separate fields of education or preparing for different professions, is joined in one unit, such a school is referred to as a university. In Pennsylvania, students may attend public, private or state-aided colleges and universities. The Pennsylvania State University, University of Pittsburgh, Lincoln University, and Temple University are state related and are supported in part by state appropriations voted by the State Legislature and approved by the Governor. The University of Pennsylvania, Drexel University, Philadelphia College of Textiles and Science, and Philadelphia College of Art are state-aided to some extent. Fourteen state Universities, owned by the state, provide instruction in liberal arts and education, training most of the teachers for public schools. These universities are located at Bloomsburg, California, Cheyney, Clarion, East Stroudsburg, Edinboro, Indiana, Kutztown, Lock Haven, Mansfield, Millersville, Shippensburg, Slippery Rock and West Chester. In 1983 the institutions were combined as part of a state university system. Community Colleges were begun with state aid during the late 1960s and now serve most of the state. They now teach much of the adult education formerly taught in night schools and two years of college courses.

There are over 100 colleges and universities within the state. These colleges differ in many ways. Some admit only men, others only women. Some of them are only for the training of church leaders. Duquesne University was founded by Roman Catholics, Bucknell University by Baptists, Westminster College by Presbyterians, Elizabethtown College by Brethern, Delaware Valley by Hebrews, and Swathmore by Quakers.

The colleges and universities of Pennsylvania, besides giving advanced general education, educate thousands of students in such professions as religion, law, public administration, education, medicine, pharmacy, nursing, engineering, business, social work and the fine arts. A great number of Pennsylvanians go to other states or nations for their college education, and in return many students from other states and countries attend Pennsylvania's colleges and universities. Pennsylvania's medical schools are extremely popular with students from other states. The Pennsylvania State University is the agricultural education center for the state and has educated hundreds of agricultural leaders. It also conducts research in a wide range of subjects. Research is carried on in most of the colleges and universities of the state to improve the life of the Commonwealth's citizens. It was at the University of Pittsburgh that Dr. Jonas Salk developed his historic vaccine for preventing infantile paralysis.

REVIEW QUESTIONS

1. Do you agree or disagree with the statement that a community must have rules to which people are expected to conform?
2. How do laws and customs differ? How are they similar?
3. Why is the family the most important unit in the community.
4. In what ways does the local community influence a person's life?
5. Why is the whole community concerned about its individual families?
6. In what ways can young people contribute to family happiness?
7. What community activities are typical of all communities?
8. What is meant by religious freedom?
9. What are moral standards?
10. In what ways do religious groups contribute to personal and community life in America today.
11. What part have religious groups played in establishing schools?
12. What evidence is there that religious groups exert a vigorous influence in our communities?
13. Why do parents send their children to non-public schools?
14. What is the difference between formal and informal education?
15. List the provisions of the compulsory school-attendance law of your state.
16. Who hires your school teachers?
17. In what class school district do you live?
18. How does the Federal government aid public education?
19. How long does a person's education continue?
20. In what way does our school help us to prepare for citizenship?
21. What is meant by the term "good citizenship"?

LIVING IN OUR LOCAL COMMUNITIES 329

Do you know the meaning of the following words or phrases?

1. family
2. citizenship
3. community
4. State-related
5. religion
6. parochial
7. tolerance
8. neighborhood
9. consolidation
10. community college
11. basic needs
12. disabled
13. rural
14. university
15. morals
16. Jonas Salk
17. cooperation
18. divorce
19. adult education
20. Ten Commandments

Maps to help us learn

1. On a map of the world, show the location of peoples of the leading religions. Let individual members of the class report on these different religions.

2. Have each student draw a map of his county, then each community to which he belongs.

3. Send a committee to visit an older resident of your community. Ask him to indicate important places of his youth on an outline map of your county. Bring this map to class and compare it with a modern map of your county to see how communities change with time.

4. After a careful study of the maps of your community, discuss major changes that should have been made in planning it. How many could be made now?

5. On your outline map of Pennsylvania, locate all the places where schools of higher education are found. Make a game of it; see who can locate the most schools.

What do you think?

1. How does attending school help in preparing people for happy family life?

2. Why do you think that it has taken people centuries to develop a world community?

3. A church or temple should be a center of community life.

4. The American plan of keeping church and state separate is an excellent idea.

5. Cooperation is the key for any kind of improvement, in the city or in the country.

6. A community is what its members make it.

7. If the people of a nation are to be self-governing, they must be educated.

8. Greater Federal aid is needed in the public schools.

9. Anyone who preaches intolerance of any religious group is not a good American.

ACTIVITIES

1. Dramatize the differences between a conforming citizen and a non-conforming citizen.

2. Draw a cartoon illustrating the difference between a community which is strictly regimented and one that is more permissive.

3. Prepare a dramatization of a family council meeting. Choose a problem and have class members discuss and finally solve it. Select subjects as "When may we use the living room"?

4. Conduct a panel discussion in class about a problem that troubles both parents and children. Choose a topic such as "How can a fair basis be established for deciding the amount of time to be spent listening to radio and television programs?"

5. Write a composition entitled "Why I am Proud of My Community."

6. Invite a member of your town council to talk to your class. Have questions prepared in advance on, "How to improve our community."

READING MATERIALS

Clint, Florence, *Pennsylvania Area Key; a Comprehensive Study of the Genealogical Record Sources of the State of Pennsylvania, Including Genealogical Maps and History*, Denver, Colo., Flak Survey, 1970.

Cox, Donald William, *The City as a Schoolhouse, The Story of the Parkway Program*, Valley Forge, Judson Press, 1972.

Leach, Leslie Duane, *School District Organization in Pennsylvania, 1834 to 1970*, Dissertation, The Pennsylvania State University, 1972.

A Conceptual Approach to Teaching About Pennsylvania, Penns Valley Publishers, 1973.

chapter XIV

The Citizen and the Voter

There are two ways to consider citizenship. First, it means membership in a political community, a township,, borough, city, state or nation. In a broader sense it means membership in the community as a whole, in the living society around us: our family, our church, our school and the other organizations to which we may belong, and, in modern times, the whole world.

The agent of the political community is the government, and the rules it enforces are laws. It is supreme ova all other organizations. It can enforce its laws by taking away one's property, liberty and even life under certain conditions. All persons are members of a political community whether they want to be or not.

From this membership they receive certain benefits. These include safety and protection from enemies both outside the political community and within, services such as water supply and sewage disposal, and the use of facilities such as streets and schools. On the other hand, the political community demands loyalty and gives its members responsibilities. They must pay taxes to support the government, take up arms in its defense when necessary and obey the laws. For after all, the political community is nothing more or less than the people themselves, organized to live the best possible life.

We speak of ourselves as citizens of the United States and as residents of the state wherein we live, for the granting of citizenship is the responsibility of the national government, and all states must accept as citizens those citizens of the United States who live within their borders.

The organization of our political community is Federal because it is made up of two entities: the nation and the states. Both are established by the Constitution of the United States which is the basic law of the land. Neither can abolish the other and each is supreme in its field of government. When there is conflict, however, the nation is supreme and this is how political unity is obtained, and maintained.

Citizens by Birth and Naturalization

All those who live in the United States are either citizens, aliens or nationals. An alien is one who lives within our borders but has not been made a member of the political community. A national is one who is a native of an American territory who has not been granted citizenship by the American government. Both aliens and nationals must obey the laws and pay taxes. Both are entitled to constitutional guaranties of personal and civil liberties. Sometimes, however, they are denied such privileges as voting, holding public office, and engaging in certain occupations. Sometimes, also, they are the victims of severe prejudicial treatment. Since 1940, all aliens are required to be registered and fingerprinted. This requirement was set up so that the authorities would know who are aliens and where they live in order to protect the nation from subversive activities of any who might work in the interests of foreign enemies. During a war the government may require citizens or subjects of enemy countries to conform with special rules.

The Constitution of the United States declares that "all persons born or naturalized in the United States, and subject to the jurisdiction thereof, are citizens of the United States and of the state wherein they reside. " Any child born in this country, who is subject to our laws, is an American citizen whether or not his parents are citizens. An example of one who is not subject to our laws is a child born here of a diplomatic representative of another country. Furthermore, persons born of American parents on foreign soil usually are considered American citizens.

Citizenship may be gained not only by birth but by naturalization. The first mandatory step in the naturalization procedure is filing a petition requesting citizenship; an investigation, preliminary hearing, and final hearing in open court then follow. Both state and Federal courts may naturalize aliens.

Before becoming a citizen, an alien must renounce all allegiance to another country. He must have lived in the United States at least five years. He must be able to read and understand English. He must not be an anarchist, polygamist, communist or other totalitarian, and he must know some of the basic facts about the American system of government. The naturalized citizen has most of the rights and privileges of a natural-born citizen, however, he never can become President or Vice President of the United States, and he may receive less protection by our government if he reenters the country of which he was once a citizen.

The Duties of Citizenship

It is not enough for a person to take his citizenship for granted, whether he has gained it by birth or naturalization. He must constantly learn to adjust his life to ideals of American democracy. This is often difficult for those who are naturalized and who lived before under different conditions. When they come to the United States, many immigrants can neither read nor understand the English language. Consequently, they know little or nothing about the American system of government. In order to help the newcomer to these shores, he is given the opportunity to learn not only the language of his chosen country but also the basic facts of American government and way of life. The public schools and patriotic organizations have taken a major part in this program of Americanization. The peak of immigration was in the first decade of the present century, and the unity of the nation during the two World Wars attests to the success of the Americanization program.

Citizens, both native and naturalized, have important duties as members of the political community. The first duty, if a person is of voting age, is to *vote*. The most important officials of our national, state, and local governments are elected by the voters at regularly scheduled elections. Each state sets up its own qualifications for voting. A citizen who has the right to vote is called an elector.

Because of the right to vote, a citizen has the duty to be *well informed*. He should have sound opinions on public questions so that he can choose the best persons to carry on our government and can express his opinions whenever he is called upon to exercise his judgment. Most of us get our opinions from our friends, the daily newspaper, magazines, radio and television. We must be always alert to the needs of the day and ways to improve conditions. So we must read, listen and think about our public policies and problems. When a nation, a state or a community has a body of citizens that is actively interested in public questions, it has gone a long way toward solving its pressing problems.

But voting is not always enough. A citizen qualified by knowledge, ability or experience must be willing to serve in a democratic society by being willing to *run for and hold public office*. To hold public office is an honor as well as a service to our nation and community. Many of the offices to be filled are not salaried or are poorly paid and carry no reward or very little except the knowledge of doing one's duty and the satisfaction of helping to get things done for the community. This is particularly true of such local offices as borough councilman, mayor, township commissioner or supervisor, and members of school boards and planning boards. Hours are spent, evening rest and relaxation are given up, enemies are made. Yet if we want to have control of our destiny, interested citizens must accept these jobs and do their best.

A political community must have rules so that it will grow in an orderly and peaceful manner. These rules, as we have seen, are the laws of our nation and state and the ordinances of our cities, boroughs and townships. Those who break these rules do so at the risk of criticism or punishment. The community tries to find ways, either by education and individual treatment or by legal punishment, by which such people will change their attitudes and ways of life. If some rules are unpopular and out of date, there usually are ways and means to get them changed through the democratic process of petitioning the governing bodies and educating the public in favor of a change. This may take a long time, during which injustices may continue but perseverance should be rewarding. Obedience to law and readiness to adapt to changing times and circumstances are required of citizens.

A citizen must be willing to defend the nation as a member of the armed forces and in other ways during national emergencies. Between 1940 and 1973 military service was expected of all qualified young men for a minimum period of two years, although an exception was made for those whose objections were based on religious grounds. Draftees were called up in an orderly procedure by the local draft boards which performed similar roles during the two World Wars. But in these days, all persons are involved if war comes—in the factory, the shop, the school and the home. War today is total and participation in both military and civil defense is expected.

Still another duty a citizen has is that of serving on juries when selected to do so.

The Voter's Job

In a democracy, it is essential that a large portion of the people have the right to vote. But even in the United States not all persons, not even all citizens, are allowed this privilege. In Pennsylvania, one must be 18 years of age, must be a United States citizen at least one month, must have lived in the state 90 days before voting, or must have lived in his election district 60 days before voting and must be registered as an eligible voter in his election district.

Out of the more than eleven million people in Pennsylvania, about 4,561,421 persons voted in the 1980 Presidential election. There were over 5,100,000 persons eligible to vote at the time. The proportion voting is usually much lower in state and local elections. Only 3,500,214 voted in the election of the Governor in 1974.

The job of the voter is not an easy one. In Pennsylvania, one votes for the following officers:

In the national government—President and Vice President every four years, one United States Representatives every two years, and two United States Senators within each six year period.

In the state government—Governor, Lieutenant Governor, Auditor Ganeral, Attorney-General and State Treasurer, every four years; one State Senator every four years; one member of the State House of Representatives every two years; and judges of the higher courts for terms of ten years.

In county government—A long list of officials such as the sheriff, coroner, recorder of deeds, register of wills, clerk of courts, county commissioners, jury commissioners, controller, or auditors, most of them every four years. In addition judges of the district courts are elected for ten-year terms.

In city, borough or township government—Members of the governing bodies such as city and borough councils, township boards of commissioners or supervisors, mayors, tax collectors, tax assessors, district justices, and constables, most of them for four-year terms but some for six.

In the national and state government, there is what is known as the "short ballot" but in our local government, it is the "long ballot," with many offices to be filled, that prevails. It is difficult for the average voter who has his own problems to worry about to know the candidates for all the offices to be filled by election. Therefore, he leans to a considerable degree on the leaders of his political party who have done most to make up the "tickets" of the parties contending in the election. That is one of the reasons most voters belong to a political party. They are inclined to follow the lead of their political leaders as a rule but always have the chance, and often use it, of voting "independently" of party dictates.

Even within his party, the voter has the opportunity by voting to help choose his party's candidates for office and the officers of the party. This he does in the primary election which is really an election within the party. It is conducted in exactly the same way as a regular election; held several months before the regular election; and a voter can cast his ballot only for candidates of his own party.

Yet there is even more work for the voter. He sometimes is called upon to vote on amendments to the Pennsylvania Constitution and often has to cast his vote on such local questions as bond issues, special tax levies, and sale of beer or liquor. Voting on policy is called a referendum.

Is it any wonder that a voter must be interested in public affairs and be well informed if he is to be an intelligent elector?

Political Parties

Political parties are organizations that have for their purpose the winning of elections. If a party wins at the polls, its candidates are elected to the offices for which they were running in the election. They control the key spots of the government—the Presidency, Congress, the Governorship, the General Assembly, the board of county commissioners, the city or borough council, the township board of commissioners or supervisors. They can carry out their ideas about how the government should be run and what government should do. If you are a member of the winning party, your candidates are likely to have your confidence in doing their job.

In the United States, the two-party system has been in existence for more than a hundred years. Since the Civil War, the Republican and Democratic parties have controlled the government—national, state and local—almost without exception. At rare intervals there is a strong third party contesting a national election, but it has never been victorious. In state elections, third parties seldom win. In local elections they have better success because local parties can be organized more easily when there is sufficient reason for such parties in the minds of the voters. People are inclined to vote more independently in local elections than in state and national elections. In fact in a great many localities, but not in Pennsylvania, local officials are elected on a non-partisan ballot, that is, one on which there is no party designation.

Once their candidates are nominated, political parties attempt to convince the voters that they are the best and should be elected. To do this, they run campaigns. A presidential campaign is a mammoth undertaking and costs millions of dollars. Hosts of speakers are sent around the country, concentrating on "doubtful" states where the contest appears close. Radio, television, newspapers, magazines are full of politics. Enthusiastic rallies are held, zealous party workers go from door to door asking people to vote for their candidates and extolling their virtues, and party members wear buttons for their favorites. Interest mounts higher and higher until the results of the election are known. Then the losing side sorrowfully folds up its tents and silently steals away—until the next election. The winning side takes charge of the government.

Local elections are not nearly so highly organized although sometimes they develop into tense struggles that divide the community into hostile camps. But not nearly so much money is spent or activity undertaken. In fact, sometimes local election campaigns

Primary Election Specimen Voting Machine Ballot
Camp Hill Borough, 1982

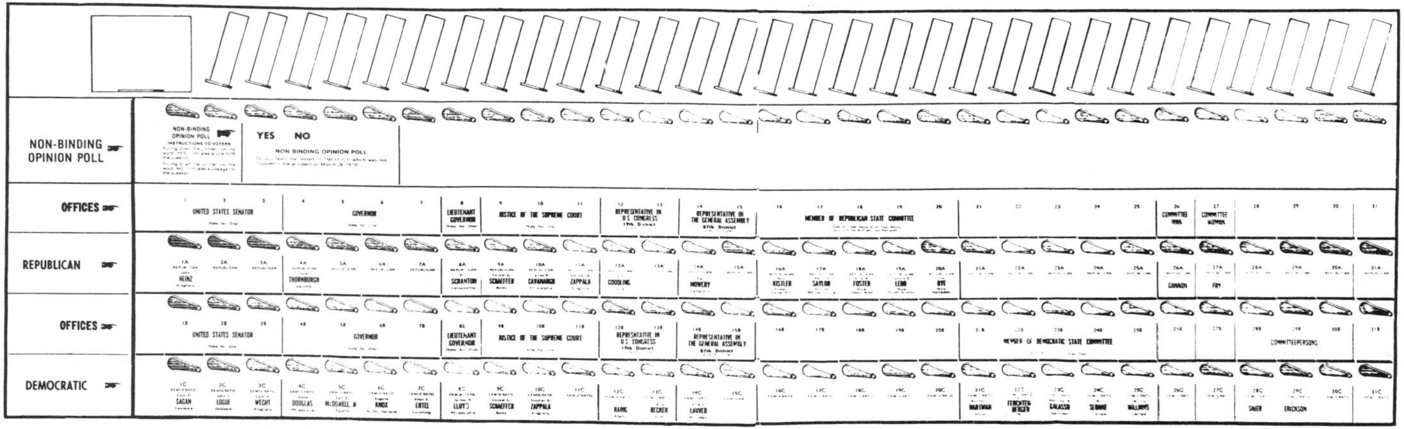

The specimen ballot shown above shows both parties, but the voting machine allows a person to only vote for members of his own party in the primary election. Persons nominated are chosen for office in the general election in November where registered voters of any party or no party may vote for candidates of any party or write in any name they wish.

THE CITIZEN AND THE VOTER

are quiet affairs, so quiet that only a handful of electors actually go to the polls.

It costs money to run election campaigns and the money to run them must come from some source. Ardent party members are solicited for funds, the richer ones often making large gifts. Party dinners are held in various localities at fifty or a hundred dollars a plate on which the food itself may cost two or three dollars. Office-holders are often asked to make "voluntary" contributions, which they do in the hope that they can keep their jobs. The national government has limited election campaign expenses for the

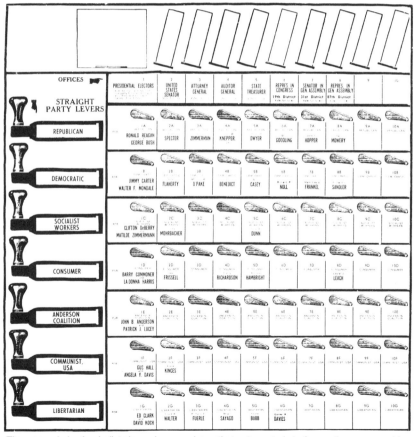

The general election ballot shown is a specimen that voters study before voting on a machine in November. A voter in a general election may vote for candidates of various parties, or pull the straight party lever. There is provision to write in other names on paper in the machines.

President, United States Senators and Representatives. State and local candidates in Pennsylvania are not limited in the amount they can spend, but they must report to the State how much they spent and for what purposes it was spent.

Elections

It is most important that elections be honest. In American history, there have been many examples of fraud and corruption in the holding of elections. Ballots have been miscounted or destroyed, election officials have handed in fictitious returns from their districts, voters have been bribed to vote the "right" way. In order to guard against such abuses, voting is secret, conducted in a booth in which the voter marks his ballot or pulls the levers on the voting machine. In Pennsylvania, the voter may vote either for a straight party ticket or for each individual office to be filled or may combine the two methods.

The state is divided into election districts in which there are polling places near the residence of the voter. There are more than 9,500 election districts in Pennsylvania. In each election district there is one judge of elections and two election inspectors. Likewise political parties may have watchers at the polls and citizens may petition to have overseers. The county government is in charge of election arrangements for all elections—national, state and local. With minor exceptions, the county pays the expenses of holding the elections. Municipalities must pay certain expenses for holding referenda on municipal questions, and the state reimburses the county a fixed amount for military ballots and veterans' ballots.

REVIEW QUESTIONS

1. What is a political party?
2. What services are performed by political parties?
3. Identify the two political parties that have dominated politics in the United States since the Civil War.
4. Explain how political parties make possible more effective cooperation within the government?
5. Of what value is an active opposition party?

THE CITIZEN AND THE VOTER

6. What is the chief difference between a boss and a leader in politics?

7. List some of the ways members of political parties show support for their candidates.

8. Why do people become politicians in the United States?

9. Why do we have political parties?

10. What is the chief work of the defeated party after election?

11. Where in our Constitution does it provide for political parties?

12. Explain the difference between the spoils system and the merit system in picking people for government jobs. Which do you prefer?

13. Identify some of the major duties of a good citizen.

14. What qualifications are required of voters in Pennsylvania?

15. Is a party member under obligation to vote for his party's candidates?

16. What is a voting district?

17. What are some of the unlawful practices that have appeared in past elections?

18. Describe the workings of the primary election.

Define or Identify:

1. nominate
2. politics
3. Americanization
4. elector
5. liberal
6. political boss
7. conservative
8. primary election
9. referendum
10. two-party system
11. campaign
12. election district
13. voting machine
14. non-partisan
15. independent
16. draft boards
17. tickets
18. ballot
19. judge of elections
20. long ballot
21. short ballot
22. convention

Maps to help us learn

1. Draw a map of your ward or borough or township showing the

location of the polling places and the boundaries of the election districts.

2. On an outline map of the United States, show the proportion of people in your state or any other state who could vote and who actually did not in the last Presidential election. Use shading or color.

3. On an outline map of your county, local community, and voting district, show the proportion of people who could vote and who actually did vote in the last Presidential election. Use shading or color.

What do you think?

1. Many qualified citizens do not even bother to vote.
2. It is often difficult today to find real differences between the ideas of the two major parties.
3. We are supposed to have "government by laws," not "government by political favors."
4. By regarding politics as a "game" many Americans are making a mistake.
5. A citizen who fails to vote should be criticized as much as a political leader who thinks only of the interests of himself and his party.
6. People who hope to be appointed to office following an election should contribute heavily to the campaign funds.
7. "Politics is a dirty business. I don't want to have anything to do with it. "
8. Whichever party wins an election, the people always lose.
9. Every citizen should be willing to accept public office.
10. We would do well to operate our government without political parties.
11. Name the last five governors of Pennsylvania and list contributions to Pennsylvania of each governor.
12. The schools should play a critical part in improving our political life.
13. The most important unit in American party organization is the county committee.
14. Loyalty to a party means support of its candidate or policies regardless of their merit.

15. In a government by the people, political parties are usually active.

ACTIVITIES

1. Make a graph showing the organization of the major political parties.
    a. Nationally
    b. In the states
    c. Locally
2. The membership of any political party will be determined by several factors. What influence do the following have:
    a. Economic factors
    b. Social factors
    c. Traditionalistic factors
    d. Sectional factors
3. American political parties in their historical development have shown a remarkable continuity in policies and sources of strength. Show how this is true by making a study of the two major political parties.
4. Plan for an election to be held in your class at the time of the regular election in your community. Observe carefully all the local requirements. Print or mimeograph your ballots.
5. Have an artistic member of your class draw cartoons showing the effect of ignorant or neglectful voters on a community.
6. Arrange a debate on the following question: "Resolved that all qualified persons who fail to vote at any election should be fined."
7. Arrange with the librarian to obtain space for a file to keep sample ballots used at each election, so that the following classes may benefit and add to the collection.
8. Explain all the steps in the nomination and election of a President. If possible, hold a convention and election in your school.
9. Have a committee draw up a party platform for state election.

READING MATERIALS

Alderfer, Harold F., *American Government for Pennsylvania*, Penns Valley Publishers, Harrisburg.

League of Woman Voters of Pennsylvania, *Key to the Keystone State, Pennsylvania*, Philadelphia, 1972.

Marsh, Elizabeth Redfield, *Geographical Isolation and Social Conservatism in Pennsylvania Small Towns, Dissertation*, The Pennsylvania State University, 1971.

Stevens, R. Michael, *The Role of Political Parties, An Exploration of Political Culture in the Pennsylvania General Assembly*, Temple University, No. 8 Philadelphia, 1970.

The Pennsylvania Manual, Department of General Services, Commonwealth of Pennsylvania, Harrisburg, Each two years.

chapter XV

Local Government in Pennsylvania

Local government in Pennsylvania is based on the English pattern. When William Penn established his proprietary colony, he brought along the form of local government organization found in the old country, much of which had been operating for centuries. Pennsylvania local government institutions are firmly rooted in the past.

For example, organized towns in England were called boroughs. The word comes from the early Anglo-Saxon *burg* which denoted a walled town in medieval days. The word county stems from the Latin *comitatus* which was a body of friends or royal escort and was the area ruled by the count in early French times. Township comes from the old Teutonic *tun*, town, and *scipe*, ship, established hundreds of years before the present nations came into being. City comes from the Latin *civitas* which is a body of citizens or a community. The constable derives from the late Roman empire *comes stabulis* or count of the stables.

Boroughs in Pennsylvania colonial days were chartered by the Proprietor or Governor under the authority granted by the King of England. Before the Revolution, there were only four boroughs in Pennsylvania: Germantown, Chester, Bristol and Lancaster. Philadelphia was chartered as a city from the first. The colony, except the western portion controlled by the Indians, was divided into counties, which in turn were subdivided into townships. Eventually the entire area of Pennsylvania was divided into counties. This general arrangement of local government still prevails.

The Number and Kinds of Local Governments

There are more than 5,000 local government units in Pennsylvania. These include 67 counties, 1,548 townships, 56 cities, 965 boroughs, 501 school districts and approximately 2,240 municipal authorities, including school building authorities. The total number varies a little from year to year. In addition, there is one incorporated town, Bloomsburg.

Having so many local governments is expensive. There are some who believe there should be fewer and stronger local governments so that they could give better services at lower costs.

There are nine classes of counties, two classes of townships, four classes of cities, one class of boroughs and five classes of school districts. All these classes are based on population. Different laws apply to different classes of local units because it is assumed that large local units need somewhat different powers than smaller units. However, the differences are not great.

Every person in Pennsylvania lives in either a city, a borough or a township. Likewise, all persons live in a county, although in Philadelphia the county and city have been consolidated. In addition, all persons live in a school district. Therefore, it can be said that everyone lives under three local governments and pays taxes to each.

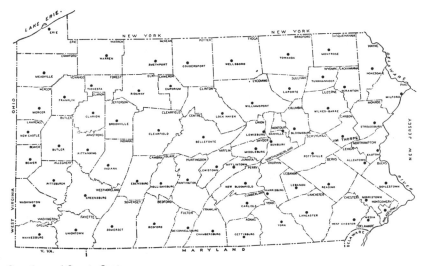

Counties and County Seats

The Pennsylvania County

The main governing body of the county is the board of county commissioners made up of three persons elected by the voters every four years. By law, only two of the commissioners may be of the same political party. The county commissioners have charge of all elections held within the county. They provide ballots, ballot boxes, polling places and pay all election expenses. They also register the voters so that accurate lists of qualified voters are available for each election. They are in charge of the assessment of real and personal property for local tax purposes. This assessment is used as the basis for real estate and personal property taxation by counties, cities, boroughs, townships and school districts. The commissioners are in charge of whatever county roads there are. They construct and maintain county buildings and have other assigned planning, development, law enforcement, health, and welfare duties.

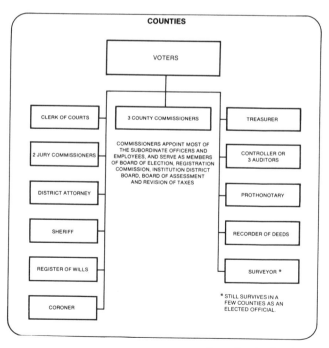

Pennsylvania Chamber of Commerce

A typical Pennsylvania county government.

The county commissioners divide authority with a number of "row officers" also elected by the people mostly for four-year terms.

The *sheriff*, an officer of the county court, has power to arrest persons violating the law, and in smaller counties is in charge of the county jail. He also carries out the orders and serves the official documents of the district court.

The *coroner* examines cases of suspicious and violent death in order to determine whether or not the cause of death was foul play or violation of law.

Two *jury commissioners* work with the sheriff to choose jurors for court sessions in which are decided the innocence or guilt of those charged with crime.

The *district attorney* brings persons accused of crime into court and prosecutes them in the name of the Commonwealth.

The *register of wills* files the wills of deceased persons, determines who is to be in charge of settling the estates of such persons and collects inheritance tax for the Commonwealth.

The *recorder of deeds* keeps a record of all real estate within the county and all property deeds. It is in this office that persons must file official records of the property they own.

The *clerk of courts* takes the records of county courts.

The *prothonotary* keeps records of the county courts.

The *controller*, or in smaller counties, *three auditors*, sees that county funds are properly spent and accounted for.

The *treasurer* keeps the money collected from taxes and from other sources, and pays it out on proper vouchers signed by the county commissioners and other officials.

The *judge of the court of common pleas*, really a state official holding court in the county, is a most important official. He hears all civil cases, involving disputes between persons; and all criminal cases, in which the innocence or guilt of persons charged with crime is determined, fixing the penalties to be imposed upon all persons found guilty.

The *district justices of the peace* are elected within magisterial districts to judge minor cases. In Philadelphia such courts are called municipal courts.

There are other elected and appointed officials such as the

surveyors, the *county clerk*, the *chief assessor*, the *county solicitor*, the *probation officer*, and a host of *assistants* and *deputies*.

The Pennsylvania Township

There are two classes of townships: first and second-class. First-class townships are found mostly in the closely settled areas outside of large cities like Philadelphia and Pittsburgh. For a township to become first class, there must be 300 persons per square mile living within the township. The governing body of the first-class township is the board of township commissioners elected by the voters for four-year terms. There are at least five commissioners in each township, elected at large, or one from each ward if the township is divided into wards. This board is assisted by a controller or three auditors, an assessor and an assistant assessor, a treasurer, who is also tax collector and constables.

The first-class township generally includes a number of unincorporated villages and stretches of countryside. Because they are well settled and near large cities, first-class townships provide many services such as police and fire protection, health care, street construction and others similar to those of cities and larger boroughs

Second-class townships are the more rural townships. They are the local government units of the open countryside, although they also contain unincorporated villages. Their governing body is the board of township supervisors, which is assisted by three auditors, the assessor, the tax collector, and the constable. Their main function is the construction and maintenance of rural roads but other local services are provided as needed.

The Pennsylvania Borough

The most important borough officers are the mayor and the borough council. The mayor is elected for four years by the voters, and he is given the power to oversee the activities of the borough, to supervise borough police and to approve or veto ordinances of the council. The real power in borough government resides in the council, composed of seven persons elected at large or from one to three elected from each ward in the borough. The term of a councilman is four years. Through committees, council directs and supervises

Expenses of Local Government

Pittsburgh Convention and Visitors Bureau

Carnegie Museum and Library was a gift of Andrew Carnegie, but its expenses today require financial aid from the City of Pittsburgh and the County of Allegheny.

Pennsylvania Department of Commerce

The Borough of Wellsboro maintains a park that houses probably the only statue of Wynken, Blynken and Nod. Parks are usually a small cost to local governments.

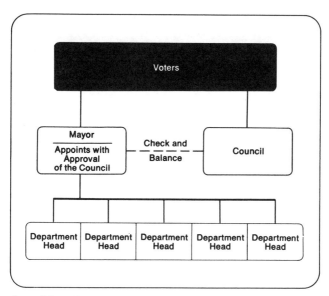

The Mayor-Council Form: legislative and executive powers are separated; executive responsbilities are centered in an elective mayor. Courtesy, McGraw-Hill Book Company.

activities of the borough government. Until 1961 the chief officer of the borough was called a burgess. By law he is now called mayor as in the cities.

Other borough officials elected by the voters included the tax collector, the assessor, the constable, auditors, or a controller.

Council appoints such officials as the treasurer, the solicitor, the engineer, the borough secretary, and, in some boroughs, the borough manager who is in charge of the administration of the borough and is responsible to the council for the operation of the government. Numerous boroughs have adopted the manager form of government. The manager plan may now be used by municipalities of all types.

The main functions of borough government are police and fire protection, construction and maintenance of streets, protection of health, refuse disposal, zoning and planning. Many boroughs also operate utilities for supplying water, electricity or gas.

City Government in Pennsylvania

There are two kinds of city government in Pennsylvania. The first is found in four of the largest cities of the Com-

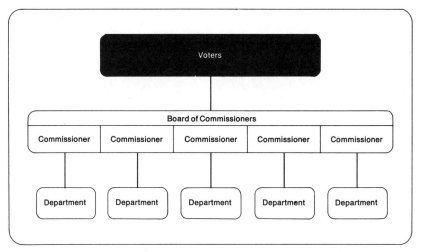

The Commission Form: legislative and executive powers are not separated; both are performed by the same group of officials, each of whom presides over an executive department for which he was elected. Courtesy, McGraw-Hill Book Company.

monwealth—Philadelphia, Pittsburgh, Erie and Scranton. This is known as the strong-mayor form of government. The governing body of the city is the city council elected by the voters, either partly from districts and partly at large as in Philadelphia, or entirely at large as in Pittsburgh, Erie and Scranton, for a term of four years. The mayor, also elected for four years, is a very powerful figure. In Pittsburgh, Erie and Scranton, he appoints the head of all major departments and so controls the work of the thousands of city employees. He makes up the budget of expenditures, which is passed upon by the council, but is enforced by him. He vetoes ordinances of council. One of the chief administrative officials of the city of Philadelphia is the managing director who is responsible to the mayor for the general operation of city government and who appoints the major department heads, with the approval of the mayor. This is a new development in the government of large American cities, and is somewhat comparable to the manager plan mentioned above.

Until 1957, according to state law, the commission form of government was required in third-class cities. In this form, five persons are elected by the voters for four-year terms to act as the governing body. One of these is the mayor. Each commissioner, including the mayor, is in charge of a department of government. Collectively

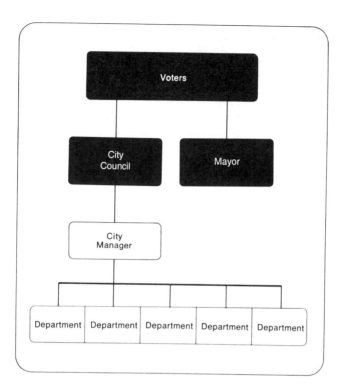

they serve as a council.

Assisting the council is an elected controller and a treasurer who acts also as the collector of taxes. Most other officials are appointed by the council.

In 1957, a law was passed that provided a way for third class cities to choose either the strong-mayor, council-manager, or commission form of government.

Home Rule for Municipalities

Constitutional changes of 1968 liberalized considerably the options available at the local level. The new provisions apply to all municipalities—counties, cities, boroughs and townships. As implemented by the State Legislature in 1972, Charter Commissions may be created by vote of the people to make studies and recommend "home rule" charters which include changes in powers and forms. The recommendations become effective when approved by referendum. Under this permissive legislation the door has been opened for modernizing local governments and making them more responsive to local needs and wishes.

Special Districts in Pennsylvania

We have noted in a previous chapter that school districts are actually local units of government that administer the local school systems, and that the school board members are elected by the voters. The school boards levy taxes, construct buildings, hire teachers and staff and generally supervise the school activities. They appoint a superintendent as the chief administrator.

There are also a number of special districts called municipal authorities which are established by municipalities to construct and operate facilities such as water works, sewers and sewage disposal plants and parking lots. Their governing body is a board appointed by the governing bodies of the local governments they represent. There are several reasons for the existence of authorities. Authorities may include more than one local government in their sphere of action. Authorities may finance their facilities and operations through revenue bonds which are paid back from the revenue collected from the services rendered by the authority. By the use of authorities, local units may be able to finance more easily large-scale facilities and utilities than would be possible by relying on general obligation bonds, which are backed by tax-paying ability as well as service charges.

Taxes and Revenue

Government costs money. Total Federal tax revenue receipts in 1992 amounted to over a trillion dollars. Total Federal social security and personal income taxes in 1992 amounted to $4,389 for every man, woman and child in the nation. Pennsylvania taxpayers paid an average of $1,160 each in 1992 for Federal social security and personal income taxes. Some pay more than others, of course, but that is the amount when the total is divided by the population.

In Pennsylvania local taxes come from several sources. The main one is the real property tax which supplies more than 70% of local revenues. Real property is land, houses and other buildings.

Local assessors are elected by the voters in all except the eight largest counties, where they are appointed by a county assessment board. The local assessor hands his figures to the chief assessor of the county board which determines the assessment for each property. The assessment of any property is usually not set at the market value of the property but only a certain percentage of it. The assessments are used as a basis for local taxes. The assessor informs the governing body of each city, borough, township and school district of the total assessed valuation of all property located there. The governing body then decides how much money will be needed from the property tax for the next year. It divides the assessed valuation into the amount needed in order to get the actual tax levy for each piece of property. For example, a borough wants to raise $300,000 in property taxes and the assessed valuation of all taxable property is $20,000,000. The tax levy would be $20,000,000 divided into $300,000 or .015 which is one and onehalf cents or 15 mills. If you owned property assessed at $50,000 you would have to pay a borough tax of $750. Your taxes are collected from you by the tax collector in your city, borough or township. He collects not only your city, borough or township tax but also the county and school taxes. You, as property owner, get a combined tax bill which you are allowed to pay in installments if you so desire in some areas.

Also there are other taxes than those on property. Pennsylvania's famous Act 511, passed first in 1947, gave local governments the right to tax almost anything that the State itself does not tax. As a result more than half of the local units levy per capita taxes, incomes taxes, amusement taxes, mercantile taxes, and others to raise over two billion dollars by 1990.

The Commonwealth itself grants large amounts of money to the local units. It gives a share of the gasoline tax to counties, cities, boroughs and townships. To school districts it makes substantial grants of money based on the assessed valuation of the school district per teaching unit. This money is to help pay for teachers' salaries and activities which are prescribed by state law.

REVIEW QUESTIONS

1. Why is every state divided into local governmental units?
2. What are the units of local government in Pennsylvania?

3. What is the greatest need of your city, borough or county? How can this need be met?

4. What are some defects of local government?

5. What are the differences between a first and second class township?

6. What are the duties of a township supervisor?

7. Why would a township board want to become a borough government?

8. What is the function of a district justice of the peace?

9. What are the important offices in borough government?

10. Why should the State retain some control over cities?

11. In what ways is the city-manager plan superior to other plans?

12. Why does a city or village need a government separate from the county government?

13. Why is it possible for a government unit to be classified as a city and yet have less people than the legal minimum for a city?

14. How are cities in Pennsylvania classified?

15. What is meant by home rule? Why is it desirable?

16. Why would a city as large as Philadelphia need a strong mayor?

17. How does a tax collector know how much tax to collect from an individual?

18. Why are counties, townships, cities and school districts classified according to population?

19. On what pattern is Pennsylvania government based, and who brought it to our state?

Do you know the meaning of these words?

1. zoning
2. home rule
3. village
4. government
5. constable
6. tax collector
7. controller
8. county seat
9. utilities
10. town
11. ordinance
12. borough council
13. assessor
14. auditor
15. burgess
16. commissioner

LOCAL GOVERNMENT IN PENNSYLVANIA

Maps to help us learn

1. On an outline map of your county draw the boundaries of the different townships and note all the cities and boroughs.
2. Using another outline map of your county draw the boundaries of the school districts.

What do you think?

1. Governments are only as good as the people that run them.
2. Local governments are merely creatures of the state, called into being for the express purpose of doing the state's will.
3. Local government deals with most things which affect our lives directly.
4. A city resembles a private corporation which is also chartered by the state and is given certain rights and duties.
5. The commission type of city government is necessarily a government of amateurs.
6. If your city does not have the city-manager type of government, do you think it should?
7. Each city of the first and second class should form a separate county. Possibly all the cities should do this.
8. No one person in county government can be held responsible for the lack of effective, coordinated administration.
9. Counties should adopt civil service for all employees who are not elected.
10. The treasurers of the county and city and the tax collectors in the township should be eliminated. A designated bank could collect taxes much more cheaply.

ACTIVITIES

1. Study the relationship of some nearby large city with the county in which it is situated. Do you find instances of unnecessary duplication or conflicts of authority?
2. Prepare charts showing the governmental organization of the three types of city government. If possible, use cities near you.
3. County government has been called the "dark continent" of American politics. Arrange a program or project for your commu-

nity which would dramatize or "glamorize" county government.

4. Take two of the larger cities in your state, find out their representation in the Legislature. Are they represented in proportion to their population?

5. A committee from the class might interview a district justice or the county judge. By preparing questions ahead of time, find out what problems confront them and any suggestions they have for changes in their work.

6. Appoint a committee from your class to attend a meeting of your local governing body (the city or borough council, the township commissioners or supervisors) and report to class.

7. Make a list of things which your county government does for you. Make another list to show what the government of your town, village, township, or city does for you.

8. List the names, titles, and duties of the chief officials in your borough, township, or city.

9. Hold a debate on the following: "Resolved, That the city-manager plan of government should be adopted in most Pennsylvania cities."

READING MATERIALS

Allison, Edward Pease, *City Government of Philadelphia*, New York, Johnson Reprint, 1973 (Reprint).

Cornell, William A., *Understanding Pennsylvania Civics*, Lansdale, PA, Penns Valley Publishers, 1994

Department of General Services, *The Pennsylvania Manual*, Commonwealth of Pennsylvania, Harrisburg, Pa., 1993.

Helstrom, Carl O. Jr., *The City in Pennsylvania Government*, Department of Community Affairs, Harrisburg, Pa., 1977.

Holcombe, William Penn, *Pennsylvania Boroughs*, New York, Johnson Reprint Corp., 1973 (Reprint).

Pennsylvania State Association of Boroughs, *Guide for Labor Relations in the Public Sector in Pennsylvania*, Arnold Addison, Harrisburg, The Association, 1972.

Pennsylvania Township News, Pennsylvania State Association of Township Supervisors, Camp Hill, Pa.,

Rogers, David, *The Management of Big Cities; Interest Groups and Social Change Strategies*, Beverly Hills, Cal., Sage Publications, 1971.

A variety of publications, Department of Community Affairs, Commonwealth of PA, Harrisburg.

chapter XVI

Government of the Commonwealth

The government of the United States is Federal in character. The Constitution of the United States established the national government with headquarters in Washington, D. C., and state governments with headquarters in the capitals of the fifty states. The capital city of Pennsylvania is Harrisburg.

On July 4, 1776, when the United States was born, the thirteen "original colonies" became states. By 1912 that number had grown to 48 states. By 1960 Alaska and Hawaii were added to create 50 states.

Each of the present 50 state governments differs somewhat from the others but generally they are much alike. Each state has a Constitution which defines the principles of the state government. These constitutions differ in wording, size and form, but they all provide the basis of the government.

Each of the 50 states of the United States has a governor as chief executive, a legislature to enact laws, and a judiciary to interpret the state laws and the state constitution. Governors usually serve terms of two to four years. Some may serve more than one term in succession, others are limited to one or two terms. The governor's powers differ in each state, but he is considered the most powerful single state official, the head of the government in name and in fact. Legislatures differ in the number of members and in other ways but they are essentially alike. In all states except Nebraska, where there is only one house, there are two houses as in the Congress of the United States. Courts differ in the various states according to how judges are selected, how long they serve and by what names they are called. Here too are similarities. All three branches work together but also act as a check against each other so that one branch will not dominate.

Our own state government is outlined in the Constitution of Pennsylvania. This Constitution was approved by the people of the Commonwealth in 1873, and went into effect January 1, 1874. It has since been modified in many respects by amendments initiated by the legislature and the Constitutional Convention of 1968. The government of the Commonwealth of Pennsylvania, like that of the other states, is patterned closely after that of the United States Government.

THE LEGISLATURE

The legislature, or lawmaking body, of Pennsylvania is called the General Assembly. It may pass any law that is not in conflict with the Constitutions of the United States and Pennsylvania. It meets in the State Capitol Building in Harrisburg. Its two houses are called the Senate and the House of Representatives. The Senate has 50 members chosen from senatorial districts for four-year terms. One half of the members are elected every two years. The Constitution calls for 203 members in the House of Representatives. All representatives are elected every two years.

Senatorial districts are provided for in the Constitution. Districts are areas of the state which are "compact and contiguous territory as nearly equal in population as may be." These districts are set up after a ratio has been obtained by dividing the total population of the state by 50. If the population of Pennsylvania were 12,281,054 each senatorial district should have 245,621 people but the Legislature which lays out the districts cannot divide the State so evenly, especially when it tries to follow county lines.

Districts for the election of members of the House of Representatives are laid out in the same manner as for the Senate, except the total state population is divided by the number 203. Prior to 1966 each county was guaranteed one representative. Hence, Forest County with less than 5,000 population had one Representative, the same as Franklin County, which had 88,000 population. The courts held this system undemocratic, and the 1968 Constitution provides

GOVERNMENT OF THE COMMONWEALTH

Pennsylvania Department of Commerce
The House chamber at the top seats the 203 members of that legislative body. The even more elaborate Senate chamber below seats the 50 senators. Visitor sections are in the back of the rooms.

for districts that are more evenly matched in population. Both Senators and Representatives are elected by the voters of the district. They must have lived within their district for one year to be elected. Further qualifications are that they must be citizens of the United States when elected, and inhabitants of Pennsylvania for at least four years. Senators must be at least 25 years old, and Representatives at least 21. Many of the Legislators are lawyers, businessmen and farmers. Until 1956, the salary of each member of the legislature was $3,000 for a two-year session, but an act of that year increased it to $3,000 a year. By 1972 the amount was changed to $15,000 per year. In 2002 state legislators were paid an annual salary of $61,889, an automotive allowance and an annual expense allowance of $10,000. Many people believe that such a generous salary is necessary to attract capable people to be full-time legislators.

How the Legislature Operates

The Pennsylvania General Assembly meets annually beginning in January. Until 1959 the legislature met only in odd-numbered years. However, as the business of the legislature grew, the members could not complete their work in one year. The 1955 session had run into 1956.

The formal meetings of the legislature usually begin Monday evening and continue through Tuesday and Wednesday of each week during the session. Committee meetings and investigations are held in the mornings and afternoons. All meetings of the General Assembly are open to the public.

The Senate is presided over by the Lieutenant Governor, elected by the people of the entire state. The Senators elect one of their own members as a President Pro Tempore to preside when the Lieutenant Governor is absent.

The members of the House of Representatives elect one of their own members to preside over their organization. He is called the Speaker. He is usually a leader of the majority party. Presiding officers in both houses decide who may speak, which committee is to study bills, and what action will take place in the chamber.

Members of the legislature may introduce bills that they wish to become law. Often a person or group outside the legislature asks a

GOVERNMENT OF THE COMMONWEALTH 363

MAPS SHOWING LEGISLATIVE DISTRICTS

Pennsylvania
House of Representatives
Districts
1992 FINAL REAPPORTIONMENT PLAN

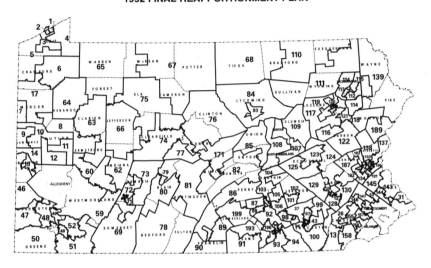

Pennsylvania
Senatorial Districts
1992 FINAL REAPPORTIONMENT PLAN

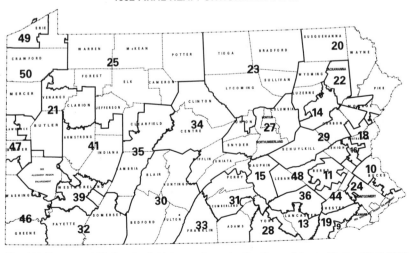

The 203 House and 50 Senate districts are drawn by the General Assembly to reflect 1990 census figures.

member of the legislature to introduce a bill. In most cases, the legislator has the bill properly drafted by the state's Legislative Reference Bureau.

After the bill is drawn up, a member may introduce it into his house by sending it to the desk of the presiding officer. This is called placing a bill in the "hopper." The presiding officer then sends the bill to a committee for study. In the process the bill is given a number. As many as 3,000 bills may be offered in one year. There are 22 standing, regular committees in the Senate and 24 in the House of Representatives. Some of the more important committees are Appropriations, Banking and Insurance, Environmental Resources, Agriculture and Rural Affairs, Urban Affairs, Judiciary, Finance, Education, Transportation, and Community and Economic Development.

A committee may either consider or ignore a bill. If it chooses to ignore a bill, there is practically nothing that can be done to have it enacted into law. If the members of a committee choose to consid-

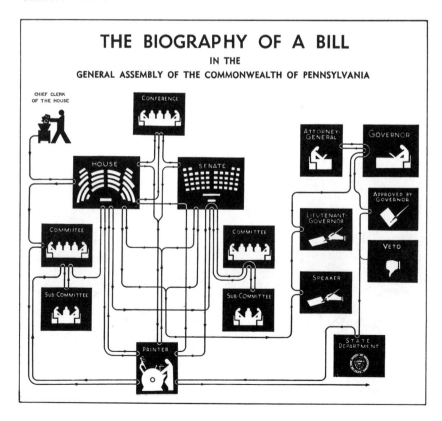

THE BIOGRAPHY OF A BILL
IN THE
GENERAL ASSEMBLY OF THE COMMONWEALTH OF PENNSYLVANIA

er a bill, witnesses may be called in or invited to tell why they feel the bill should or should not be enacted. Legislative proposals are often complicated and difficult for the average person to understand. Therefore, the legislators need the help of experts and persons who understand the proposals. Some bills are very short, a page or two. Other bills are long and involved with over a hundred pages.

When a committee decides that a bill is worth considering and feels that it should be brought before the whole house, the committee so votes and sends it to be placed on the calendar for formal action on the "floor," this is, in open meeting of the whole house. When its time arrives, it is to be considered on three separate days, according to the Constitution. Usually only the title is read on the first and second readings. On the third, the bill may be debated and the vote then taken. If the bill passes by a majority vote, it is then sent to the other house of the legislature where it must pass in the same manner. If the second house amends or changes the bill, a conference is held with members from the two houses in what is called a conference committee. That committee usually compromises the differences so that the bill is repassed in both houses.

When the bill has been approved by both the Senate and the House of Representatives, it is sent to the Governor. He has three choices of action with the bill. He may approve it and it becomes a law; he may allow it to become a law by simply not signing it; or he may veto it. When a bill is vetoed, it cannot become a law unless two-thirds of the members of each of the two houses of the Legislature vote favorably for the bill. In Pennsylvania a bill rarely is passed over the veto of the Governor.

Pennsylvania's Governor has an item veto power that even the President of the United States does not have. That is, the Governor of Pennsylvania has the power to veto or reduce special items within appropriation bills. For an example, he may find that the General Assembly has passed a bill providing $50,000 for a special celebration. The Governor has the power, and often exercises it, to change the amount to any lower figure, or veto the entire amount. This power is especially useful in that if he had to veto the entire bill, the legislature might not have the time to pass another.

EXECUTIVE BRANCH

The Governor as the Chief Executive

Pennsylvania state government is headed by a chief executive called the Governor and is elected by the voters of the entire state for a term of four years. After 1968 the Governor was entitled to be elected to two succeeding terms. At the same election the voters elect a Lieutenant Governor who succeeds the Governor if he should die in office or leave the office for any reason, and who is a member of the same political party as the Governor. In order for a person to hold either of these offices, he must meet the qualifications that are stated in the State Constitution: he must be a citizen of the United States; he must have attained the age of 30 years; he

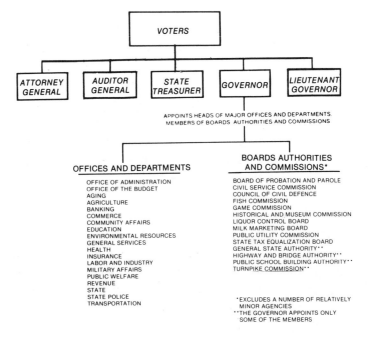

Pennsylvania Chamber of Commerce

must have lived the previous seven years in Pennsylvania, unless on public business of the United States or Pennsylvania.

The Governor takes office the third Tuesday in January following his election. On that day, called the Inauguration Day, the Governor outlines in a speech what he hopes to accomplish during his four-year term. Later, the Governor usually goes before a joint meeting of the General Assembly to state his program to the legislators. He also delivers in person, or by messenger, a message in which he gives his suggested ideas as to how the income and the expenses of the state should be balanced. This is called the budget message. It is drawn up with the aid of the Governor's Secretary of Administration and Budget Secretary who have reviewed the requests for appropriations from the various departments of the state government.

The Governor of Pennsylvania, as the head of the executive branch of the state government, is one of the most powerful state executives in the country. Under the present State Constitution, and numerous reorganization acts, the Governor has been made responsible for the administration of almost the entire state government. For his work, the Governor is paid a salary of $138,270 per year and is provided with an executive mansion in the capital city. The former home for the Governor at Indiantown Gap, near Harrisburg, is used as a home for the Lieutenant Governor.

The Governor is the personal leader of the state government, and has more than 85,000 permanent employees working in the departments and agencies responsible to him. The Governor appoints the heads of nearly all departments, boards and commissions of the state. If he wishes, the Governor may further appoint the deputies and the numerous assistants. Usually the department chiefs and their deputies appoint officers and employees under them, but even when that is true, the Governor's approval is required.

Many appointees are "political" in the sense that they reflect the Governor's point of view and usually his partisanship. Some are active party workers whose sponsorship by precinct, ward, county and State chairmen is required. About half of all State jobs are filled on the basis of merit as demonstrated by open competitive examinations. These employees may not be dismissed for political reasons and may look forward to having careers in public service.

Cabinet officers, heads of other agencies, and most bureau chiefs remain outside the merit system. In some departments and agencies, notably the Departments of Education, Environmental Resources, Public Welfare, State Police and Liquor Control Board, all but a few top officials are appointed on the basis of merit.

The Governor has the duty to maintain law and order within the State and does so with the aid of the State Police. He has the power to grant pardons and reprieves and commute sentences. He fills vacancies in certain state and local offices.

Other Elected Administrative Officers

In addition to the Governor and the Lieutenant Governor, the voters of the state elect three other state-wide administrative officers. These are the Auditor-General, the State Treasurer and beginning in 1980, the Attorney-General. These officers are elected for four years, but their election takes place two years before and after the election of the Governor. These three officials appoint their own assistants and conduct their offices independently of the Governor and report directly to the General Assembly.

The Attorney General

The Attorney General is the chief law officer of the state. When the state is involved in court cases, the Attorney General or one of his assistants represents the state before the court.

Prior to 1980, the Attorney General was appointed by the Governor, but a Constitution change voted by the citizens now provides for an elected Attorney General. By being separate from the Governor's appointment, the Attorney General is expected to check the legal functioning of all public officials.

The State Treasurer

The State Treasurer audits all requests for expenditures and has custody of State monies and securities. All collections made by the Department of Revenue are turned over to the Treasurer. After the Treasurer receives the money, it is deposited in banks designated by the Board of Finance and Revenue. The Commonwealth keeps its money in a number of banks throughout the state. The Treasurer pays out the money for legally incurred expenditures.

The Treasurer may serve two successive terms but may not be elected Auditor General until four years have elapsed.

Departments of State Government

To assist the Governor in his duties, the following departments of the state Government have been established:

State	General Services	Community Affairs
Aging	State Police	Banking
Corrections	Insurance	Commerce
Education	Public Welfare	Revenue
Agriculture	Health	Conservation and
Transportation	Labor and Industry	Natural Resources
Military Affairs	Environmental Protection	

The heads of all of these departments are appointed by the Governor, subject to approval by the Senate. All can be removed by the Governor at any time.

The *Department of State*, headed by the Secretary of the Commonwealth, keeps certain official records and documents of the state government. He also has duties connected with elections and charters all corporations organized within the state.

The Department of State has a Bureau of Professional and Occupational Affairs which issues licenses and enforces laws that relate to medical doctors, dentists, pharmacists, certified public accountants, barbers, veterinarians, nurses and other recognized professions.

The *Department of Aging* was established in 1978 to advance the well being of Pennsylvania older citizens to effect coordination in the administration of federal and state aging programs, to promote the creation and growth of organizations designed to maximize independence and involvement of older Pennsylvanians.

The department develops advocacy programs that are consistent with the mandates of the federal and state legislation. It provides for advocacy for older citizens and the adult handicapped.

The Department of Corrections was established in 1984 to administer corrections institutions of the state, formerly called prisons, the institutions would like to have the inmates correct their habits and become good citizens. Education, counseling and training programs are used.

The *Department of Education* expends more money than any other department. The greatest expense is direct payments to public school districts according to the number of students and financial needs of the school district. The Department works with state-owned universities and community colleges of Pennsylvania. It also aids and guides state-related universities of the Commonwealth System of Higher Education, state-aided institutions, and private institutions.

The Department administers all laws, regulations and policies dealing with education, prescribes courses of study for schools, licenses private schools, deals with non-public schools, administers programs for libraries in the state and issues teaching certificates.

There is a State Board of Education, appointed by the Governor, to make regulations within the school laws.

The *Department of Agriculture* is designed to help the farmers of the state. It makes studies and publishes bulletins on many agricultural subjects. To protect the non-farmers as well, the Department quarantines diseased cattle, works to control plant diseases, and inspects food, milk and beverages to see that they hold to the standards set by law. When next you purchase any baked goods note that the maker has had his ingredients approved by the Department.

The *Department of Transportation* (PennDot) has as its purpose to develop programs to assure adequate, safe and efficient transportation facilities and services at reasonable costs. The coordination of various forms of transportation is sought on highway, rails, buses and in the air. The largest job is building and maintaining over 60,000 miles of highway. Mass transportation systems are encouraged in and near cities to aid travellers and reduce the need for even more highways. The Department cooperates with the Federal government in building interstate highways and with other interstate and mass transportation systems. The Department funds a daily passenger train to and from Pittsburgh and Philadelphia.

The *Department of General Services* is the Commonwealth's builder-purchasing agent. It buys in bulk and as cheaply as possible all materials and supplies used by the various state agencies. Further, the Department establishes standards of quality for purchases, publishes state reports and bulletins, and is responsible for major building construction and alteration. The idea of such a central system is to save money by purchasing supplies and materials in bulk and at the best possible prices.

The *Department of Insurance* regulates all insurance companies doing business in Pennsylvania. All insurance agents are licensed by the Department. Complaints against companies for violations of laws, regulations or policies are investigated. The Department regulates rates of all types of insurance. Out-of-state companies have the same regulations and cannot do business in Pennsylvania unless approved.

The *Department of Public Welfare* is the second most expensive department. The Department aids citizens with both Federal and State funds who cannot care for themselves. Working through County Boards of Assistance, appointed by the governor, the Department grants money to needy persons over 65 years of age, to dependent children up to 18 years of age if one or more parents is missing, to the blind, and to those generally in need who do not fit the above categories.

The Department also maintains several state general hospitals and institutions for those who are mentally ill or retarded. It sets standards, licenses, and supervises nursing homes, and hospitals. It maintains Youth Development Centers and Youth Forestry Camps to care for youthful offenders of the law.

The *Department of Health* conducts an advisory service for county and local health units and enforces public health laws. The Department is responsible also for public health education, medical education and nutrition. It maintains records of vital statistics such as birth, deaths, marriages, adoptions, divorces, and annulments within the state. Special health services include divisions of communicable diseases, alcoholism, dental health, chronic diseases, chronic respiratory diseases, maternal and child health, and physical therapy.

The *Department of Military Affairs*, headed by the Adjutant General, is really the National Guard of Pennsylvania. The latter is a military organization made up of persons who receive military training and instruction in state armories throughout the State. In time of war and emergencies, the "Guard" may be activated. The Department also keeps war records of military organizations and veterans. Most of the funds and equipment for this Department are provided by the national government.

The *Department of Community Affairs* is the smallest Department. The Department is to develop inter government relations between the state and counties, boroughs, cities and townships. Assistance in legal, fiscal, public works, administrative, and other local governmental activities is offered through consultants and training. Aid is granted to help communities apply for State and Federal grants for housing, renewal or related physical improvements of the community.

The *Department of Banking*, headed by the Secretary of Banking, supervises all state banking and savings institutions. Since most of the banks are part of the national banking system, the number supervised by the state has been reduced to about 300. Other companies that loan money are also supervised. This Department examines the financial dealings of the companies and banks to see that they are properly conducted and managed. The Department has the power to close questionable institutions.

The *Department of Revenue*, headed by the Secretary of Revenue, collects all money that is due the state in the way of taxes and license fees. Once the money is collected, it is turned over to the State Treasurer for deposit. This Department, which was founded in 1927, abolished the many collection agencies of the state and reduced the cost of such collections. It is in charge of titling and registering motor vehicles and issues drivers' licenses. In addition, it supervises the issuing of hunting, fishing and dog licenses and conducts the lottery.

The *Department of Commerce* has as its purpose to advance the growth of business and industry in the State. Through the Pennsylvania Industrial Development Authority (PIDA) the organization, location and expansion of industry is encouraged with loans. Promotion of travel in Pennsylvania by out-of-staters is a major duty since tourists spend millions of dollars in the state. The Department helps state businesses to export into the world market and promotes federal purchases in Pennsylvania.

The *Department of Labor and Industry*, headed by the Secretary of Labor and Industry, was set up to protect workmen in manufacturing and mining industries from bad working conditions, unfair labor practices, unemployment, and unsafe and unsanitary working conditions. Special sections of the Department help enforce the laws to protect women and children from hazardous work and long hours. Unemployment insurance and workmen's compensation are also administered. This Department tries to improve the conditions of workers throughout the state. In addition to this, it protects the public by supervising the construction of most buildings other then private dwellings. It inspects elevators and steam boilers, regulates the storage and use of explosives, and supervises the manufacture of bedding and upholstered furniture.

The *Department of Conservation and Natural Resources* and the *Department of Environmental Protection* were created in 1995 out of the former Department of Environmental Resources. The conservation function includes care of the 2,000,000 acres of State owned forest lands, 250,000 acres in 108 State parks and soil and water conservation. The environmental protection function is to enforce land use, mining, air and water quality, and water and sewer treatment plant laws and regulations.

The *State Police*, although technically not a department, has similar status. It aids the Governor, state departments and agencies upon request and has primary responsibility for enforcing certain state laws, particularly those related to highway safety. When called upon, the State Police go to the aid of local officials.

Independent Agencies of the State Government

In addition to the departments noted above, there are a number of independent agencies, the members of which the Governor appoints. In most cases the members of commissions are appointed for terms that overlap in such a manner that the Governor cannot appoint all members at one time. A person wishing to make an extensive study into any of these agencies should consult the Pennsylvania Manual, which is published by the Commonwealth every two years.

Pennsylvania Commissions include:

Civil Service	Horse Racing
Ethics	Human Relations
Public Utility	Securities
Pennsylvania Turnpike	Public Television
Historical and Museum	Game
Delaware River Basin	Fish and Boat
Pension Study	Women
Heritage Affairs	Independent Regulatory Review

The Public Utility Commission is perhaps best known because it approves the rates for such essential services as electricity, water, natural gas, and public transportation.

Other Agencies include:

Council on the Arts	Health Care Cost Council
Board of Probation and Parole	Pennsylvania Industrial Development Authority
Tax Equalization Board	Emergency Management Office
Milk Marketing Board	
Higher Education Assistantce Agency	Public School Building Authority
Higher Education Facilities Authority	Governor's Council on Drug and Alcohol Abuse
Housing Finance	State Employees' Retirement Board
State System of Higher Education	Public School Employees' Retirement System
Energy Office	
Tax Equalization Board	Inspector General

The School Building, and Highway and Bridge Authorities were set up to borrow money beyond the former one-million dollar debt limit imposed upon the state until 1968. The Liquor Control Board operates the state-owned monopoly for the sale of alcoholic liquors. The Board of Probation and Parole supervises former prisoners who have been returned to society before their terms of punishment are completed. The Milk Marketing Board sets the price of milk sold within the state.

THE JUDICIAL BRANCH

The General Assembly makes the laws of Pennsylvania; the

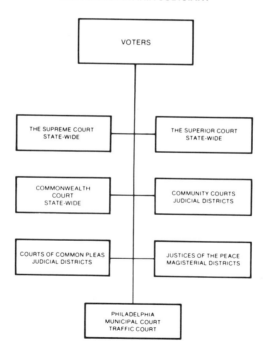

Pennsylvania Chamber of Commerce

Governor is responsible for seeing that the laws are executed; and the judiciary interprets the law.

The Supreme, Superior, and Commonwealth Courts have statewide jurisdictions; common pleas, community, and district justice of the peace courts serve smaller areas. Philadelphia has two special courts, municipal and traffic, which may be displaced by a community court if the voters prefer one. The General Assembly may establish such other special courts as it considers appropriate. Constitutional changes of 1968 brought the courts mentioned into a single unified system headed by the Supreme Court. An Administrative office of the court assists the Supreme Court in overseeing the unified system.

All judges are elected except those appointed by the Governor to fill and complete temporary vacancies. Regular terms for judges are 10 years; those of district justices of the peace are six years.

The Supreme Court consists of seven justices and settles cases appealed to it from the lower courts. The Superior Court has fifteen judges who consider lesser appeals, thus easing the burden upon the highest court. The Commonwealth Court, a newcomer authorized by the Constitution in 1968, has nine judges, and considers cases brought against the Commonwealth and appeals from district courts involving local governments.

JUDICIAL DISTRICTS

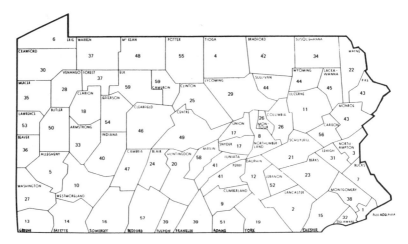

Each county is a judicial district except a few which are sparsely populated. The 59 districts are drawn by the General Assembly.

Courts of Common Pleas are popularly known as district or county courts. One usually exists in each county, but where populations are small one court may serve two counties. There are at present 59 judicial districts. Each Common Pleas Court has divisions for handling civil and criminal cases of various types. It is in these courts that all but minor cases are tried.

The minor judiciary was overhauled by the Constitutional Convention of 1968. Each county and Philadelphia may have, if the voters approve, a community court manned by justices who are lawyers. Where the voters prefer, district justices of the peace courts exist, each serving within a magisterial district whose boundaries are drawn according to guidelines prescribed by the Supreme Court. These district justices need not be lawyers, but henceforth they must pass prescribed tests before they can run for election.

Minor offenses and civil cases involving small amounts of money are settled by these justices without a jury. Preliminary hearings may be held for more serious offenses, but trial occurs in an appropriate division of the Court of Common Pleas. District justices were formerly paid from fees they collected, but salaries were mandated in 1968.

How Courts Operate

A person accused of committing a crime has the right to a jury-trial and also an appeal. At the trial, the state is represented by a locally-elected district attorney. The accused person must hire his own defense lawyer, or, if he is poor the court will appoint one to defend him. A person found guilty is sentenced by the judge according to laws of the State of Pennsylvania.

In civil trials one person brings legal action against another. The court acts as an arbitrator according to the laws of the state. The Constitution guarantees the right of trial by jury when substantial sums are involved, although the right often is waived by the parties involved. When used, the jury decides the party wronged. Otherwise, the judge makes the decision. The person who had been wronged may be awarded money and one or both parties have to pay trial costs. Appeals may be taken in both criminal and civil cases. Appeals are first taken to the Superior Court in most instances, thence to the Supreme Court. Appeals may be taken in some instances to United States courts, usually where constitutional rights are in dispute.

CHECKS AND BALANCES

Each of the three branches of state government has a check over the actions of the other two. This arrangement is intended to keep the branches equal and limited.

The Supreme Court may nullify a law if it feels that the State Constitution is violated. The Court may also declare an action of a member of the executive department unconstitutional and thereby regulate administrative officials.

The Governor, to a certain extent, has a check over the courts by having the power to appoint persons to the vacancies within the courts when such vacancies occur between elections. We already have noted that the Governor may veto a bill of the General Assembly and may reduce the appropriation of any department or branch of state government. Since the courts must rely upon the Governor to carry out their decisions, they may find that a person sentenced to jail by them is later released by the Governor.

The General Assembly has the power to decide how much money is to be spent by either the judicial or executive branches. However, it may not reduce or raise the salary of individuals already in office. The Legislature may set up additional courts and administrative agencies. It may regulate procedures in both courts and in the executive branch. The Legislature may also impeach and remove executives and judges from office. The procedure set forth in the Constitution authorizes the House of Representatives to impeach, or bring charges of wrong doing, and the Senate to conduct the trial.

WHAT THE STATE DOES FOR US

It is the American belief that the government exists for the good of the people, and not that the people exist for the government. It is a natural question then to ask what is done for us by the state government.

Intellectual development and education are the greatest expense of Pennsylvania State government. This is true despite the fact that Pennsylvania does not spend as much per student as do other states, and despite the fact that much of the money spent on education in Pennsylvania is provided by local sources. Pennsylvania does not have an integrated university system similar to many states. Education costs Pennsylvania about half of its General Fund income, and probably will continue to do so.

Health and human services are the second greatest expenses of state government in Pennsylvania. This care of unfortunates, through provision for institutions for the sick, the poor, the handicapped, the aged, the blind, orphaned and criminals, costs the taxpayers increased millions each year. It is a necessary but in many ways a gracious, work of the state. This is an increasing expense.

Highways make up another great expense of the state. All money that is spent on state highways comes from the gasoline tax, vehicle and operators' licenses, and from grants from the Federal government. Sometimes money is borrowed to build highways. The motor license fund is separate from the general fund.

These three functions of state government alone account for all but a small portion of expenditures. Many persons feel that salaries of legislators and other elected officials make up the greatest expense but this is a misconception. The total cost of the whole legislative and judicial branches account for a small fraction of total expenditures. Citizens should realize that state government is expensive, but most of the money is spent for direct services to individuals, communities and institutions.

PAYING FOR OUR STATE GOVERNMENT

Every year it is the job of the General Assembly, with the aid of the Governor, to decide how the state can raise the money to carry out its duties.

Pennsylvania spent more than 20 billion dollars in 2002. Since there are about 12,000,000 people in Pennsylvania, this amounts to an expense of about $1667 per person. Therefore, if each man, woman and child contributed $1667 to the state, there would be no

GENERAL FUND FINANCIAL STATEMENT

(Dollar Amounts in Thousands)

	2001-02 Available	2002-03 Enacted Budget
Beginning Balance	$336,467	$136,766
Revenue:		
Revenue Receipts	$20,059,967	$21,803,300
Less Refunds Reserve	(967,200)	(934,800)
Total Revenue	$19,092,767	$20,868,500
Prior Year Lapses	105,000	—
Funds Available	$19,534,234	$21,005,266
Expenditures:		
Appropriations	$20,693,451	$20,695,750
Supplemental Appropriations	88,817	—
Less Current Year Lapses	(347,000)	—
Total Expenditures	$20,435,268	$20,695,750
Preliminary Balance	(901,034)	$309,516
Transfer to Budget Stabilization Reserve Fund	—	(300,000)
Transfer from Tax Stabilization Reserve Fund	1,037,800	—
25% Transfer to Budget Stabilization Reserve	—	(2,379)
Unappropriated Surplus	$136,766	$7,137

taxes. However, we know that some people could not, and others would not, make such an offer. For that reason, taxes are levied and collected in many different ways.

Formerly, the greatest source of state revenues was taxes on business and industry. The emphasis shifted from business and industry to individuals with the enactment of a sales tax in 1953. Business levies on such items as capital stock, franchises, and corporation income, still provide large sums.

Many other states have had a personal income tax for some years. A graduated income tax, which taxes according to a scale that increases with the amount of an individual's income, is unconstitutional in Pennsylvania. The only type of income tax that could be levied under the present constitution would be one that taxes everyone's income at the same rate. Such a tax was levied for the first time in 1972. In 1976 the income tax was 2% of each individual's income. In 1994 it was 2.8%.

The sales tax is the largest single source of state income.

REVIEW QUESTIONS

1. List several definitions of the word "state."
2. What protective service does the Commonwealth render its citizens?
3. What system is used to determine the size of State House and Senatorial Districts?
4. How many members does your state legislature have? How does it compare in size with the legislatures of other states? Does your Constitution place any limitations on the length of legislative sessions?
5. What is the function of committees in the General Assembly? What is their importance in the law-making process?
6. What are the qualifications of the Governor of Pennsylvania?
7. How does the Governor influence and control the work of the General Assembly?
8. What is the extent of the Governor's power of appointment? Of the power of removal?
9. What are the functions of the Lieutenant Governor?

10. List the qualifications that must be met by State Senators and Representatives.

11. What are the numerous functions of the Department of Public Welfare?

12. Why have our governments been enterprises of "increasing costs?"

13. How are our state funds safeguarded?

14. What department spends most of the money collected by the state?

15. What is the highest court in your state? Of how many judges does it consist? How are they selected?

16. Does your state have an intermediate court of appeals? If so, why?

17. What types of cases are presented to the State Supreme Court? To the State Superior Court?

18. What are the many functions of a District Court judge?

Do you know the meaning of these words?

1. checks and balances
2. president pro tempore
3. budget
4. revenue
5. mental hospital
6. legislature
7. authorities
8. orphans' court
9. special session
10. conference committee
11. item veto
12. public utilities
13. Court of Common Pleas
14. judicial
15. Liquor Control Board
16. income tax
17. environmental resource

Maps to help us learn

1. Make a list of all the State officials that your parents may help vote into office, such as Governor and Representatives. On an outline map of Pennsylvania, draw lines from your home to locations of state institutions controlled by these men.

2. On a map of your county, place all state roads, state hospitals, state parks and anything else that is operated or controlled by the state.

GOVERNMENT OF THE COMMONWEALTH

What do you think?

1. We use the word "state" to mean one of the parts of our country. But any independent political power may also be spoken of as a "state."
2. It is possible to conceive of the state without thinking of its government.
3. It would seem a simple process to make all men good by making good laws.
4. Every citizen should know the main features of his State Constitution.
5. There should be a limit on the number of states that may enter the union.
6. It was natural that the framers of the first constitution should continue the organization of their legislatures in two houses.
7. The system of Federal aid to the states has stimulated state activity.
8. Almost all of the limitations to be found in state constitutions are limitations upon state legislative power.
9. The sales tax is considered a fair and reasonable tax.
10. The courts are a conservative influence.

ACTIVITIES

1. Find out how much money it costs to educate you for one day or one year. Then find out how much the state government contributes to the cost.
2. Appoint a committee to interview your representative to the General Assembly.
3. Secure information concerning the Governor's Cabinet; membership, duties of each member, names of present members, and a brief biographical sketch of each.
4. Secure for class bulletin board and individual scrapbooks, clippings in the form of newspaper articles, editorials, cartoons and other illustrative material dealing with your State Government.
5. Ask your Representative or Senator for a copy of a bill that has gone through your state legislature. Trace the progress of a similar bill for the class.

6. Some persons want a new State Constitution; draw up a model constitution of the American states. Compare it with your present State Constitution.

7. Hold a debate on this question: "Resolved, That the state legislature should meet only once every two years."

8. Do a study of Pennsylvania government in the last ten years and list the departments that have been abolished and the new departments that have been established. Explain the changes.

READING MATERIALS

Commonwealth of Pennsylvania, *Pennsylvania Manual*, Published Biennially, Harrisburg, Pa.

Cornell, William A., *Understanding Pennsylvania Civics*, Lansdale, PA, Penns Valley Publishers, 1994.

Jackson, Richard, *An Historical Review of the Constitution and Government of Pennsylvania, from Its Origin*, New York, Burt Franklin, (Reprint).

McGeary, Martin Nelson, *Pennsylvania Government in Action, Governor Leader's Administration (1955-1959)*, State College, Penns Valley Publishers, 1972.

Pennsylvania Economy League, *Financing Pennsylvania Highway Construction*, Philadelphia, The League, 1977.

Stevens, R. Michael, *Occupation, "Legislator,"* Temple University, Center for the Study of Federalism, Research Report No. 3, Philadelphia, 1971.

Wolf, George D., *Constitutional Revision in Pennsylvania; the Dual Tactic of Amendment and Limited Convention*, State Constitutional Convention Studies No. 2, New York, National Municipal League, 1969.

APPENDIX
LIST OF EXECUTIVES OF THE PROVINCE AND COMMONWEALTH OF PENNSYLVANIA

William Penn, Proprietor		1681-	1693
Benjamin Fletcher, Governor of New York and Pennsylvania		1693-	1695
William Penn, Proprietor		1695-	1718
John, Richard, and Thomas Penn, Proprietors		1718-	1776

The Committee of Safety

Benjamin Franklin, Chairman	Sept.	1776 - March	1777

The Supreme Executive Council

Thomas Wharton, Jr., President	March	1777 - May	1778
George Bryan, V.P. for Wharton, deceased	Oct.	1778 - Dec.	1778
Joseph Reed, President	Dec.	1778 - Oct.	1781
William Moore, President	Nov.	1781 - Oct.	1782
John Dickinson, President	Nov.	1782 - Oct.	1785
Benjamin Franklin, President	Oct.	1785 - Oct.	1788
Thomas Mifflin, President	Nov.	1788 - Dec.	1790

Governors of the Commonwealth Home County

Thomas Mifflin, Democrat-Republican	Philadelphia	1790-	1799
Thomas McKean, Democrat-Republican	Philadelphia	1799-	1808
Simon Snyder, Democrat	Northumberland	1808-	1817
William Findlay, Democrat	Franklin	1817-	1820
Joseph Hiester, Democrat	Berks	1820-	1823
John A. Shulze, Democrat	Lebanon	1823-	1829
George Wolf, Democrat	Northampton	1829-	1835
Joseph Ritner, Anti-Mason	Washington	1835-	1839
David R. Porter, Democrat	Huntingdon	1839-	1845
Francis R. Shunk, Democrat	Allegheny	1845-	1848
William F. Johnston, Whig	Armstrong	1848-	
William Bigler, Democrat	Clearfield	1852-	1855
James Pollock, Whig	Northumberland	1855-	1858

Name	County	From	To
William F. Packer, Democrat	Lycoming	1858-	1861
Andrew G. Curtin, Republican	Centre	1861-	1867
John W. Geary, Republican	Westmordand	1867-	1873
John F. Hartranft, Republican	Montgomery	1873-	1879
Henry M. Hoyt, Republican	Luzerne	1879-	1883
Robert E. Pattison, Democrat	Philadelphia	1883-	1887
James A. Beaver, Republican	Centre	1887-	1891
Robert E. Pattison, Democrat	Philadelphia	1891-	1895
Daniel H. Hastings, Rep.	Centre	1895-	1899
William A. Stone, Rep.	Allegheny	1899-	1903
Samuel W. Pennypacker, Republican	Philadelphia	1903-	1907
Edwin S. Stuart, Republican	Philadelphia	1907-	1911
John K. Tener, Republican	Washington	1911-	1915
Martin G. Brumbaugh, Republican	Philadelphia	1915-	1919
William C. Sproul, Republican	Delaware	1919-	1923
Gifford Pinchot, Republican	Pike	1923-	1927
John S. Fisher, Republican	Indiana	1927-	1931
Gifford Pinchot, Republican	Pike	1931-	1935
George H. Earle, Democrat	Montgomery	1935-	1939
Arthur H. James, Republican	Luzerne	1929-	1943
Edward Martin, Republican	Washington	1943-	Jan.3, 1947
John C. Bell, Republican	Philadelphia	Jan. 3-21,	1947
James H. Duff, Republican	Allegheny	1947-	1951
John S. Fine, Republican	Luzerne	1951-	1955
George M. Leader, Democrat	York	1955-	1959
David L. Lawrence, Democrat	Allegheny	1959-	1963
William W. Scranton, Republican	Lackawanna	1963-	1967
Raymond Shafer, Republican	Crawford	1967-	1971
Milton Shapp, Democrat	Montgomery	1971-	1979
Richard Thornburgh, Republican	Allegheny	1979-	1987
Robert Casey, Democrat	Lackawanna	1987-	1995
Thomas J. Ridge, Republican	Erie	1995	Oct 5, 2001
Mark S. Schweiker	Bucks	2001	—

INDEX

ALCOA, 44, 246, 266
Abbey, Edwin A., 256
Abington Township, 21
Abolitionists, 215, 216, 217
Academy of Fine Arts, 183
Act, 511, 355
Adams Counq, 47, 55, 72, 81
Adams, John, 186
Administrative Code, 267
Aging, 296
Agencies, State, 374-375
Agriculture, 55
Airplanes, 271-272
Airports 27
Alaska, i9, 359
Algeria, 24
Aliens, 332
Aliquippa, 76
Allegewi Indians, 59
Allegheny, College, 182, 191
County, 22, 23, 35, 37, 45-49, 51 59, 96, 181, 245, 350; Mountains, 14, 73, 184, 201; National Forest, 14;
Plateau, 14; River, 17, 24, 25, 38, 75, 133-135, 141, 143, 198, 199, 201, 283
Allentown, 21, 72, 161, 205, 220; Products 47
Alpern, Anne X., 296
Alter, George, 266
Altoona, 21, 205, 220, 300
AlunAinum, 44, 246
Ambridge, 137, 196, 291
American Federation of Labor (AFL), 249
American Sterilizer Co., 50
Amish, 10, 55, 95, 96, 324
AMP, 47, 299
Anabaptists, 96
Anti-Federalists, 171-172
Anti-Masons, 191-193, 385
Architecture, 125
Armstrong County, 181, 193, 203, 208,
Armstrong, John, 141, 142, 166
Arnold, Henry H., 289
Articles of Confederation, 161, 169-170
Assessor, 349, 351, 354
Atlantic Oil, 50
Attorney-General, 366, 368
Atterbury, William, 264
Auditor-General, 234, 268
Auditors, 348-349, 351
Audubon, J. J., 183
Austria, 248
Austin, 263
Authorities, 354

Autocar Company, 258
Automobiles, 258
Automobile Insurance, 293

Bache, Sarah, 167
Baldwin Locomotives, 203-205, 247
Baldwin, Matthias, 203
Ballots, 338, 339
Baltimore 119,187 207
Baltimore Lord, 92, 146
Baltimore and Ohio Railroad, (see also Chessie System), 205, 235
Banking Department, 240
Banks, 39, 275
Baptists, 95, 324
Barnard, G. G., 256
Barry, John, 166
Barton, Clara, 239
Bartram, John, 122
Battle of Lake Erie, 188
Bayer, USA, 48
Beaver County, 38, 51, 196, 244
Beaver, J. A., 236-237, 238, 386
Beaver River, 17, 198, 202
Bedford, 14, 107, 129 139 185, 198
Bedford County, 51, 129; 173
Beissel, Conrad, 123
Bdl Atlantic, 53
Bell, John C., 294, 386
Bellefonte, 202
Benet, S. V., 271
Benner, Philip, 166
Bensalem, 21-22
Berkman, Alexander, 249
Berks County, 46-48, 50-52, 72, 109, 112, 119, 129, 134, 145, 173
Berry, William H., 260, 261
Berwick, 247
Bessemer and Lake Erie Railroad, 26, 243
Bethlehem, 21, 42, 97, 123, 168, 242, 297
Bethlehem Steel Company, 44, 244
Bicycling, 258
Bigler, William, 385
Bingham, William, 197
Birds, 66
Big Business, 242
Black, Chauncey F., 237
Black, Jeremiah S., 217-219, 233
Blacks, 22, 234, 255, 297, 300
Blair County, 33, 45, 50, 201, 208
Blane, Ephraim, 166
Blatt, Genevieve, 296
Bliss, Tasker, 264
Bloomsburg, 14, 46, 234, 327
Blue Laws, 295

Blue Mountain, 14, 140-141,
Boeing Helicopters, 48
Bonnewell, e. c., 268
Book-of-the-month, 43
Boone, Daniel, 109, 112, 118
"Bootleg" Coal, 287
Bouquet, Henry, 142-143, 145,
Boroughs, 345-346, 349
Borough Council, 349
Boston, 119
Boston Tea Party. 156
Braddock, 140
Braddock, Edward, 139-140
Braddock Road, 76, (See also National Road)
Bradford County, 28, 37,187, 216
Bradford, Andrew, 124
Bradford, David, 185
Bradley, Andrew, 297
Brady, Sam, 73, 164
Bradys Bend, 208
Brandywine Battle, 28, 161, 166
Brant Joseph 164
Breck Samuei, 189
Brethren Church, 327
Bristol, 202, 345
Bristol Township, 21
British, 24, 160-162, 187
Broadtop, 207
Brodhead, Daniel, 164
Brooklyn Bridge, 202
Brown, Jacob, 188
Brown, John, 217
Brownsville, 139, 199, 277
Brumbaugh, Martin G. 264, 386
Bryan, George, 169 170, 385
Bryn Mawr College 250
Buchanan, James, 193, 194, 217, 218
Bucknell University, 327
Bucks County, 9, 22, 24, 27, 49, 51, 71, 72, 95, 100, 115, 126, 129, 186, 266, 300
Buckshot War, 192
Bucktails, 220, 223
Budd Company, 284
Budget, 380
Burd, James, 139, 206
Burrowes, Thomas, 190
Bush, George, 295
Bushy Run Battle, 28, 143
Business Services, 41
Butler, 17, 182, 247, 258
Butler County, 22, 37, 46, 49, 181-182, 196, 202, 245
Butler, John, 164
Butler, Zebulon, 164

Cabinet, 368
Cadman, C. W., 271
Cadwalader, John, 166

Calgon, 48
California, 19, 44, 295
California (PA), 327
Cambria Countv, 35. 48. 187
Cameron County, 18, 220
Cameron, Donald! 232
Cameron, Simon, 217, 218, 219, 226, 232
Camp Curtin 220
Camp Reynolds, 289
Canada, 75, 133-135, 142, 143, 165, 166, 187, 300
Canals, 199, 200, 202, 203
Canonburg, 190
Capitalism, 34
Capitol Building, 39, 256, 257; Fire, 240, Scandal, 260
Carbon County, 35, 39, 72, 73
Carbondale, 203
Carlisle, 46, 129, 141, 142, 143, 161, 166, 167, 221, Barricks, 161
Carnegie, Andrew, 226, 242-244 248, 250
Carnegie Institute (Carnegie-Mellon University), 250
Carnegie Museum, 42, 350
Carpenters' Hall, 125, 157
Carter, James, 295
Casey, Robert, 294
Cassatt Muy, 249
Caterpillar Corporation, 46
Catholics, 96, 189, 192-193, 250, 322, 324, 327
Celoran de Bedinville, 135
Cement Industry, 50
Centennial Exposition, 249
Centre County, 36, 51, 73, 181, 208
Central High School, 191
Chadd's Ford, 161
Chambersburg, 14, 198, 217, 220, 221, 224-226, 235
Charles II, 86, 87, 89, 99
Charter, 89
Charter Commission, 353
Charter of Privileges, 101
Checks and Balances, 378
Chemical Industry, 44, 47
Chemung, 164
Chesapeake Bay, 161
Chessie System, 26
Chester, 22, 87, 90, 91, 95, 115, 128, 145, 154, 297, 34
Chester County, 22, 36, 47, 49, 71, 91, 93, 119, 129, 300
Chew House, 125
Cheyney, 327
Chicago, 25, 26, 29
China, 33
Christiana, 217
Christiana, Queen, 83
Christians, 92

Church (See individual names)
Church of England, 88, 141
Citizenship, 331-344
City, 346, 351-353
Civil Service, 259
Civil War, 215-230
Civilian Conservation Corps (CCC), 279
Clarion, 327
Clarion County, 50, 245
Clarion River, 17
Clark's Ferry, 201
Clarks, Joseph S., 294
Clay Products, 35, 37, 49
Clearfidd, 182
Clearfield County, 35, 37, 47, 50, 187, 190, 207, 209
Clerk of Courts, 348
Climate, 15
Clinton County, 18, 19, 209
Clymer, George, 160, 170
Coal, 25, 35, 200, 206-207, 227, 299, 309
Coal and Iron Police, 277
Coal Strikes, 255, 269, 277
Coatesville, 39
Cobalt, 39
Coke, 25, 207-208
Colebrook Furnace, 119
College of Philaddphia (See University of Pennsylvania)
Colonial Life, 107
Columbia, 201, 203, 217
Columbia County, 35, 73, 187, 225
Commissioner, County, 352
Communities, 317-330
Committee of Correspondance, 158
Committee of Safety, 158, 168
Committees, General Assembly, 363
Communication Industry, 39, 53
Communist Party, 275
Community Colleges, 308, 327
Conemaugh River, 17, 74, 75, 210, 238,
Conestoga Creek, 63, 75
Conestoga Indians, 144
Conestoga Wagon, 116, 117, 139, 167,
Conewango Creek, 76, 134
Confedaates, 220-224
Congress, U. S., 359
Congress of Industrial Organizations (CIO), 282
Conneaut Lake, 18
Connecticut, 86, 95, 125, 147-148
Connellsville, 46, 207
Connelly, John, 147,165
Conrail, 53, 302
Conrad, Frank, 271
Conservation, 262
Consolidated Coal Co., 55
Constables, 349, 351
Constitution, State, 168, 172, 191, 233

Constitution, U.S., 171, 172
Construction Industry, 39, 52
Continental? Congress, 155, 157, 158, 163,64, 167
Controller, 348-349, 351-352
Conway, 247
Cook Forest, 269
Cooke, Jay, 226, 235
Copper, 39
Coplay, 246
Corn, 54, 73, 111, 114
Cornplanter, Chief, 75, 165
Cornwall Furnace, 119, 207
Cornwallis, Lord, 161
Coroner, 348
Corrections, 370
Council-Manager, 353
Council of Censors 168 173
County, 91, 346, 347, 348, (See also names of counties)
County Clerk, 348
County Commissioners, 348
County Government, 336
Court, Common Pleas, 375-377
Court, Commonwealth, 376
Court, District, 376
Court State Supreme, 92, 173, 191, 216, 234 376, 378
Court, Superior, 376-377
Coventry Furnace, 119
Cramp Ship Yards, 227
Cranberry Township, 22
Crawford County, 18, 36, 45, 53, 59, 181, 182
Creighton, 46
Cresap, Thomas, 146
Cressona, 290
Croghan, George, 110, 141
Cumberland County, 43, 49, 72, 129, 173, 181, 221
Cumberland Valley, 107,128
Cumberland Valley Railroad, 204
Curtin, Andrew G., 190, 224, 226, 386
Custaloga, 136, 137
Custaloga, Chief, 143
Customs, 317
Curriculum, 325 Czechoslovakia, 248

Dallas, A. J., 186
Dallas, George Mifflin, 193
Damato, A. P., 289
Danville, 40, 290
Dauphin County, 23, 35, 36, 47, 51, 72, 73, 173, 181
Davis, Phineas, 203
De La Warr, Lord, 87
Decatur, Stephen, 188
Dedaration of Independence, 158, 168
Delaware, 12, 77, 81, 87, 90, 146, 172

Delaware Bay, 81
Delaware County, 45, 48, 50, 71, 93, 180, 181
Delaware Indians, 60, 63, 64, 70, 72, 74, 135, 140, 141, 143, 145, 164, 165
Delaware and Hudson, Canal, 200; Railroad, 26, 203
Delaware River, 11, 12, 13, 24, 35, 63, 72, 73, 75, 85, 128, 129, 160, 161, 199
Delaware Valley College, 327
Delaware Water Gap, 28
Democrats, 186, 188, 189, 191, 193, 217, 237, 337, 385
Declaration of Rights and Grievances, 155
Departments,__Aging, 369
—Agriculture, 240, 369, 370
—Banking, 240, 369 370
—Commerce, 369, 3;3
—Community Affairs, 300, 369, 372
—Corrections, 370
—Education, 368, 370
—Environmental Resources, 309, 368, 373
—Health, 309, 369, 373
—General Services, 369, 371
—Insurance, 369, 371
—Labor and Industry, 264, 369-372
—Military Affairs, 369, 372
—Public Welfare, 51, 281, 306, 368, 369, 371
—Revenue, 268, 369, 372
—State, 369
—Transportation, 51, 302, 369, 370
Depression, 276-288
Dewey, Thomas, 295
Dickens, Charles, 201
Dickinson College, 190, 234
Dickinson, John, 155-157, 160, 169, 170,
Dinwiddie, Robert, 136
District Attorney, 348
District Justices, 348, 377
Divesting Act, 169
Divorce, 321
Donation Lands 182
Doylestown, 254, 256
Drake, Edward L., 244
Drakes Well, 28, 244-245
Drexel, A. J., 250
Drexel Institute (University), 250, 327
Drugs, 48
Duff, James H., 294, 386
Dunbar, Thomas, 140
Dunkers, 225
Dunmore Lord, 147
Duportail General, 161
DuQuesne, Marquis, 136, 138
Duquesne University, 327
Durham Boats, 128
Durham Furnace, 119, 128

Duryea, Charles, 258
Dutch, 70, 81, 85, 87, 91, 96
Dutch West India Company, 81, 86

Eakins, Thomas, 249
Earle, George H. 281, 303, 386
Eastern Airlines, 27
Easton, 20, 128, 129, 141, 159, 161, 164, 191, 202, 205 264
Easton Conference, i 53
East Stroudsburg, 327
Eberhard Faber, 298
Economy Village, 196
Eddystone, 299
Edinboro University, 327
Education, 125, 263, 305-309, 322, 379; Services, 41
Eisenhower, Dwight D., 28, 295
Electrical Products, 44, 47
Elections, 340
Electronics 299
Elfreth's Ailey, 80
Elizabethtown College, 327
Elk County, 18, 45, 245
Elkin, John, 256
Elkland Leather Company, 47
Ellman, Amos, 191
Employment, 39-55
Engineering Services, 41
England, 33, 92, 94, 99, 142, 154
Entertainment, 4142
Environment, 309
Ephrata, 28, 97, 123, 168
Erie, 14, 15, 18, 20, 21-22, 27, 45, 75, 136, 182, 187, 202, 265, 351
Erie Canal, 200
Erie County, 16, 20, 39, 45, 48-50, 136, 181
Erie Indians, 62
Erie-Pittsburgh Expressway, 27
Erie Thruway, 27
Erie Triangle, 73, 149
Evans, Lewis, 135
Everett, Edward, 224

Family, 318
Farmers High School (See also Pennsylvania State University), 191
Farming, 16, 55, 113-115, 194-196, 300
Farm Museum, 28
Fayette County, 38, 50, 96, 135, 172, 173, 187, 198, 243, 277, 300
Federalist, 172, 173, 188
Finance, 39, 52
Findlay, William, 172, 173,185,186 188, 199, 385
Fine, John S., 294, 386
Finland, 85, 87, 91
Firmstone, William, 207
First Defenders, 220

First Frame of Government 90
Fisher, John S., 260, 268, 2;0, 277, 386
Fitch, John, 199
Fitzsimmons, Thomas, 170
Fletcher, Benjamin, 99, 100, 285
Floods, 283, 310-312
Flower, Enoch, 125
Floyd, John B., 215
Fogel Grip (Bird Griffin), 83
Food Products Industry, 44, 47
Forbes, John, 142-143
Foreign Born, 23
Forest County, 18, 22, 36, 245, 360
Forests, 18
Forts,
—Bedford, 142
—Beversrede, 82
—Casimir, 83, 87
—Christina, 83
—Detroit, 160
—Duquesne, 138, 142, 147
—Durkee, 148
—Leboeuf, 147
—Ligonier, 142-143
—Littleton, 142
—Loudon, 142
—Machault, 136-137, 142-143
—Necessity, 28, 139
—New Gothenburg, 84
—Niagara, 165
—Pitt, 142-145, 164, 206
—Presque Isle, 143
—Prince George, 138
—Shirley, 141
—Stanwix, 73
—Sumter, 219
—Venango, 143
Forty Fort, 148
Foster, Stephen, 227
Frame of Government, 168
France (French) 87, 89, 133, 138 161
Frankford, 291; Land Company 93
Franklin, Benjamin, 121, 124, 127, 136, 139, 141, 145, 155, 158, 160, 166, 168-170, 191, 385
Franklin County, 72 181, 360
Frankstown Road, 1;0
Fraser, John, 110, 136, 137
Free Enterprise, 33-34
Free Public Schools, 189
Free Society of Traders, 93
French (See France)
French Creek, 136, 202
French and Indian War, 138, 153
Frick, Henry C., 243, 248
Friends (See Quakers)
Friendship Hill, 187
Fries, John, 186
Fulton County, 22, 32

Fulton, Robert, 199, 200
Furniture Industry, 44, 49

GTE, 47
Gabreski, Francis, 289
Gallatin, Albert, 173, 185, 186, 198
Galloway, J., 157
Gamster, Clay, 38, 46
Geisinger Medical Center, 40
Geary, J. W., 224, 231, 386
General Assembly, 7, 51, 91, 98, 141, 145, 173 183, 192, 297, 309, 337, 359-366, 375 378-379
General Electric Company, 47, 48
General Fund, 380
General Motors, 48
Genesee River, 17
Germany, 24, 83, 87, 94, 96, 98, 118
Germans, 140, 186, 189, 193, 195, 248, 265
German Reform Church (Church of Christ), 96, 97, 125
Germantown, 93, 145, 165, 203, 345
Gettysburg, 14, 28, 190-191, 214, 221-224
Gettysburg College, 191
Girard, Stephen, 188
Girty, Simon, 165
Gist, Christopher, 135, 138
Glackens, William, 250
Glass Industry, 44, 50
Godfrey, Thomas, 122
Gold, 39
Gore, Obadiah, 206
Gorsuch, Edward, 217
Government, State, 359-384
Governor, 99-100, 173, 191, 234, 311, 324, 335, 359, 363, 366-30, 376, 378-380, 385-386
Government Employees, 39, 51
Grant, James, 142
Granite, 36
Great Britain, 138
Great Lakes, 133
Great Law, 91, 92
Great Runaway, 164
Great Treaty of 1683, 70
Greek, 24
Greencastle, 221
Greene County, 35, 36, 96, 147, 181, 245
Greensburg, 22, 48, 165, 215, 261, 298
Greenville, 46
Grenville, George, 154
Greyhound Bus Line, 27, 53
Groghan, George, 135
Grow, Galusha A., 219
Grumman LLV, 48
Grundy, Joseph, 266
Guffey, Joseph, 281, 294
Gulf Oil Corporation, 50, 245
Gustavus Adolphus, 82-84

Guyasuta, Chief, 143, 165

Half-King, 71, 74, 137
Halefax, (N.S.) 154
Hall, Charles Martin, 246
Hamilton, Alexander, 185
Hancock, W. S., 223
Hand, Edward, 166
Hannastown, 129, 147, 165
Hanover, 147, 221,
—Foods, 47- Shoes, 49
Harley-Davidson, 48
Harmer, Josiah, 181
Harmony Society, 196-197
Harpers Ferry, 217
Harris, John, 271
Harrisburg 14, 16, 21, 22, 27 128 144, 183 193, 205, 219, 22;, 233, 247, 297, 359; Hospital, 40
Harrison, C. C., 250
Harrison, William H., 193
Hartranft, John, 231, 236, 386
Harvey's Lake, 18
Hastings, Daniel, 239, 240, 386
Haverford, 21
Hawaii, 359
Health Service Industry, 40
Hebrews (Jews) 98, 169, 322, 324, 327
Heinz, Foods, 47, 49; H. John, 294
Helicoptas, 27, 48, 299
Henry, William, 118
Hershey, Foods, 47, 291
Hessians, 161
Hiawatha, 62
Hiester, Joseph, 189, 385
Higher Education, 326-327
Highway Department, 258, 376
Highways, 26-27, 265, 301, 379-380
Historical Commission, 8, 268
Hindus, 24
Holland, 81, 86
Holland Land Company, 182
Hollender, Peter, 83
Hollidaysburg, 201
Holy Experiment, 99
Home Rule, 353
Homestead, 249
Honesdale, 200, 203
Hopewell Village, 28
Hopkinson, Francis, 123
Horseracing, 295
Hot Water Rebellion, 186
Hotels, 41
House of Representatives, State, 173, 360-365, 378
House of Representatives, U.S., 295
Houston, Joseph, 260
Howe, William, 161
Hoyt, Henry M., 231, 236, 386

Hudson, Henry, 81
Hudson River; 81, 96, 199
Human Relations Commission, 374
Humphrey, Hubert, 295
Hunters, 107
Huntingdon, 181
Huntingdon County, 37, 192, 207, 208

Iceland, 43
Illinois, 15, 26
Income Tax, (See Taxes)
Immigration, 247
Independence Hall, 28, 125, 157, 158, 172, 183, 219, 241
Indiana County, 35, 54, 187
Indiana University of Pennsylvania, 327
Indians, 59-79, 108, 163, 181, (See Individual tribe names)
Indiantown Gap, 289
Ingersoll, Jared, 170
Insurance Industry, 39 52
Intermediate Units, 324
Internal Affairs, 234
Interstate Highways, 27
Ireland, 98
Irish, 24, 248
Iron (see also steel) 39, 119, 207
Iroquois Indians, 135, 163, 165
Irvine, William, 149, 166
Irvis, Leroy, 297
Irwin, 284 Italy, 24, 248

Jacks Mountain, 14
Jackson, Andrew, 193
Jacob Creek, 199
James, Arthur H., 287, 386
James 11, 99
Jamestown, (VA),81, 87
Jeanette, 144
Jefferson County, 50, 187, 190, 234, 244
Jefferson, Thomas 158, 185, 186
Jews (See Hebrews)
Johnson, Lyndon B., 295
Johnson, William F., 193, 385
Johnstown, 15, 21, 201, 238, 242, 311
Johnstown Flood, 28, 238-239
Jones, Bill, 242
Jones, Walter A., 284
Judge of Common Pleas, 348
Judicial Branch, 375, 378
Judicial Districts, 376
Jumonsville, Coulon de, 138
Jumiata County, 22 75
Juniata River, 17, ;41, 201, 208, 221, 311
Jury Commissioners, 348

KDKA, 271
Kalmar Nyckel, (Key of Calmar), 83
Keimer, Samuel, 124

Kelly, "Commando", 289
Kendall, Oil, 51
Kennedy, John F., 295
Kent, Atwater, 271
Kentucky, 110
Keystone Shortway, 27
Keystone State, 12
Kier, Samud, 244
King George's War, 133
King Ranch, 300
King William's War, 133
Kinzua, 18, 75
Kirkbridge, Mabelle M., 296
Kiskiminetas River, 17, 74, 76,134, 147-201
Kittanning, 24, 76, 141, 182
Knappenberger, A. W., 289
Knox, Philander, C., 260, 266
Kutztown, 327
Koppers Chemicals, 49

Labor, 41, 235; Organizations, 41
Lackawanna, 75
Lackawanna County, 23, 39, 46, 49, 225
Lackawanna River 17
Lafayette College, ;91
Lake, Chautauqua, 134
— Erie, 13, 14, 16, 18, 38, 134, 147, 149
— Ontario, 17, 149
Lancaster, 21, 42, 48, 161, 167, 183, 187, 191, 193, 197, 199, 214, 248, 268, 297,
Lancaster County, 10, 45, 47-49, 63, 72, 96, 97, 110, 116, 128-129, 144, 146, 191, 199, 207, 217, 240, 246
Langley, S. P., 271-272
Laurd Ridge, 15, 107, 129, 133, 142, 147
Lawrence County, 48-50, 182, 245
Lawrence, David, 294, 296, 308, 309, 312,
Lawrenceville, 219, 227, 246
Lawrey, James, 110
Leader, George M., 294, 310, 386
Leather Products, 44, 49
Lebanon, 42
— County, 36, 38, 72, 98, 119, 187, 207
Le Boeuf, 136, 137
Lee, Robert E., 221
Legislature (See General Assembly)
Legislative Reference Bureau, 354
Lehigh Coal and Navigation Company, 200, 206
Lehigh County, 36, 38, 46, 48, 50, 72, River, 17, 60, 203, 206, 226; University 250' Valley Railroad, 205, 207, 247,
Lehighton, 72
Lemoyne, 221
Lemoyne, F. J., 216
Leslie Fay, 43
Letterkenny, 290
Lewis, John L., 269, 270

Lewisburg, 264
Lewistown, 220
Liberty Bell, 102, 158, 159, 161
Lieutenant Governor, 234, 237, 239, 362 366, 367
Ligonier, 181
Limestone, 36, 49, 208, 246
Lincoln, Abraham, 218, 219, 222, 224,
Lincoln Highway, 76
Lincoln University, 307, 327
Liquor Control Board, 280, 368, 375
Lithuania, 248
Lititz, 97, 125, 168
Lloyd, David, 103
Local Government, 336, 345, 384
Lock Haven, 14, 299, 327
Locomotives, 25, 48
Log Cabin, 86, 111
Logan, James, 102, 125
Logstown, 137
London, 119, 135, 155
Longstreth, Morris, 193
Lower Counties, 101
Lower Merion Township, 21
Loyalists, 165
Luks, George, 250
Lumber Industry, 44, 49, 208-209
Lutheran Church, 86, 96, 97, 125, 189, 324
Luzerne County, 18, 35, 46, 47, 49, 181, 225, 231, 235
Lycoming County, 47, 75, 181, 209

MacFarlane, James, 185
Machinery Industry, 44, 46
Mack Truck Company, 48
Mackinac, 133
Madison College, 191
Magee Carpets, 46
Managing director, 352
Mansfield, 327
Manufacturing, 44
March, Peyton C., 264
Marcus Hook, 47, 48
Margiotti, Charles, 287
Marin, Pierre, 136
Markham, William, 90, 100
Markham's Frame, 100
Marriage, 320
Marshall, George C., 289
Marshall College, 191
Martin, Edward, 291, 294, 386
Maryland, 86, 92, 95, 141, 142, 146, 185, 216, 311
Masland, 46
Mason-Dixon Line, 12, 147
Maybridge, Edward, 271
Mayor, 349, 352
McCausland, General, 224
McClellan, George, 226

McKean County, 18, 37, 187, 220, 245
McKean, Thomas, 172,186,187, 385
McKee, Alexander, 165
McNarney, Joseph 289
McParlan, James, 236
Meade, George G., 220, 223
Meadville, 182, 187,191, 290
Medicine, 48
Mellon, Andrew, 266- Bank, 52- W. L., 245, 266
Membership Organizations 41
Mennonites, 55, 96, 189, 215, 225, 324
Mercer County, 181, 182, 245
Mercer, Henry, 254, 256
Mercersburg, 191
Mesta Machine Company, 291
Mdal Products Industry, 44
Methodist Church, 95
Metropolitan Areas, 20-22
Mexican War, 193
Middlesex, 284
Middletown, 200, 290
Miffin County, 37, 181
Mifflin, George, 169
Mifflin, Thomas, 166, 170, 173, 174, 186, 187, 385
Milford, 266
Milk Control Commission, 286
Millersville Univasity, 190, 307, 327
Mills, 116
Minerals, 34
Mingo Indians, 143
Mining Industry, 39, 55
Minority Groups 297
Minuit, Peter, 83
Mississippi River, 133
Mitchdl, John, 255-256
Monmouth, 163, 166
Molly Maguires, 235
Monongahela River, 17, 24, 37, 198, 199, 283, 309
Monroe County, 22, 27, 39
Montgomery County, 22, 27, 36, 45-47, 49,50,72,93, 181,231
Montour County, 40
Montreal, 133
Moore, William, 169, 385
Moravians, 97, 113, 123, 125, 128, 144, 168
Morgan, William, 123
Morris Gouverneur 170-171
Morris Robert H., 141, 160, 166, 172,
Morrisville, 128
Morton, John, 160
Mount Davis, 15,
—Union, 221
Mt. Pleasant House, 125, 126
Muhlenberg Frederick, 172
Muhlenberg Peter, 166
Muncy, 73

Muncipal Authorities, 354
Municipal Reform League, 259
Murraysville, 246
Museum of Art, 42

Nanticoke Indians, 61 71
National Guard, 249, 255, 262
National Government, 335
National Park Service, 224
National Road, 76, 198
Nationalities, 23
Native Americans, 192
Naturalization, 332
Natural Gas, 36, 54
Navigation Acts, 154
Nazareth, 97
Nazareth Hall, 125
Nebraska, 359
Negro Mountain, 14
Neville, John, 185
Netherlands, 24 (see also Dutch)
Nemacolin (Path), 76, 136, 139, (See also National Road)
New Amsterdam, 83, 85, 86
New Brighton, 198
New Castle, 205
New Castle, (Del), 12, 87, 89, 91, 146, 147
New Cumberland Army Depot, 52
New Geneva, 186
New Holland, 46, 268
New Jersey, 12, 13, 19, 20, 27, 81, 89, 93, 160, 185
New Kensington, 246
New Orleans, 25, 133
New Process Company, 43
New Stamton, 46, 240, 299
New Sweden, 82, 84
New York Central Railroad, 205 (See also Penn Central)
New York City, 12, 26, 27, 77, 87, 200, 302
New York State, 11, 12, 13, 14, 19, 44, 61, 73 75, 93, 119, 128, 129, 160, 163
Niagara Falls, 246
Nigeria, 24
Nix, Robert, 297
Nixon, Richard M., 295
Norfolk Southern Railroad, 26
Normal Schools, (See also State Universities), 190
Norristown, 183, 223
Northampton County, 36, 46, 50, 51, 73, 129, 130, 181, 186, 296
Northumberland County, 35, 36, 47, 70
Nova Scotia, 154
Nuclear Energy, 303
Nursing, 40

Oakley, Violet, 256
Ohio, 12, 13, 74, 145, 165

Ohio Company, 135
Ohio River, 12, 17, 18, 59, 133, 134, 135, 147, 185, 197, 199, 283
Oil, 24, 35, 36, 55, 244, 245
Oklahoma, 74
Old Ironsides, 188
Ontario, Canada 13
—Watershed, 17
Ord, Edward O.C., 220
Orientals, 23, 57
Oxen, 113

PNC Financial, 52
Packer, Asa, 250
Packer, William F., 386
Paine, Thomas, 158
Paoli, 161
Paper Money, 154
Paper Industry, 44, 45
Pardee, Ario, 250
Parliament, 154, 155
Pastorius, F.D., 93
Pattison, Robert E., 237, 239, 256, 386
Paxton (Boys), 144
Peale Charles Wilson, 160, 183
Peale Rembrandt, 183
Pearl Harbor, 288
Peat, 35, 38
Penn, Hanna, 100, 102
—John, 102, 385
—Richard, 102, 385
—Thomas, 102, 385
—William, 61, 70, 80, 81, 87, 93, 99 120, 169, 312, 345, 385
Pennamite War, 147
Penn Central Railroad, (Also see Pennsylvania Railroad), 302
Penn Hills, 21
Pennsbury Manor, 100, 101, 125
Pennsy-care, 306
Pennsylvania Abolition Society, 215
Pennsylvania Associators, 157, 158
Pennsylvania College (See Gettysburg College)
Pennsylvania Gazette, 116, 121, 124
Pennsylvania Higher Education Assistance Agency (PHEAA), 308
Pennsylvania House Furniture, 49
Pennsylvania History, 325
Pennsylvania Horticultural Society, 195
Pennsylvania Industrial Development Authority (PIDA), 291, 373
Pennsylvania Line, 166 Pennsylvania Plan, 188
Pennsylvania Railroad, 202, 205, 235, 243, 247, 284, 302 (See also Conrail and Penn Central)
Pennsylvania Rifle, 117
Pennsylvania State University, 51, 306, 307, 327
Pennsylvania Turnpike, 26, 243, 285
Pennsylvania Turnpike Commission, 284
Pennypacker, Samuel, 256, 386
Pennzoil, 51
Penrose, Boise 241, 256, 259, 261, 266
Pepper, G. W. 266-267
Perry, Oliver Hazard, 187-188
Personal Services, 41
Pders, Richard, 195
Petroleum, 25, 36, 50, 55
Pew, Joseph, 245
Philadelphia, 25, 27, 28, 39, 4548, 51, 52 54, 71 80 82 90 91 94 95 96 98, 107, 113, 115, 119-120 122-123, 127-128, 129, 140, 144-146, 155-156, 161-163, 166-168, 172, 181-185 190-193, 197-206, 215-219 221-225 233, 258-260, 297, 302, 308, 324, 345, 351
Philadelphia College of Art, 327
Philadelphia College of Textiles and Science, 46, 327
Philadelphia and Erie Railroad, 247
Philadelphia Navy Yards, 52, 291, 292
Philadelphia and Reading Railroad (See Reading Railroad)
Picketts Charge 223
Pike County, 18, 22, 27, 187, 320
Pinchot, Gifford, 266, 267, 275-280, 368
Pinkerton Detectives, 248
Piper Aircraft Company, 299
Pitcaim, Harold F., 272
Pitcher, Molly, 166
Pithole City, 244
Pitt, William 142
Pittsburgh, 9 13, 15, 20, 21-22, 25, 27, 39,52,138,156,181,184,188,191 197, 198, 199, 205, 207, 208, 219, 2,- 225, 227, 235, 242, 244, 246, 247, 260, 291, 297, 309, 350, 351; University, 191, 250, 307, 327
Pittsburgh and Lake Erie Railroad, 26
Pittsburgh Plate Glass Company, 50
Plastic Products Industry, 44, 49
Pocono, 14,16 22, 27, 76
Poland, 24, 248
Political Bosses, 232
Political Parties, 336, (See also party by names)
Pollock, James, 385
Pontiac, Chief, 143
—War, 153
Poor Richard's Almanac, 121
Population, 19-24, 179, 295
Port Carbon, 199
Portage Railroad, 202, 204-205
Porter, David, 192, 385
Post, C. F., 141
Portugal, 98

Potomac River, 17, 128, 172
Potter County 18,187, 209, 245, 263
Potter, Ellen, 296
Pottery, 50
Pottsville, 206, 220
Presbyterians (Church), 98, 182
President of Pennsylvania, 168, 169, 385
President of U. S., 333, 335
President Pro Tempore, 362
Presque Isle, 19, 25, 136, 149
Primary Elections, 259, 338
Printing Industry, 44, 45
Printz, Johan, 84-85
Proclaimation Line of 1763, 153, 154
Prohibition, 239, 265, 267, 280
Project 70, 309
Proprietors, Pennsylvania, 385
Protestants, 322
Prothonotary, 348
Provincial Court, 92
Public Admimstration Jobs, 39, 51
Public Authorities, 283
Public Utilities, 39, 53, 54, 302
Public Utilities Commission, 264
Public Welfare, 303-305, 368, 369
Puerto Ricans, 297, 300
Punxsutawney, 76, 261
Pymatuming, 18, 28, 76, 279, 291

Quakers, 75, 88, 89, 90, 91, 92, 94, 95, 98, 100, 120, 125, 129, 140, 141, 165, 189, 215, 225, 324, 327
Quaker State Oil, 51
Quay, Matthew S., 233, 237, 241, 256, 259
Quebec (Act), 136, 156
Queen Anne's War, 133
Quitrent, 93

Radio, 271
Railroads, 25, 53, 203, 204, 205, 247, 302
Railroad Museum, 28
Rapp, George, 196,
Raystown, 110
Reading, 21, 25, 49, 72, 129, 200, 220, 235, 262, 296, 297
Reading Raulroad, 72, 204, 206, 236, 302
Reagan, Ronald, 295
Real Estate Industry, 39, 52
Real Estate Taxes, (See Taxes)
Recorder of Deeds, 348
Reed, Joseph, 169, 170, 385
Redstone (See Brownsville)
Referendum, 336, 353
Reformed Church, 86, 189
Register of Wills, 348
Registration, Voter, 259
Reibman, Jeanette, 296
Religion, 319, 322
Republican Party, 194, 217, 227, 231, 237, 241, 267, 294, 337, 386
Retail Trade 39, 42
Revere, Pau; 156
Revenue, 354
Revolutionary War, 153-170
Reynolds, John, 214, 220, 223
Rinehart, Mary Roberts, 270
Rite-Aid, 43
Ritner, Joseph, 191, 385
Rittenhouse, David, 122, 146, 172
Roads, 128,198, 258, 278, 279
Robertshaw Thermostat Company, ' _
Rocky Mountains, 15
Roebling, John, 202
Roffsdale, 240
Rohm and Haas, 49
Roman Catholic (See Catholics)
Roosevelt, Franklin, 281
Roosevdt, Nicholas, 199
Roosevelt, Theodore, 255, 256, 261
Roosevelt Park, 23
Ross, Betsy, 167
Ross, George, 160
Rothrock Joseph T., 240
Royal Coiony, 99
Rubber Industry, 44, 49
Rural Free Delhery (RFD), 2__
Rush, Benjamin, 123, 160
Russia, 33, 83, 248
Rutter, Thomas, 119

Safe Harbor Dam, 54, 284
St. Clair, Arthur, 147, 166, 181
St. Francis College, 250
St. Lawrence River, 25, 133
St. Louis, 26
Sales Tax, 310, 380, 381
Salk, Jonas, 328
Salomon, Haym, 166
Sand, 25, 35, 37, 50
Sanderson, John, 260
Saudia Arabia, 24
Savings and Loan, 39
Sawdust War, 235
Saxonburg, 202
Saylor, David, 246
Schaefferstown, 98
Scholarships, 308
Schools (See education)
School Boards, 324
School Code, 263
School Superintendent, 354
Schuylkill County, 35, 73, 187, 199, 225
Schuylkill River, 17, 60, 77, 81, 82, 93 128, 145, 198, 206, 311
Schwab, Charles M., 242, 250
Schweiker, Richard, 294
Schwenkfelder Church, 97
Scotch Irish, 23, 87, 94, 98, 111, 140, 144,

185
Scott, Hugh, 294
Scott Paper Company, 45
Scott Thomas, 226
Scott, Winfield 193
Scranton, 21, 2;, 205, 235, 351
Scranton, W. W., 294, 310, 386
Second Frame of Government, 98
Secretary of Education, 324
Secret Ballot, 239-240
Sectarians, 96
Sdinsgrove, 187
Sellers, Coleman, 271
Senate, 173, 360-365
Seneca Indians, 62, 75,145,164,165
Service Industries, 39
Shafer, Raymond 294, 308, 309, 386
Shaler, Charles, 219
Shamokin, 110
Shapp Milton J., 294, 299, 310, 386
Sharon, 21, 42; Hills, 45
Shawnee Indians, 61, 73, 74, 135, 140, 141, 143, 145, 146
Shenango River, 74, 202
Sheriff, 348
Shippen, William, Jr., 123
Shippensburg, 110, 327
Shoes, 49
Shoemaker, George, 206
Shulze, John A., 189, 202, 385
Shunk, Francis, 193, 385
Singerly, William M., 240
Slate, 36, 46
Slavery, 169, 215-217
Slippery Rock, 327
Sloan, Grace, 296
Smilie, John, 172-174, 185
Smith, James, 160
Snowfall, 16
Snyder, Simon 186, 187, 385
Social Security 321
Social Services, 41
Society of Friends, (See Quakers)
Soil, 18
Soil Conservation Commission, 293
Solicitor, 348, 351
Somerset, 15, 16
Somerset County, 66,181, 198, 217
Somerset Museum, 28
South Penn Railroad, 243, 284
South Mountains, 14 223
Southwark Theatre, 124
Spain, 24, 120
Spaatz, Carl, 289
Spanish American War, 241
Speaker of House, 362
Special Districts, 354
Special Instruments, 44, 50
Spector, Arlen, 294

Spinning Wheels, 113
Spiegla, Caesar, 271
Springdale, 266
Sproul, William C., 265-266
Stamp Act, 155-156
Standard Oil Company 245
Stanton, Edwin, 217, 219, 221, 226
Stark, Harold R., 280
State Board of Education, 263
State College Borough, 21
State Colleges, (See State Universities)
State Constitution, (See Constitution, State)
State Government, 335
State House, 171 (See also Capitol and Independence Hall)
State Legislature (See General Assembly)
State Parks, 28
State Police, 261, 282, 368, 369, 373
State School Building Authority 307
State Treasurer, 369 (See also Treasurer)
State-related Universities, 307
State Universities, 243, 257, 288, 299, 300, 307, 318, 327, 359
Steamboats, 199
Steel Industry, 44, 242-244
Steelton, 244
Stewart Charles 188
Stewart John, 237
Stevens, Thaddens, 190, 218, 231
Stockton, Frank, 250
Stoddardsville, 200
Stone Industry, 36 44 49
Stone, William A. 241, 386
Strikes, Labor, 235, 248-249, 269, 277
Strong Mayor, 253
Stroudsburg, 14
Stuart, Edwin S., 260, 386
Stuart, J. E. B., 220-221
Stvyvesant, Peter, 85, 86
Suburbs, 297-298
Sugar, 24
Sullivan County, 18, 22
Sullivan, John, 164
Sully, Thomas, 183
Sun Company, 50 245
Sunbury, 130, 182, 311
Superior Court, (See Court)
Superintendent, School, 354
Supreme Court (See Court)
Susquehanna Company, 148, 187
Susquehanna County, 22, 187
Susquehanna River, 15, 17, 19, 27, 63, 69, 75, 96, 129, 149, 163, 179, 199, 201, 205, 206, 209, 221, 283, 311
Susquehanna Expressway, 27
Susquehannock Indians, 63, 70
Swallow, Silas C., 239
Swathmore College, 327
Swedes (Sweden) 33, 70, 77, 81, 82, 91

Switzerland, 96, 186

Tammany, 70, 93
Tarbdl, Ida, 244
Taxes, 154, 166, 184-186, 231, 232, 286, 301, 310, 354, 379
Tax Collector, 349, 351, 354
Taylor Baynard 250
Taylor George, ;60
Taylor, Joseph, 250
Teacher Tenure, 282
Telephone, 53, 243
Television, 291, 299-300
Temple University, 307, 327
Tener, John K., 260, 386
Texas, 11, 19, 26, 36, 295
Textile Industry, 44, 46, 227
Thaw, William, 250
Thiel, A. L., 250
Thiel College, 250
Thomson, Charles, 157, 158, 159
Thornburgh, Richard, 294, 386
Three Mile Island, 303
Tinicum Island, 84, 85
Tioga County, 36, 49, 75, 164, 187, 207, 209, 245
Titusville, 244-245
Torkillus, (Rev.) Roerus, 83
Townships, 93, 345, 349
—Commussioners, 349
—Supervisors, 349
Tories, 102, 165
Traders, 110
Trailways Bus Lines, 27, 53
Transportation, 24, 128, 199, 301; Industry 44, 48
Trans-World Airlinu, 27
Treasurer, 234, 260, 348, 349, 351, 352, 368, 369
Treaty of Easton, 141
Treaty of Greenville, 181
Trenton, (N.J.) 148, 161
Tucker, C. De Lores, 297
Turnpikes, 198
Tuscarora Indians, 62
Tuscarora Mountain, 14
TV Guide, 45
Twenty-eighth Division, 264, 288, 292

Underground Railroad, 216-217
Unemployment, 276, 281
Union Canal, 200
Union County, 49, 187
Union Switch Signal Company, 246
Unions (see AFL, CIO, and United Mine Workers)
Uniontown, 191
Unisys Corporation, 46
United Marine Workers, 255

United States Steel Corporation, 9, 44, 300
University of Pennsylvania, 123, 127, 190, 250, 327
USAir, 27, 53
Upper Darby Township, 20-21
Upland, (See Chester)
Valley Forge, 48, 162, 163, 167
Van Dyke, Henry, 270
Vanity Fair, 46
Vare, Flora, 296
Vare, William, 267
Venango County, 37, 38, 51, 136, 181, 244
Vermont, 11
Veto, 365
Virginia, 87, 96, 107, 110, 116, 133, 134, 137, 142, 147, 185, 219
Voters, 335
Voting, 334
Von Steuben, Baron, 163
Von Kyaphawsen, General, 161
Voting Machines, 268

WCTU, 267
Walking Purchase, 72-73
Wallenpaupack, Lake, 18
Wampum, 246
Wanamaker, John, 241, 247
War of 1812, 187
Warren County, 18, 37, 51, 75, 181, 294
Washington, 191, 245
Washington College, (See Washington and Jefferson College)
Washington County, 35, 37, 96, 181, 185, 216
Washington Crossing Park, 28
Washington, D. C., 172, 183
Washington, George, 134, 136, 138, 140, 142, 158, 160, 161, 162, 164, 171, 172
Washington and Jefferson College, 190, 234
Waterford, 136
Wayne, Anthony 166,181
Wayne County, 18, 181
Weather, 16
Weiser, Conrad, 134-135
Welcome, 90, 91
Welfare Department (See also Departments), 266
Wellsboro, 350
Welsh, 24, 93
West, Benjamin, 71, 123
West Chester, 327
West Germany, 24
West Indies, 94, 116
West Virginia, 12, 24
Western University of Pennsylvania, (See Pittsburgh University)
Westinghouse, George, 246
Westinghouse Electric Company, 47, 246
Westminister College 327

Westmordand Countj, 35, 49, 50 59 129, 144, 165, 172, 173, 179, 231, 240,
Wetherill, Samuel, 167
Wharton, Joseph, 250
Wharton, Thomas, 169, 385
Wheeling, W. Va., 199
Whig Party, 102, 191, 193, 385
Whiskey Rebellion, 184-185
Wholesale Trade 39, 42
Wiggins, Kate, 2;0
Wilkes-Barre, 21, 27, 164, 235, 311
William and Mary, 99
William Penn Charter School, 125
William Penn Highway, 76
William Penn Museum, 28
Williamsburg, (VA), 119, 127
Williamsport, 21, 48, 163, 209 235, 290
Will Creek (Cumberland, MD;, 136, 137,
Wilmington (Del.), 83
Wilmot, David, 216-218
Wilson, James, 157, 160, 170-173
Wilson, William B., 261
Wilson, Woodrow, 261
Wister, Owen, 270
Wolf, George, 189, 191, 202, 385

Women's Rights, 296
Wood Products, 25, 110, (See also Lumber)
Woolworth, F. W., 248
Works Progress Administration, (WPA),
World War I, 264-265
World War II, 288-292
Wrightstown, 72
Wrightsville, 221
Wyandot Indians, 164
Wyoming, 261
Wyoming Massacre, 164
Wyoming Valley, 164

Yankee-Pennamite War, 148
Yellow Fever, 183
York, 21, 22, 4547,161,187,199, 203, 221
York County, 4547, 72, 95, 129, 146
York Haven, 199
Youghiogheny River, 17, 136
Youth, 296
Yugoslovia, 248

Zinc, 35, 38, 300, 309
Zion Luthern Church, 193
Zurn Industries, 46